Symbolic Computing with Lisp

Robert D. Cameron
Anthony H. Dixon

School of Computing Science
Simon Fraser University

PRENTICE HALL, Englewood Cliffs, New Jersey 07632

Library of Congress Cataloging-in-Publication Data

Cameron, Robert D.
    Symbolic computing with Lisp / Robert D. Cameron, Anthony H.
  Dixon.
      p.   cm.
    Includes bibliographical references and index.
    ISBN 0-13-877846-9
    1. Lisp (Computer program language)   I. Dixon, Anthony H.
  II. Title.
  QA76.73.L23C36   1992
  005.13'3--dc20   91-44555
                                                              CIP

Editorial/production supervision
  and interior design: Carol L. Atkins
Cover design: Wanda Lubelska Design
Manufacturing buyers: Linda Behrens and David Dickey
Freelance Coordinator: Nancy Menges
Copy Editor: Zeiders & Associates
Acquisitions Editor: Marcia Horton

LIMITS OF LIABILITY AND DISCLAIMER OF WARRANTY

The author and publisher of this book have used their best efforts in preparing this book and software.
These efforts include the development, research, and testing of the theories and programs to determine
their effectiveness. The author and publisher make no warranty of any kind, expressed or implied, with
regard to these programs or the documentation contained in this book. The author and publisher shall not
be liable in any event for incidental or consequential damages in connection with, or arising out of, the
furnishing, performance, or use of these programs.

ISBN 0-13-877846-9

Prentice-Hall International (UK) Limited, *London*
Prentice-Hall of Australia Pty. Limited, *Sydney*
Prentice-Hall Canada Inc., *Toronto*
Prentice-Hall Hispanoamericana, S.A., *Mexico*
Prentice-Hall of India Private Limited, *New Delhi*
Prentice-Hall of Japan, Inc., *Tokyo*
Simon & Schuster Asia Pte. Ltd., *Singapore*
Editora Prentice-Hall do Brasil, Ltda., *Rio de Janeiro*

To

Carol and Jessa

Patty, Kirsten, Victoria, and Kimberly

Contents

Preface

Symbolic Computing began as notes for a one-semester third-year computing science course at Simon Fraser University. Initially, the goals of the course were to teach list processing and symbol manipulation with the Lisp programming language, in preparation for subsequent work in artificial intelligence. What began as a typical introductory course on programming in Lisp has evolved into one where the emphasis is now placed on symbolic computing as a discipline in itself. The topic of Lisp programming is now presented in this context, with the focus being placed on those aspects of programming languages, particularly functional languages, which are most significant to the implementation of programs that act on symbolic representations of objects.

As more software products are developed that can be characterized in whole or in part as symbolic computing, the need for systematic ways of employing suitable tools and for developing appropriate programming paradigms has become increasingly important. Furthermore, the value of adopting good software engineering practices has become more evident as implementations originally developed for personal use have evolved into commercial products. Thus the role of our course today is to introduce students to a formal, systematic way of problem solving and programming in this environment. This book is the result.

Symbolic computing is fundamentally concerned with techniques for the automated processing of symbolic notation. This book emphasizes techniques applicable to formally defined notation systems, which include the grammar-based definition and representation of such systems, recursive programming on symbolic data domains, environment data structures and their use in interpretation and evaluation applications, transformation techniques such as expression simplification and program transformation, and language-to-language translation, among others. It also emphasizes the software engineering approach to constructing symbolic computing applications through techniques such as functional programming, data abstraction, data-driven design, and rapid prototyping.

The application of the techniques developed in this book to various notation systems are illustrated by examples from four important areas—mathematics, logic, grammars, and programming languages. Although space prevents us from being able to provide a thorough treatment of these topics in their own right, we do try to provide enough background to make our symbolic computing problems in these areas self-contained. Nevertheless, our examples will perhaps be most beneficial to students who have had prior exposure to these areas. Such exposure helps to motivate the use of many of the symbolic computing techniques described. Furthermore, with a basic understanding of these areas, studying the application of symbolic computing techniques to them can complement and reinforce this knowledge.

The book adopts two notation systems for the representation of algorithms which act on symbolic data domains. In Chapter 2, a purely functional dialect of Lisp, called Small Lisp, is introduced and used for all examples presented until Chapter 7. In that chapter we turn to Common LISP as the notation system for the remainder of the book.

Two key characteristics of Small Lisp are its size and syntax. The small size of the language permits the entire language to be introduced completely yet quickly, minimizes the overhead involved in learning it, and allows us to move almost immediately into the consideration of symbolic computing applications rather than to dwell on the syntactic details of a tool. Patterned after McCarthy's original m-Lisp notation, Small Lisp uses a syntax for programs that is distinct from the syntax of Lisp data objects. This also aids in learning the language quickly without the confusion that can arise from the more common *S-Lisp* representation of Lisp programs as Lisp data objects. This does not, however, deemphasize the "programs as data objects" theme; on the contrary, it allows us to explore it in greater detail. For example, in Chapter 4, we are able to derive the S-Lisp representation by applying symbolic computing principles to the problem of representing Small Lisp programs as Lisp data objects. The S-Lisp form is then used as the basis for the Lisp-in-Lisp interpreter presented in Chapter 6 and for other metaprogramming applications discussed in Chapter 9. In addition, the S-Lisp representations of Small Lisp expressions correspond almost directly to their Common LISP counterparts. This leads in to Chapters 7 and 8, which focus on some of the more important and useful features for symbolic computing that can be found in modern Lisp systems such as Common LISP.

There is a temptation on the part of knowledgeable Lisp programmers initially to interpret this method of development as a requirement that the reader learn two languages. However, we would argue that this is not really the case, and that the reader is actually learning how to program in Lisp while working in the Small Lisp notation system. As noted previously, Chapter 4 demonstrates the equivalence of Small Lisp definitions and expressions with Common LISP definitions and expressions. Following this chapter students are immediately able to read Common LISP programs, even though Common LISP is not introduced until Chapter 7. So there is very little time required of the reader to "relearn" the Common LISP representations of the Small Lisp language constructs. This is a point frequently made by our own students, who often elect to continue using Small Lisp as a descriptive language for clarifying algorithms presented in the later chapters.

The purely functional nature of Small Lisp also has important pedagogical advantages. Throughout the book, we stress a functional programming style in the development of elegant solutions to symbolic computing problems. By initially restricting our language to exclude imperative features, we require students to use and hopefully appreciate the merits of the functional approach.

We also place a heavy emphasis on recursive programming techniques throughout. Of course, the ability to apply recursion to problem solving is an important skill for any computer scientist, but it is particularly relevant to symbolic computing because of the recursive nature of the data structures involved. Unfortunately, we have found that students tend to avoid recursion whenever an alternative is available. We have hence made recursion the only repetitive control structure available in Small Lisp. We have also delayed until Chapter 8 the introduction of high-level iteration facilities, such as mapping functions and the reduce operation, even though those facilities are preferable to recursion in many cases.

As mentioned previously, we advocate a software engineering approach to symbolic computing problems. In particular, we emphasize throughout the book the value of data abstraction in developing readable, maintainable, and translatable programs. We discuss the role of Lisp in rapidly prototyping symbolic computing applications for which production versions might ultimately be developed in some other more common implementation language, such as Pascal. We also show how design problems in symbolic computing can be tackled using a data-driven approach, based on a grammatical notation developed for symbolic data domains in Chapter 4. Although many of the examples discussed are relatively small, the techniques employed can be scaled up if a software engineering perspective is followed consistently.

The implementation of Small Lisp itself provides a significant example of the application of many of the techniques described. In particular, it serves as an illustration of the software development process in the context of symbolic computing, beginning with the formulation of a prototype interpreter, described in Chapter 6, through to its complete Pascal implementation, highlighted in Appendix C. The accompanying diskette provides the resulting Small Lisp interpreter with which students and faculty can execute their own Small Lisp programs. The source code for many of the examples in the book is also included. Small Lisp therefore serves two roles: that of a notation system for which an interpreter is to be designed (a symbolic computing problem), and that of a programming language for teaching the fundamentals of sound functional programming (a symbolic computing tool). Thus through our description of the implementation of Small Lisp, we have attempted to provide a relatively complete treatment of the development of a symbolic computing application from inception, design, and prototype through to the production version.

Finally, although our emphasis is on symbolic computing, we believe that a course organized around our book could complement or provide a feasible alternative to the ubiquitous "principles of programming languages" course. Certainly, our book does not cover nearly the breadth of programming language concepts that such a course would normally cover. However, we have found that students with a procedural language background often gain a considerable appreciation of programming language issues from an in-depth exposure to programming in Lisp languages and more specifically, Small Lisp. In particular, such exposure provides a deeper understanding of the possibilities inherent in purely functional and recursive programming paradigms compared with the traditional imperative and iterative approaches. Small Lisp is also useful in illustrating a radically different approach to data structures and in showing that a very small programming language can, in fact, be quite powerful.

Furthermore, by considering programming languages as an application domain for symbolic computing techniques, we have attempted to illustrate a number of programming language issues from an implementation perspective. In particular, a number of semantic issues are explored as modifications to the Lisp-in-Lisp interpreter discussed in Chapter 6. We also discuss such issues as typing, program transformation, and language-to-language translation in Chapter 9, and grammatical ambiguity and parsing in Chapter 12. Although we have not attempted to provide an exhaustive survey of these issues, we feel that an in-depth exploration of a number of programming language topics may be as useful as an in-breadth treatment of the entire field.

Our experience with teaching this subject has been that there is insufficient time to address all the topics presented here during a one-semester session. Therefore, the final four chapters provide an opportunity for the instructor to tailor his or her presentation of the subject according to interest. All of these chapters develop the theme of symbolic computing with respect to programming language applications to some extent. However, Chapters 9 and 12 emphasize the manipulation of programs as data objects, whereas Chapters 10 and 11 introduce alternative control structures for programs whose initial formulations were due, in large measure, to a need for such techniques to address important problems in artificial intelligence.

Thus, the book should appeal both to students planning to pursue further studies in artificial intelligence, the traditional realm of Lisp programmers, and also to those interested in the theory of programming languages. Today, at Simon Fraser University, *Symbolic Computing* is a prerequisite or strongly recommended for all students planning advanced studies in these discipline areas of computing science.

ACKNOWLEDGEMENTS

We would like to extend sincere thanks to the following groups and individuals whose assistance was instrumental in the successful completion of this book:

- The School of Computing Science at Simon Fraser University for providing an environment supportive of its faculty, which permitted us to devote the considerable time required to preparing a textbook.

- Our colleague, Dr. Fred Popowich, who made many valuable contributions to the style and accuracy of the book, and who volunteered to use the work in his lectures to assess its pedagogical merits.

- The students of CMPT 384 and CMPT 418 who suffered through ambiguities, errors, and ill-defined exercises during the development of the course material that led to this book. In spite of the problems, they provided many constructive suggestions which have improved the final manuscript.

Robert D. Cameron
Anthony H. Dixon

School of Computing Science
Simon Fraser University

1

Introduction

1.1 A PARADIGM FOR SYMBOLIC COMPUTING

Symbolic computing is concerned with the representation of information in symbolic form and how that information can be processed using computers and human-computer (interactive) systems. An example application is that of symbolic differentiation, in which the computer might be expected to take an algebraic expression such as $\sin x^2$ as input and generate the derivative with respect to x, represented symbolically by $2x \cos x^2$, as output.

In symbolic computing, we are typically dealing with a data domain which is some sort of *symbolic notation* system. In our symbolic differentiation example, the data domain consists of "algebraic expressions" written in a particular style of mathematical notation. In fact, the manipulation of algebraic expressions in various ways is one of the most important symbolic computing application areas and is known in general as *computer algebra*. Other areas of application involve other sorts of notation systems. For example, *automatic theorem proving*, or the computerized proof of logical statements, involves logical notation systems such as those of the *propositional calculus* and the *predicate calculus*. More esoterically, perhaps, but still within the paradigm of symbolic computing, is the manipulation of musical notation for the computerized processing of music and of *labanotation* for the computerized choreography of dance.

In this book, our emphasis will be on general techniques for the computerized processing of all such symbolic notation systems. To illustrate the application of these

1

techniques, we will often focus on examples that are important or interesting in their own right. In particular, we shall develop examples from formal logic, from computer algebra, and from another important application of symbolic computing, the processing of programming languages, since these too are really just notation systems for algorithms and data structures. We shall refer to this latter type of symbolic computing as *metaprogramming*; that is, the writing of programs about programs. Indeed, an important aspect of the implementation of any symbolic computing application is the *notation system* or choice of representation used for defining objects in the input or output domain. We will demonstrate that a particularly powerful notation system is a *formal grammar*. By defining an appropriate grammar, it will be possible to specify the data access functions of an abstract data type corresponding to the input or output domain.

1.2 CLASSIFICATION OF PROBLEMS

For any given area of symbolic computing, a taxonomy of application types can be provided based on the input/output characteristics of the application. For a particular notation, this generally results in a classification of applications into four categories: analyzers, generators, translators, and manipulators.

Analysis applications are those in which the symbolic notation is analyzed to determine characteristics of the notation or of what it represents. For example, software metric programs exist which quantify the complexity of a given source program; that is, they read as input a source program and output a numeric quantity that reflects the effort that can be expected to be required subsequently to maintain it. In such applications, the input is in symbolic form, but the output is nonsymbolic. An important special case of analysis applications is the *interpretation* application, in which the symbolic notation is interpreted to produce what is represented by the notation. As examples, musical notation can be interpreted to produce music through a synthesizer, while programs can be interpreted to produce the desired effect of their execution.

Generation applications are, in a sense, the "inverse" of analysis applications, taking nonsymbolic input and generating symbolic output. For example, computer programs which produce their own music can be written to generate their output in symbolic form; in this case the input might merely be a random number. Alternatively, the symbolic representation of a polynomial of given degree which fits a set of points in the Cartesian plane is an example of a programming problem whose solution is provided by a generator.

The third type of application is that of *translation*, in which input in one system of symbolic notation is translated to output in a different system of notation. For example, one might want to translate programs from Pascal to FORTRAN, or one might want to translate music from one notation system to another.

The fourth and final type of application is that of *manipulation*, in which symbolic input is processed in some fashion to generate symbolic output in the same notation system. An important special case here is that of *transformation*, in which the output is in some way equivalent to the input. For example, logical expressions can be transformed to other equivalent but distinct logical expressions using the laws of

Boolean algebra. Other examples include programs which can be transformed to generate semantically equivalent but more efficient versions, while musical notation can be transformed to recast a score in a different key.

The manipulation category includes many interactive applications wherein the symbolic notation system is used as a vehicle of communication between human being and computer. The computer is used to do the detailed work of complicated manipulation under the direction of the human being. This, for example, is the way in which computer algebra and program transformation systems work.

At this point, it must be emphasized that the classification of a given application is based on the choice of representation for the inputs and outputs. Once we have established a suitable notation system for representing symbolically the inputs or outputs of an implementation, a classification is made from the point of view of those representations. In the case of analyzers, only the inputs will be defined by a notation system; in the case of generators, only the outputs. Translators and manipulators employ symbolic representations for both their inputs and outputs. However, translators are distinguished from manipulators by the number of notation systems required to represent the inputs as well as the outputs.

It is of course also possible to argue that generators and analyzers are but special cases of translation, where the input (or output) domain is "degenerate." Alternatively, it is possible to view translation as a kind of "pipeline" wherein an input expression is supplied to an analyzer whose output is in turn the input to a generator which produces the symbolic output. The described taxonomy is not intended to be a formal partition of problems in a mathematical sense. Rather, its purpose is to provide a way of characterizing the nature of problems with symbolic domains. What we wish to do is to find features which are common to many of the problems in a given class. This permits us to take advantage of previously developed techniques that work well for that particular class of problems, when we can identify a new problem at hand as being yet another instance of a familiar type.

In fact, the very issue of what one actually means by symbolic data is not so easily dismissed as might be inferred from the examples cited so far. It is clear that one aspect of symbolic expressions is that they represent something else, such as a concept or a "real world" object, or are made up of tokens which in turn represent something else. However, one can argue that a numeric output, for example, is a symbolic representation (a graphic, or printed character in a particular font) of the concept of the number itself. Philosophically, this issue is unresolved and considerable discussion and debate is devoted to it in academic circles.

Nevertheless, we will require some sort of operational definition which will permit us to adopt the taxonomy we have described. Therefore, we will define an input or output as being nonsymbolic if it is self-referential. Informally, this suggests the input or output is not being used to represent something else. For example, a nonsymbolic use of the object X is to represent the character "X," whereas a symbolic application might be to denote the Roman numeral for "10." This definition illustrates an important operational distinction. Nonsymbolic objects can be passed as arguments to system utilities or returned as values from them, a characteristic not shared by symbolic objects within the context of their domain of interpretation. Instead, symbolic elements usually require *conversion* before (and possibly after) the computer's "arithmetic logic" is used.[1] Thus the operation expressed by "10 + 5" can be performed immediately without conversion of the operands using the standard system utilities available, while evaluating "X + V" (as the addition of two Roman numerals) requires prior conversion of the operands.

It should also be apparent that nonsymbolic applications can have symbolic solutions. This book does not address whether it is appropriate to treat a given problem as a symbolic computing application. It is certainly possible to determine symbolically that the result of input "10 + 5" is "15" by using the common addition table to identify the appropriate substitutions to make, rather than using the built-in computer arithmetic addition function. However, there is some question as to whether this is a sensible thing to do and in any case our focus will instead be on providing ways for developing a solution when the software engineer has already chosen to view a problem as an application for symbolic computing.

One should not conclude from the proposed taxonomy that a given symbolic computing problem is resolved by a program which belongs to just one of the classes described. This is not usually the case; rather, a complete solution is frequently a sequence of programs or modules, each of which is the implementation of a solution to a simpler symbolic computing subproblem. This is because it is common practice to partition a large problem into smaller, simpler ones. From a software engineering point of view two questions arise: how to partition the problem, and how simple to make each partition. The taxonomy of symbolic computing applications suggests the following design strategy. Partition a problem into a sequence of subproblems, where the solution to each subproblem can be classified according to the taxonomy given. As will be seen later, the class of an application influences the type of data access functions needed for processing objects in the input or output domains.

Finally, it should be noted that symbolic computing applications do not always run in isolation; they are commonly found as components of larger systems. For example, in an operating system, the command language processor is indeed a symbolic computing subsystem which provides a user interface to other operating system components.

1.3 SYMBOLIC COMPUTING WITH LISP

A major theme in the following chapters is the virtue of using a functional programming language as at least the initial implementation language for symbolic computing applications. Such a decision will be shown to provide many software engineering benefits over using a more conventional procedural language. While there are a number of contemporary functional languages available (e.g., Miranda [Tur85] and Standard ML [MTH90]), we will focus on a group of languages or dialects which shall collectively be referred to as the *Lisp family*. By a Lisp language, or just Lisp, we shall mean a language whose native data types include atoms, and lists, and whose primary control structures are conditionals and recursion.

---

[1]In Chapter 4, *converter* functions will be defined to provide such a capability for user-defined symbolic representations.

Historically, Lisp has been the programming language of choice for many symbolic computing applications. The representation of abstract objects as lists was proposed by John McCarthy [McC60] in the late 1950s and resulted in the first implementation of the programming language LISP (for LISt Processor). Its long history as a language for the implementation of symbolic applications, particularly in the area of artificial intelligence, has resulted in many examples distributed throughout the literature on computing. This background combined with the ready availability of efficient interpreters and compilers on every size of machine accounts, in part, for its popularity today.

A Lisp language's usefulness for symbolic computing applications stems from the facilities it provides in supporting such applications. In particular, it supports the *symbolic expression*, or *S-expression* data type, in terms of which all kinds of notation systems can be recast. In particular, a *list* is a special type of S-expression. In providing the S-expression data type, Lisp makes available both a representation scheme for symbolic data and a convenient set of operations for manipulating such data. Lisp also provides a built-in facility for reading and writing arbitrary S-expressions (including lists); this means that whenever a symbolic notation system is implemented in Lisp, input and output routines are automatically defined for that notation system. Furthermore, Lisp provides a built-in symbol table system that allows one easily to associate arbitrary properties and values with the symbols used in a notation system. Finally, Lisp supports a programming style which we shall see is conducive to symbolic computing, namely a style emphasizing functional programming and recursion. The combination of these factors, then, has lead to Lisp's dominance in symbolic computing applications.

As we shall see, however, implementing a symbolic notation system in terms of Lisp S-expressions involves some distortion of the original notation. This results in notation systems which are somewhat more awkward than the original, but nevertheless represent a good compromise between information formats that are easy to process and ones which are easy for humans to read. Even if such a compromise is ultimately unacceptable in an application requiring a high degree of "user friendliness," it may still be advisable to use Lisp for rapidly *prototyping* the application.

1.4 SYMBOLIC COMPUTING WITH PASCAL

This book is not about "clever" Lisp programming, but rather about techniques for symbolic computing. The role of Lisp is that it encourages a particular style of programming. Other languages possess the capability to represent lists and to define recursive functions. Such languages, however, also provide other ways to formulate a solution. It is our contention that because of the nature of the problem specification in symbolic computing applications, the programming style imposed by Lisp provides benefits that are important to the effective engineering of the software product. We shall endeavor to support this claim through the examples we present in later chapters.

Nevertheless, we shall also examine how symbolic computing applications can be programmed in a procedural language: Pascal. In this regard, we shall be using Pascal primarily as an example of a conventional procedure-oriented language not specifically designed for symbolic computing; the techniques we use can apply equally well to other procedural languages, such as C or Modola-2. Thus we shall use Pascal to generalize our study of symbolic computing techniques beyond the domain of Lisp. At the same time, this should also give us a better understanding of the special nature of Lisp for symbolic computing applications and also the compromises we need to make in using Lisp.

In our study of symbolic computing with Pascal, we shall be particularly interested in the translation of applications programmed in Lisp to Pascal. The ability to do such translations can be motivated by reasons of efficiency or portability. In doing such translations, however, we will also study how we can deal with notation systems that are more faithful to the original objects of the input/output domains than the Lisp representations. This will then provide us with the ideal scenario for the software engineering of symbolic computing applications: development of a rapid prototype in Lisp, followed by translation of this prototype to Pascal and concomitant improvement of the notation system to achieve a production version of the application.

1.5 PROGRAMMING STYLE FOR SYMBOLIC COMPUTING

In this book, we shall be emphasizing two points of programming style that are particularly important to symbolic computing, namely recursion and data abstraction. The importance of recursion to symbolic computing arises from the observation that symbolic data objects are themselves recursive in nature. For example, the general form of a product as an algebraic expression has two subexpressions as components (operands), and these subexpressions can in turn be products which have their own subexpressions.

Throughout we shall also place a heavy emphasis on the implementation of symbolic data domains as abstract data types. In doing so, we will demonstrate that our programs reap the well-recognized software engineering benefits of employing abstract data types in general; that is, our programs will be readable and modifiable and hence maintainable. We will also see that we can take a systematic approach to the implementation of the abstract data types for our various symbolic data domains and hence speed up our implementation work considerably. In addition, it should become evident that the use of abstract data types makes the translation of applications between source languages considerably easier and hence will strengthen our argument for the effectiveness of Lisp as a rapid prototyping language.

1.6 EXERCISES

1.1. For each of the following computing applications, identify the principal symbolic data domain, and classify the application with respect to this domain.

(a) A calculator program which accepts arithmetic expressions such as 10 + 5, 12 * 63, or (1 + 2 + 3 + 4 + 5) / 5.

(b) A program which accepts Lisp programs as input and produces Pascal programs as output.

(c) A program which produces a cross-reference dictionary of variable identifiers and the location of their usage in a source program.

(d) A program which accepts as input a digitized image from a television camera and outputs a description of the image.

(e) A program which accepts as input a digitized image of the planet Neptune and produces as output an enhanced image of the planet.

(f) A program which accepts as input the labanotation of a dance sequence and outputs an animated graphics display of the sequence.

(g) A word processor.

1.2. Consider the problem of representing positive integers using Roman numerals.

(a) Devise an algorithm to transform a Roman numeral, expressible with the characters I, V, X, L, C, D, and M, into its corresponding Arabic form.

(b) Explain why the input domain is symbolic. Discuss whether the output domain should be considered a symbolic domain.

(c) Compare the virtues of different composite data structures found in typical programming languages, for the representation of Roman numerals. Examine each from the point of view of utility (how easily can operations required by an application be performed with the representation) and readability (how well does the representation preserve the notational conventions that are likely to be familiar to a human user).

(d) Choose a particular data structure and describe what data access functions you would expect to define to complete the implementation of your representation of Roman numerals as an abstract data type. Explain if the complexity of the implementation is influenced by the choice of data structure.

2

Small Lisp

Many of the symbolic computing applications discussed throughout this book will be implemented in a purely functional dialect of Lisp called Small Lisp. Small Lisp provides a small, but sufficient set of features for symbolic computing. In common with other Lisp languages, it supports the key Lisp data types for symbolic computing and the basic operations on those data types. It also supports Lisp programming in its purest form, using only recursion for repetition and only the Lisp conditional expression for decision making and control. The small size of Small Lisp allows it to be learned very quickly. Nevertheless, Small Lisp is quite a powerful language for implementing symbolic computing applications, as we shall see in constructing a symbolic differentiation program in Section 2.6. Furthermore, the small size of Small Lisp makes it possible to conveniently consider symbolic computing applications on the domain of Small Lisp programs themselves; in particular, the implementation of a complete Small Lisp interpreter will be presented in Chapter 6.

Small Lisp uses a separate syntax for programs and data, adapted from McCarthy's original syntax for Lisp [McC60]. This is in contrast to other Lisp languages in which Lisp programs are directly represented as Lisp data objects in what we call the *S-Lisp* (symbolic Lisp) representation. The S-Lisp approach makes it easy to write Lisp programs to process other programs (i.e., *metaprograms*), which is why Lisp systems often provide a large collection of software tools not commonly found in other programming environments. For studying symbolic computing, however, there are three advantages to the separate program syntax of Small Lisp. First of all, it avoids confusion while learning the language and makes it easier to read and write programs generally. Second, it provides an opportunity to apply the concepts of symbolic computing to the problem of representing and manipulating Small Lisp programs as data objects. As we shall see in Chapter 4, this allows us to develop the S-Lisp representation of Small Lisp programs from first principles. Thus the third advantage of our approach is that it provides a deeper understanding and appreciation of the S-Lisp representation—which can be of considerable benefit when programming in an S-Lisp-based system.

Sections 2.1 through 2.5 describe the syntax and semantics of Small Lisp. An important aspect of this description is the use of an EBNF (extended Backus-Naur form) grammar for defining Small Lisp syntax.[1] Such a grammar will first of all provide a clear and concise description of the allowable Small Lisp constructs. In addition, however, it will serve as the first example of a general theme in symbolic computing, namely the use of grammars to define the syntax of symbolic notation systems. This theme will play an important role in our approach to symbolic computing; in Chapter 4, we shall refine it to provide a powerful grammatical tool for the design of symbolic computing applications.

Our semantic description of Small Lisp will generally be informal and presented through the use of examples. A formal reference manual for Small Lisp is presented as Appendix B of this book.

2.1 SYMBOLIC DATA

In symbolic computing, we want to treat symbolic information as data just as we treat numbers as data in conventional computing. One possible approach is to use character strings to represent symbolic information, an alternative considered by McCarthy [McC60], who discussed some of the advantages and disadvantages as compared with using lists. The principal disadvantage of strings is the difficulty of extracting subexpressions from a given expression. This task is central to symbolic computing and can be implemented simply and efficiently using lists.

In Lisp, *atoms* are the basic data elements out of which lists are composed. The following are all examples of Lisp atoms.

3   -42   ATOM   LongerAtom   R2D2   ++

There are two basic types of atom, namely *numeric atoms*, such as 3 and -42, and *symbolic atoms* (also called *literal atoms*), such as ATOM, R2D2, and ++. In Small Lisp, the exact syntax of atoms is as follows:

$$
\begin{aligned}
\langle\text{atom}\rangle &::= \langle\text{numeric-atom}\rangle \mid \langle\text{symbolic-atom}\rangle \\
\langle\text{numeric-atom}\rangle &::= [-]\,\langle\text{digit}\rangle\,\{\,\langle\text{digit}\rangle\,\} \\
\langle\text{symbolic-atom}\rangle &::= \langle\text{letter}\rangle\,\{\,[-]\,\langle\text{letter}\rangle \mid [-]\,\langle\text{digit}\rangle\,\} \mid \\
&\qquad \langle\text{special}\rangle\,\{\,\langle\text{special}\rangle\,\}
\end{aligned}
$$

---

[1] EBNF is defined in Appendix A.

$$\langle\text{letter}\rangle \ ::= \ \text{A} \mid \text{B} \mid \text{C} \mid \ldots \mid \text{Z} \mid \text{a} \mid \text{b} \mid \text{c} \mid \ldots \mid \text{z}$$
$$\langle\text{digit}\rangle \ ::= \ 0 \mid 1 \mid 2 \mid 3 \mid 4 \mid 5 \mid 6 \mid 7 \mid 8 \mid 9$$
$$\langle\text{special}\rangle \ ::= \ + \mid - \mid * \mid / \mid < \mid > \mid = \mid \& \mid \mid \mid ! \mid @ \mid$$
$$\# \mid \$ \mid \% \mid ? \mid :$$

Note that Small Lisp supports only integer numeric atoms; it does not provide any "real" or floating-point numeric types. Symbolic atoms have two possible forms in Small Lisp. In the first form, a symbolic atom consists of a series of letters, digits, and hyphens starting with a letter and subject to the constraint that there may not be two consecutive hyphens, nor may the last character of the atom be a hyphen. The second form of symbolic atoms allows so-called "operator" atoms, consisting of strings of one or more special characters. The exact nature of atoms varies among Lisp implementations, but most Lisps allow the forms above.

In general, atoms in symbolic computing applications will serve as *symbols* representing particular objects in the application domain. An important special case of this occurs in the representation of the Boolean data domain (truth values) in Small Lisp. Small Lisp represents the truth values "true" and "false" by the the atoms T and F. This convention is actually built-in to the Small Lisp interpreter so that all facilities which deal conceptually with Boolean values actually deal with these atoms instead. Note, however, that this convention only defines the interpretation of T and F in the Boolean domain, and does not preclude a different use for these atoms in some other application domain (although such a different interpretation could be confusing).

While atoms are the primitive data objects in Lisp, it is the *list* data type which gives Lisp both its flavor and its name (recall that LISP stands for "LISt Processor"). A list is a (possibly empty) sequence of atoms and other lists. As we argued in Chapter 1, an important reason for choosing Lisp for the implementation of a symbolic computing algorithm is the merit of representing objects in a symbolic domain with lists. For this reason, a list or atom which represents an object in such a domain is called a *symbolic expression* or, more simply, an *S-expression*. Formally, S-expressions and lists are defined as follows:[2]

$$\langle\text{list}\rangle \ ::= \ (\ \{ \ \langle\text{S-expression}\rangle \ \} \ )$$
$$\langle\text{S-expression}\rangle \ ::= \ \langle\text{atom}\rangle \mid \langle\text{list}\rangle$$

The following are all examples of Lisp lists.

```
(A List of 5 Atoms)

((VANCOUVER 4) (CALGARY 3))

(sin (power x 2))

((I am) (a (partially parsed) sentence))

()
```

The last example denotes the empty list.

---

[2]Spaces and end-of-line characters are delimiters in Lisp and may be placed anywhere except inside atoms.

Symbolic computing applications with Lisp generally involve presenting symbolic information in list-notation format. For example, a Lisp symbolic differentiation program might process expressions represented in a *prefix-keyword* notation. Here the list representation of an algebraic expression consists of an operator denoted by a keyword atom followed by an appropriate number of operand subexpressions. Thus the program would accept as input the following list representation of the algebraic expression $\sin x^2$:

$$\text{(sin (power x 2))}$$

and generate a list representation of $2x \cos x^2$ as output in the form

$$\text{(times 2 x (cos (power x 2)))}$$

Prefix-keyword notation is often used in Lisp applications because it allows the type of expression to be easily determined just by looking at the keyword atom.

There is, however, considerable flexibility here for designing different symbolic data formats. For example, a more readable notation for algebraic expressions might use operator symbols such as +, -, *, and so on, in *infix* position (i.e., between the operand subexpressions). The symbolic differentiation application would then expect the following input and produce the following output expressions:

$$\text{(sin (x ** 2))}$$

$$\text{(2 * (x * (cos (x ** 2))))}$$

Lisp list notation has proven itself very useful in symbolic computing applications over the years. This is probably because it represents a good compromise between information formats that are easy to process with computers and those which are easy for humans to read. Contrast this with a character string representation, which requires a fair bit of relatively complex processing to determine the basic symbols of the string and how they are grouped. Even so, list notation is still a compromise and some people find the plethora of parentheses rather irksome (which is why they say Lisp really means "Lots of Irritating Silly Parentheses").

2.2 BASIC EXPRESSIONS

Now we present the basic types of expression that Small Lisp provides. There are five types of expression in Small Lisp:

⟨expression⟩ ::= ⟨value⟩ | ⟨variable⟩ | ⟨function-call⟩ |
⟨conditional-expression⟩ | ⟨let-expression⟩

We will discuss only the first three of these now, deferring the presentation of the ⟨conditional-expression⟩ and ⟨let-expression⟩ constructs until after the built-in functions have been described. A ⟨value⟩ is simply an expression which represents an atom or a list as a literal constant. Numeric atoms and lists can be used directly as values in Small Lisp expressions, but symbolic atoms need to be placed in quotation marks:

$$\langle value \rangle ::= \langle numeric\text{-}atom \rangle \mid " \langle symbolic\text{-}atom \rangle " \mid \langle list \rangle$$

In the following examples—and throughout this book—the notation "$\Rightarrow$" means "evaluates to":

$$4 \Rightarrow 4$$

$$\text{"RED"} \Rightarrow \text{RED}$$

$$(A\ B) \Rightarrow (A\ B)$$

The quoting of symbolic atoms is necessary to distinguish them from variable identifiers, which have a similar syntax:

$$\langle variable \rangle ::= \langle identifier \rangle$$
$$\langle identifier \rangle ::= \langle letter \rangle \{ [-] \langle letter \rangle \mid [-] \langle digit \rangle \}$$

So if the current value of a variable x is 3, we have

$$x \Rightarrow 3$$

$$\text{"x"} \Rightarrow x$$

Strictly speaking, quoting is also necessary if the atoms T and F are to be used as expressions to denote "true" and "false."

$$\text{"T"} \Rightarrow T$$

$$\text{"F"} \Rightarrow F$$

However, in order to avoid using these quoted forms—and to improve readability—Small Lisp predefines the variables T and F to have the values T and F, respectively.

$$T \Rightarrow T$$

$$F \Rightarrow F$$

Furthermore, the variable otherwise is also predefined to have the value T; this aids the readability of conditional expressions, as we shall see later in the chapter.

The third type of Small Lisp expression is the function call. Function calls have a straightforward syntax using square brackets to surround the arguments and semicolons to separate them:[3]

$$\langle function\text{-}call \rangle ::= \langle function\text{-}name \rangle [\langle argument\text{-}list \rangle]$$
$$\langle function\text{-}name \rangle ::= \langle identifier \rangle$$
$$\langle argument\text{-}list \rangle ::= \langle expression \rangle \{ ; \langle expression \rangle \}$$

With this notation, we can now illustrate the Small Lisp built-in functions in action.

2.3 FUNCTIONS ON SYMBOLIC DATA

Small Lisp provides twenty built-in functions as primitives. This includes groups of functions for analyzing and constructing lists, for performing integer arithmetic on numeric atoms, and for comparing and manipulating symbolic atoms. It also includes

---

[3]Note that a different typeface is used to distinguish between the square brackets that are part of Small Lisp ("[ ]") and the square brackets that are used to indicate optional phrases in the EBNF ("[ ]").

functions to determine whether an arbitrary S-expression is a symbolic atom, a numeric atom or a list as well as a special error-reporting primitive.

The function cons[s-exp; list] is used to construct a new list from a given one by adding a new element to the front of it:

$$\text{cons[\"A\"; (B C)]} \Rightarrow \text{(A B C)}$$

$$\text{cons[(X Y); (Z)]} \Rightarrow \text{((X Y) Z)}$$

$$\text{cons[(A B); ((C D) (E F))]} \Rightarrow \text{((A B) (C D) (E F))}$$

$$\text{cons[\"A\"; ()]} \Rightarrow \text{(A)}$$

Note that a single element list can be created by "consing" that element onto an empty list. Also note that the second element to cons must be a list; a run-time error results otherwise.

Lists can be analyzed using the first, rest, and endp functions. The first function selects the first element of a list, while the rest function selects the tail sublist after the first element:

$$\text{first[(A (B C) D)]} \Rightarrow \text{A}$$

$$\text{rest[(A (B C) D)]} \Rightarrow \text{((B C) D)}$$

$$\text{first[rest[(A (B C) D)]]} \Rightarrow \text{(B C)}$$

$$\text{rest[rest[(A (B C) D)]]} \Rightarrow \text{(D)}$$

$$\text{rest[rest[rest[(A (B C) D)]]]} \Rightarrow \text{()}$$

Of course, first and rest make sense only if applied to a list which has at least one element; a run-time error results if either of these functions is applied to the empty list or to an atom.

To recognize when you have reached the end of a list, Small Lisp provides the endp function, mnemonic for "end predicate."[4] Specifically, endp[x] determines whether the list x is empty or not, returning the atom T if x is empty, or the atom F otherwise. (Recall that T and F, respectively, represent "true" and "false" in Small Lisp.) It is often used to check whether the tail sublist of a given list is empty after one or more applications of the rest function.

$$\text{endp[()]} \Rightarrow \text{T}$$

$$\text{endp[(A B)]} \Rightarrow \text{F}$$

$$\text{endp[rest[(A B)]]} \Rightarrow \text{F}$$

$$\text{endp[rest[rest[(A B)]]]} \Rightarrow \text{T}$$

If endp is given an atom as its argument, a run-time error results.

When an element is extracted from a list it may be any S-expression; that is, it may be a numeric atom, a symbolic atom, or another list. In order to distinguish these cases, the predicates numberp, symbolp, and listp are defined.[5] Each of these predicates takes an an arbitrary S-expression as an argument and returns T or F to indicate whether it is of the appropriate type.

---

[4]A predicate is a function that returns a truth value.

[5]Note the use of a "p" suffix as a standard naming convention for predicate functions in Lisp. Of the Small Lisp primitives, only the eq predicate does not follow this convention. For user-defined predicates, a similar convention using a "-p" suffix is used throughout this book.

$$numberp[-8] \Rightarrow T$$
$$numberp[(1\ 3)] \Rightarrow F$$
$$symbolp["A"] \Rightarrow T$$
$$symbolp[72] \Rightarrow F$$
$$symbolp[()] \Rightarrow F$$
$$listp[()] \Rightarrow T$$

Those familiar with other Lisp languages should note that in Small Lisp, the empty list is not an atom.

Once an object is known to be a symbolic or a numeric atom, various operations apply. For testing the equality of symbolic atoms, Small Lisp provides a dyadic comparison predicate eq. At least one of the arguments must be a symbolic atom.

$$eq["A";\ "A"] \Rightarrow T$$
$$eq["A";\ "a"] \Rightarrow F$$
$$eq["X";\ 4] \Rightarrow F$$
$$eq[(X\ Y);\ "A"] \Rightarrow F$$

If neither argument is a symbolic atom, a run-time error occurs. Note that it is inappropriate to return F in this case, since this would be misleading as the result of eq[(X Y); (X Y)], for example.

Small Lisp provides five integer arithmetic operations and three numeric comparison predicates for processing numeric atoms. The functions plus, minus, times, divide, and rem perform addition, subtraction, multiplication, integer division, and integer remainder, respectively:

$$plus[5;\ 2] \Rightarrow 7$$
$$minus[5;\ 2] \Rightarrow 3$$
$$times[5;\ 2] \Rightarrow 10$$
$$divide[5;\ 2] \Rightarrow 2$$
$$rem[5;\ 2] \Rightarrow 1$$

Note that the use of functions rather than operators for integer arithmetic emphasizes the fact that Small Lisp is focused primarily on symbolic rather than numeric processing. Similarly, equality, less-than, and greater-than comparisons are provided by the eqp, lessp, and greaterp predicates:

$$eqp[5;\ 2] \Rightarrow F$$
$$lessp[5;\ 2] \Rightarrow F$$
$$greaterp[5;\ 2] \Rightarrow T$$
$$greaterp[2;\ 2] \Rightarrow F$$

Each of these arithmetic and comparison functions requires two numeric atoms as arguments; if either argument is nonnumeric, a run-time error will result.

In symbolic computing applications it is sometimes necessary to process the character string representation of symbols. For this purpose, Small Lisp provides a lexicographic comparison predicate and functions for converting atom names to and from lists of their individual characters. The `sym-lessp` predicate determines whether the first of two symbolic atoms is lexicographically less than the second:

$$\text{sym-lessp}["A"; "B"] \Rightarrow \text{T}$$
$$\text{sym-lessp}["B"; "A"] \Rightarrow \text{F}$$
$$\text{sym-lessp}["AX"; "AX5"] \Rightarrow \text{T}$$
$$\text{sym-lessp}["A"; "A"] \Rightarrow \text{F}$$

A run-time error results if either of the arguments provided to `sym-lessp` is a numeric atom or a list. Given a symbolic atom, the `explode` function returns a list of characters which make up its name.

$$\text{explode}["R2D2"] \Rightarrow (\text{R 2 D 2})$$

Each element of the returned list is either a one-character symbolic atom or a single-digit numeric atom. The `implode` function performs the complementary operation to `explode`, constructing a symbolic atom by concatenating together the names and values of a list of symbolic and numeric atoms.

$$\text{implode}[(\text{L i s p})] \Rightarrow \text{Lisp}$$
$$\text{implode}[(\text{CAT CH - 22})] \Rightarrow \text{CATCH-22}$$

As shown, multicharacter and multidigit atoms can be used in the list of atoms for implosion.

The final "function" built-in to Small Lisp is `error`, an error-reporting facility. Whenever `error[message]` is called, the indicated `message` is printed out and the program is halted. The `message` may be an atom or a list.

$$\text{error}[(\text{This case has not been implemented yet})]$$

Note that `error` is not really a function since it never returns a value. Alternatively, you can think of the value of a call to `error` as always being undefined.

2.4 STRUCTURED EXPRESSIONS

In addition to values, variables, and function calls, Small Lisp has two types of structured expression, the *conditional expression* and the *let expression*. Conditional expressions are the basic decision mechanism in Small Lisp, taking the place of IF statements in conventional languages:

$$\langle\text{conditional-expression}\rangle ::= [\ \langle\text{clause-list}\rangle\ ]$$
$$\langle\text{clause-list}\rangle ::= \langle\text{clause}\rangle\ \{\ ;\ \langle\text{clause}\rangle\ \}$$
$$\langle\text{clause}\rangle ::= \langle\text{expression}\rangle \dashrightarrow \langle\text{expression}\rangle$$

A conditional expression thus is made up of a number of *conditional clauses*, each of which has two expressions, called the *predicate* and the *result* expressions, respectively. The predicate of a conditional clause is a Boolean condition which determines if its corresponding result is to be evaluated. Thus the predicate expression must evaluate to either T (representing "true") or F (representing "false"); any other result produces a run-time error. Evaluation of a conditional expression proceeds by successively evaluating the predicates of each clause until one of them returns T. When this happens, the value of the corresponding result expression is then computed and returned as the value of the entire conditional expression. For example, consider the following conditional expression, which returns the larger of two numeric atoms x and y:

```
[lessp[x; y] --> y;
 T --> x]
```

If x is less than y, the first predicate evaluates to T and y is returned. Otherwise, the T predicate in the second clause forces the value of the corresponding result expression x to be returned. Note that if none of the predicates in a conditional expression evaluates to T, the value of the expression is undefined and a run-time error occurs.

Lisp programs often use T in the final clause of a conditional expression as a standard "programming idiom" to specify the default case when none of the preceding cases apply. To make such default cases stand out more clearly, the variable otherwise—which Small Lisp predefines to have the value T—may be used:

```
[lessp[x; y] --> y;
 otherwise --> x]
```

Throughout the Small Lisp examples of this book, we will adopt the convention of using otherwise as the predicate of our default clauses.

Conditional expressions often have several branches and may also be nested. Consider a test to determine whether a given Lisp object x is either a numeric atom, or a list whose first element is a numeric atom. Such a test may be implemented using conditional expressions as follows:

```
[numberp[x] --> T;
 listp[x] -->
    [endp[x] --> F;
     otherwise --> numberp[first[x]]];
 otherwise --> F]
```

If x is a numeric atom, T is returned from the first clause and the remaining clauses are skipped. The second clause applies if x is a list. In this case, we must have additional logic nested in the result part of the clause to determine if the list has at least one element and, if so, if that element is a numeric atom. Finally, the third clause catches the default case that the object is neither a numeric atom or a list and returns F in that case.

Let expressions are the mechanism for introducing local variables in Small Lisp:[6]

⟨let-expression⟩ ::= { ⟨let-list⟩ : ⟨expression⟩ }
⟨let-list⟩ ::= ⟨local-definition⟩ { ; ⟨local-definition⟩ }
⟨local-definition⟩ ::= ⟨variable⟩ = ⟨expression⟩

Each ⟨local-definition⟩ introduces a new local variable and assigns that variable a value. These variables may then be used in evaluating the final expression (following the :) within the let expression. The value resulting from this evaluation is then returned as the value of the entire let expression. For example, to compute the square of the difference between two numbers n1 and n2, the following let expression can be used.

```
{diff = minus[n1; n2] :
 times[diff; diff]}
```

This can be read as "let `diff` have the value of `minus[n1; n2]` in evaluation of `times[diff; diff]`." Once the let expression has been evaluated, its local variables are no longer defined.

Let expressions may have multiple assignments and may be nested. The multiple assignments are conceptually carried out in parallel; all of the values being assigned are computed before any of the assignments are actually made. For example, suppose that `numlist` is a list of two numeric atoms and we want to compute the sum of the squares of the sum and difference of the two numbers. This can be accomplished as follows:

```
{n1 = first[numlist];
 n2 = first[rest[numlist]] :
 {sum = plus[n1; n2];
  diff = minus[n1; n2] :
  plus[times[sum; sum]; times[diff; diff]]}}
```

Note that the nesting of the let expressions is necessary to make the values of the local variables n1 and n2 available for computing the values of `sum` and `diff`.

2.5 DEFINITIONS AND PROGRAMS

A program in Small Lisp is simply a list of constant and function definitions.

⟨definition-list⟩ ::= { ⟨definition⟩ }
⟨definition⟩ ::= ⟨function-definition⟩ | ⟨constant-definition⟩

Both constant and function definitions may be preceded by comments which consist of one or more source lines beginning "; ; ;".

⟨comment⟩ ::= { ⟨comment-line⟩ }
⟨comment-line⟩ ::= *a line of source text beginning* ; ; ;

---

[6]Again, different typefaces are used to distinguish between the ("{}") symbols appearing in Small Lisp and the ("{}") symbols which denote repeated phrases in EBNF.

The syntax of constant definitions is similar to that of local definitions used inside let expressions.

$$\langle\text{constant-definition}\rangle \ ::= \ [\,\langle\text{comment}\rangle\,]\ \langle\text{variable}\rangle = \langle\text{expression}\rangle$$

However, in the context of the program's definition list, the definitions establish their variables as globally defined constants. The value of such a constant may be specified by an arbitrary expression using any constants and functions which have previously been defined.

Small Lisp's function definition mechanism is the only component of the language remaining to be described.

$$\langle\text{function-definition}\rangle \ ::= \ [\,\langle\text{comment}\rangle\,]\ \langle\text{function-name}\rangle$$
$$[\ \langle\text{parameter-list}\rangle\ ] = \langle\text{expression}\rangle$$
$$\langle\text{parameter-list}\rangle \ ::= \ \langle\text{variable}\rangle\ \{\ ;\ \langle\text{variable}\rangle\ \}$$

The value of a function applied to a given set of arguments is determined by evaluation of the ⟨expression⟩ comprising its body. In that evaluation, the function parameters serve as variables standing for the values of the corresponding arguments.

Consider, for example, the following definition of the square function, which squares its argument.

```
square[x] = times[x; x]
```

If the function call square[3] is issued, the parameter x will be given the value 3 and the defining expression will be evaluated in the context of that assignment, yielding 9 as the result. This result is then returned as the value of the function.

Small Lisp functions may be–and frequently are–recursive. In fact, recursion is the only mechanism for performing iterative computations in Small Lisp. For example, consider the function listsum to add up all the elements in a list of numeric atoms. Such a function might be programmed using a loop construct in other languages, but has a straightforward recursive definition in Small Lisp.

```
listsum[nums] =
 [endp[nums] --> 0;
  otherwise --> plus[first[nums]; listsum[rest[nums]]]]
```

Of course, recursion can also be used in situations for which loops are inappropriate. For example, consider the following function to check for the equality of arbitrary Lisp S-expressions.

```
equal[x; y] =
 [numberp[x] -->
    [numberp[y] --> eqp[x; y];
     otherwise --> F];
  numberp[y] --> F;
  symbolp[x] --> eq[x; y];
  symbolp[y] --> F;
  endp[x] --> endp[y];
```

```
endp[y] --> F;
equal[first[x]; first[y]] --> equal[rest[x]; rest[y]];
otherwise --> F]
```

This doubly recursive formulation is quite straightforward, and would be the preferred approach even in languages with iterative constructs.

The order in which global function definitions occur in a Small Lisp program is generally unimportant. In particular, a call to one function may appear in the definition of a second function even before the first function is defined. This allows mutually recursive functions to be programmed in a straightforward fashion.[7]

A Small Lisp program is "run" by reading it into a Small Lisp interpreter and then evaluating Small Lisp expressions in the context of the globally defined variables and functions. Typically, the program will contain one "main" function, which conventionally appears as the last one in the program. Calling this function on an appropriate set of arguments will compute and print out the result of the program. However, any other function can be called from the interpreter as well, allowing each function to be tested individually.

2.6 SMALL LISP APPLIED: SYMBOLIC DIFFERENTIATION

We will now consider how a Small Lisp program to perform symbolic differentiation might be constructed. Let us assume that our program must compute derivatives according to the rules shown in Table 2.1. This table uses the symbol n to stand for an arbitrary numeric constant and the symbol v to stand for an arbitrary mathematical variable. The symbols f and g stand for arbitrary algebraic expressions of any type. The symbols n, v, f, and g are called *metavariables*, that is, variables whose possible "values" are notational phrases rather than mathematical variables which assume numeric values. For the time being, assume that these are all the differentiation rules with which we are concerned.

The basic data type in this example is that of the algebraic expression, of which there are several possible variations. Each of these variations can be thought of as a data type in its own right. Thus, we also have data types such as `constant`, `variable`, or `cosine`, corresponding to the algebraic expressions illustrated in each rule of differentiation. We can further classify these types of algebraic expression into two broad groups, namely the *primitive* expressions, consisting of constants and variables, and the *composite* expressions, which are constructed in terms of the primitives. In order to build our Small Lisp differentiator, then, we will define Lisp representations for each of these various types of algebraic expression.

As we have indicated previously, there are a variety of ways that algebraic expressions could be represented using Lisp S-expressions; we will take a straightforward approach using infix notation. Quite naturally, the primitives of the algebraic expression domain will be represented using primitives of the S-expression domain, namely, atoms. Thus, numeric atoms will represent constants, while symbolic atoms represent variables.

---

[7]Mutual recursion is discussed in Chapter 3.

TABLE 2.1   DIFFERENTIATION RULES

$$\frac{dn}{dx} = 0 \qquad \text{(constants)}$$

$$\frac{dv}{dx} = \begin{cases} 1 & \text{if } v = x \\ 0 & \text{if } v \ne x \end{cases} \qquad \text{(variables)}$$

$$\frac{d(-f)}{dx} = -\frac{df}{dx} \qquad \text{(negations)}$$

$$\frac{d(f \times g)}{dx} = f \times \frac{dg}{dx} + g \times \frac{df}{dx} \qquad \text{(products)}$$

$$\frac{d(f/g)}{dx} = \frac{g \times df/dx - f \times dg/dx}{g^2} \qquad \text{(quotients)}$$

$$\frac{d(f + g)}{dx} = \frac{df}{dx} + \frac{dg}{dx} \qquad \text{(sums)}$$

$$\frac{d(f - g)}{dx} = \frac{df}{dx} - \frac{dg}{dx} \qquad \text{(differences)}$$

$$\frac{d(f^n)}{dx} = n \times f^{n-1} \times \frac{df}{dx} \qquad \text{(powers)}$$

$$\frac{d(\exp f)}{dx} = (\exp f) \times \frac{df}{dx} \qquad \text{(exponentials)}$$

$$\frac{d(\sin f)}{dx} = (\cos f) \times \frac{df}{dx} \qquad \text{(sine functions)}$$

$$\frac{d(\cos f)}{dx} = (-\sin f) \times \frac{df}{dx} \qquad \text{(cosine functions)}$$

Composite algebraic expressions will be represented by the composite S-expressions, namely, lists. Algebraic expressions with only one subexpression will be represented by a two-element list whose first element is a keyword or operator atom indicating the type of algebraic expression and whose second element is the representation of the subexpression. Algebraic expressions with two subexpressions will have representations as three-element lists with representations of the subexpressions as the first and third elements, and with an operator symbol for the expression type located in infix position as the second element. The representations can be summarized as shown in Table 2.2. In this table, the metavariables F, G, and N stand for the Lisp representations of the corresponding algebraic expressions, f, g, and n, respectively.[8]

---

[8]In essence, the rules in this table describe the notation for algebraic expressions using a notation of its own. This notation for describing notations is called a *metanotation*. Metavariables are particular features of the metanotation which stand for items in the notation being described.

TABLE 2.2 REPRESENTATION OF
COMPOSITE ALGEBRAIC
EXPRESSIONS

Expression	Representation
$-f$	(- F)
$f \times g$	(F * G)
f/g	(F / G)
$f + g$	(F + G)
$f - g$	(F - G)
f^n	(F ** N)
$\exp f$	(exp F)
$\sin f$	(sin F)
$\cos f$	(cos F)

This scheme now allows us to represent complex algebraic expressions using list notation. For example, the representation for $\cos(\exp 2x + 3)$ can successively be built up as shown in Table 2.3.

TABLE 2.3   REPRESENTATION OF $\cos(\exp 2x + 3)$

Expression	Representation
2	2
x	x
$2x$	(2 * x)
3	3
$2x + 3$	((2 * x) + 3)
$\exp 2x + 3$	(exp ((2 * x) + 3))
$\cos(\exp 2x + 3)$	(cos (exp ((2 * x) + 3)))

2.6.1 Algebraic Expressions as an Abstract Data Type

The scheme described above is just one possible way of representing algebraic expressions as lists. If we were to program directly in terms of this representation, our algorithms would be unnecessarily cluttered with representation details, hampering both readability and modifiability. Instead, however, we will define an abstract data type (ADT) for algebraic expressions as a symbolic data domain and implement the ADT using our representation. This approach is now an accepted design technique in software engineering which exploits the concept of *information hiding*. That is, a data type is defined in terms of a set of access functions which provide the sole means of using instances of the data type elsewhere. Since the actual implementation of the data type is "hidden" from other routines, it is possible to make modifications or even completely change the implementation without affecting the rest of the program.

For our example, the ADT definition involves four groups of functions for manipulating algebraic expressions as data objects, namely *recognizers*, *selectors*, *constructors*, and *converters*.

Before defining the ADT functions, however, some auxiliary functions for selecting the second and third elements of lists will be useful. These functions are quite simply defined, as follows:

$$second[list] = first[rest[list]]$$

$$third[list] = second[rest[list]]$$

The first group of ADT functions to be defined is a set of predicates called *recognizers*, whose purpose is to distinguish among the various types of algebraic expression. As predicates, these functions take an algebraic expression as input and return T if the expression is of the appropriate type, F otherwise. These functions are named using the particular type of algebraic expression to be recognized together with the "-p" suffix for predicates. For example, the constant-p function must check that its argument is a numeric atom, while the variable-p function checks for a symbolic atom.

$$constant\text{-}p[expr] = numberp[expr]$$

$$variable\text{-}p[expr] = symbolp[expr]$$

The recognizer negation-p sets the pattern for recognition of the composite algebraic expressions. It checks that an algebraic expression given as input is a two-element list whose first element is the atom "-".

```
negation-p[expr] =
  [listp[expr] -->
    [endp[rest[rest[expr]]] --> eq[first[expr]; "-"];
     otherwise --> F];
   otherwise --> F]
```

Once we have determined that the input expression is a list, we know that as an algebraic expression, it must have two or three elements. The expression endp[rest[rest[expr]]] then asks the question: Are we at the end of the list after removing two elements? If the answer is yes, the list has exactly two elements and we hence check for the "-" symbol as the first element.[9] In all other cases, we return F to indicate that the given expr is not a negation.

The logic for the recognizers exponential-p, sine-p, and cosine-p is the same except that a different prefix symbol is involved. We define an auxiliary function unary-math-p to capture the common logic:

---

[9]In general, we cannot assume that the first element is a prefix symbol unless the list has only two elements; for example, (sin / purity) should not be recognized as a sine function but as a quotient expression.

```
unary-math-p[expr; prefix] =
  [listp[expr] -->
    [endp[rest[rest[expr]]] --> eq[first[expr]; prefix];
     otherwise --> F];
   otherwise --> F]


exponential-p[expr] = unary-math-p[expr; "exp"]


sine-p[expr] = unary-math-p[expr; "sin"]


cosine-p[expr] = unary-math-p[expr; "cos"]
```

The remaining composite expressions are all structured as lists of three elements with an operator symbol in infix position. We define dyadic-math-p to check for this possibility and implement the corresponding recognizers accordingly:

```
dyadic-math-p[expr; infix-sym] =
  [listp[expr] -->
    [endp[rest[rest[expr]]] --> F;
     otherwise --> eq[second[expr]; infix-sym]];
   otherwise --> F]


product-p[expr] = dyadic-math-p[expr; "*"]


quotient-p[expr] = dyadic-math-p[expr; "/"]


sum-p[expr] = dyadic-math-p[expr; "+"]


difference-p[expr] = dyadic-math-p[expr; "-"]


power-p[expr] = dyadic-math-p[expr; "**"]
```

It is important to note that in every definition of a recognizer function, the tacit assumption was made that the argument being tested, expr, was in fact a valid S-expression representation of some algebraic expression. The purpose of a recognizer is to identify whether an algebraic expression is one of several possible alternatives, not to test the validity of the representation itself. Clearly, in a robust system it is important to ensure the syntactic correctness of the input before applying any functions which assume valid data. We will call such predicates *input validaters* and reserve the term "recognizer" for the role described previously.

The second group of ADT functions needed are the *selector* functions for algebraic expressions, whose purpose is to select component expressions from the various composite expression types. In processing negations, there is only one component expression, which we will refer to as the operand of the negation. Thus we define the operand selector as follows:

```
operand[expr] = second[expr]
```

Whether the expression type is a product, quotient, sum, or difference, we will use the same selector functions operand1 and operand2. The use of the same selector names for related but different expression types is referred to as *overloading*. The selector implementation is straightforward since the representations for all these types of algebraic expressions are similar.

$$operand1[expr] = first[expr]$$

$$operand2[expr] = third[expr]$$

If the representations for the expression types were different (i.e., not all using infix-notation lists), the overloaded selectors would be more complicated.

The remaining selector implementations follow the general pattern. The two selectors base and exponent are used for selecting the components of a power expression, and the overloaded selector argument is used for selecting the single argument of exponential, sine, and cosine expressions.

$$base[expr] = first[expr]$$

$$exponent[expr] = third[expr]$$

$$argument[expr] = second[expr]$$

The third group of functions in our algebraic expression ADT is a group of *constructor* functions for constructing new algebraic expressions from their components. In general, the structured algebraic expressions are represented using two- and three-element lists, so we define the following auxiliary functions:

$$list2[e1; e2] = cons[e1; cons[e2; ()]]$$

$$list3[e1; e2; e3] = cons[e1; list2[e2; e3]]$$

The make-negation constructor, for example, is now straightforward.

$$make-negation[expr] = list2["-"; expr]$$

The remaining constructors are implemented following the same pattern.

$$make-product[expr1; expr2] = list3[expr1; "*"; expr2]$$

$$make-quotient[expr1; expr2] = list3[expr1; "/"; expr2]$$

$$make-sum[expr1; expr2] = list3[expr1; "+"; expr2]$$

$$make-difference[expr1; expr2] = list3[expr1; "-"; expr2]$$

$$make-power[expr1; expr2] = list3[expr1; "**"; expr2]$$

```
make-exponential[expr] = list2["exp"; expr]

make-sine[expr] = list2["sin"; expr]

make-cosine[expr] = list2["cos"; expr]
```

As these examples illustrate, the general convention for naming constructor functions is to append the type of the item being constructed to the `make-` prefix.

The final group of ADT functions to be defined are *converter* functions to convert between the primitive expression types in the algebraic expression domain (i.e., constants and variables) and appropriate values for manipulation in our programming language. For the numeric constants, it is appropriate to convert to numeric atoms in Small Lisp, so that we can perform arithmetic on them. Now it so happens that we have already chosen to represent constant algebraic expressions as numeric atoms! Nevertheless, from the ADT point of view, we are not supposed to know what the representation is; that is, we are trying to hide the representation details in the data access functions. Therefore, we define the function `const-val` to convert a numeric constant as an algebraic expression to a numeric atom, and the function `make-constant` to perform the inverse operation.[10] These functions have the following straightforward implementations.

```
const-val[const-expr] = const-expr

make-constant[numeric-atom] = numeric-atom
```

Similarly, in order to manipulate variables in Small Lisp it is appropriate to convert them to symbolic atoms so that we can compare them with the `eq` and `sym-lessp` functions. We thus define the functions `var-name` and `make-variable` to perform the conversions.

```
var-name[variable] = variable

make-variable[symbolic-atom] = symbolic-atom
```

This completes the definition of the ADT and auxiliary functions for manipulating algebraic expressions.

2.6.2 The Symbolic Differentiation Program

We now define our main function `deriv`, which takes an algebraic expression E and a variable V and returns the derivative of E with respect to V. The implementation is a straightforward recursive definition using case analysis on the type of the expression E and logic which parallels the differentiation rules given earlier. For example, consider the rule for sum expressions:

---

[10]The `make-` prefix emphasizes the similarility of the `make-constant` converter to the constructor functions: each `make-` function builds and returns a symbolic object of a specified algebraic expression type. However, `make-constant` is not technically a constructor because it does not construct its resultant expression from other algebraic expression components.

$$\frac{d(\boldsymbol{f}+\boldsymbol{g})}{dx} = \frac{d\boldsymbol{f}}{dx} + \frac{d\boldsymbol{g}}{dx}$$

This is implemented using a conditional clause which recognizes the expression E as a sum and then builds the derivative expression as the sum of the derivatives of the operands:

```
sum-p[E] -->
    make-sum[deriv[operand1[E]; V]; deriv[operand2[E]; V]];
```

Similar analysis for the other cases allows the complete implementation of `deriv` as follows:

```
deriv[E; V] =
  [constant-p[E] --> make-constant[0];
   variable-p[E] -->
     [eq[var-name[E]; var-name[V]] --> make-constant[1];
      otherwise --> make-constant[0]];
   negation-p[E] --> make-negation[deriv[operand[E]; V]];
   product-p[E] -->
     make-sum
       [make-product[operand1[E]; deriv[operand2[E]; V]];
        make-product[operand2[E]; deriv[operand1[E]; V]]];
   quotient-p[E] -->
     make-quotient
       [make-difference
          [make-product[operand2[E]; deriv[operand1[E]; V]];
           make-product[operand1[E]; deriv[operand2[E]; V]]];
        make-power[operand2[E]; make-constant[2]]];
   sum-p[E] -->
     make-sum[deriv[operand1[E]; V]; deriv[operand2[E]; V]];
   difference-p[E] -->
     make-difference[deriv[operand1[E]; V]; deriv[operand2[E]; V]];
   power-p[E] -->
     make-product
       [make-product[exponent[E]; deriv[base[E]; V]];
        make-power
          [base[E]; make-constant[minus[const-val[exponent[E]]; 1]]]];
   exponential-p[E] --> make-product[E; deriv[argument[E]; V]];
   sine-p[E] -->
     make-product[make-cosine[argument[E]]; deriv[argument[E]; V]];
   cosine-p[E] -->
     make-negation
       [make-product[make-sine[argument[E]]; deriv[argument[E]; V]]]]
```

Our symbolic differentiation program is now complete. It consists of the data access functions for algebraic expressions (recognizers, selectors, constructors, and

converters), a few auxiliary functions (second, third, not, list2, and list3), and
the main function deriv. Using a Small Lisp interpreter, we can now run our program
and calculate derivatives of algebraic expressions.

Consider, for example, what happens when we evaluate the following expression:

```
deriv[(cos (x ** 2)); "x"]
```

The deriv function will be applied and each recognizer which is a predicate in the
conditional expression of deriv will be tried until one returns T. Such a predicate, in
this case cosine-p, is said to *succeed*. The corresponding result of the clause whose
predicate succeeded will then be evaluated. The effect will be just as if we had evaluated the following expression:

```
make-negation
  [make-product [make-sine[(x ** 2)];
                 deriv[(x ** 2); "x"]]]
```

This is the original result part of the clause, with (x ** 2) substituted for the expression argument [E] and "x" for V. Similarly, substitution of the inner application of
deriv with the expression corresponding to power-p can be performed.

```
make-negation
  [make-product
    [make-sine[(x ** 2)]];
     make-product
       [make-product[2; deriv["x"; "x"]];
        make-power["x"; make-constant[minus[2; 1]]]]]]]
```

The expression deriv["x"; "x"] of course yields 1, so the final result of executing
our program is

```
(- ((sin (x ** 2)) * ((2 * 1) * (x ** 1))))
```

The function deriv returns an algebraic expression which correctly represents
the derivative of the given expression. As in the example, however, the form of this
resulting expression is generally more complex than it needs to be. This is because a
purely mechanical set of rules is being used, without applying any simplifications. As
we shall see in Chapter 5, there are many simplifications that can be used to reduce
the complexity of the resulting algebraic expressions.

2.7 EXERCISES

2.1. Sometimes it is convenient to treat symbolic and numeric atoms the same way, that is,
to process them as atoms without distinction as to their kind.

   (a) Implement the predicate atom, which recognizes whether or not a given object is
   an atom.[11]

---

[11]We use atom rather than atom-p in keeping with historical convention.

    (b) Implement the predicate `eql` which checks for equality of two atoms.

    (c) Show how the implementation of the `equal` function defined on page 36 can be simplified through the use of the `atom` and `eql` functions.

2.2. What two kinds of errors can result if recognizers are applied to incorrectly formed representations of algebraic expressions? Give examples.

2.3. Implement `good-expr-p`, an input validater for algebraic expressions. It should take an arbitrary S-expression as input and return `T` or `F`, depending on whether that S-expression is a well-formed algebraic expression. An algebraic expression is well-formed if it is either a symbolic or a numeric atom (representing a variable or a constant), or if it is constructed from well-formed subexpressions according to the scheme given in Table 2.2.

2.4. A ⟨vector⟩ is an ordered sequence of numbers, and a ⟨matrix⟩ is an ordered sequence of ⟨vector⟩s. Define representations as lists for these abstract data types if the numbers can only be integers. Write functions in Small Lisp to perform the following tasks:

    (a) Add two vectors of length n.

    (b) Compute the dot product of two vectors of length n.

    (c) Transpose an $n \times n$ matrix.

    (d) Multiply an $m \times n$ matrix by a (column) vector of length n.

    (e) Multiply two $n \times n$ matrices.

2.5. The `deriv` program and all the data access functions it uses assume that the arguments given to them are well-formed mathematical expressions. If the expression supplied to `deriv` is not well formed, a run-time error may occur or erroneous results may be produced. How can this be avoided?

2.6. In Small Lisp define a function `atoms[x]` which returns a list of all the atoms in `x`. The argument `x` can be an atom or a list whose components, in turn, can be atoms or lists. Assume there are no multiple occurrences of atoms within `x`.

$$\texttt{atoms[(A (B (C D)) E)]} \quad \Rightarrow \quad \texttt{(A B C D E)}$$

2.7. To implement a "Student Grades" system in a list processing language requires a suitable representation for a student in the context of keeping track of marks received for the different kinds of work submitted for grading.

    (a) Propose a suitable list structure for the abstract data type ⟨student⟩ which includes the student's first and last name, student number and provision for identifying specific grades for previously completed work. Each grade should have associated with it an identifier to enable subsequent retrieval of the grade rather than finding the grade by its position in the structure. Use a formal notation, such as BNF, to describe your structure in terms of Small Lisp primitive data types and illustrate with two examples: (1) using your own name, with no grading information yet entered; and (2) using your own name, with grades for `ASST1` and `QUIZ1`.

    (b) A ⟨class⟩ is an abstract data type represented by a list consisting of the course name followed by the ⟨student⟩s (as defined in part a) registered in the course. Write a function in Small Lisp to retrieve from a student number and a list of ⟨class⟩es, a list of all course names in which the student is registered.

2.8. The following grammar describes a representation for expressions entered into a simple calculator:

$$\langle\text{calculation}\rangle \ ::= \ \langle\text{numeric-atom}\rangle \mid \langle\text{expr}\rangle$$
$$\langle\text{expr}\rangle \ ::= \ (\ \langle\text{calculation}\rangle\ \langle\text{operator}\rangle\ \langle\text{calculation}\rangle\ )$$
$$\langle\text{operator}\rangle \ ::= \ + \mid - \mid \times \mid /$$

(a) The calculator is likely to be what type of symbolic computing problem? Why?

(b) Define in Small Lisp a set of data access functions required to implement the abstract data type $\langle\text{calculation}\rangle$.

(c) Define in Small Lisp a validater function which returns true if its argument is a valid list representing a $\langle\text{calculation}\rangle$ as defined by the grammar.

(d) Define in Small Lisp an interpreter for evaluating $\langle\text{calculation}\rangle$s. That is, implement a function `interpret[calc]` which returns as its value the result of evaluating `calc`, if it represents a valid $\langle\text{calculation}\rangle$. Otherwise, return the argument unevaluated.

2.9. Write a Small Lisp function `multiples` that returns a list of the multiply occurring atoms in a given list of symbolic atoms. The order of elements in the result list is unimportant. For example:

$$\text{multiples}[(Z\ B\ C\ Z\ D\ X\ B)] \quad \Rightarrow \quad (B\ Z)$$

Choose suitable test cases to demonstrate your function.

2.10. Consider the representation of sets of atoms by lists.

(a) Implement a function `intersect` which returns the members common to two sets of elements. The order of the atoms in the result list is unimportant.

$$\text{intersect}[(A\ B\ C\ D);\ (C\ D\ E\ F)] \quad \Rightarrow \quad (C\ D)$$

(b) Implement a function `union` which returns the union of two sets without duplicate members.

$$\text{union}[(A\ B\ C\ D);\ (C\ D\ E\ F)] \quad \Rightarrow \quad (A\ B\ C\ D\ E\ F)$$

(c) Implement a function `setdiff[S1; S2]` which returns a set consisting of all the elements in S1 that are not in S2.

$$\text{setdiff}[(A\ B\ C\ D);\ (A\ D\ E)] \Rightarrow (B\ C)$$

(d) Implement a function `exclusive-union[S1; S2]` which returns the set of all elements that are in either S1 or S2 but not both sets.

$$\text{exclusive-union}[(A\ B\ C\ D);\ (A\ D\ E)] \Rightarrow (B\ C\ E)$$

(e) Implement a function `powerset[S]` which returns the power set of the set S.

$$\text{powerset}[(A\ B)] \Rightarrow ((A\ B)\ (B)\ (A)\ ())$$

(f) Suggest, but *do not implement*, a way of representing the complement of a set.

2.11. Notice that the final conditional clause in the `deriv` function explicitly uses a call to the recognizer `cosine-p` rather than simply using the `otherwise` constant to catch the final case. Explain the advantages of this approach. Pay particular attention to the issue of maintenance (e.g., the possibility that tangent functions could be introduced as a new type of algebraic expression).

2.12. Extend the Lisp representation of algebraic expressions to include the natural logarithm
(ln) function. Define and implement suitable data access functions. Modify the `deriv`
program to incorporate the appropriate differentiation rule for logarithmic expressions,
as well as a modified rule for powers, as follows:

$$\frac{d(f^g)}{dx} = g \times f^{g-1} \times \frac{df}{dx} + \ln f \times \frac{dg}{dx} \times f^g \qquad \text{(powers)}$$

$$\frac{d(\ln f)}{dx} = \frac{df/dx}{f} \qquad\qquad\qquad \text{(ln functions)}$$

3

Recursive Programming Techniques

The examples of the preceding chapter illustrate what is a general phenomenon of symbolic computing applications—that implementations are frequently recursive. Such recursive algorithms arise naturally from the recursive nature of the data structures involved. For example, symbolic data domains such as the set of algebraic expressions can give rise to recursive functions (such as `deriv`), which are applied to objects from those domains. In addition, intermediate or internal data structures can be implemented using lists and recursive functions (such as `listsum` and `equal`) on those structures. Because of the importance of recursion to symbolic computing, this chapter describes and illustrates a variety of techniques that are useful in such applications.

3.1 THINKING RECURSIVELY

Recursion and induction are actually practical techniques of formal reasoning, and their informal application is commonly observed in the problem-solving activities of children as well as adults. Unfortunately, our natural ability to use these techniques is often adversely affected when we are required to apply these skills in formal settings. Such settings include proof by induction and the use of recursion in programming.

Many programmers find recursive programming difficult to comprehend and apply, especially if they have only programmed in iteration-based languages such as Pascal, as opposed to recursion-based languages such as Small Lisp. One reason for this is that they try to understand the nature of recursion in the wrong way, by elaborating the effect of successive calls of a recursively defined function, that is, by tracing recursive programs through all their steps in order to see that they work. This is the wrong approach, for at best it merely verifies the correctness of the function for but a single input. While it might be argued that it also illustrates what happens during the execution of a recursive step, this is already conveyed by the definition of the step itself—all one is really doing is "executing" the step, that is, interpreting the recursive definition for a given input. Viewed in a more natural way, recursive programming can become a simple, elegant, and effective tool for the software developer. The "natural" way to think about recursion is to use *inductive reasoning*. This is the approach that most of us use (often unconsciously) when we perform such tasks as identifying the generating rule for a pattern by examining a few instances. Indeed, the idea of using a pattern as an aid to formulating recursive definitions has proven to be a useful technique to employ in programming. However, inductive reasoning actually encompasses at least two related activities, and it is important to make a distinction between them in order to understand more precisely the activity being employed.

Initially, when trying to find the general solution to a problem, a process which we shall call *informal induction* is often used to identify some sort of pattern, general property, or relationship that can be used. In its simplest application this process is generative in nature; that is, a generalization or pattern is proposed based on a study of the problem and its solution in a few instances. For more experienced problem solvers, the process may be somewhat different. Based on past experiences and known solutions to other problems, such individuals often know what kinds of problem instance to study and what types of pattern to look for. While such reasoning is still informal, experience often allows the problem solver to have reasonable confidence in the "correctness" of a proposed solution developed by this means.

A very general approach to use when solving a problem by informal induction is to look for patterns which express properties about complex instances of the problem in terms of the same properties in simpler cases. This is the essence of recursive problem solving. Once an appropriate property has been identified, it then needs to be formulated as a recursive statement describing the complex case in terms of the simpler one. This in turn can lead to an implemented solution to the problem as a recursive function in a suitable programming language such as Small Lisp.

As a simple example of the inductive process leading to a recursive Small Lisp function, consider the problem of determining the number of ways n different things can be ordered.[1] Let us denote our proposed solution to this problem as *orderings*(n). We might begin by examining the problem in a few instances:

Two objects A and K can be ordered in two ways, namely (A K) and (K A), so *orderings*$(2) = 2$.

Three objects A, K, and Q can be ordered in six ways: (A K Q), (A Q K), (K Q A), (K A Q), (Q A K), and (Q K A). Thus *orderings*$(3) = 6$.

---

[1]In mathematical terms, this is known as the number of *permutations* of n objects.

Four objects A, K, Q, and J can be ordered in 24 ways, so *orderings*(4) = 24.
and so on.

A comparison of the relationship between the number of objects and the number of orderings of them leads to the following observations:

1. There are three times as many orderings of three objects compared with orderings of two objects.

2. There are four times as many orderings of four objects as there are of three objects.

Examination of these examples (and a few more) might lead to the hypothesis that if $n - 1$ objects can be ordered in m ways, n objects can be ordered in $n \cdot m$ ways. Further observing that a single object A can be ordered in one way, namely (A), we could propose the following recursive definition for calculating the number of orderings of n objects.

Termination Rule.   *orderings*(1) = 1.

Recursion Rule.   *orderings*(n) = $n \cdot$ *orderings*($n - 1$), for $n > 1$.

The recursion rule allows us to calculate the number of orderings for case n in terms of the number of orderings for the simpler case $n - 1$. Of course, this process of reducing to a simpler case cannot continue forever, so the termination rule specifies our solution in the base case $n = 1$.

Given the recursive statement for calculating *orderings*(n), a corresponding Small Lisp implementation follows easily:

```
orderings[n] =
  [eqp[n; 1] --> 1;
    otherwise --> times[n; orderings[minus[n; 1]]]]
```

From an examination of a few cases for *orderings*(n), we have *induced* or proposed a general rule for its calculation and implemented this proposal as a recursive function.

3.2 RECURSIVE DEFINITIONS AND INDUCTIVE PROOFS

When a proposed solution has been developed using informal inductive reasoning, an important question that remains is: How can we be certain that our solution is correct? Fortunately, we can use a process called *formal induction* to verify properties of our solution. If our problem involves calculations or properties involving the positive integers, the process is called *mathematical induction*. As we shall see in Section 3.4, there is also a corresponding process called *structural induction*, which can be used when our problems involve recursively defined data structures such as lists or algebraic expressions.

The basis for mathematical induction is the following *inductive* definition of the positive integers.

Base Rule.   The number 1 is a positive integer.

Inductive Rule.   If k is a positive integer, $k + 1$ is a positive integer.

Completeness Rule.   No other numbers belong to the set of positive integers except those that may be determined using the base and inductive rules.

This is the mathematician's way of saying that the positive integers consist of $1, 2, 3, \ldots$ and no others. Now let P_n be some statement related to the positive integer n and suppose that we wish to show that P_n is true for all n.[2] Based on the inductive definition of the positive integers, this can be accomplished as follows:

Base Step.   Prove P_1.

Inductive Step.   Prove that if k is a positive integer and P_k is true, so is P_{k+1}.

If both these steps have been successfully taken, we can now reason as follows. The base step establishes P_1. Knowing that P_1 is true, the inductive step establishes P_2. Since P_2 is now known to be true, the inductive step further establishes P_3, and so on. In fact, the base and inductive steps establish P_n for all positive integers described by the base and inductive rules of the definition of the positive integers. Since the completeness rule specifies that there are no other positive integers, the base and inductive steps complete the proof for all positive integers.

The inductive step is clearly the critical element in carrying out a proof by induction. The goal is to prove that P_{k+1} is true whenever P_k is true for any positive integer k. This is achieved by assuming that P_k is true and then trying to show that P_{k+1} is true based on this assumption. The assumption that P_k is true is called the *inductive hypothesis*. Reflecting this approach in the proof process, we can rephrase the steps of an inductive proof as follows:

Base Step.   Prove P_1.

Inductive Step.   Assume that P_k is true, for arbitrary positive integer k. Prove P_{k+1}.

In carrying out the proof that P_k implies P_{k+1}, it is also essential to make sure that the argument is valid for any arbitrary integer k. If this is done, the inductive step will establish P_k for all k assuming that the base case P_1 has been verified.

For example, suppose that we want to prove the statement P_n defined as follows:

The recursive statement defining *orderings*(n) correctly specifies the number of different orderings of n objects.

The proof proceeds by mathematical induction.

Base Step.   Prove P_1. By the termination rule of the recursive statement, *orderings*$(1) = 1$. This is the correct number of ways a set consisting of a single object can be ordered. Therefore, P_1 is established.

Inductive Step.   Assume that P_k is true for arbitrary positive integer k. Prove P_{k+1}. That is, assume that *orderings*(k) specifies the correct number of orderings of k

---

[2]As a function of n, P_n is often called a *predicate*, that is, a function whose value is either true or false.

objects and then prove that *orderings*$(k + 1)$ specifies the correct number of orderings for $k + 1$ objects.

Let $m = orderings(k)$ be the correct number of orderings of k objects. For any of these m orderings an additional object may be added in several ways. It may be placed before the first object, between the first and second objects, between the second and third objects, and so on. More precisely, the additional object may be added to the ordering in $k + 1$ ways (i.e., before any of the k existing objects or after the last one). This is true for all m orderings of the original k objects, so there are $(k+1) \cdot m$ orderings of $k + 1$ objects.

By the recursion rule in our definition of *orderings*(n), we have

$$orderings(k + 1) = (k + 1) \cdot orderings(k)$$
$$= (k + 1) \cdot m$$

This is the correct number of orderings for $k + 1$ objects as established above. Therefore, P_{k+1} is true, whenever P_k is true, completing the inductive step.

This completes our proof by mathematical induction. Notice that the base step of our proof dealt with the termination rule of our recursive definition, while the inductive step dealt with the recursion rule. Also note that the argument used in the inductive step applies for any arbitrary positive integer k, including $k = 1$.

We can also use formal induction to verify the correctness of programs. For example, we could let P_k be the statement

The function `orderings[k]` correctly computes the number of different orderings of k objects.

An inductive proof of this statement is only slightly more complex than the one given above. However, in cases like this one, where there is a direct correspondence between the recursive definition and its implementation in Small Lisp, and the definition is known to be correct, most programmers feel reasonably confident in trusting the implementation without formal verification.

The decision as to whether to verify a program formally is usually based on our confidence in the validity of our problem solutions. In most everyday activities, including the writing of many recursive functions, we usually rely on our past experience and the apparent "obviousness" of the final result to defer a proof. The important thing in such cases is our confidence that a proof can be produced if required. This confidence is aided by structuring the recursive functions so that it is easy to see what the base and inductive steps in an inductive proof would be. In the case of functions on the positive integers, a termination rule for the case 1 corresponds to the base step, while a recursion rule for the case n in terms of the case $n - 1$ corresponds to the inductive step. Of course, there also exist situations (see, e.g., Section 5.2) where it is not at all evident that the recursive definition does in fact define the set or property desired. In such cases we can employ mathematical or structural induction (which will be defined in Section 3.4) to verify formally the desired property of our program.

In summary, then, informal inductive reasoning can be used to formulate hypotheses about problems and their solutions. Many problems can be solved recursively, by finding a way to solve a complex case of the problem by first solving a simpler case. Properties of our proposed solution can then be verified using the principle of formal induction. There is a close relationship between the rules specified in a recursive definition and the formal cases to be considered in a proof using the principle of formal induction. It is this relationship that permits properties of recursive programs to be easily verified.

3.3 VARIATIONS ON MATHEMATICAL INDUCTION

As illustrated in the preceding section, formal induction can be used to prove properties of recursive programs. More important, formal induction provides a basis for having confidence in the correctness of recursive programs, whether they are formally verified or not. Because of the central importance of formal induction to recursive thinking, then, this section examines a number of variations on recursive definitions and inductive proofs.

In many applications, the recursive definitions obtained depend on more than one of the previously defined cases. In such situations, a more convenient form of induction, known as *strong induction*, can be used. A proof by strong induction proceeds in the following steps.

Base Steps.   Prove $P_1, \ldots, P_b$. More precisely, for some given integer $b : b \geq 1$, prove P_k for all integers $k : 1 \leq k \leq b$.

Inductive Step.   Assume that for an arbitrary positive integer $k : k \geq b$, P_i is true for all $i : 1 \leq i \leq k$. Prove P_{k+1}.

There are two differences between this form of induction and that given earlier. First of all, this form allows an arbitrary number of base cases to be proven individually. Second, the inductive hypothesis is stronger. In the earlier form, sometimes called *linear induction*, one proves P_{k+1} assuming only that P_k is true. In strong induction, one is allowed to assume that P_i is true for all $i \leq k$.

For example, strong induction can be used in proving properties about the Fibonacci numbers, defined as follows:

Termination Rule 1. $x_1 = 1$.

Termination Rule 2. $x_2 = 1$.

Recursion Rule. $x_n = x_{n-1} + x_{n-2}$ for all $n > 2$.

Now consider the proposition, P_n, that the nth Fibonacci number, x_n, is given by

$$x_n = \frac{(1 + \sqrt{5})^n - (1 - \sqrt{5})^n}{2^n \sqrt{5}}$$

Strong induction can be used to prove that the proposition P_n holds for all n, as follows:

Base Step 1.   By termination rule 1, $x_1 = 1$. By the formula,

$$x_1 = \frac{(1 + \sqrt{5})^1 - (1 - \sqrt{5})^1}{2^1\sqrt{5}}$$

$$= \frac{1 + \sqrt{5} - (1 - \sqrt{5})}{2\sqrt{5}}$$

$$= 1$$

Base Step 2.   By termination rule 2, $x_2 = 1$. By the formula,

$$x_2 = \frac{(1 + \sqrt{5})^2 - (1 - \sqrt{5})^2}{2^2\sqrt{5}}$$

$$= \frac{1 + 2\sqrt{5} + 5 - (1 - 2\sqrt{5} + 5)}{4\sqrt{5}}$$

$$= 1$$

Inductive Step.   Assume that for any $k : k \geq 2$, P_i is true for all $i : 1 \leq i \leq k$. Prove P_{k+1}.

By the inductive hypothesis, the following are true:

$$x_k = \frac{(1 + \sqrt{5})^k - (1 - \sqrt{5})^k}{2^k\sqrt{5}}$$

$$x_{k-1} = \frac{(1 + \sqrt{5})^{k-1} - (1 - \sqrt{5})^{k-1}}{2^{k-1}\sqrt{5}}$$

By the recursion rule, $x_{k+1} = x_k + x_{k-1}$. Substituting in yields

$$x_{k+1} = \frac{(1 + \sqrt{5})^k - (1 - \sqrt{5})^k}{2^k\sqrt{5}} + \frac{(1 + \sqrt{5})^{k-1} - (1 - \sqrt{5})^{k-1}}{2^{k-1}\sqrt{5}}$$

$$= \frac{2(1 + \sqrt{5})^k - 2(1 - \sqrt{5})^k + 4(1 + \sqrt{5})^{k-1} - 4(1 - \sqrt{5})^{k-1}}{2^{k+1}\sqrt{5}}$$

$$= \frac{(1 + \sqrt{5})^{k-1}(2(1 + \sqrt{5}) + 4) - (1 - \sqrt{5})^{k-1}(2(1 - \sqrt{5}) + 4)}{2^{k+1}\sqrt{5}}$$

$$= \frac{(1 + \sqrt{5})^{k-1}(1 + 2\sqrt{5} + 5) - (1 - \sqrt{5})^{k-1}(1 - 2\sqrt{5} + 5)}{2^{k+1}\sqrt{5}}$$

$$= \frac{(1 + \sqrt{5})^{k-1}(1 + \sqrt{5})^2 - (1 - \sqrt{5})^{k-1}(1 - \sqrt{5})^2}{2^{k+1}\sqrt{5}}$$

$$= \frac{(1 + \sqrt{5})^{k+1} - (1 - \sqrt{5})^{k+1}}{2^{k+1}\sqrt{5}}$$

This is just the value for x_{k+1} predicted by the formula, proving that P_{k+1} holds. This completes the proof by strong induction.

Strong induction is useful because it sometimes allows proofs to be constructed more readily than with linear induction. Whenever strong induction applies, however, an equivalent, albeit more complex proof can also be constructed using linear induction.

Another variation on mathematical induction is that it may be employed on other integer domains besides the domain of the positive integers. For example, suppose that we wish to verify a predicate Q_n for all integers $n \geq a$, where $a \neq 1$. We could do this by letting $P_n = Q_{n+a-1}$ and using mathematical induction on the positive integers to verify P_n. Alternatively, we can use the following more direct approach, which is entirely equivalent:

Base Step.   Prove P_a.

Inductive Step.   Assume that P_k is true for an arbitrary integer $k : k \geq a$. Prove P_{k+1}.

The concept of mathematical induction can be extended to any domain which maps to the positive integers. Suppose that f is a function mapping values from a domain D to the positive integers. In general, f can be many-to-one; that is, many values from D can be mapped to a particular positive integer, but it must be total (i.e., a mapping must be defined for every element of D). To show that a property Q_x holds for all elements x of D, we can use mathematical induction to establish P_n defined as

Q_x is true for all x in D such that $f(x) = n$.

As we shall see in the next section, however, it may be more convenient to use formal induction directly on the inductive structure of D itself, rather than working through the mapping f.

3.4 STRUCTURAL INDUCTION

Structural induction is a technique of formal induction which can be used to verify statements on recursive data structures such as lists, S-expressions, and algebraic expressions. In general, a recursive data structure can be analyzed by breaking it down into simpler data structures of the same type. Correspondingly, the domains for data structures can be inductively defined by specifying all the ways in which complex data structures may be generated from simpler ones. For any such data domain, a proof by structural induction is based on an inductive definition for that domain, just as a proof by mathematical induction is based on the inductive definition of the integers.

Let us first consider structural induction on lists, based on the following inductive definition:

Base Rule.   ( ) is a list.

Inductive Rule.   If x is a list, cons $[a; \ x]$ is a list for any S-expression a.

Completeness Rule.   No objects are lists other than those that can be determined using the base and inductive rules.

Note that this specification parallels the inductive specification for positive integers given earlier. Now let P_x be some statement related to the list x and suppose that we wish to show that P_x is true for all x. Based on the inductive definition of lists, this can be accomplished as follows:

Base Step.   Prove $P_{()}$.

Inductive Step.   Assume that P_x is true for an arbitrary list x. Prove that $P_{\mathtt{cons[a;\ x]}}$ is true for any S-expression a.

In a similar fashion to the positive integers, the base and inductive steps establish P_x for all lists described by the base and inductive rules of the definition of lists. Since the completeness rule specifies that there are no other lists, the base and inductive steps complete the proof for all lists.

To illustrate, consider the problem of appending two lists, as in the following example:

$$\mathtt{append[(A\ B);\ ((C)\ D)]}\ \Rightarrow\ \mathtt{(A\ B\ (C)\ D)}$$

Suppose that we wish to verify the property

$$\mathtt{append[x;\ append[y;\ z]]\ =\ append[append[x;\ y];\ z]}$$

for any lists x, y, and z, given the following definition of append:

```
append[list1; list2] =
  [endp[list1] --> list2;
   otherwise --> cons[first[list1]; append[rest[list1]; list2]]]
```

It is apparent from an examination of this definition that append recurs on the first parameter, list1, so it is natural to employ structural induction on x rather than y or z, the variables used in the original statement of the property to be proved. The property to be proved by structural induction can now be stated more precisely in terms of the variable x. That is, we wish to prove

$$\forall x P_x$$

where P_x is the property about a list x that

$$\mathtt{append[}x\mathtt{;\ append[y;\ z]]\ =\ append[append[}x\mathtt{;\ y];\ z]}$$

for any lists y and z.

Base Step.   Prove

$$\mathtt{append[();\ append[y;\ z]]\ =\ append[append[();\ y];\ z]}$$

From the first clause of the recursive function append, we can see that $\mathtt{append[();\ }w\mathtt{]}$ is equal to w, for any list w. Therefore,

$$\mathtt{append[();\ append[y;\ z]]\ =\ append[y;\ z]}$$

and

$$\text{append[append[(); y]; z]} = \text{append[y; z]}$$

This establishes $P_{()}$.

> **Inductive Step.** Assume that
>
> $$\text{append[}x\text{; append[}y\text{; }z\text{]]} = \text{append[append[}x\text{; }y\text{]; }z\text{]}$$

is true for an arbitrary list x. Prove

$$\text{append[cons[}a\text{; }x\text{]; append[}y\text{; }z\text{]]}$$
$$= \text{append[append[cons[}a\text{; }x\text{]; }y\text{]; }z\text{]}$$

From the recursive definition of append, observe that

$$\text{append[cons[}a\text{; }x\text{]; } w\text{]} = \text{cons[}a\text{; append[}x\text{; }w\text{]]}, \text{ for any } w$$

So we have

$$\text{append[append[cons[}a\text{; }x\text{]; }y\text{]; }z\text{]}$$
$$= \text{append[cons[}a\text{; append[}x\text{; }y\text{]]; }z\text{]}$$
$$= \text{cons[}a\text{; append[append[}x\text{; }y\text{]; }z\text{]]}$$
$$= \text{append[cons[}a\text{; }x\text{]; append[}y\text{; }z\text{]]}$$

This establishes $P_{\text{cons[}a\text{; }x\text{]}}$.

This completes the proof by structural induction on lists.

The inductive treatment of lists is illustrative of the general case for recursive data domains. In general, an inductive definition for such a domain will consist of a number of base rules specifying the primitive elements of the domain, and a number of inductive rules specifying how complex objects of the domain can be generated from simpler ones. If the domain is specified as an abstract data type (ADT), the inductive rules will be defined in terms of constructor functions. In the list domain, for example, the base rule defines the primitive element (), while the inductive rule defines the generation of more complex lists in terms of the constructor cons.

Now consider the domain of algebraic expressions introduced in the symbolic differentiation example of Section 2.6. An inductive definition of this domain can be formulated as follows:

Base Rules.

1. A constant n is an algebraic expression.
2. A variable v is an algebraic expression.

Inductive Rules.

1. If x is an algebraic expression, so is make-negation$[x]$.
2. If x and y are algebraic expressions, so is make-sum$[x; y]$.
3. If x and y are algebraic expressions, so is make-difference$[x; y]$.
4. If x and y are algebraic expressions, so is make-product$[x; y]$.

5. If x and y are algebraic expressions, so is `make-quotient[x; y]`.

6. If x and y are algebraic expressions, so is `make-power[x; y]`.

7. If x is an algebraic expression, so is `make-exponential[x]`.

8. If x is an algebraic expression, so is `make-sine[x]`.

9. If x is an algebraic expression, so is `make-cosine[x]`.

Completeness Rule.   No objects are algebraic expressions other than those that can be determined from the application of the base rules 1 and 2, and inductive rules 1 through 9.[3]

Based on this inductive definition, a property P_x on algebraic expressions can be proven by structural induction in the following steps.

Base Steps.

1. Prove P_n for any constant n.

2. Prove P_v for any variable v.

Inductive Steps.

1. Assume that P_x is true for an arbitrary algebraic expression x.
Prove $P_{\texttt{make-negation}[x]}$.

2. Assume that P_x and P_y are true for arbitrary algebraic expressions x and y.
Prove $P_{\texttt{make-sum}[x;\ y]}$.

3. Assume that P_x and P_y are true for arbitrary algebraic expressions x and y.
Prove $P_{\texttt{make-difference}[x;\ y]}$.

4. Assume that P_x and P_y are true for arbitrary algebraic expressions x and y.
Prove $P_{\texttt{make-product}[x;\ y]}$.

5. Assume that P_x and P_y are true for arbitrary algebraic expressions x and y.
Prove $P_{\texttt{make-quotient}[x;\ y]}$.

6. Assume that P_x and P_y are true for arbitrary algebraic expressions x and y.
Prove $P_{\texttt{make-power}[x;\ y]}$.

7. Assume that P_x is true for an arbitrary algebraic expression x.
Prove $P_{\texttt{make-exponential}[x]}$.

8. Assume that P_x is true for an arbitrary algebraic expression x.
Prove $P_{\texttt{make-sine}[x]}$.

9. Assume that P_x is true for an arbitrary algebraic expression x.
Prove $P_{\texttt{make-cosine}[x]}$.

Although a proof on the domain of algebraic expressions involves considerably more steps than one on the domain of lists, the principle of structural induction is the same in both cases. Fortunately, it is not often necessary to carry out a formal proof of the properties of a symbolic computing application. With a good understanding of the principles of formal induction, one can instead make informal arguments with full confidence that the details of a formal proof could be worked out if necessary.

---

[3]Remember that we are using the term *algebraic expression* as the formal name of a particular symbolic input domain described in Chapter 2, not in the more general sense of all possible mathematical expressions that one might encounter.

Consider, for example, an informal proof of correctness for the `deriv` program implemented in Section 2.6. By inspection, we can see that it consists of a conditional expression with clauses for each possible type of algebraic expression. For constants and variables, the result returned is exactly that specified in Table 2.1. Thus the base cases of the inductive proof can be verified. For each of the composite expression types constructed with a `make...` constructor, the `deriv` program specifies how the derivative is computed in terms of the components from which the object is constructed. By the inductive hypotheses for each inductive step, we can assume that the derivatives are correctly calculated for these components. We can then see that the various rules implement exactly the specifications of symbolic differentiation specified in Table 2.1. Therefore, the correctness of the program is shown by structural induction.

As we shall see in the next chapter, the input domain for a symbolic computing problem can often be viewed as a set of elements which are defined by a grammar. A grammar thus becomes a notational system for defining symbolic data domains. Since grammars are inherently recursive in nature, they provide a logical and elegant way of defining recursive data domains. Grammars can also be interpreted in an inductive fashion to generate all the objects of such a domain. Thus structural induction will be applicable to such grammar-defined data domains, providing a basis for verification of the properties of symbolic computing programs on those domains.

One further point should be made regarding the representation of data with recursive definitions as well as the recursive implementations that can be based on that representation. It is fairly evident that, in general, the representation of an abstract object will influence the implementation. However, as any software engineer or programmer knows, several different implementations are possible from even a single representation. The decision on which approach to adopt is based on the relative importance of sometimes conflicting factors associated with software quality: simplicity, readability, and efficiency, for example. Just as there exist "good" and "bad" ways to program using the iterative and branching mechanisms of a programming language, there are also techniques and conventions which influence the quality of recursive function definition.

It is the purpose of the rest of this chapter to survey some of these techniques. With the advent of compilers capable of recognizing certain types of recursion, it is now possible for recursive coding segments to be implemented as efficiently as iterative ones. This allows the software designer to exploit the advantages of a recursive specification, with less concern for the effect of such a decision on the efficiency of the implementation. As we will demonstrate further, in the area of symbolic computing at least, there are significant benefits to be gained by the liberal, yet intelligent application of recursion.

3.5 LINEAR RECURSION

In this section and the rest of the chapter we shall examine various forms of recursive programming. The simplest general form of recursion is *linear recursion*, in which the function may make at most one recursive call from any level of invocation. For example, the previously defined function to determine all the orderings of n elements, `orderings[n]`, is linearly recursive:

```
orderings[n] =
  [eqp[n; 1] --> 1;
   otherwise --> times[n; orderings[minus[n; 1]]]]
```

As an example with lists, consider the function count-sublists, which determines the number of elements of a list which are themselves lists.

$$\text{count-sublists[(A (B C) 1 D E (F 2))]} \Rightarrow 2$$

This function requires two recursive clauses in its definition.

```
count-sublists[list] =
  [endp[list] --> 0;
   listp[first[list]] --> plus[count-sublists[rest[list]]; 1];
   otherwise --> count-sublists[rest[list]]]
```

Even though there are two recursive clauses, the definition is linearly recursive because there is no more than a single recursive call in any clause. Recall that when a conditional expression is evaluated, only one result expression is evaluated, namely that of the first clause containing a predicate that succeeds. Thus, as long as the recursive calls are confined to the result expressions of a conditional expression and each result expression contains at most one recursive call, the function is always linearly recursive.[4]

In recursive programming style, linear recursion is used in place of the iteration (looping) used in more traditional programming styles. In fact, a direct correspondence can be established between iteration and a particular type of linear recursion known as *tail recursion*. Tail recursion occurs when the value to be returned by a function is the value directly computed by a recursive call. Consider, for example, the following definition of the member function, which determines whether a symbol occurs within a given list of symbols.

```
member[sym; symbolset] =
  [endp[symbolset] --> F;
   eq[first[symbolset]; sym] --> T;
   otherwise --> member[sym; rest[symbolset]]]
```

The termination conditions for this function are that the list of symbols to be considered is empty or else that the first element of the list is the symbol sought. If neither of these conditions holds, the function calls itself recursively on the rest of the list, directly returning the result of the call as the result. Because there is no further work to be done after a tail recursive call, however, the call can instead be interpreted as an instruction to loop back to the beginning of the member function with new values for its parameters.

Compare, for example, the following iterative version of the member function, implemented in Pascal:[5]

---

[4]The recursive call can be made either directly by the result expression, or indirectly by another function called by the result expression.

[5]For the purposes of exposition we assume the prior definition of types atom and list, and ADT functions first, rest, endp and eq.

```
function member(sym: atom; symbolset: list): boolean;
  var symbolfound : boolean;
begin
  symbolfound := false;
  while not endp(symbolset) and not symbolfound do
    begin
      symbolfound := eq(sym, first(symbolset));
      symbolset := rest(symbolset)
    end;
  member := symbolfound;
end;
```

Note that the conditions which lead to each iteration of the loop in this version of member are exactly those which lead to the corresponding recursive call in the preceding version. When the loop terminates, the value returned is the same as that would be returned in the recursive version, albeit with slightly different logic. This example illustrates a general approach which can be applied to recast any tail-recursive function into iterative form.

There is a tendency for some programmers to criticize recursion as being more inefficient than iteration. Every time a function is called, it is generally necessary to save not only the return address, but also the values of all local variables before transferring control to the function body. Consequently, there is a computational overhead introduced by the need to execute instructions which perform these tasks, as well as an overhead when control is returned to the calling function, at which time the values of the local variables are restored to their saved values. It is this overhead that is often referred to when talking about the inefficiency of recursion as compared to more traditional iterative constructs such as while loops. Although the overhead is generally small, it can be significant in the performance-critical regions of a program.

Often, however, concern about the efficiency of recursive programs is misplaced. Because compilers can detect tail recursion easily and automatically, they can therefore implement tail recursive functions just as efficiently as if they were iteratively programmed.[6] This eliminates the overheads due to the saving and restoring of local variables in tail-recursive calls. From a software engineering point of view, then, it may be counterproductive to seek iterative implementations when tail-recursive ones are simpler, if the objective is improved efficiency. The result is frequently a longer and less readable program, as the example of member illustrates.

At this point it is also useful to review the examples of this section whose input domain is the set of lists; in particular, comparing them with respect to the structural organization of recursive functions as described in the preceding section. Each case is an example of linear recursion; however, the data type returned by member is boolean, while an integer is returned by count-sublists. As yet another illustration, consider the following example of linear recursion where the value returned is a list:

---

[6]Unfortunately, not many compilers outside the Lisp world actually do perform such tail-recursion optimization.

```
numeric-elements[list] =
  [endp[list] --> ();
   numberp[first[list]] -->
     cons[first[list]; numeric-elements[rest[list]]];
   otherwise --> numeric-elements[rest[list]]]
```

These examples all illustrate a type of organization that is common to most linear recursive functions whose inputs are lists, no matter what type of data is returned:

1. A termination clause which tests whether the value of the formal parameter is a primitive element[7] of the input domain. This is often just the empty list. If so, an instance of the output domain is returned.

2. A recursive clause whose result is invoked when the leading component of the list argument satisfies a given property.

3. A recursive clause whose result is invoked when the leading component of the list does *not* satisfy the property.

An awareness of the existence of standard structural organizations for recursive functions makes their implementation an almost mechanical procedure when working from a well-defined recursive specification. This observation helps to explain why a formal specification can simplify the task of recursive programming.

3.6 AUXILIARY FUNCTIONS

An important technique in recursive programming is the definition of functions through the introduction of recursive auxiliaries. In such cases, the main function itself is not recursively programmed but simply calls an auxiliary function, which is recursive, to carry out the major work.

An important use of auxiliary functions is to allow the introduction of an *accumulating parameter*. Such a parameter is used to build up the value of a recursive function as it recursively calls itself; when a termination condition is satisfied, the value of the accumulating parameter becomes the final value to be returned. For example, the `factorial` and `count-sublists` functions could be defined using accumulating parameters as follows.

```
factorial[n] = fact-aux[n; 1]

fact-aux[n; accum] =
  [eqp[n; 0] --> accum;
   otherwise --> fact-aux[minus[n; 1]; times[n; accum]]]

count-sublists[list] = count-aux[list; 0]
```

---

[7]A *primitive element* of a set is one which cannot be further decomposed into other "simpler" elements which are also members of the set.

```
count-aux[list; accum] =
  [endp[list] --> accum;
   listp[first[list]] --> count-aux[rest[list]; plus[accum; 1]];
   otherwise --> count-aux[rest[list]; accum]]
```

In each case, the main function calls the recursive auxiliary with an appropriate initial value for the accumulating parameter accum. The value to be returned is gradually built up within the auxiliary functions each time a recursive call is made. When a recursion terminates, the final value of accum is returned as the value of the function.

An important application of accumulating parameters is illustrated by these examples. In each case their use has allowed the definitions of the factorial and count-sublists functions to be recast in tail-recursive form. As observed previously, once in this form a compiler can translate them into efficient iterative code. Use of accumulating parameters in this way is often said to be a *recursion removal* technique, because it allows general linear recursions to be recast in a form which compiles to nonrecursive code.

The factorial and count-sublists functions illustrate the accumulation of numeric results; accumulation can be even more useful in constructing data structures. Consider, for example, the reverse function, which reverses a list.

$$\text{reverse}[(A\ B\ C)] \Rightarrow (C\ B\ A)$$

A straightforward recursive implementation of this function would proceed by asking how the first element of the list, A, and the reverse of the rest of the list (i.e., reverse[(B C)] or in other words (C B)) could be combined to reverse the entire list. The answer is to place the first element after the reverse of the rest of the list. List reversal by this means requires the following auxiliary function, which appends a single element to the end of a list:

```
append1[list; elem] =
  [endp[list] --> cons[elem; ()];
   otherwise --> cons[first[list]; append1[rest[list]; elem]]]
```

Using append1, the recursive implementation of reverse follows easily.

```
reverse[list] =
  [endp[list] --> ();
   otherwise --> append1[reverse[rest[list]]; first[list]]]
```

Using an accumulating parameter allows a much more efficient version of reverse to be implemented, however. In the straightforward version, note that $\Theta(n^2)$ time and space are used (where n is the length of the list), since n calls to append1 are made and these calls average $\Theta(n)$ time and space.[8] On the other hand, suppose that

---

[8]For the reader unfamiliar with big-*theta* notation, an informal definition is that the expression "$\Theta(f(n))$ time (or space)" describes the rate at which execution time (or memory space) increases as a function of the size, n, of the input. For example, the expression "$\Theta(n^2)$ time," read "order n squared time," means the execution time increases as the square of the size of the input, while $\Theta(1)$ time means that execution time is independent of input size. (Footnote continued on p. 47.)

an accumulating parameter is used to accumulate the reverse of the list seen so far as the recursion proceeds down the list. In reversing the list (A B C D E), for example, the accumulating parameter would be (B A) after processing the first two elements. Processing the next element, namely C, would then simply require a cons operation to add it to the beginning of the accumulated list (giving (C B A)). This inexpensive $\Theta(1)$ updating of the accumulating parameter would thus allow the following $\Theta(n)$ implementation of reverse.

```
reverse[list] = revaux[list; ()]


revaux[list; accum] =
  [endp[list] --> accum;
   otherwise --> revaux[rest[list]; cons[first[list]; accum]]]
```

Note also that this implementation of reverse is tail recursive, so that it can be compiled into efficient iterative code.

In addition to acting as accumulators, another use for an additional formal parameter occurs when the value returned by a function call is required more than once in the body of another function. The traditional solution is to store the result in a temporary, local variable, which is subsequently referenced wherever the value of the result is needed. In Small Lisp ⟨let-expression⟩s are used to define local variables, as described in Chapter 2. As an alternative, however, an additional parameter can be used. While not as elegant as using a local variable, it is preferable to calling the function repeatedly with the same arguments, particularly if the call is to a recursive function.

Consider, for example, a hypothetical function fn[x] defined as follows:

```
fn[x] =
  [predicate-p[costly-calc[x]] --> g[x];
   otherwise --> h[costly-calc[x]]]
```

From an examination of the function body of fn it is apparent that the function call costly-calc[x] might need to be made twice as a result of a call to fn. Consequently, we can instead define fn[x] as follows:

```
fn[x] = fn-aux[x; costly-calc[x]]


fn-aux[x; y] =
  [predicate-p[y] --> g[x];
   otherwise --> h[y]]
```

The use of an auxiliary function allows us to introduce a local variable which is bound to the value returned as a result of evaluating costly-calc[x], and at the same time

---

More formally, $\Theta(f(n))$ denotes the set of all functions which grow at the same rate as $f(n)$. That is, $g(n) \in \Theta(f(n))$ whenever there exists positive constants C_1, C_2, and N such that $C_1 |f(n)| \le |g(n)| \le C_2 |f(n)|$, for all $n \ge N$. Thus the expression "$\Theta(n^2)$ time" formally means that the execution time as a function of input size n is expressed by some function h such that $h(n) \in \Theta(n^2)$.

to preserve the requirement for only a single parameter in the definition of `fn`. Of course, a let expression provides the means for us to do this without the need to introduce an auxiliary function:

```
fn[x] =
  {y = costly-calc[x] :
   [predicate-p[y] --> g[x];
    otherwise --> h[y]]}
```

3.7 TREE SEARCHING: AN EXAMPLE

A data structure that occurs commonly in symbolic computing is the tree, or more precisely, the *rooted tree*. Trees are important because they provide a means of representing objects whose components are organized in a nonlinear, hierarchical fashion. Trees also have the virtue of being a well-studied mathematical subject in their own right, and this provides an opportunity for using the results of graph theory in the design of data structures, and development of provably correct algorithms.[9] Finally, trees can be represented by diagrams, and such a means of representation is often convenient for gaining insights into their behavior and organization.

Briefly, a rooted tree consists of two sets—a set of *nodes* and a set of ordered pairs called *directed edges*. Each directed edge (v, w) specifies a successor relation between a pair of nodes v and w, and w is said to be the *successor* of v. No node v can be the successor of more than one node w. Only one node, called the *root*, is not the successor of some other node. A node without a successor is called a *leaf*.

The versatility of the tree in programming applications comes from the fact that nodes can have any data type, and the directed edges can specify any hierarchical relationship among the nodes. This organization can be illustrated graphically in line drawings. For example, let {A, B, C, D, E, F} denote a set of nodes, and let {(A,B), (A,C), (C,D), (C,E), (C,F)} be a set of directed edges defined on the nodes. Then the tree is represented graphically in Figure 3.1.

While there are many ways to define a tree data type, for our purposes in the rest of this section, the following specification will be used:

$$\langle tree \rangle ::= (\ \langle root\text{-}name \rangle\ \{\langle tree \rangle\}\ )$$
$$\langle root\text{-}name \rangle ::= \langle symbolic\text{-}atom \rangle$$

The data type is easily represented as a list consisting of a ⟨root-name⟩, to be represented by a symbolic atom, followed by an indefinite number of lists, each corresponding to a subtree. A list of just the root name will correspond to a leaf; that is, a tree with no subtrees. The existence of a root name allows us to label all the nodes of the tree. The tree in Figure 3.1 is thus represented by the list (A (B) (C (D) (E) (F))).

We begin by defining a validater and suitable data access functions (a constructor and two selectors) for a ⟨tree⟩. From the specification given for a ⟨tree⟩, there is only

---

[9]Many references are available to the interested reader. See Harary [Har69] for a comprehensive summary of terms and results, and Gibbons [Gib85] or Read [Rea72] for some algorithms and computer-related problems.

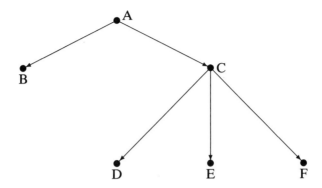

Figure 3.1   Graphical representation of a tree.

one possible representation, specifically a list whose first element is a symbolic atom.
Therefore, there are no recognizers to define since the purpose of recognizers is to
distinguish among different valid alternative subtypes of an abstract data type.

```
tree-p[obj] =
  [listp[obj] -->
     [endp[obj] --> F;
      symbolp[first[obj]] --> tree-list-p[rest[obj]];
      otherwise --> F];
   otherwise --> F]

tree-list-p[list] =
  [endp[list] --> T;
   tree-p[first[list]] --> tree-list-p[rest[list]];
   otherwise --> F]

make-tree[name; subtree] = cons[name; subtree]

root-name[tree] = first[tree]

subtrees[tree] = rest[tree]
```

Because of the usefulness of trees for representing the objects of a problem domain,
this simple representation of the tree ADT as a restricted kind of list is yet another
argument for the suitability of the list data type in the implementation of symbolic
computing applications.

Consider now the problem of finding a node with given label. This is a simple
form of the general problem of tree traversal. In this case we would like to find the
node, if it exists, with as little effort as possible. In the absence of predictive information, the search is usually performed in one of two ways: depth-first or breadth-first.
With depth-first search we endeavor to reach a leaf as "quickly" as possible:

```
depth-first-search[tree; label] = depth-aux[cons[tree; ()]; label]

depth-aux[treelist; label] =
  [endp[treelist] --> F;
   eq[root-name[first[treelist]]; label] --> T;
   otherwise -->
     depth-aux
       [append[subtrees[first[treelist]]; rest[treelist]]; label]]
```

The strategy reflected by this implementation is to maintain a list of candidate sub-trees, among which we hope to find the node whose name is label. If it is not the name of the root node of the first tree on the list, any subtrees of this node are placed on the list before we examine the remaining trees (which, of course, may now include some new ones, unless the current node is a leaf). A key feature of this implementation is that the order in which nodes are examined is controlled exclusively by the third clause of our conditional expression. Since our desire in depth-first search is to reach a leaf as soon as possible, it seems appropriate to examine the subtrees of the root of the current subtree first.

In a breadth-first search, we wish to examine the nodes which are the roots of all subtrees of the current node, before examining their subtrees. Therefore, if we examine one such subtree without success, then, although we may need to examine its subtrees of its root at a later time, we should look at the next subtree of the current node first. This strategy results in the following implementation:

```
breadth-first-search[tree; label] = breadth-aux[cons[tree; ()]; label]

breadth-aux[treelist; label] =
  [endp[treelist] --> F;
   eq[root-name[first[treelist]]; label] --> T;
   otherwise -->
     breadth-aux
       [append[rest[treelist]; subtrees[first[treelist]]]; label]]
```

Comparison of this implementation with that for depth-first search reveals that the only difference is in the third clause, where we have reversed the order of arguments in append. In fact, we took advantage of the observation made for the implementation of depth-first-search, that order of search was controlled exclusively by its third clause, and merely rewrote the result expression to provide the search candidates in a different order.

Other search strategies are possible, based on more elaborate decision mechanisms for selecting the next node to examine. Nevertheless, when that selection is based on the current candidates, it is possible to express the search algorithm in a way that defers specification of the search strategy:

```
search[treelist; label] =
  [endp[treelist] --> F;
   eq[root-name[first[treelist]]; label] --> T;
   otherwise --> search[candidates[treelist]; label]]
```

This is an important technique in software engineering, particularly in situations where the "correct" choice of algorithm can only be determined empirically, that is, by testing an implementation and measuring its performance. The substitution of new function definitions for old is generally preferable to modifying the code of existing functions because the latter procedure is more prone to the introduction of new coding errors into previously debugged programs.

The function `candidates` arranges a list of subtrees so that the next tree to be examined is at the front of the list. The ordering depends on the search strategy to be followed. For example, to define breadth-first search for testing as our initial prototype, the definition of `candidates` can be based on the result expression of the previous implementation:

```
candidates[treelist] =
   append[rest[treelist]; subtrees[first[treelist]]]
```

To obtain a revised definition for the function `breadth-first-search` itself, treat `search` as the auxiliary, and simply replace `breadth-aux` in the original definition by `search`:

```
breadth-first-search2[tree; label] = search[cons[tree; ()]; label]
```

Notice that while it is possible to define `depth-first-search` in a similar manner, both functions cannot be defined simultaneously using `search`, since each requires a different `candidates` function. It would seem that a logical extension to the development of a general search algorithm would be to provide the `search` function with the name of the `candidates` function to use. This is obviously necessary if we ever wish to mix different search strategies in processing a complex tree. To do so will require that our programming language provide the facility for us to define functions which can take functions as arguments. As this is not a feature of Small Lisp, we shall defer this topic to Chapter 8.

3.8 DOUBLE RECURSION

In the design of algorithms which employ recursion, it is desirable to develop solutions which are linear, since these generally lead to the most efficient solutions. However, many solutions are based on recursive definitions having a recursion rule which includes two (or more) self-references. The recursive definition of the Fibonacci numbers, mentioned earlier, is an example. Such definitions lead to implementations which require more than one recursive call per iteration. In particular, *double recursion* occurs when it is possible to make two recursive calls in a given invocation of a function. This situation is most evident when the recursive calls occur in a single clause. Both calls may be embedded in the predicate expression or the result expression of the clause, or we may find a recursive call in each. This commonly occurs in Lisp when both a list and all its sublists (and their sublists, etc.) have to be processed. For example, consider the `deleteall` function, which deletes all occurrences of a given symbol throughout a list structure.

```
deleteall["C"; (A C (B (D C) F C) B A)] ⇒ (A (B (D) F) B A)
         deleteall["A"; (((((A)))))] ⇒ (((((())))))
```

This function can easily be implemented using a doubly recursive implementation as follows:

```
deleteall[sym; list] =
  [endp[list] --> ();
   numberp[first[list]] -->
     cons[first[list]; deleteall[sym; rest[list]]];
   symbolp[first[list]] -->
     [eq[first[list]; sym] --> deleteall[sym; rest[list]];
      otherwise --> cons[first[list]; deleteall[sym; rest[list]]]];
   otherwise -->
     cons[deleteall[sym; first[list]]; deleteall[sym; rest[list]]]]
```

After dealing with the simple cases in which the list is either empty or its first element is atomic, the final clause contains recursive calls for processing the first element of the list as a sublist and for processing the remaining elements of the original list. The pattern of applying cons to the results of recursively processing the first and rest of the list occurs frequently.

As with linear recursion, accumulating parameters can also be useful with double recursion. Consider a function to return a list of all the distinct symbols that occur throughout a given list structure.

```
symbols-used[((X C B) ((B B) (A B X)))] ⇒ (A B C X)
```

Each symbol is to occur only once in the result list, but the order of the elements in the result list is unimportant. The key issue in such a problem is how to combine the recursion on the rest of a given list and on a sublist occurring as the first element of that list. In the example above, the recursive computations would give the following results:

```
symbols-used[(X C B)] ⇒ (B C X)
symbols-used[(((B B) (A B X)))] ⇒ (X A B)
```

In general, if the two recursive steps are handled independently, the results will have to be merged in a process which discards redundant symbols.

Using an accumulating parameter, however, the result of one recursion can be passed as the initial accumulation value for the other. Using accumulating parameters in this fashion leads to the following implementation:

```
symbols-used[list] = symbols-aux[list; ()]

symbols-aux[list; accum] =
  [endp[list] --> accum;
   numberp[first[list]] --> symbols-aux[rest[list]; accum];
   symbolp[first[list]] -->
```

```
        [member[first[list]; accum] --> symbols-aux[rest[list]; accum];
        otherwise -->
          symbols-aux[rest[list]; cons[first[list]; accum]]];
      otherwise -->
        symbols-aux[rest[list]; symbols-aux[first[list]; accum]]]
```

Note the nested nature of the final doubly recursive clause in this solution and compare it with the nonnested double recursion in `deleteall`.

Just as double recursion arises from a recursive definition based on two self-references, so it is possible for more than two recursive calls to be possible in each iteration of a recursive function. Any recurrence relation which is defined in terms of more than two previous elements is such a situation. The term *multiple recursion* will be used to describe implementations which may employ more than two recursive calls per iteration.

Although double recursion is natural and appropriate when dealing with tree-like data structures or lists and their sublists, one should be wary of double or multiple recursion in other contexts. In such situations, each additional function call per iteration can dramatically and adversely affect the efficiency of an implementation. For example, consider the following two alternative recursive definitions for the calculation of binomial coefficients:

Definition 1
$$binom(m, 0) = 1$$
$$binom(m, m) = 1$$
$$binom(m, n) = binom(m - 1, n) + binom(m - 1, n - 1)$$
$$\text{for } 0 < n < m$$

Definition 2
$$binom(m, 0) = 1$$
$$binom(m, n) = m \cdot binom(m - 1, n - 1)/n \text{ for } n > 0$$

Given straightforward recursive implementations of these definitions, what are the efficiency implications?

The first definition in effect counts the number of recursive calls made to *binom*, so the number of such calls equals the value of the binomial coefficient calculated. On the other hand, the second definition calls *binom* each time n is decremented by 1, until $n = 0$, so $binom(m, n)$ is determined after n recursive calls. This is significantly fewer in general than the number of calls required using definition 1.

3.9 PREDICATE RECURSION

In the previous sections, a recursive function was classified in terms of the number of recursive calls that occur in a typical implementation. However, it is also possible to classify a recursive function by the location of the the recursive calls within the body of the implementation. In particular, *predicate recursion* occurs when the function body includes a recursive call in the predicate term of a conditional clause. Predicate recursion can occur at the same time as linear, double, or multiple recursion. One important reason for studying predicate recursion is that it can often disguise a doubly recursive implementation so that, at first glance, it appears to be linearly recursive.

Consider, for example, a function `deepmember` which determines whether a symbol occurs anywhere within a given list structure. Supposing that the first element of a given list is a sublist, `deepmember` should return T if either the symbol being sought occurs in that sublist or it occurs in the remainder of the original list after the first element. Such a condition is easily programmed using predicate recursion as follows:

```
deepmember[sym; list] =
  [endp[list] --> F;
   numberp[first[list]] --> deepmember[sym; rest[list]];
   symbolp[first[list]] -->
     [eq[first[list]; sym] --> T;
      otherwise --> deepmember[sym; rest[list]]];
   deepmember[sym; first[list]] --> T;
   otherwise --> deepmember[sym; rest[list]]]
```

To ascertain whether this implementation is employing double recursion, we must determine whether there are a set of conditions for which two of the three recursive calls to `deepmember` observed in the function body will actually be invoked during a single evaluation of the function body. If the `list` is empty or its first element is atomic, then clearly a double recursion does not arise. However, if the first element is a list structure, the predicate recursive call in the fourth clause is made. Now consider what happens if the symbol `sym` is not contained within this list structure. In this case, the predicate recursion returns F, causing a second call to `deepmember` to be invoked in the final clause of the function body. If, however, the result of the final clause were not a call to `deepmember`, no set of conditions could be found which would result in the invocation of both of the remaining self-references, and hence the function would be an example of linear recursion. A correct recursive implementation of `deepmember`, however, requires the result of the final clause given in the definition, so double recursion is employed.

Predicate recursion occurs commonly in implementations which employ data structures whose components are themselves data structures of the same type. For example, since the components of a list can also be lists, any examination of the deep structure of a list of lists can be expected to involve predicate recursion, particularly when execution is to be terminated by recognizing the existence of a feature in some sublist. Since a list is formally a structure possessing two components, `first` and `rest`, the typical approach is to test for the existence of the feature in `first[list]` in the predicate of a clause with a recursive call. If the predicate evaluates to F, the second component, `rest[list]`, is tested in a subsequent clause, again via a recursive call. Since the "final" outcome of the function call will be determined by the value returned by this second recursive call, it is usually found in the result of the last clause of the function body. The example of `deepmember` above is a case in point.

As a second example, compare the structural organization in the implementation of `search` for traversing trees with some previous examples in this chapter. It should not be surprising to find some similarity with functions such as `member` and deepmember, because we have chosen to represent trees by lists. These "tree" lists differ from arbitrary lists only in the requirement that the first element be a symbol. Such insights can often be exploited to obtain more efficient implementations.

For example, because append is $\Theta(n)$, it would be desirable if we could eliminate the evaluation of append that occurs with every recursive call. The definition of deepmember suggests a solution for depth-first search based on using predicate recursion in a new version of the auxiliary function that defines depth-first-search:

```
fastdepth-aux[treelist; label] =
  [endp[treelist] --> F;
   eq[root-name[first[treelist]]; label] --> T;
   fastdepth-aux[subtrees[first[treelist]]; label] --> T;
   otherwise --> fastdepth-aux[rest[treelist]; label]]
```

To obtain a breadth-first solution, we need only interchange the arguments of the recursive calls to fastsearch-aux in the third and fourth clauses. Renaming the auxiliary function to fastbreadth-aux, the result is

```
fastbreadth-aux[treelist; label] =
  [endp[treelist] --> F;
   eq[root-name[first[treelist]]; label] --> T;
   fastbreadth-aux[rest[treelist]; label] --> T;
   otherwise --> fastbreadth-aux[subtrees[first[treelist]]; label]]
```

Once again, it is possible to generalize the search algorithm by deferring the decision of how selection is to be made. From our two examples, fastdepth-aux and fastbreadth-aux, we observe that the candidates are always divided into two sets: the preferred-candidates, as determined by the search strategy adopted, and the other-candidates. As before, we can now define a generalized search algorithm, whose behavior is determined by two "user-defined" functions which specify the candidates to try

```
fast-search[treelist; label] =
  [endp[treelist] --> F;
   eq[root-name[first[treelist]]; label] --> T;
   fast-search[preferred-candidates[treelist]; label] --> T;
   otherwise --> fast-search[other-candidates[treelist]; label]]
```

For depth-first and breadth-first search strategies, the definition of preferred-candidates and other-candidates in each case is easily determined by comparing the function body of fastsearch with either fastdepth-aux or fastbreadth-aux.

In concluding this section we should review one motive for developing this new version of search, namely to develop a more efficient implementation. The question is, have we really achieved this goal? It is not a simple matter to ascertain this. It is true that we eliminated the need to call the function append. But careful inspection of fast-search reveals a potential double recursion that is realized every time the predicate of the third clause is false. Essentially, the append operations have been replaced using the stack of recursive activations which arise from the first recursive call. Since this stacking is more efficient than the append operation, our new solution is indeed more efficient.

3.10 MUTUAL RECURSION

Mutual recursion exists when two or more functions are recursively defined in terms of each other. For example, consider functions odd-elems and even-elems, which return a list of the elements which are, respectively, at successive odd and even positions in a given list.

$$\text{odd-elems}[(A\ B\ C\ D\ E)] \Rightarrow (A\ C\ E)$$

$$\text{even-elems}[(B\ C\ D\ E)] \Rightarrow (C\ E)$$

$$\text{odd-elems}[(C\ D\ E)] \Rightarrow (C\ E)$$

Note that the odd elements of a nonempty list consist of the first element of a list followed by the even elements of the remainder of the list. Also note that the even elements of a nonempty list are exactly the odd elements of the list after the first element. These observations allow a simple mutually recursive implementation of the functions as follows:

```
odd-elems[list] =
  [endp[list] --> ();
   otherwise --> cons[first[list]; even-elems[rest[list]]]]


even-elems[list] =
  [endp[list] --> ();
   otherwise --> odd-elems[rest[list]]]
```

As can be seen from this simple example, mutual recursion occurs when two sets are defined inductively, each in terms of the other. The following example illustrates how such a situation arises among a large class of problems commonly called *game playing*.

In the preceding section, two tree searching strategies, breadth-first search and depth-first search, were implemented. More complex strategies are possible when predictive information is used. One method that is commonly used in the implementation of game-playing programs is move selection based on look-ahead. Look-ahead requires a means of generating some or all of the possible moves for a player and an opponent for some number of moves ahead. The resulting outcomes or positions, as a result of look-ahead, are then evaluated for their strategic advantage.

The sequences of alternative moves and the resulting outcomes or positions can be represented by a tree called a *game tree*. Each node represents a possible game position or configuration. A directed edge connects one node, say N_1, to a different node, say N_2, if there exists a move which will transform the game configuration from that represented by node N_1 to that represented by node N_2. Every path from the root to some other node of the tree defines a sequence of moves from the initial game configuration. If the player starts first, nodes an even distance from the root define the positions encountered by the player during that sequence of moves. At the same time, those nodes an odd distance from the root define the positions encountered by the opponent during the same sequence of moves.

If one quantifies the "strategic advantage" to the player of a given position or configuration by assigning some value to each node of the game tree, a derived tree called an *AND/OR tree* results. The determination of "best" move can be implemented as a search of the AND/OR tree. When the AND/OR tree is defined for all possible outcomes in a game, the leaves of such a tree reflect a termination of play (and therefore the end of the game), and wins can be distinguished from losses simply by using truth values. In particular, we can represent winning positions for the player by the truth value T, and losing positions for the player (but winning for the opponent) by the truth value F.

To find the "winning" path, the player's strategy is to make the most advantageous move from among the choices available. This corresponds to the player choosing a node which "evaluates" to T. Meanwhile the opponent tries to choose moves that provide no opportunity for the player to win; in other words, he seeks nodes that correspond to game positions from which there are no paths to T nodes. Thus the player tries to control the alternatives available to her opponent so that at least one node evaluates to T, and the opponent tries to choose nodes from which all alternatives evaluate to F.

A node which corresponds to the player's turn is called an *OR node* to reflect the calculation that must be performed to determine whether a node is "advantageous". An "advantageous" node for a player is one where the root of at least one subtree is T. At the same time, an "advantageous" node for the opponent is one where ALL subtree roots evaluate to F. A node which corresponds to the opponent's turn is thus called an *AND node*. It is these observations and the role played by the value associated with each node that give the AND/OR tree its name.

Figure 3.2 illustrates an AND/OR tree for the game known as Grundy's Game. The game begins with a single pile of n objects (in Figure 3.2, $n = 7$). Two players take turns dividing one of the piles containing more than two objects into two smaller piles each containing an unequal number of objects. As the game progresses the number of piles increases until every pile contains only one or two objects. The first player unable to make a move loses. To identify game positions with the nodes of the AND/OR graph, an m-digit number is used, where m is the current number of piles in the game. Each digit in the number corresponds to the number of objects in a pile. Thus the root is labeled 7 to indicate that the game begins with one pile containing seven objects. One possible move for the starting player is to partition the single pile of seven objects into two piles, one containing two objects, the other containing five objects. This configuration is represented by the two-digit number 25 in Figure 3.2. All leaves of the tree that are OR nodes correspond to losing positions for the starting player; all AND nodes, to winning positions.

In searching the AND/OR tree, each node is assigned a truth value based on the truth values of its subtrees. If a node corresponds to the player's turn (i.e., an OR node), it is assigned a value equal to the *disjunction* of all the roots of its subtrees. If the node corresponds to the opponent's turn (i.e., an AND node), its value is the *conjunction* of all the roots of its subtrees. The effect of this effort to assign a truth value to the root of an AND/OR tree is to traverse that tree to the leaves, that is, to

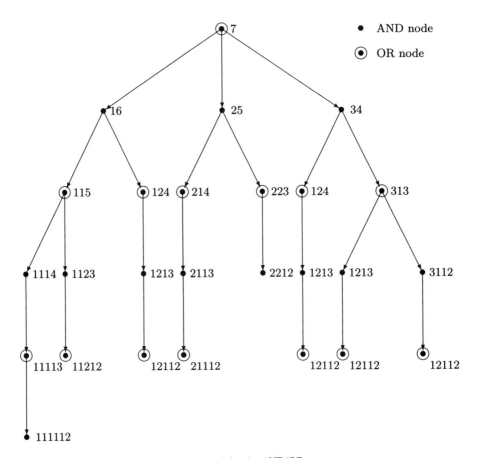

Figure 3.2 An AND/OR tree.

perform a look-ahead. If the root node of the AND/OR tree is assigned the value true as a result of this look-ahead, the player's position is a winning one.

From this description it is clear that a natural way to implement the tree search is recursively. Observe that the value assigned to a node can be calculated in two ways. The choice depends on whether the node corresponds to a player's turn or to an opponent's turn. However, if the current turn being considered is the player's, the next will be the opponent's, and vice versa. From this observation it is evident that the node values can be evaluated using mutual recursion. Consider, for example, a decision function to determine if a move is a winning one. Only leaves will initially have values associated with them; we first define a function to recognize a leaf.[10] Using the previous definition of a tree, this is simply

$$\texttt{leaf-p[tree]} = \texttt{endp[subtrees[tree]]}$$

---

[10]Notice that `leaf-p` is a recognizer and not a validater; that is, its argument is assumed to be a valid instance of a `tree`.

We now define evaluator functions for AND nodes and OR nodes using mutual recursion:

```
disj[list] =
  [endp[list] --> F;
   winning-AND[first[list]] --> T;
   otherwise --> disj[rest[list]]]

conj[list] =
  [endp[list] --> T;
   winning-OR[first[list]] --> conj[rest[list]];
   otherwise --> F]

winning-AND[node] =
  [leaf-p[node] --> T;
   otherwise --> conj[subtrees[node]]]

winning-OR[node] =
  [leaf-p[node] --> F;
   otherwise --> disj[subtrees[node]]]
```

In this implementation we have used the same representation of a tree that was described in Section 3.3. If we adopt the convention that it is the player's turn to move, the root node of an AND/OR tree being evaluated corresponds to an OR node. The initial call is therefore made to winning-OR, which is applied to the AND/OR tree. The truth value returned thus indicates if there is a winning move from the current position. An actual winning move would correspond to a subtree of the root node that evaluated to true.

The simple example above assumes the existence of a complete game tree. However, for all "interesting" games it is not possible to develop such a tree since the number of possible configurations is astronomical. For those cases where a complete game tree can be defined, one knows before play begins who will be the winner, so there is not much point to playing. Nevertheless, the technique is also applicable to partially developed game trees. Such trees are called *look-ahead trees* because they do not represent all alternatives, but rather only those alternatives for a given number of moves ahead. In such trees, the leaves may not represent terminal configurations. Therefore, a truth value cannot be assigned to indicate a winning position. Instead, a numeric value based on the game configuration associated with that leaf is derived which attempts to measure the relative advantage of that position to the player as compared with other positions at the same stage of the game. We can modify our functions above to evaluate the nodes of look-ahead trees by returning the value of a "position evaluator" function instead of a truth value whenever a leaf is reached. The argument of such a function is some representation of the game configuration associated with that leaf.

3.11 EXERCISES

3.1. Provide an inductive definition for ⟨S-expression⟩s. Use this definition and structural induction to verify that the function `equal[expr1; expr2]`, defined in Section 2.5, does compare any two S-expressions for equality.

3.2. The *weight* of a binary sequence is the number of bits set to 1. Use informal inductive reasoning to obtain a recursive definition for the number of n-bit binary sequences with weight k; then verify your result formally using the induction principle.

3.3. **(a)** Revise the definition given in Section 3.7 to obtain a representation for trees that requires trees consisting only of a root node to be represented by a symbolic atom. Based on this new definition, write a function `terminals[tree]` that returns the number of subtrees of `tree` (i.e., its immediate successors) that consist only of a root node. Your implementation should use auxiliary functions and accumulator parameters.

(b) Write a function `count-nodes[tree]` that returns the number of nodes in the entire tree, `tree`.

3.4. **(a)** Implement the function `last` which returns the last element of a list and the complementary function `butlast` which returns the sublist of a list consisting of all but its last element. Both functions may assume that the argument they are given is a list with at least one element.

$$\text{last}[(A \ (B \ C) \ (D \ E))] \Rightarrow (D \ E)$$
$$\text{butlast}[(A \ (B \ C) \ (D \ E))] \Rightarrow (A \ (B \ C))$$

(b) Provide an identity relating the `last` and `butlast` functions with the `append1` function, described in Section 3.6, which appends a single element to a list. Use structural induction to prove the validity of your identity.

3.5. Implement a recursive function `palindrome-p` which determines if a given list of atoms is a palindrome; that is, it contains the same atoms reading from left to right as from right to left.

$$\text{palindrome-p}[(A \ B \ C \ B \ A)] \Rightarrow T$$
$$\text{palindrome-p}[(A \ A \ C \ B \ A)] \Rightarrow F$$

3.6. Implement the function `deep-replace[struct; old; new]`, which replaces all occurrences of an `old` element with a `new` one throughout (all levels of) a given list `struct`.

$$\text{deep-replace}[(A \ (B \ (X \ A)) \ E); \ "A"; \ "Y"] \Rightarrow (Y \ (B \ (X \ Y)) \ E)$$
$$\text{deep-replace}[(A \ (B \ C) \ B \ C); \ (B \ C); \ (G \ F)] \Rightarrow (A \ (G \ F) \ B \ C)$$

3.7. A *binary tree* is an abstract object that consists of a unique node label and up to two binary subtrees. A binary tree without any subtrees is called a leaf. The number of leaves in a nonleaf binary tree is equal to the number of leaves in its subtrees.

(a) Give an inductive definition for binary trees.

(b) Give a formal definition as an EBNF grammar for ⟨binary-tree⟩ that requires leaves to be represented as symbolic atoms, and trees with subtrees to be represented as lists.

(c) Based on the definition given in part (b), define the following data access functions:

   i. Selector functions `subtree1` and `subtree2` to retrieve the subtrees of a given tree.

   ii. Constructors `make-one-node-tree` and `make-two-node-tree`, which construct list representations, respectively, for trees with one subtree, and trees with two subtrees.

   iii. Recognizers `leaf-p`, `one-node-tree-p`, and `two-node-tree-p` which return `T` whenever their arguments (trees) are, respectively, a leaf, a tree with one subtree, or a tree with two subtrees.

(d) Write a function `leaf-count[tree]` that returns the number of leaves of `tree`.

(e) Use structural induction to verify that your function `leaf-count[tree]` does indeed return the number of leaves in `tree`.

3.8. Use informal induction to obtain a recursive definition for finding the greatest common divisor of two numbers, m and n. Implement this definition as a Small Lisp function `gcd[m; n]`, and verify its correctness formally. *Hint*: This may be easier to prove using a proof technique other than induction.

3.9. Define a representation of Boolean (i.e., logical) expressions and implement in Small Lisp a function `eval` which applies an assignment of truth values to the variables of the Boolean expression and returns the truth value of the expression for that assignment. Assume that the expression is built from variables and the logical operators "AND," "OR," and "NOT."

3.10. As indicated in Section 3.10, it is not practical to construct the complete game tree for any interesting games; otherwise, there would be no point in playing since the outcome would be known. One way the AND/OR tree search strategy can be employed in more complex games is to develop only a part of the game tree. This subtree consists of all nodes within a given distance from the root, and this distance is called the *look-ahead* distance.

   The leaves of the subtree correspond to all leaves of the game tree which are within the look-ahead distance from the root as well as all internal nodes which are exactly the look-ahead distance from the root. The leaves of this subtree are assigned values which measure the quality of the position corresponding to the node in a manner similar to the assignment of truth values for the AND/OR tree.

   Internal nodes of the subtree are assigned values in the following way:

   If it is the starting player's turn to move, the value assigned to the corresponding node is the maximum value of all successors.

   If it is the opponent's turn to move, the value assigned to the corresponding node is the minimum value of all successors.

   Define a representation for subtrees (of game trees) that permits integer values to be associated with the labels of the leaves. Using this representation, write a function `minimax[tree]` that evaluates the subtree, `tree` of a game tree, and returns the value assigned to its root according to the strategy described.

4

The Data Abstraction Approach

One of our objectives is to present an approach to symbolic computing based on *data abstraction*. In fact, we have already seen an example of this approach in Section 2.6 with the development of the `deriv` program for algebraic expressions; we now describe this approach in general.

4.1 PRINCIPLES OF DATA ABSTRACTION

Data abstraction is a software engineering technique in which an application is programmed in terms of the logical properties of the data without knowing the physical data representation being used. This involves defining a set of *data access functions* whose specifications reflect the logical structure of the data and whose implementation provides a representation of the physical data in terms of the native data types of the programming language used. The application is then programmed entirely in terms of these data access functions, which are said to implement an *abstract data model* for the application.

In Section 2.6.1 we identified four basic types of data access function for manipulating symbolic data, namely *recognizers*, *selectors*, *constructors*, and *converters*. In general, recognizers are functions which distinguish among the various possibilities of an abstract data type. For example, `constant-p` and `quotient-p` are recognizers for two of our algebraic expression types. Selectors, such as the `operand1` and `argument` functions for algebraic expressions, extract components of a structured data object. Constructor functions, exemplified by `make-negation` and `make-power`, build new instances of structured objects out of their components. Finally, converters such as `value-of` and `make-constant` are used to convert between primitive elements of a symbolic application domain and appropriate values in the host language for manipulation.

The `deriv` example illustrates the independence from a physical data representation achieved by programming the main algorithm entirely in terms of the data access functions. In fact, this separation of logical and physical data characteristics contributes to software engineering advantages in four important ways: programs are more writable, more readable, more easily modified, and more easily translated.

Writability is the ease of implementation of programs. The effect of data abstraction is to split the implementation effort into two independent parts: implementation of the data access functions in terms of a physical data representation, and implementation of the main algorithms in terms of the logical data properties specified by the data access functions. The fact that the implementations of these two parts are noninteracting and can be tackled in any order considerably simplifies the overall implementation effort.

In addition to splitting up the implementation work, data abstraction also provides advantages in the implementation of the resultant parts. In particular, implementation of the main algorithms can proceed without worrying about the physical properties of the data; this can substantially reduce the effort involved in implementing such algorithms. Also, the small size of the data access functions themselves often makes their implementation a simple matter.

Readability is that quality of a program that characterizes how easy it is to infer a program's purpose and operation from an inspection of its source code. Data abstraction has important advantages for program readability. First of all, the main algorithms of a program are not cluttered with details of the physical data representation, but rather are more abstractly programmed in terms of logical data properties, using data access functions suitably named to reflect their function. Second, the small size of the data access functions again is an advantage, this time making them easy to understand.

The ability to modify programs is also enhanced by data abstraction. In particular, a desired change to the physical data representation can be made simply by changing the data access function implementations; no change to the main algorithms is needed as long as the logical properties of the data remain unchanged. For example, in the `deriv` program, we might want to change from an infix to a prefix representation for algebraic expressions, say for example, from $(F + G)$ to (SUM F G). This could be done simply by changing the data access functions without changing the main algorithms. Data abstraction also allows changes to the main algorithms to be carried out without affecting the data access functions. Furthermore, such changes are simplified by not having the main algorithms cluttered with physical representation details.

A fourth advantage of our data abstraction approach is that it provides a basis for the *source-to-source* (e.g., Lisp to Pascal) translation of programs. In particular, the main algorithms of an application are generally easy to translate when they are programmed abstractly, because they rely on no special language features for data manipulation. For example, given an appropriate definition of the Pascal type MathExprType for representing mathematical expressions, the following program could result from the translation of deriv from Lisp to Pascal:

```
function deriv (expr, vrbl : MathExprType) : MathExprType;
begin
if ConstantP(expr) then deriv := MakeConstant(0)
else if VariableP(expr) then
  if VarName(expr) = VarName(vrbl)
    then deriv := MakeConstant(1)
    else deriv := MakeConstant(0)
else if NegationP(expr) then deriv :=
  MakeNegation(deriv(Operand(expr), vrbl))
else if ProductP(expr) then deriv :=
    MakeSum
      (MakeProduct(Operand1(expr), deriv(Operand2(expr),vrbl)),
       MakeProduct(Operand2(expr), deriv(Operand1(expr),vrbl)))
else if QuotientP(expr) then deriv :=
    MakeQuotient
      (MakeDifference
         (MakeProduct
             (Operand2(expr), deriv(Operand1(expr), vrbl)),
          MakeProduct
             (Operand1(expr), deriv(Operand2(expr), vrbl))),
       MakePower(Operand2(expr), MakeConstantExpression(2)))
else if SumP(expr) then deriv :=
   MakeSum(deriv(Operand1(expr), vrbl), deriv(Operand2(expr), vrbl))
else if DifferenceP(expr) then deriv :=
  MakeDifference
      (deriv(Operand1(expr), vrbl),
       deriv(Operand2(expr), vrbl))
else if PowerP(expr) then deriv :=
    MakeProduct
      (MakeProduct(Exponent(expr), deriv(Base(expr), vrbl)),
       MakePower
         (Base(expr),
          MakeConstant(ConstVal(Exponent(expr)) - 1)))
else if ExponentialP(expr) then deriv :=
    MakeProduct(expr, deriv(Argument(expr), vrbl))
else if SineP(expr) then deriv :=
    MakeProduct
      (MakeCosine
         (Argument(expr)), deriv(Argument(expr), vrbl))
else if CosineP(expr) then deriv :=
    MakeNegation
```

```
                  (MakeProduct(MakeSine(Argument(expr)),
                     deriv(Argument(expr), vrbl)))
         end;
```

This program uses the same algorithm and the same data access functions (with a slight change in naming conventions) as our earlier Lisp version.

It is the hiding of language-dependent details of data manipulation in data access functions that makes source-to-source translation easy using the data abstraction approach. As in the `deriv` example, main algorithms free of explicit data manipulations can generally be translated in a straightforward fashion. On the other hand, in dealing with the data access functions, the approach is not to attempt a literal translation between languages, but rather to reimplement these functions in terms of the natural data structuring mechanisms of the output language. For example, in translating our `deriv` application from Lisp to Pascal, we need to provide a Pascal type definition for `MathExprType` and to reimplement the various data access functions for algebraic expressions in terms of this type definition.

```
     type
       MathExprType = ^ MathExprCell;
       MathExprCell =
         record
           case ExprKind : ExprKindType of
             constant : (constval : integer);
             variable : (varname : SymbolicNameType);
             negation: (operand : MathExprType);
             product, quotient, sum, difference:
               (operand1, operand2 : MathExprType);
             power: (base, expon : MathExprType);
             exponential, sine, cosine:
               (argument : MathExprType)
         end;
```

This type declaration defines algebraic expressions with the same abstract structure as our original Lisp data type, but with quite a different physical structure. Implementation of the data access functions in terms of this type definition is straightforward, however, as the following examples illustrate:

```
     function NegationP(exp : MathExprType) : boolean;
     begin
       NegationP := exp^.ExprKind = negation
     end;

     function Operand1(exp : MathExprType) : MathExprType;
     begin
       Operand1 := exp^.operand1
     end;
```

```
function MakePower(base, expon : MathExprType) : MathExprType;
var newcell : MathExprType;
begin
  new(newcell);
  newcell^.ExprKind := power;
  newcell^.base := base;
  newcell^.exponent := expon;
  MakePower := newcell
end;

function ConstVal(cnst : MathExprType) : integer;
begin
  ConstVal := cnst^.constval
end;
```

The various other data access functions could be implemented similarly.

Using these techniques, then, the data abstraction approach allows the systematic source-to-source translation of main algorithms and data access functions. In translating our deriv application from Lisp to Pascal, however, what we have not translated is an ability to read and print algebraic expressions as data objects. This ability comes for free in Lisp if we accept the compromise of representing our symbolic data objects using Lisp S-expressions. We then automatically have a way of reading and printing such objects. In Pascal, however, we must make some effort to implement our own readers and printers for the physical representation we have chosen for the symbolic data objects. On the other hand, we need not stay with a compromise representation for our symbolic data objects, but could just as well design readers and printers for whatever notational conventions we desire. We shall consider techniques for constructing such readers and printers in Chapter 12.

The ability to perform such source-to-source translation suggests a *rapid prototyping* methodology for developing symbolic computing applications. Lisp is used to prototype an application, without making any commitment to the language ultimately used for the production version. This takes advantage of Lisp's built-in I/O capabilities and other features to rapidly implement the initial version. The prototype then represents an initial design of a system which can be evaluated and modified based on user feedback. Such prototypes can be particularly important in designing good user interfaces, which are hard to specify correctly the first time through. Once the prototype has been developed to an acceptable form, work on a production version can begin, with a relatively free choice of implementation language. Even if a language other than Lisp is chosen, use of the data abstraction approach during prototype development allows the translation techniques described above to be employed, reusing much of the work in constructing main algorithms and data access functions.

4.2 GRAMMAR-BASED DATA ABSTRACTION

Although the manual construction of an abstract data model for algebraic expressions in the deriv example was somewhat tedious, there were significant payoffs in the development of an application as outlined in the preceding section. Nevertheless, an even greater improvement in the efficiency of software development of symbolic computing applications can result if a systematic way of expressing abstract data models can be formulated. Fortunately, this is possible using *grammar*-based techniques and a formal notation system, such as GRAIL (GRAmmars In Lisp), which we shall describe presently.

A *grammar* is a formal set of rules describing the formation of valid strings in a notation system or language. Of course, the grammar rules themselves must be written using some notational conventions; a notation system for grammars is typically called a *grammatical formalism*. Such grammatical formalisms are examples of *metalanguages* (i.e., languages for describing languages). For the examples we have discussed so far, we have been using one of the most common such formalisms, EBNF (extended Backus-Naur form) metalanguage, which is widely used for describing the syntax of programming languages. In fact, the grammar of Small Lisp, as presented in Chapter 2, is written in EBNF.

In this section we will be introducing GRAIL, a grammatical formalism specifically designed for describing symbolic notations in Lisp. In comparison to other grammatical formalisms, GRAIL has two unusual aspects. First of all, it restricts the strings which can be described in a grammar to those which represent valid Lisp data objects. For example, GRAIL terminal symbols are restricted to be either Lisp atoms or parentheses ("(" and ")") and parentheses must be balanced. The second unusual aspect of GRAIL is that it is designed not only to represent symbolic notations, but also to specify the ADT on the corresponding symbolic data domain. That is, a GRAIL grammar for a given symbolic notation specifies all the data access functions necessary for manipulating the items of that notation as data objects. Before describing GRAIL in detail, however, let us review some terminology common to all grammatical formalisms.

Typically, a grammar is written using three types of symbols, namely, *terminal symbols*, *nonterminal symbols*, and *metasymbols*. A *terminal symbol* is a symbol in the grammar which directly denotes a corresponding symbol in the language being defined. For example, --> is a terminal symbol in the following EBNF rule for conditional clauses in Small Lisp.

$$\langle \text{clause} \rangle \; ::= \; \langle \text{expression} \rangle \; \text{-->} \; \langle \text{expression} \rangle$$

Nonterminal symbols, on the other hand, do not directly denote objects of the language being defined, but rather, stand for a whole class of language phrases. For example, the EBNF rule above defines the class of phrases that correspond to the ⟨clause⟩ nonterminal in terms of phrases corresponding to the ⟨expression⟩ nonterminal.

In contrast to both terminal and nonterminal symbols, *metasymbols* do not stand for any part of the language being defined, but are symbols which have some special meaning in the metalanguage. For example, in the EBNF rule above, the metasymbol "::=" serves to introduce, on its right-hand side (R.H.S.), the definition for the left-hand side (L.H.S.) nonterminal ⟨clause⟩.[1] Other EBNF metasymbols include "|" to

---

[1]The need to reference the right-hand or left-hand sides of a rule occurs so frequently that we will adopt the convention of representing these phrases by the abbreviations "R.H.S." and "L.H.S."

separate alternative phrases, "[" and "]" to enclose optional phrases, and "{" and "}" to enclose phrases which may be repeated zero or more times.

Now let us consider the GRAIL formalism in detail. In a GRAIL grammar, there are four types of rule for defining Lisp objects, namely, *alternation* rules, *list* rules, *construction* rules, and *lexical* rules. Each of these types of rule is essentially a restricted form of EBNF rule. In addition, GRAIL further extends EBNF by adding *component names* to the R.H.S. nonterminals of construction rules and by allowing special *repetition* metasymbols in list and construction rules.

4.2.1 Alternation Rules

The first type of rule in the GRAIL formalism is the *alternation* rule. It specifies a symbolic data type as one of several alternatives, as the following rule listing the various algebraic expression types illustrates:

⟨expression⟩ ::= ⟨constant⟩ | ⟨variable⟩ | ⟨negation⟩ | ⟨product⟩ | ⟨quotient⟩ | ⟨sum⟩ | ⟨difference⟩ | ⟨power⟩ | ⟨exponential⟩ | ⟨sine⟩ | ⟨cosine⟩

Each alternative within an alternation rule consists of a single nonterminal symbol. These nonterminal symbols thus provide names for distinguishing between the alternatives whenever a choice must be made. The general form of an alternation rule can be expressed by describing its syntax[2] using the following EBNF rules.

⟨alternation-rule⟩ ::= ⟨nonterminal⟩ ::= ⟨nonterminal⟩ { | ⟨nonterminal⟩ }
⟨nonterminal⟩ ::= < ⟨identifier⟩ >

Note that this specification requires an alternation rule to consist of at least two alternatives separated by vertical bars ("|").

In the GRAIL formalism, alternation rules are used to specify the recognizer functions that are necessary for distinguishing between the various alternatives for a symbolic object type. In using a GRAIL grammar as a software specification tool, conventions for the naming of the data access functions should be adopted. Each recognizer is typically named by adding the suffix "-p" to the name of the appropriate subtype. For example, the alternation rule given above for ⟨expression⟩ specifies ten recognizers. For the first three alternatives defined in the rule, the corresponding recognizers are named `constant-p`, `variable-p`, and `negation-p`, respectively. The remaining seven are similarly named. Each recognizes a different type of algebraic expression as a data object. Note, however, that alternation rules do not provide any information on how such recognizers are to be implemented. This must be determined by reference to the rules which describe the actual formation of the subtypes.

4.2.2 List Rules

The second type of rule in the GRAIL formalism is the *list rule*. It defines an object as a list of components of a given type, called the *base* type of the list. For example, the following list rule defines an ⟨expression-list⟩ as a list of one or more expressions.

---

[2]The syntax of GRAIL rules is more precisely referred to as a *metasyntax* since it is the syntax of a notation which is in turn used to describe the syntax of symbolic data objects.

$$\langle\text{expression-list}\rangle ::= (\langle\text{expression}^+\rangle)$$

The R.H.S. of a list rule always contains a single nonterminal symbol naming the base type of the rule and augmented with one of the special metasymbols * or +. The * metasymbol is used to denote repetition of the base type zero or more times, while the + metasymbol denotes one or more repetitions, as in the example.

The exact syntax of list rules is given by the following EBNF grammar.

$$\langle\text{list-rule}\rangle ::= \langle\text{nonterminal}\rangle ::= (\langle\text{list-nonterminal}\rangle)$$
$$\langle\text{list-nonterminal}\rangle ::= < \langle\text{identifier}\rangle \langle\text{repetition-metasymbol}\rangle >$$
$$\langle\text{repetition-metasymbol}\rangle ::= * | +$$

Note that a list rule must always include the parentheses necessary to the syntax of a valid Lisp list.

From an abstract point of view, the objects that correspond to list rules in the GRAIL notation are sequences of elements of a given base type which happen to be implemented as Lisp lists. Thus one might propose appropriate abstract operations for processing these sequences that are divorced from the concrete operations on their implementation. However, we shall take an alternative view that the functions `first` and `rest` are selector functions for the abstract lists whether or not the physical data structure is a linked list or some other linear structure. Remember, this is the essence of data abstraction; instances of a data type are manipulated only through the data access functions defined for that type.

By a similar argument, we take the view that the function `cons` is the constructor function for lists of any type, and `endp` is the generic recognizer of an empty list, that is, a list of no copies of the base type. With the further proviso that () represents the empty list of any base type, these primitives are sufficient to manipulate any subobject that corresponds to a list defined using the * metasymbol.

If a list object is defined using a + metasymbol, it is required to have at least one element. In this case, the `first`, `rest`, and `cons` functions are all meaningful and appropriate, but it is inappropriate to specify the empty list () as a list of this type or to use `endp` as a recognizer on such lists. Instead, we specify appropriate data access functions: a constructor `list1` to return a single-element list given its element, and a recognizer `single-p` to determine if a list has only a single element. Of course, lists requiring at least one element are represented using the ordinary list structure, which allows empty lists, but this knowledge is hidden inside the data access function implementations.

```
list1[elem] = cons[elem; ()]

single-p[list] = endp[rest[list]]
```

Once a single-element list has been constructed using `list1`, larger lists may be recursively constructed from it using `cons` in the same way that they would be constructed from () if empty lists were allowed. Conversely, `single-p` replaces `endp` to recognize the terminating case in recursively analyzing lists.

4.2.3 Construction Rules

The third type of rule to be described is the *construction rule*. Construction rules are the basic rules used to describe structured objects in the GRAIL formalism; most often, they define fixed-format list objects as compositions of other objects. An example of a construction rule in the standard EBNF is that describing the Lisp syntax of a product from the domain of algebraic expressions:

$$\langle product \rangle \; ::= \; (\; \langle expression \rangle \; * \; \langle expression \rangle \;)$$

To ensure that the object represented is a valid list, the first and last symbols of a construction rule must always be a balancing set of parentheses. Within the parentheses, terminal symbols representing atoms or parentheses, and nonterminal symbols representing subconstructs, may appear. However, construction rules do not allow any of the conventional metasymbols that may appear on the R.H.S. of an EBNF rule. This excludes optional phrases ("[" "]") and repeated phrases ("{" "}") as well as alternative phrases which are covered by alternation rules in the GRAIL formalism.

In the GRAIL formalism, construction rules are extended by augmenting their R.H.S. nonterminal symbols with *component names*. For example, the EBNF rule just defined for $\langle product \rangle$ can be recast in the GRAIL formalism as follows:

$$\langle product \rangle \; ::= \; (\; \langle operand1{:}expression \rangle \; * \; \langle operand2{:}expression \rangle \;)$$

Component names are used to specify components unambiguously in the context of a given type of symbolic object; in this example, "operand1" and "operand2" are the component names for the two expression components of a product expression.

Once a construction rule has been defined for a given type of symbolic data object, the definition of appropriate constructor and selector data access functions follows automatically. For each construction rule, one constructor is needed to construct symbolic objects of the type defined by the rule; this constructor will have one argument corresponding to each R.H.S. nonterminal in the rule. In addition, one selector function is needed for each R.H.S. nonterminal to select the corresponding component from the composite object.

A typical convention for naming constructors is to add the prefix "make-" to the name of the type. For example, the constructor for the rule above would be called make-product. Its arguments would be the two algebraic expressions which are to become components of the resulting product expression.

```
make-product[expr1; expr2] = list3[expr1; "TIMES"; expr2]
```

Selectors are typically named by using the component names directly, or by adding the suffix "-of" to the component name. Following the first convention, the rule above specifies the selectors operand1 and operand2 for selecting component subexpressions of product expressions.

```
operand1[expr] = first[expr]
operand2[expr] = third[expr]
```

Although selector implementations such as these are generally straightforward, they may be complicated by the possibility of overloading. In general, the implementation of selector functions must consider all the construction rules in a given GRAIL grammar.

A more complicated example of a construction rule is the following definition of two-by-two matrices of "values":

$$\langle matrix\rangle ::= ((\langle x11:value\rangle \langle x12:value\rangle)$$
$$(\langle x21:value\rangle \langle x22:value\rangle))$$

Here, extra parentheses have been introduced to group pairs of values into rows. This introduces an extra level of list structure, and thus results in somewhat more complicated data access functions.

```
x11[matrix] = first[first[matrix]]
x12[matrix] = second[first[matrix]]
x21[matrix] = first[second[matrix]]
x22[matrix] = second[second[matrix]]

make-matrix[x11; x12; x21; x22] =
    list2[list2[x11; x12]; list2[x21; x22]]
```

Whenever extra parentheses are introduced in a construction rule, they must be balanced to ensure that a well-formed Lisp object is represented.

Sublist components.   It is entirely feasible that list objects described by list rules will be used as components in construction rules. For example, consider the following definition for series sums:

$$\langle series\text{-}sum\rangle ::= (\text{SIGMA} \langle summands:expression\text{-}list\rangle)$$
$$\langle expression\text{-}list\rangle ::= (\langle expression^+\rangle)$$

Note that the selector and constructor for this rule are implemented following the standard pattern.

```
summands[series] = second[series]

make-series-sum[summands] = list2["SIGMA"; series]
```

The following are typical examples of series sums according to this definition:

```
(SIGMA (X Y 5))

(SIGMA ((Z TIMES 2) 1))
```

The GRAIL formalism allows list subobjects to be directly represented within construction rules using *sublist* nonterminal symbols. For example, the structure of series sums may be expressed more concisely as follows:

$$\langle series\text{-}sum\rangle ::= (\text{SIGMA} (\langle summands:expression^+\rangle))$$

Note that a sublist nonterminal denotes a list by its base type and one of the repetition metasymbols * or $^+$, in a similar fashion to list nonterminals within list rules. Sublist nonterminals are also augmented with component names to specify the selector name for the list.

The chief reason for sublist nonterminals, however, is that they allow selection of a sublist as the tail part of a list including other items. This can often avoid the insertion of an extra level of list structure in a notation. For example, suppose that it is desirable to use more concise representations for series sums, such as the following:

```
(SIGMA X Y 5)
```

```
(SIGMA (Z TIMES 2) 1)
```

Now the summand expressions do not appear as a list on their own, but rather appear as the tail part of the top-level list representing the series sum.

The new representation for series sums can be described by the following GRAIL rule, which uses the sublist nonterminal as the tail part of the top-level list.

⟨series-sum⟩ ::= (SIGMA ⟨summands:expression⁺⟩)

Of course, the selector and constructor implementations must change for the new form of representation.

```
summands[series] = rest[series]
make-series-sum[summands] = cons["SIGMA"; series]
```

These definitions reflect the inclusion of the summands as part of the top-level list rather than as a separate component list on their own.

Metagrammar of construction rules.   The various possibilities for construction rules as described above are summarized by the following EBNF rules:

$$
\begin{array}{rcl}
\langle\text{construction-rule}\rangle & ::= & \langle\text{nonterminal}\rangle ::= \langle\text{list-phrase}\rangle \\
\langle\text{list-phrase}\rangle & ::= & (\ \{\langle\text{list-item}\rangle\}\ [\langle\text{sublist-nonterminal}\rangle]\ ) \\
\langle\text{list-item}\rangle & ::= & \langle\text{atom}\rangle \mid \langle\text{augmented-nonterminal}\rangle \mid \\
& & \langle\text{list-phrase}\rangle \\
\langle\text{augmented-nonterminal}\rangle & ::= & <\langle\text{identifier}\rangle : \langle\text{identifier}\rangle > \\
\langle\text{sublist-nonterminal}\rangle & ::= & <\langle\text{identifier}\rangle : \langle\text{identifier}\rangle \\
& & \langle\text{repetition-metasymbol}\rangle >
\end{array}
$$

Augmented and sublist nonterminal symbols appear only in construction rules. Note that parentheses as terminal symbols can only be introduced in a balanced fashion as part of a ⟨list-phrase⟩. Also note that a sublist nonterminal must be followed immediately by a right parenthesis terminal symbol in every case.

4.2.4 Lexical Rules

The final type of rule in the GRAIL formalism is the *lexical rule*. This type of rule defines those items of the symbolic input or output domain which are to be treated as atomic or unstructured objects. In the GRAIL specification of an abstract data model, such items are also called *lexemes*. In most cases, the R.H.S. of a lexical rule consists of a single augmented nonterminal symbol, whose type name is usually "symbolic-atom" or "numeric-atom," indicating how the lexeme is represented. The component name of the augmented nonterminal is used to specify the converter function which converts the lexeme to the indicated type. Lexical rules also specify the inverse converter function, named by prefixing the type of the lexical rule with the "make-" prefix.

In the domain of algebraic expressions, for example, the lexical types are the constants and variables. The following lexical rules could be used to define them in the GRAIL formalism.

$$\langle\text{constant}\rangle \ ::= \ \langle\text{const-val:numeric-atom}\rangle$$
$$\langle\text{variable}\rangle \ ::= \ \langle\text{var-name:symbolic-atom}\rangle$$

These rules specify the `const-val` and `make-constant` converters for constants and `var-name` and `make-variable` converters for variables just as described in Section 2.6.1.

Alternatively, the R.H.S. of a lexical rule may consist of a single atom, as in the following examples.

$$\langle\text{asterisk}\rangle \ ::= \ *$$

Rules of this form do not specify any data access functions, but instead, specify a data access "constant."[3]

```
asterisk = "*"
```

Just as with data access functions, however, these constant definitions allow the representation to be changed without affecting algorithms programmed in terms of the constant.

4.3 ALGEBRAIC EXPRESSIONS IN GRAIL

The full GRAIL grammar for algebraic expressions as Lisp data objects is shown in Figure 4.1. This grammar exhibits a fairly common pattern for GRAIL grammars: it

$$
\begin{aligned}
\langle\text{expression}\rangle \ &::= \ \langle\text{constant}\rangle \mid \langle\text{variable}\rangle \mid \langle\text{negation}\rangle \mid \langle\text{product}\rangle \mid \\
&\quad \langle\text{quotient}\rangle \mid \langle\text{sum}\rangle \mid \langle\text{difference}\rangle \mid \langle\text{power}\rangle \mid \\
&\quad \langle\text{exponential}\rangle \mid \langle\text{sine}\rangle \mid \langle\text{cosine}\rangle \\
\langle\text{negation}\rangle \ &::= \ (\ -\ \langle\text{operand:expression}\rangle\ ) \\
\langle\text{product}\rangle \ &::= \ (\langle\text{operand1:expression}\rangle\ *\ \langle\text{operand2:expression}\rangle\ ) \\
\langle\text{quotient}\rangle \ &::= \ (\langle\text{operand1:expression}\rangle\ /\ \langle\text{operand2:expression}\rangle\ ) \\
\langle\text{sum}\rangle \ &::= \ (\langle\text{operand1:expression}\rangle\ +\ \langle\text{operand2:expression}\rangle\ ) \\
\langle\text{difference}\rangle \ &::= \ (\langle\text{operand1:expression}\rangle\ -\ \langle\text{operand2:expression}\rangle\ ) \\
\langle\text{power}\rangle \ &::= \ (\langle\text{base:expression}\rangle\ **\ \langle\text{exponent:expression}\rangle\ ) \\
\langle\text{exponential}\rangle \ &::= \ (\text{exp}\ \langle\text{argument:expression}\rangle) \\
\langle\text{sine}\rangle \ &::= \ (\ \text{sin}\ \langle\text{argument:expression}\rangle\ ) \\
\langle\text{cosine}\rangle \ &::= \ (\ \text{cos}\ \langle\text{argument:expression}\rangle\ ) \\
\langle\text{constant}\rangle \ &::= \ \langle\text{const-val:numeric-atom}\rangle \\
\langle\text{variable}\rangle \ &::= \ \langle\text{var-name:symbolic-atom}\rangle
\end{aligned}
$$

Figure 4.1 GRAIL grammar for algebraic expressions.

---

[3]Of course, if $\langle\text{asterisk}\rangle$ is found on the R.H.S. of an alternation rule, the recognizer `asterisk-p` is required.

begins with a single alternation rule defining the major syntactic class of the notation, and continues with construction and lexical rules describing the representation of the various alternatives for this class. Following the GRAIL method, then, we could now use this grammar to specify the complete set of data access functions needed for processing algebraic expressions as data objects. Using the conventions described above, the data access functions defined by the grammar are exactly the same as the ones we have defined in Section 2.6.1.

This example highlights the essential value of a GRAIL grammar—that it provides a concise specification of a symbolic ADT and its Lisp representation. For the implementer of an ADT, it provides a complete requirements specification for the set of data access functions needed and their functional characteristics. For the users of an ADT, it provides a convenient reference guide to the data access functions. In contrast, a written specification listing all the data access functions and their verbal descriptions would be long-winded and tedious.

4.4 THE PROPOSITIONAL CALCULUS IN GRAIL

As a second example of the GRAIL method for representing notation systems in Lisp, we consider how it might be applied to the representation of logical formulas of the propositional calculus.

Propositional calculus is the branch of logic concerned with logical relationships between simple statements or *propositions*. For example, "This book describes symbolic computing" and "Symbolic computing is easy" are propositions which might be related in a logical implication such as "If this book describes symbolic computing, then symbolic computing is easy." In the propositional calculus, propositions are the primitive entities out of which logical formulas are built. They are typically represented by *proposition symbols* such as p, q, and r. From the viewpoint of the propositional calculus, the actual statement represented by a propositional symbol is unimportant; the only thing of concern is that a proposition may be either true or false.

Logical relationships may be formed in the propositional calculus using five different operators, giving five different types of composite logical formula. The "not" operator ("$\sim$") is used to construct logical *negations* which invert the truth value of their subformulas. For example, the formula "$\sim p$" is true when "p" is false, and vice versa. The "and" operator ("$\wedge$") is used to form the logical *conjunction* of two operands; "$p \wedge (\sim q)$" is true only if "p" is true and "q" is false. Similarly, the logical *disjunction* of two operands is formed using an "or" operator ("$\vee$") and is interpreted as true if either or both disjuncts are true. The fourth type of logical formula is the *implication* formed using the "implies" ("$\rightarrow$") operator. An implication is true whenever its L.H.S. subformula (called its *antecedent*) is false, or its R.H.S. subformula (called its *consequent*) is true. Finally, the "equivalence" operator ("$\leftrightarrow$") is used to construct logical *equivalences*; such a formula is true whenever both of its subformulas have the same truth value: either both are false or both are true.

A GRAIL grammar can now be used to define an abstract data model for propositional formulas as data objects. At the same time, the GRAIL method also provides a suitable representation of such formulas as Lisp data objects and specifies the data access functions necessary for manipulating them. Choosing a representation scheme based on an infix-keyword notation, an appropriate GRAIL grammar is shown in Figure 4.2. Note that this grammar follows the same pattern exhibited by the grammar for algebraic expressions, consisting of a single alternation rule followed by construction and lexical rules describing the representation of each alternative. Because it is defined in GRAIL, this grammar specifies all the data access functions necessary for manipulation of propositional formulas. The alternation rule specifies that six recognizers are necessary for distinguishing among formula types, namely, `proposition-p` through `equivalence-p`. The nine component names identified in the construction rules define nine selectors named `negend` through `condition2`, and the five construction rules themselves require five constructors, named `make-negation` through `make-equivalence`. Finally, the lexical rule for propositions specifies the converters `prop-name` and `make-proposition`.

$$
\begin{array}{rcl}
\langle\text{formula}\rangle & ::= & \langle\text{proposition}\rangle \mid \langle\text{negation}\rangle \mid \langle\text{conjunction}\rangle \mid \\
& & \langle\text{disjunction}\rangle \mid \langle\text{implication}\rangle \mid \langle\text{equivalence}\rangle \\
\langle\text{negation}\rangle & ::= & (\ \texttt{NOT}\ \langle\text{negend:formula}\rangle\ ) \\
\langle\text{conjunction}\rangle & ::= & (\langle\text{conjunct1:formula}\rangle\ \texttt{AND}\ \langle\text{conjunct2:formula}\rangle\ ) \\
\langle\text{disjunction}\rangle & ::= & (\langle\text{disjunct1:formula}\rangle\ \texttt{OR}\ \langle\text{disjunct2:formula}\rangle\ ) \\
\langle\text{implication}\rangle & ::= & (\langle\text{antecedent:formula}\rangle\ \texttt{IMPLIES}\ \langle\text{consequent:formula}\rangle\ ) \\
\langle\text{equivalence}\rangle & ::= & (\langle\text{condition1:formula}\rangle\ \texttt{EQUIV}\ \langle\text{condition2:formula}\rangle\ ) \\
\langle\text{proposition}\rangle & ::= & \langle\text{prop-name:symbolic-atom}\rangle
\end{array}
$$

Figure 4.2   GRAIL grammar for formulas of the propositional calculus.

In addition to specifying the abstract data model for propositional formulas, the GRAIL grammar also describes a concrete scheme for their representation in Lisp. Based on this representation scheme, implementation of the data access functions follows easily. In particular, the various selectors and constructors are quite straightforward, as illustrated by the following definitions for processing implication formulas:

```
antecedent[formula] = first[formula]

consequent[formula] = third[formula]

make-implication[ante; conseq] = list3[ante; "IMPLIES"; conseq]
```

The implementation of the recognizers is somewhat more complex, as they depend on the unique structural representation in Lisp of each alternative identified in the alternation rule. For example, propositions can be recognized as the only formula represented by (symbolic) atoms:

```
proposition-p[formula] = symbolp[formula]
```

If a formula is not an atom, it must be a list with at least two elements. Negations can be recognized as the only formula type with exactly two elements:

```
negation-p[formula] =
 [symbolp[formula] --> F;
  otherwise --> endp[rest[rest[formula]]]]
```

If a formula representation is neither an atom nor a two-element list, it must be a three-element list, in which case it can be recognized by the appropriate keyword atom. The recognizer for conjunctions is typical:

```
conjunction-p[formula] =
 [symbolp[formula] --> F;
  endp[rest[rest[formula]]] --> F;
  otherwise --> eq[second[formula]; "AND"]]
```

Finally, the converters for propositions have straightforward implementations:

```
prop-name[proposition] = proposition
```

```
make-proposition[symbolic-atom] = symbolic-atom
```

Recall that the use of converter functions is a fundamental aspect of data abstraction: although we know that propositions are already represented as symbolic atoms, the converter functions allow us to hide this information from our algorithms.

This example illustrates how a GRAIL grammar is used as a design tool for constructing representations of formulas of the propositional calculus. It identifies a suitable Lisp representation for such formulas together with the data access functions needed to process that representation. The software engineer need only work out the details of the functions, based on the constraints imposed by the specification. The development of applications involving propositional formulas can now proceed in a straightforward fashion. We shall see examples of such applications later, including, in particular, an automated theorem prover for theorems of the propositional calculus.

4.5 THE GRAIL REPRESENTATION OF LISP IN LISP: S-LISP

In this section we develop a representation of Small Lisp programs as Lisp data objects. This representation is called S-Lisp (symbolic Lisp) to distinguish it from the representation we have been using so far (m-Lisp or metalanguage Lisp[4]). In fact, all large Lisp systems require that programs be expressed using an S-Lisp representation, so this will be a good introduction to that approach. Later, we will develop programs that interpret and manipulate Small Lisp programs in S-Lisp form.

The symbolic data domain of Small Lisp programs is more complex than the domains for algebraic expressions or propositional formulas. However, the same basic approach applies: analyze the abstract nature of the domain outside of its representation in Lisp, and then synthesize a GRAIL grammar reflecting both the abstract form

---

[4]The term *metalanguage* in this context is somewhat misleading. It refers to the common practice of using notation in the style of Small Lisp to describe the semantics of S-Lisp based systems. Nevertheless, for the lack of a better term, we will use m-Lisp to refer to the Small Lisp notation presented in Chapter 2.

and an appropriate Lisp representation. To analyze the form of Small Lisp programs, we can work from the original EBNF grammar for Small Lisp given in Chapter 2.

Small Lisp has two principal types of construct, expressions and definitions. Expressions are used to specify the computation of values, while definitions are used to establish the names of constants and functions that can be used in evaluating expressions. As we shall see, both expressions and definitions will be defined by alternation rules, and their alternative forms will be defined by construction and lexical rules in much the same fashion as the expressions of the algebraic expression domain and the formulas of the propositional formula domain. We begin by considering the representation of Small Lisp expressions.

4.5.1 Expressions

Recall that expressions in Small Lisp come in five varieties as defined by the following EBNF rule:

$$\langle expression \rangle ::= \langle value \rangle \mid \langle variable \rangle \mid \langle function\text{-}call \rangle \mid$$
$$\langle conditional\text{-}expression \rangle \mid \langle let\text{-}expression \rangle$$

Variables are just identifiers and values are just S-expressions (atoms and lists), except that symbolic atoms must be enclosed in quotation marks.

$$\langle variable \rangle ::= \langle identifier \rangle$$
$$\langle value \rangle ::= \langle numeric\text{-}atom \rangle \mid " \langle symbolic\text{-}atom \rangle " \mid \langle list \rangle$$

The EBNF rules defining the remaining expression types are as follows:[5]

$$\langle function\text{-}call \rangle ::= \langle function\text{-}name \rangle \, [\, \langle argument\text{-}list \rangle \,]$$
$$\langle function\text{-}name \rangle ::= \langle identifier \rangle$$
$$\langle conditional\text{-}expression \rangle ::= [\, \langle clause\text{-}list \rangle \,]$$
$$\langle clause\text{-}list \rangle ::= \langle clause \rangle \, \{ \, ; \, \langle clause \rangle \, \}$$
$$\langle clause \rangle ::= \langle expression \rangle \, \text{-->} \, \langle expression \rangle$$
$$\langle let\text{-}expression \rangle ::= \{ \, \langle let\text{-}list \rangle : \langle expression \rangle \, \}$$
$$\langle let\text{-}list \rangle ::= \langle local\text{-}definition \rangle \, \{ \, ; \, \langle local\text{-}definition \rangle \, \}$$

So there are seven types of Small Lisp expression in all, and the problem is to devise a unique S-Lisp representation for each of these expression types.

The major difficulty in devising a suitable S-Lisp representation for Small Lisp expressions is in dealing with the representation of symbolic atoms and lists. It seems reasonable to use symbolic atoms to represent themselves. On the other hand, it also seems reasonable to use symbolic atoms to represent identifiers, just as they represent variables in the domain of algebraic expressions and propositions in the domain of propositional formulas. A similar situation arises with lists; it would be nice to use Small Lisp lists to represent themselves directly. However, if lists are reserved to represent themselves, how are the composite expression types such as function calls and conditional expressions to be represented?

The m-Lisp syntax of Small Lisp exhibits a similar problem in distinguishing between identifiers and symbolic atoms when used in the context of an expression. The

---

[5] Recall that different typefaces are used to distinguish between the ("{}") symbols appearing in Small Lisp and the ("{}") symbols which denote repeated phrases in EBNF.

m-Lisp solution is to enclose symbolic atoms in quotation marks in such contexts. This solution can be adapted to the S-Lisp representation by enclosing symbolic atoms in lists whose first element is the keyword atom `quote`. Thus, in the S-Lisp form, the list (`quote A`) will be used to represent the atom `A`, while the atom `A` standing alone will be used to represent the identifier `A`.

The same process of quotation can also be used to resolve the problem of representing lists in S-Lisp, even though there is no corresponding problem in using lists directly as expressions in the m-Lisp syntax. For example, if we want to represent the list (`quote A`) in m-Lisp, we can simply use (`quote A`) itself. In S-Lisp, however, (`quote A`) represents the atom `A`, so to represent (`quote A`), we must quote it once more:

(quote (quote A))

Similarly, the S-Lisp notation will use lists such as (`first x`) to represent function calls such as `first[x]`, so the list (`first x`) must itself be represented:

(quote (first x))

These examples of quotation are summarized in Table 4.1. With this resolution of the representation of symbolic atoms and lists, we are free to use any list structures not beginning with `quote` to represent the other composite expression types.

TABLE 4.1   QUOTED FORMS IN S-LISP

m-Lisp	S-Lisp
A	A
"A"	(quote A)
(quote A)	(quote (quote A))
first[x]	(first x)
(first x)	(quote (first x))

Using a prefix-keyword style of notation, a suitable Lisp representation of Small Lisp expressions can now be developed. As described above, `quote` will be used as a keyword atom for symbolic constants (i.e., symbolic atoms or lists). Conditional expressions and let expressions, respectively, will be represented as lists beginning with the keyword atoms `cond` and `let`. Rather than using a keyword atom such as `func` for function calls, however, we will follow the historical convention that any list not beginning with `quote`, `cond`, or `let` represents a function call with the function name as the keyword atom.[6] With these decisions, the remaining details of the S-Lisp representation of Small Lisp expressions can easily be worked out and are summarized by the GRAIL grammar of Figure 4.3.

The seven types of expression have been given unique representations which can be identified with the following recognizer implementations.

---

[6]This does have the effect, however, of precluding the use of `quote`, `cond`, and `let` as function names.

⟨expression⟩ ::= ⟨identifier⟩ | ⟨numeric-atom-expr⟩ |
⟨symbolic-atom-expr⟩ | ⟨list-expr⟩ | ⟨fn-call⟩ |
⟨cond-expr⟩ | ⟨let-expr⟩
⟨identifier⟩ ::= ⟨id-name:symbolic atom⟩
⟨numeric-atom-expr⟩ ::= ⟨numeric-val:numeric atom⟩
⟨symbolic-atom-expr⟩ ::= (quote ⟨symbolic-val:symbolic-atom⟩)
⟨list-expr⟩ ::= (quote ⟨list-val:list⟩)
⟨fn-call⟩ ::= (⟨callee:identifier⟩ ⟨arguments:expression⁺⟩)
⟨cond-expr⟩ ::= (cond ⟨clauses:clause⁺⟩)
⟨clause⟩ ::= (⟨predicate:expression⟩ ⟨result:expression⟩)
⟨let-expr⟩ ::= (let (⟨local-defs:local-def⁺⟩)
⟨final-expr:expression⟩)
⟨local-def⟩ ::= (⟨local-var:variable⟩ ⟨local-val:expression⟩)

Figure 4.3   GRAIL grammar for Small Lisp expressions.

```
identifier-p[expr] = symbolp[expr]

numeric-atom-expr-p[expr] = numberp[expr]

symbolic-atom-expr-p[expr] =
  [listp[expr] -->
    [eq[first[expr]; "quote"] --> symbolp[second[expr]];
    otherwise --> F];
  otherwise --> F]

list-expr-p[expr] =
  [listp[expr] -->
    [eq[first[expr]; "quote"] --> listp[second[expr]];
    otherwise --> F];
  otherwise --> F]

fn-call-p[expr] =
  [listp[expr] -->
    [eq[first[expr]; "quote"] --> F;
    eq[first[expr]; "cond"] --> F;
    eq[first[expr]; "let"] --> F;
    otherwise --> T];
  otherwise --> F]

cond-expr-p[expr] =
  [listp[expr] --> eq[first[expr]; "cond"];
  otherwise --> F]

let-expr-p[expr] =
  [listp[expr] --> eq[first[expr]; "let"];
  otherwise --> F]
```

Note, however, that no recognizers `clause-p` and `local-def-p` are defined. This follows from the GRAIL method because recognizers are specified only for data types which appear on the R.H.S. of an alternation rule. Alternatively, it can be seen that clauses and local definitions appear only in contexts in which no other alternatives may appear (i.e., in clause lists and local-definition lists, respectively). Once an element has been selected from a clause list, for example, there is no need to apply a recognizer, because the element is already known to be a clause.

Lexical rules are used to define both the representation of identifiers and that of numeric atoms. This results in the following converter function definitions:

```
id-name[ident] = ident

make-identifier[id-name] = id-name

numeric-val[num-atom] = num-atom

make-numeric-atom-expr[val] = val
```

Even when numeric atoms are being used to represent themselves, we use the converter functions to hide this knowledge inside the S-Lisp ADT.

The representations for symbolic atoms and lists are defined by similar construction rules. According to the GRAIL method, the data access function definitions are straightforward.

```
symbolic-val[sym-atom-expr] = second[sym-atom-expr]

make-symbolic-atom-expr[sym] = list2["quote"; sym]

list-val[list-expr] = second[list-expr]

make-list-expr[list] = list2["quote"; list]
```

Note, however, that the objects selected by `symbolic-val` and `list-val` are not other symbolic data types defined by the GRAIL grammar, but are the symbolic atom and list data types, respectively. Thus the selectors can also be viewed as converters, taking the S-Lisp representation of a symbolic atom or list, and returning the represented object. Similarly, the constructors `make-symbolic-atom-expr` and `make-list-expr` can be viewed as the inverse converters, taking a symbolic atom or list and converting it to its S-Lisp representation.

The rule for function calls uses a sublist nonterminal to indicate that the function arguments immediately follow the function name in the top-level list. For example, the function call `endp[x]` is represented `(endp x)`, while `cons[KEYWORD; list]` is represented `(cons (quote KEYWORD) list)`. In this representation, the argument list of a function call is simply the sublist remaining after removing the function name. This is illustrated by the data access functions defined according to the GRAIL method.

```
make-fn-call[func; args] = cons[func; args]

callee[fn-call] = first[fn-call]

arguments[fn-call] = rest[fn-call]
```

Conditional expressions have a slightly more complex structure, defined using both a sublist nonterminal and an auxiliary rule for clauses. Consider, for example, how the conditional expression

$$[\text{symbolp}[x] \; \text{--> eq}[x; \; \text{"A"}]; \; \text{otherwise --> F}]$$

is represented. The first clause has function calls for both its predicate and result expressions. These are represented (symbolp x) and (eq x (quote A)), respectively. The entire clause is then represented as follows:

$$((\text{symbolp} \; x) \; (\text{eq} \; x \; (\text{quote} \; A)))$$

The second clause, which has variables for both its predicate and result expressions, is simply represented as (otherwise F). Putting together the pieces gives the representation of the the entire conditional expression.

$$(\text{cond} \; ((\text{symbolp} \; x) \; (\text{eq} \; x \; (\text{quote} \; A))) \; (\text{otherwise} \; F))$$

The data access functions for conditional clauses follow from the GRAIL grammar in a straightforward fashion.

```
make-cond-expr[clauses] = cons["cond"; clauses]

clauses[cond-expr] = rest[cond-expr]

make-clause[pred; result] = list2[pred; result]

predicate[clause] = first[clause]

result[clause] = second[clause]
```

Let expressions are also defined using a sublist nonterminal and an auxiliary data type. In this case, however, the sublist nonterminal is enclosed in its own list instead of being part of the top-level list as in the representation of function calls and conditional expressions. This is reflected in the data access functions.

```
local-defs[let-expr] = second[let-expr]

final-expr[let-expr] = third[let-expr]

make-let-expr[defs; expr] = list3["let"; defs; expr]

local-var[local-def] = first[local-def]

local-val[local-def] = second[local-def]

make-local-def[var; val] = list2[var; val]
```

Consider, for example, how the expression

```
{e1 = first[list];
 e2 = second[list] :
 list2[list2[e1; e2]; list2[e2; e1]]]}
```

is represented in S-Lisp. Each of the local definitions is represented as a two-element list [i.e., (e1 (first list)) and (e2 (second list))]. A list of these local definitions is then constructed and embedded together with the representation of the final expression as follows:

```
(let ((e1 (first list))
      (e2 (second list)))
  (list2 (list2 e1 e2) (list2 e2 e1)))
```

4.5.2 Definitions

Recall that a Small Lisp program is just a list of function and constant definitions, as defined by the following EBNF rules:

$$
\begin{aligned}
\langle\text{definition-list}\rangle &::= \{\ \langle\text{definition}\rangle\ \} \\
\langle\text{definition}\rangle &::= \langle\text{function-definition}\rangle \mid \langle\text{constant-definition}\rangle \\
\langle\text{function-definition}\rangle &::= [\langle\text{comment}\rangle]\ \langle\text{function-name}\rangle \\
&\quad\ [\ \langle\text{parameter-list}\rangle\ ] = \langle\text{expression}\rangle \\
\langle\text{parameter-list}\rangle &::= \langle\text{variable}\rangle\ \{\ ;\ \langle\text{variable}\rangle\ \} \\
\langle\text{constant-definition}\rangle &::= [\langle\text{comment}\rangle]\ \langle\text{variable}\rangle = \langle\text{expression}\rangle
\end{aligned}
$$

Working out suitable Lisp representations for these rules will complete the development of the S-Lisp representation of Small Lisp. For simplicity, however, we will ignore the possibility of comments in the S-Lisp representation of constant and function definitions.

In order to set up distinct representations for function and constant definitions, we again use prefix-keyword notation. Function definitions will be represented by a list beginning with a keyword defun, short for "define function," followed by representations of the name, parameters, and body of the function. Constant definitions will use the keyword setc ("set constant"), followed by the constant name and its value expression. These representations are summarized in the GRAIL grammar of Figure 4.4. Note that a list rule is used to define definition lists as the top-level construct. The data access functions for function and constant definitions follow easily from the GRAIL method. They are presented below in S-Lisp form.

```
(defun fn-def-p (def)
  (eq (first def) (quote defun)))

(defun const-def-p (def)
  (eq (first def) (quote setc)))

(defun fn-name (fndef)
  (second fndef))

(defun parameters (fndef)
  (third fndef))

(defun body (fndef)
  (fourth fndef))
```

```
(defun make-fn-def (name parms body)
  (list4 (quote defun) name parms body))

(defun const-name (constdef)
  (second constdef))

(defun const-val (constdef)
  (third constdef))

(defun make-const-def (name value)
  (list3 (quote setc) name value))
```

$\langle$definition-list$\rangle$ ::= ($\langle$definition*$\rangle$)
  $\langle$definition$\rangle$ ::= $\langle$fn-def$\rangle$ | $\langle$const-def$\rangle$
   $\langle$fn-def$\rangle$ ::= (defun $\langle$fn-name:identifier$\rangle$
        ($\langle$parameters:identifier$^+$$\rangle$) $\langle$body:expression$\rangle$)
  $\langle$const-def$\rangle$ ::= (setc $\langle$const-name:identifier$\rangle$ $\langle$const-val:expression$\rangle$)

Figure 4.4   GRAIL grammar for Small Lisp definitions.

This completes the development of the S-Lisp form of Small Lisp. The data access functions on this representation allow us to process Small Lisp programs as data objects, as we shall do in Chapters 6 and 9. Furthermore, as we shall see in Chapters 7 and 8, Common LISP and other Lisp systems are programmed in an S-Lisp form which is substantially similar to that presented here for Small Lisp. In fact, whenever difficulties arise in dealing with the S-Lisp syntax of such systems, it can be beneficial to apply the representation principles described here to rederive the S-Lisp form from a suitable m-Lisp representation.

4.6 EXERCISES

4.1. Suppose that our original Small Lisp implementation of `deriv` had not used converter functions, but had instead manipulated constants and variables directly in terms of their representation as numeric and symbolic atoms. How would this affect the translation of `deriv` to Pascal presented in Section 4.1?

4.2. In the GRAIL formalism, a sublist nonterminal symbol within a list phrase must be followed immediately by a right parenthesis. Consider what would happen if this restriction were relaxed so that a sublist nonterminal symbol could appear anywhere within a list phrase, but no more than one such symbol could appear in the phrase directly. Show how the EBNF metagrammar for GRAIL construction rules needs to be changed to accommodate this relaxation. Describe how this relaxation affects the implementation techniques for selector and constructor data access functions, in general. Analyze the costs of such implementations assuming unit costs for the `symbolp`, `numberp`, `listp`, `endp`, `cons`, `first`, and `rest` functions and compare these costs with the corresponding costs arising from the more restricted GRAIL approach.

4.3. Consider a further relaxation of the GRAIL formalism to that described in Exercise 4.2, allowing any number of sublist nonterminals appearing within list phrases. What are the implementation difficulties and costs for data access functions following this approach?

4.4. Write a function `find-vars[expr]` which constructs a list of one copy of all the distinct variables in a given logical expression, `expr`, as defined by the GRAIL grammar of Figure 4.2.

4.5. Suppose you are given a function `logic-eval[expr; env]` which evaluates a logical expression, `expr`, given an assignment of truth values to the logical variables in the expression. This assignment is passed to the function through the parameter `env`, which is a list of those variables which are to be assigned the value "true." Define a function `exception[expr; var-list]` which returns T if there is an assignment of truth values to the variables in `var-list` that makes the logical expression `expr` "false." Otherwise, the function returns F if no such assignment can be made.

4.6. Any logical expression can be represented using only disjunction, conjunction, and negation. However, in some environments, such as theorem proving and functional programming languages, the implication operator, $\rightarrow$, is encountered more frequently. In particular, it is possible to define any logical expression using only implication and negation ($\sim$).

   (a) Write a function `implies[p1; p2]` which takes two truth values as arguments and returns the truth value of their logical implication, p1 $\rightarrow$ p2. Your solution should not call any other logical functions.

   (b) Propose a GRAIL grammar for list representations of logical expressions which employ only conjunction, disjunction, and negation. Use the symbolic atoms AND, OR, and NOT to distinguish among the alternatives.

   (c) Propose a GRAIL grammar for list representations of logical expressions which employ only implication and negation. Use the symbolic atoms --> and - to distinguish among the alternatives.

   (d) Implement a function `translate` which accepts as input a logical expression as defined by the grammar of part (b) and produces as output an equivalent logical expression as defined by the grammar of part (c).

4.7. De Morgan's laws for Boolean expressions provide a means for transforming the negation of such expressions into disjunctions and conjunctions of literals. A literal is a propositional variable or its complement. Let `expr` be a Boolean expression, represented as a list using the grammar for propositional logic given Fig. 4.2.

   (a) Define a GRAIL grammar to represent the output domain, which consists of Boolean expressions where only the variables themselves may be complemented.

   (b) Write a function `negate[expr]` that transforms `expr` into its complement, expressed as a list with the output grammar of part (a).

4.8. Suppose that `function-list` is a list of Small Lisp functions represented according to the grammar of Section 4.5. Implement `scan-for-globals[function-list]`, which determines the "global" variables of each function, that is, variables which are not defined within the scope of the function in which they appear. The value returned by `scan-for-globals` should be a list consisting of each global variable encountered paired with the name of the function in which it occurs.

4.9. The following GRAIL grammar provides a list representation for functions of one argument:

$$\langle\text{fn-def}\rangle ::= (\text{FUNCTION} \langle\text{fname:id}\rangle \langle\text{param:id}\rangle \langle\text{body:expr}\rangle)$$
$$\langle\text{expr}\rangle ::= \langle\text{const}\rangle \mid \langle\text{id}\rangle \mid \langle\text{fn-call}\rangle \mid \langle\text{cond-expr}\rangle$$
$$\langle\text{const}\rangle ::= (\text{CONSTANT} \langle\text{item:datum}\rangle)$$
$$\langle\text{fn-call}\rangle ::= (\text{CALL} \langle\text{fn:id}\rangle \langle\text{arg:expr}\rangle)$$
$$\langle\text{cond-expr}\rangle ::= (\text{IF} \langle\text{pred:expr}\rangle \text{ THEN} \langle\text{caseT:expr}\rangle \text{ ELSE} \langle\text{caseF:expr}\rangle)$$
$$\langle\text{id}\rangle ::= \langle\text{name:symbolic-atom}\rangle$$
$$\langle\text{datum}\rangle ::= \langle\text{value:S-expression}\rangle$$

(a) Rewrite the following Small Lisp function as a list according to the GRAIL grammar given:

```
nmbrlist-p[x] =
  [single-p[x] --> numberp[first[x]];
   numberp[first[x]] --> nmbrlist-p[rest[x]];
   otherwise --> F]
```

(b) Assuming the existence of the data access functions specified by the grammar, write a Small Lisp function `recursive-p[fn]`. This function accepts as input a function definition `fn`, represented as a list according to the grammar above, and returns T if `fn` is a recursive function definition (F otherwise).

4.10. Define and implement a function `mutual-recursion-p[fn-list]` which returns T if mutual recursion is exhibited among a list of functions, `fn-list`. Each function on the list is represented according to the grammar of Exercise 4.9. Not all functions on the list need be part of a mutual recursion.

4.11. Define and implement in Small Lisp a function `recursion-type` which returns an atom indicating the type of recursion exhibited by the argument, which is a list representation of a function as defined by the grammar of Section 4.5 with the exclusion of let-expressions. Also exclude mutual and multiple recursion as possible inputs. Thus the type can be one of the following:

NON-RECURSIVE: The function is not recursive.
TAIL-RECURSIVE: The function is tail recursive.
LINEAR-RECURSIVE: The function is linear but not tail recursive.
PREDICATE-RECURSIVE: The function is predicate recursive but not linear.
DOUBLE-RECURSIVE: The function is double but not predicate recursive.

4.12. Using the GRAIL grammar notation, define a list representation for GRAIL grammars themselves. Suppose that G is a GRAIL grammar to define the objects in some symbolic domain. Your task is to devise a GRAIL grammar $meta\text{-}G$ that shows how any arbitrary G can be expressed as a list structure. Show how the GRAIL grammar for the propositional calculus—defined in Figure 4.2—can be represented in your notation.

4.13. Consider the GRAIL grammar defined in Exercise 4.12 as a definition for the abstract data type $\langle\text{GRAIL-grammar}\rangle$. Design and implement the data access functions necessary for manipulating GRAIL grammars as data objects.

4.14. Write a program in Small Lisp which generates list representations of the selector functions for the $\langle\text{GRAIL-grammar}\rangle$ ADT defined in Exercise 4.12. As an added feature, your program should check for the multiple occurrence of a selector function name. This corresponds to an overloaded function definition, but is valid only if all definitions define the same function. Your program should allow overloaded selectors only if they have the same implementation in every case. If this assumption is violated, your program should report the error.

4.15. Extend the program of Exercise 4.14 to generate list representations of the constructor functions specified by the grammar. Since your program should generate the selectors and constructors from the GRAIL grammar of any ADT, it should generate the selectors for the ⟨GRAIL-grammar⟩ ADT itself. Use this grammar as a test case. Describe briefly the problems and possible approaches to modifying the program so that it generates the other types of data access functions specified by a GRAIL grammar.

4.16. Construct a program which performs the following substitutions on the S-Lisp form of Small Lisp programs. Any occurrences of the predefined variables `otherwise` and `F` are replaced by `T` and `NIL`, respectively. Any occurrences of function names for the arithmetic primitives are replaced by operators as indicated in the following table:

Function Name	Replacement
eqp	=
greaterp	>
lessp	<
plus	+
minus	−
times	*
divide	/

For example, the S-Lisp function call `(plus x y)` becomes `(+ x y)`. The result of this process will almost always be a valid Common LISP program which corresponds to the original Small Lisp one.[7] Why would it be inappropriate to perform this conversion process using the global search-and-replace facilities of a text editor?

---

[7]With a few exceptions as described in Section 7.1.

5

Notation Systems and Transformations

5.1 NOTATION SYSTEMS

A *notation system* is a means of representing information in a given application domain. Since there may be many alternative notation systems possible for a given domain, an important aspect of a "good" notation system is that syntactic manipulations of the notation produce semantically meaningful results. For example, the standard Arabic numeral system is a notation for representing natural numbers (positive integers). As we all learn in our early school years, there are straightforward algorithms for adding and multiplying numbers which involve the syntactic manipulation of the corresponding Arabic numerals. However, another notation system which is equally capable of representing natural numbers is the Roman numeral system. This system is inferior to the Arabic system, however, because there is no simple way of performing the semantically useful operations of addition and multiplication as simple syntactic manipulations of Roman numerals.

Informally, we often think of the transformation of an object as any manipulation which changes the shape or representation of that object. However, with the transformation of symbolic expressions it is important that the result of such manipulation be meaningful in the context of the problem domain. Therefore, we shall constrain the term *transformation* to mean any systematic manipulation of a notation system which achieves a semantically useful result. Symbolic differation is one example of a transformation because it involves the systematic manipulation of an expression in order to compute its derivative.

There are many examples of transformations, like symbolic differentiation, whose usefulness is confined to a particular application domain. However, there are also certain general categories of transformation that are common to many application areas. In particular, three important types of transformation occur so often in symbolic computing that they merit special attention as their method of application depends on the nature of the transformation rather than on the input domain. Hence it is possible to define each using a programming paradigm that can be associated with the tranformation type. Two problem domains that require the same particular transformation type will possess structural similarities in the implementation of that transformation type. That is, they can be implemented in essentially the same way irrespective of the problem domain. These transformation types are *simplification, reduction*, and *conversion to canonical form*. It is the purpose of this chapter to describe the nature of these transformation types and to provide examples of their implementation which illustrate how they can be effectively employed.

5.2 SIMPLIFICATION

Simplifications are transformations which produce equivalent but simpler forms of given notational phrases. For example, the following are all valid simplifications in the realm of algebraic expressions:

$$x \times (y/x) \;\mapsto\; y$$
$$(\sin x)^2 + (\cos x)^2 \;\mapsto\; 1$$
$$3 + 4 \;\mapsto\; 7$$

In these examples—and throughout the book—the symbol $\mapsto$ means "transforms to." As a second example, the following simplifications apply in the propositional calculus:

$$\sim\sim p \;\mapsto\; p$$
$$p \wedge p \;\mapsto\; p$$

As illustrated by these examples, simplifications generally result in notational phrases which are less complex syntactically than the expressions from which they were derived.

5.2.1 Algebraic Expression Simplification

In Chapter 2 the function `deriv` was developed for computing the derivative of algebraic expressions with respect to given variables. However, `deriv` left the results in unsimplified form. For example,

```
deriv[(cos (3 * (X ** 2))); X]
```

would yield as output

```
( -
  ((sin (3 * (X ** 2)))
```

```
            *
        ((3 * ((2 * 1) * (X ** 1)))
            +
        ((X ** 2) * 0)))))
```

However, by applying a systematic method for algebraic expression simplification, much more "useful" output can be generated, such as the following simplified form of the derivative above.

$$\text{(- ((sin (3 * (X ** 2))) * (6 * X)))}$$

The basis for expression simplification is the existence of various simplification rules for each type of mathematical expression. Typically, the most useful rules are those which evaluate an expression given numeric operands and those which apply various algebraic laws. For example, simplification of the `deriv` output above involved the following evaluations and algebraic manipulations:

$$\text{(2 * 1)} \; \mapsto \; 2$$

$$\text{(X ** 1)} \; \mapsto \; \text{X}$$

$$\text{(3 * (2 * X))} \; \mapsto \; \text{(6 * X)}$$

$$\text{((X ** 2) * 0)} \; \mapsto \; 0$$

$$\text{((6 * X) + 0)} \; \mapsto \; \text{(6 * X)}$$

Other simplification rules come from the application of trigonometric identities such as the following:

$$\text{(((sin X) ** 2) + ((cos X) ** 2))} \; \mapsto \; 1$$

Many more simplification rules are possible using known mathematical laws. In fact, there is no finite set of simplification rules that can achieve all possible simplifications of algebraic expressions. This also means that there is no algorithm which can completely simplify any arbitrary algebraic expression. Nevertheless, very good simplification can be achieved in practice through the systematic application of a suitable finite set of simplification rules.

A particularly important technique is the *inside-out method* for simplifying expressions, so-called because simplification starts with the innermost subexpressions and proceeds outwards. Given an expression to be simplified, then, the first step is to simplify all the subexpressions of that expression. For example, the simplification of the expression

$$\text{((2 - 1) * (X + 2))}$$

would proceed by first of all simplifying the subexpressions (2 - 1) and (X + 2) to 1 and (X + 2), respectively. Using the simplified subexpressions, then, the second step is to apply the simplification rules in reconstructing an expression equivalent to the original in simplified form. Given the subexpressions 1 and (X + 2), for example, reconstruction of their product would simply mean returning (X + 2) directly. In this fashion, the inside-out algorithm systematically applies simplifications throughout an expression.

A program to simplify algebraic expressions can be organized in the following way. A recursive driver routine performs the inside-out method, while a set of auxiliary functions implement the various simplification rules to be used. For example, given simplified operands of a sum expression, let the two argument function make-simplified-sum be responsible for applying the various simplification rules for sums. Then the driver routine is simply responsible for simplifying the operands of the sum expression before passing them on to make-simplified-sum. This leads to a Small Lisp formulation of the driver routine as follows:

```
simplify[expr] =
 [constant-p[expr] --> expr;
  variable-p[expr] --> expr;
  negation-p[expr] -->
    make-simplified-negation[simplify[operand[expr]]];
  product-p[expr] -->
    make-simplified-product
      [simplify[operand1[expr]]; simplify[operand2[expr]]];
  quotient-p[expr] -->
    make-simplified-quotient
      [simplify[operand1[expr]]; simplify[operand2[expr]]];
  sum-p[expr] -->
    make-simplified-sum
      [simplify[operand1[expr]]; simplify[operand2[expr]]];
  difference-p[expr] -->
    make-simplified-difference
      [simplify[operand1[expr]]; simplify[operand2[expr]]];
  power-p[expr] -->
    make-simplified-power
      [simplify[base[expr]]; simplify[exponent[expr]]];
  sine-p[expr] --> make-simplified-sine[simplify[argument[expr]]];
  cosine-p[expr] -->
    make-simplified-cosine[simplify[argument[expr]]];
  exponential-p[expr] -->
    make-simplified-exponential[simplify[argument[expr]]]]
```

Note that simplification of subexpressions terminates when constants and variables, which are the primitive algebraic expression types, are reached. In such cases, no simplifications are possible and the expressions are returned unmodified.

An important property of the inside-out algorithm is that for a given set of rules, it systematically performs all possible simplifications according to those rules. Let us say that an expression is in *simplified form* if it cannot be further simplified according to the given rule set. Assume that each of the make-simplified-... functions faithfully implements its simplification rules, returning an expression in simplified form given argument expressions in simplified form. Then it can be proven inductively that `simplify` always returns expressions in simplified form. The proof is an application of structural induction on the domain of algebraic expressions. As discussed in Chapter 3, proofs on this domain have two base steps and nine inductive steps. In our case, the proof proceeds as follows:

Base Steps.

1. Prove `simplify[expr]` is a simplified expression for any constant `expr`.
2. Prove `simplify[expr]` is a simplified expression for any variable `expr`.

    From the definition of the function `simplify`, these cases are processed, respectively, by the clauses whose predicates are `constant-p[expr]` and `variable-p[expr]`. In either case, `expr` is returned unmodified as the expression in simplified form. This is correct because there are no simplifications that can be applied to constants or variables.

Now, let P_x be a predicate denoting "`simplify[x]` is the simplified form of the algebraic expression x." Then there are nine cases to consider; four involve expressions having one operand, five correspond to expressions with two operands. We examine the cases with one operand first, using the negation of an expression as a typical example.

Inductive Steps.

1. Assume that P_x is true for an arbitrary algebraic expression x.
    Prove $P_{\texttt{make-negation}[x]}$.

    Let `expr` = `make-negation[x]` = `(- x)`, where x is an arbitrary expression. Then

    $$\texttt{operand[expr]} \Rightarrow x$$

    From the function definition, `simplify[expr]` returns the value of

    $$\texttt{make-simplified-negation[simplify[x]]}$$

    since only `negation-p[expr]` is true. By the induction hypothesis, `simplify[x]` returns a correctly simplified expression, say `e1`. Now since `make-simplified-negation` is assumed to return correctly simplified expressions, it is the case that `make-simplified-negation[e1]` must be a correctly simplified expression.

In a similar fashion, we can establish the following inductive inferences for the simplification of the other algebraic expressions having one operand:

2. Assume that P_x is true for an arbitrary algebraic expression x.
    Prove $P_{\texttt{make-exponential}[x]}$.
3. Assume that P_x is true for an arbitrary algebraic expression x.
    Prove $P_{\texttt{make-sine}[x]}$.

4. Assume that P_x is true for an arbitrary algebraic expression x. Prove $P_{\texttt{make-cosine}[x]}$.

To address the algebraic expressions having two operands, we choose the sum of two expressions as typical and prove the following:

5. Assume that P_x and P_y are true for arbitrary algebraic expressions x and y. Prove $P_{\texttt{make-sum}[x;\ y]}$.

Let $\texttt{expr} = \texttt{make-sum}[x;\ y] = (\texttt{+}\ x\ y)$, where x and y are arbitrary expressions. Then

$$\texttt{operand1[expr]} \Rightarrow x$$
$$\texttt{operand2[expr]} \Rightarrow y$$

From the function definition, $\texttt{simplify[expr]}$ returns the value of

$$\texttt{make-simplified-sum[simplify}[x]\texttt{;\ simplify}[y]\texttt{]]}$$

since only $\texttt{sum-p[expr]}$ is true.

Again, by the induction hypothesis, $\texttt{simplify}[x]$ and $\texttt{simplify}[y]$ each return correctly simplified expressions, say e1 and e2. Since make-simplified-sum is assumed to return correctly simplified expressions, $\texttt{make-simplified-sum[e1;\ e2]}$ must be a correctly simplified expression.

A completely equivalent argument can be made for each of the following induction steps:

6. Assume that P_x and P_y are true for arbitrary algebraic expressions x and y. Prove $P_{\texttt{make-difference}[x;\ y]}$.

7. Assume that P_x and P_y are true for arbitrary algebraic expressions x and y. Prove $P_{\texttt{make-product}[x;\ y]}$.

8. Assume that P_x and P_y are true for arbitrary algebraic expressions x and y. Prove $P_{\texttt{make-quotient}[x;\ y]}$.

9. Assume that P_x and P_y are true for arbitrary algebraic expressions x and y. Prove $P_{\texttt{make-power}[x;\ y]}$.

This completes the proof that $\texttt{simplify[expr]}$ always returns simplified expressions assuming only the correctness of the make-simplified-... auxiliary functions. The interesting aspect of this proof is that it verifies the inside-out method itself, regardless of which particular simplification rules are used.[1] Thus, given a particular set of rules, we can ensure that they are applied systematically to an expression in all possible ways by making use of the inside-out method.

This proof illustrates another reason to implement with recursive functions: namely, to exploit the close relationship between recursion and induction to prove correctness of programs. Program verification is an important objective in the engineering of a software product. However formal proofs of correctness of iterative

---

[1] The simplification rules must be consistent, however, so that the notion of "expressions in simplified form" is well defined.

programs are extraordinarily difficult in all but the simplest cases. As a consequence, such programs are typically "verified" using lengthy, custom-designed testbeds. Such verification is usually incomplete unless the test data accounts for all alternatives. This practical consideration underscores the virtue of a recursive, rather than an iterative implementation, even when standard recursion removal techniques are subsequently used to improve efficiency.

The nature of the various `make-simplified-...` functions depends, of course, on the simplification rules that they implement. Consider, for example, the simplification of negations using the following rules:

$$(- \ 0) \ \mapsto \ 0$$
$$(- \ (- \ e)) \ \mapsto \ e$$
$$(- \ (e_1 \ - \ e_2)) \ \mapsto \ (e_2 \ - \ e_1)$$

In these rules, the metavariables e, e_1, and e_2 denote arbitrary algebraic expressions. The implementation of these rules in the `make-simplified-negation` function is quite straightforward.

```
make-simplified-negation[expr] =
  [zero-p[expr] --> 0;
   negation-p[expr] --> operand[expr];
   difference-p[expr] -->
     make-simplified-difference[operand2[expr]; operand1[expr]];
   otherwise --> make-negation[expr]]

zero-p[expr] =
  [constant-p[expr] --> eq[value-of[expr]; 0];
   otherwise --> F]
```

The first three clauses of `make-simplified-negation` implement the simplification rules, while the final clause indicates what to do when no simplification applies; in that case just construct a negation using the given operand.

In constructing auxiliary functions such as `make-simplified-negation`, it is important to ensure that the output is always in simplified form given that the inputs are in simplified form. This can generally be done using a clause-by-clause analysis. In the body of `make-simplified-negation`, the first clause returns 0, which is in simplified form because it is a constant. The second clause returns `operand[expr]`, which is in simplified form because `expr` is in simplified form and a subexpression of an expression in simplified form must also be in simplified form. The third clause returns an expression in simplified form because `operand2[expr]` and `operand1[expr]` are each in simplified form, and we assume that `make-simplified-difference` returns an expression in simplified form given two arguments in simplified form. Note the importance of using `make-simplified-difference` here instead of `make-difference`; if the latter function were used it would be hard to prove that the result is in simplified form without further information. Finally, the last clause returns a result in simplified form because it constructs a negation whose negend is in simplified form and there are no simplification rules which apply directly to the negation (they are all caught by the first three clauses).

In a similar way it is possible to construct `make-simplified-...` functions for each of the other types of algebraic expression. Some sample rules of simplification for use in defining constructor functions for each operator are given in Figures 5.1 through 5.6.

$$
\begin{aligned}
(n_1 + n_2) &\mapsto n, \\
&\quad \text{where } n = n_1 + n_2 \\
(0 + e) &\mapsto e \\
(e + 0) &\mapsto e \\
(n_1 + (e_1 + n_2)) &\mapsto (e_1 + n), \\
&\quad \text{where } n = n_1 + n_2 \\
((e_1 + n_1) + n_2) &\mapsto (e_1 + n), \\
&\quad \text{where } n = n_1 + n_2 \\
((e_1 + n_1) + (e_2 + n_2)) &\mapsto ((e_1 + e_2) + n), \\
&\quad \text{where } n = n_1 + n_2 \\
((- e_1) + e_2) &\mapsto (e_2 - e_1) \\
(e_1 + (- e_2)) &\mapsto (e_1 - e_2)
\end{aligned}
$$

Figure 5.1   Some simplification rules for addition.

$$
\begin{aligned}
(n_1 - n_2) &\mapsto n, \\
&\quad \text{where } n = n_1 - n_2 \\
(0 - e) &\mapsto (- e) \\
(e - 0) &\mapsto e \\
((- e_1) - (- e_2)) &\mapsto (e_2 - e_1) \\
(e_1 - (- e_2)) &\mapsto (e_1 + e_2)
\end{aligned}
$$

Figure 5.2   Some simplification rules for subtraction.

$$
\begin{aligned}
(n_1 * n_2) &\mapsto n, \\
&\quad \text{where } n = n_1 * n_2 \\
(0 * e) &\mapsto 0 \\
(e * 0) &\mapsto 0 \\
(1 * e) &\mapsto e \\
(e * 1) &\mapsto e \\
(n_1 * (n_2 * e_1)) &\mapsto (n * e_1), \\
&\quad \text{where } n = n_1 * n_2 \\
((n_1 * e_1) * n_2) &\mapsto (n * e_1), \\
&\quad \text{where } n = n_1 * n_2 \\
((n_1 * e_1) * (n_2 * e_2)) &\mapsto (n * (e_1 * e_2)), \\
&\quad \text{where } n = n_1 * n_2 \\
((- e_1) * (- e_2)) &\mapsto (e_1 * e_2)
\end{aligned}
$$

Figure 5.3   Some simplification rules for multiplication.

$$
\begin{aligned}
(n_1 \ / \ n_2) &\mapsto n, \\
&\text{where } n = n_1/n_2 \\
(0 \ / \ e) &\mapsto 0 \\
(e \ / \ 1) &\mapsto e \\
((- \ e_1) \ / \ (- \ e_2)) &\mapsto (e_1 \ / \ e_2)
\end{aligned}
$$

Figure 5.4   Some simplification rules for division.

$$
\begin{aligned}
(n_1 \ ** \ n_2) &\mapsto n, \\
&\text{where } n = n_1{}^{n_2} \\
(0 \ ** \ e) &\mapsto 0 \\
(1 \ ** \ e) &\mapsto 1 \\
(e \ ** \ 0) &\mapsto 1 \\
(e \ ** \ 1) &\mapsto e \\
(e_1 \ ** \ (- \ e_2)) &\mapsto (1 \ / \ (e_1 \ ** \ e_2))
\end{aligned}
$$

Figure 5.5   Some simplification rules for exponentiation.

$$
(\cos \ (- \ e)) \ \mapsto \ (\cos \ e)
$$

Figure 5.6   A simplification rule for cosine.

This "incomplete" list only serves to emphasize the need for more efficient ways of expressing the rules of simplification. In many implementations, simplification is frequently combined with another transformation type, *conversion to canonical form*, because the latter can reduce the number of "special cases" that require additional simplification rules. In other words, the simplification rule set can itself be simplified by restricting the number of valid alternatives that might require simplification. Conversion to canonical form will be discussed in Section 5.4, where we shall again return to the problem of simplification of algebraic expressions. In the next section, however, we shall describe another transformation type that also is commonly applied to reduce the number of alternative symbolic representations of objects, appropriately called *reduction*.

5.3 REDUCTION

Reductions are transformations that eliminate "higher-level" operators of a notation system. In doing so, however, the notation becomes syntactically more complex than the original. For example, the following reductions can be used in the propositional calculus to eliminate implication and equivalence operators.

$$
\begin{aligned}
p \rightarrow q &\mapsto (\sim p) \lor q \\
p \leftrightarrow q &\mapsto (p \land q) \lor ((\sim p) \land (\sim q))
\end{aligned}
$$

Another example is the rewriting of a for loop in Pascal using an equivalent while loop as illustrated in Figure 5.7.[2]

```
for v := e1 to e2 do body
            ↦
begin
    TEMP1 := e1;
    TEMP2 := e2;
    if TEMP1 <= TEMP2 then
        begin
            v := TEMP1;
            body;
            while v <> TEMP2 do
                begin
                    v := SUCC(v);
                    body
                end
        end
end
```

Figure 5.7　A reduction rule for Pascal programs.

5.3.1 Theorem Proving Using Reductions

The implementation of a theorem prover for the propositional calculus is an interesting example of reduction transformation techniques. The method to be described is based on the application of a set of rules of inference defined by Hao Wang [Wan60]. Before describing the method, however, it is necessary to characterize what is meant by the phrase "a theorem to be proven."

An *interpretation* for a logical formula is an assignment of truth values to each of its constituent propositions. An interesting type of logical formula is one which is true for every possible interpretation. Such a formula is often called a *tautology*, because it represents a fact which is trivially true about the world. For example, the (tautological) formula (P1 OR (NOT P1)) might stand for the statement "Either Fermat's Last Theorem is provable or Fermat's Last Theorem is not provable." This is an obviously true statement which provides no real information about its subject. On the other hand, tautological formulas are very interesting from a logical viewpoint because they are formulas which are true purely by virtue of their logical form. Such statements are true not because of any interpretation assigned to their constituents, but rather because of the logical relationships among them. Such formulas are also called *logical truths* or *theorems*.

The nature of a logical formula can be studied by constructing its *truth table*. Such a table lists the truth value of a formula for every possible interpretation of its

---

[2]This reduction transformation actually comes from the 1983 Pascal Standard, wherein it is used to define the semantics of **for** loops.

propositions. Consequently, one possible strategy for proving that a logical formula is a theorem in the propositional calculus is to evaluate the logical formula for all possible assignments of truth values to its propositions; in other words, construct its truth table. Note that the truth table method requires 2^n steps, where n is the number of propositions.

As a general-purpose algorithm for determining logical truth, the truth table method is unsuitable for two reasons. First, the size of the table grows exponentially with the number of propositions. Second, it reveals nothing about the structural reasons that make a logical formula always true. The truth table method is useful as a decision procedure of last resort, however; to show, for example, the truth of rules used in a framework of logical deduction.

In the late 1950s, Hao Wang formulated an alternative algorithm for proving whether any given logical formula is a theorem of the propositional calculus. The Wang algorithm actually verifies or refutes *proof conjectures* rather than theorems. In fact, a theorem is just a special case of a proof conjecture. Thus, a proof conjecture is really a generalization of what is meant by the phrase "a theorem to be proven." Therefore, in what follows, we shall address the issue of proving proof conjectures, with the understanding that this includes theorems to be proved as special cases.

Formally, a *proof conjecture* is expressed by a pair of lists, an *hypothesis list* and a *goal list*, both of which are lists of logical formulas. The hypothesis list specifies formulas whose role is comparable to the hypotheses in standard mathematical theorem proving; every formula in the hypothesis list can be assumed to be true in proving the proof conjecture. The goal list, on the other hand, specifies alternative formulas to be proven; the proof conjecture is verified when any one of the goals is shown to follow from the hypotheses.

As indicated above, a theorem is a tautology and its proof consists of showing that it can be inferred from its logical structure alone, without regard to premises. As a special case of a proof conjecture, a theorem to be proved therefore consists of a empty hypothesis list and a goal list which contains only the logical formula (purported tautology). Any verified proof conjecture can also be turned into a tautology by constructing a "new" logical formula, specifically an implication whose antecedent is the conjunction of all the hypotheses and whose consequent is the disjunction of all the goal formulas.

The concept of goal list in the context of theorem proving is a bit unusual but provides a computationally convenient representation for the Wang algorithm. The idea of interpreting a theorem to be proved as a "goal" transforms the process of logical inference into a search among a set of symbolic expressions. The effectiveness of this alternative representation of the problem comes from the fact that it is possible to control the search in a manner analogous to the derivation of intermediate results during the development of a proof. The search is controlled by the applicability of a set of rules which define the allowable ways a proof conjecture can be transformed to an equivalent proof conjecture.

The basis of the Wang algorithm consists of a set of reduction rules whose application will successively reduce the complexity of goal and hypothesis formulas until one of the following two rules applies:

Rule 1a.   If the goal list contains a proposition which is also in the hypothesis list, the theorem is true.

Rule 1b.   If both the goal list and the hypothesis list contain only propositions, and have no common propositions, the theorem is false.

The Wang algorithm recursively applies suitable reduction rules to formulas in the goal or hypothesis lists, with the rules above being used as terminating conditions. Each reduction rule specifies how a proof conjecture may be reduced to either one or two simpler proof conjectures. The reductions are rules of equivalence; that is, if the reduced conjecture or conjectures are true, then the original is true, and if a reduced conjecture is false, then the original is false. For each of the five types of logical formula (negation, conjunction, disjunction, implication, and equivalence) there is a reduction rule for such a formula appearing in the hypothesis list and a reduction rule for such a formula appearing in the goal list, for a total of ten reduction rules.

We now summarize these reduction rules for the Wang algorithm. In the following, H and G are metavariables standing for arbitrary lists of hypothesis formulas and goal formulas, respectively, and f, f_1, and f_2 are metavariables standing for individual formulas. The notation "$H \models G$" represents a proof conjecture with hypothesis list "H" and goal list "G":

Rule 2a. $H, (\text{NOT } f) \models G \mapsto H \models G, f$

Rule 2b. $H \models G, (\text{NOT } f) \mapsto H, f \models G$

Rule 3a. $H, (f_1 \text{ AND } f_2) \models G \mapsto H, f_1, f_2 \models G$

Rule 3b. $H \models G, (f_1 \text{ AND } f_2) \mapsto H \models G, f_1$ and $H \models G, f_2$

Rule 3b requires that the truth of both reduced theorems be shown to show the truth of the original theorem. Rules 4a, 5a, 6a, and 6b have similar requirements.

Rule 4a. $H, (f_1 \text{ OR } f_2) \models G \mapsto H, f_1 \models G$ and $H, f_2 \models G$

Rule 4b. $H \models G, (f_1 \text{ OR } f_2) \mapsto H \models G, f_1, f_2$

Rule 5a. $H, (f_1 \text{ IMPLIES } f_2) \models G \mapsto H, f_2 \models G$ and $H \models G, f_1$

Rule 5b. $H \models G, (f_1 \text{ IMPLIES } f_2) \mapsto H, f_1 \models G, f_2$

Rule 6a. $H, (f_1 \text{ EQUIV } f_2) \models G \mapsto H, f_1, f_2 \models G$ and $H \models G, f_1, f_2$

Rule 6b. $H \models G, (f_1 \text{ EQUIV } f_2) \mapsto H, f_1 \models G, f_2$ and $H, f_2 \models G, f_1$

The validity of these proof rules may not be obvious at first, but can be verified by careful analysis or through the use of truth tables.

These rules can be used to verify or refute proof conjectures in the following way. To determine whether a given conjecture is true, first check for common propositions on the hypothesis and goal lists. If a common proposition is found, the current proof conjecture is verified by Rule 1a. If not, look for composite logical formulas on the hypothesis list. If such formulas exist, choose one (e.g., the first one encountered) and apply the appropriate reduction rule on the hypothesis formula. This will involve the recursive verification of one or two subproof conjectures. If there are no composite hypothesis formulas, look for a composite goal formula, and if found, apply the appropriate goal reduction rule. If all these cases fail, the hypothesis and goal lists must contain only disjoint sets of propositions; the proof conjecture is therefore refuted by Rule 1b.

5.3.2 Implementation of the Wang Method

Now consider the implementation of the Wang algorithm as a Small Lisp function theorem-p which takes an hypothesis list and a goal list of formulas[3] and determines whether the corresponding proof conjecture is valid. First a number of auxiliary functions need to be defined. The predicate have-common-props implements Rule 1a and checks whether two lists of formulas have common propositions, using the function hasprop:

```
have-common-props[hlist; glist] =
  [endp[hlist] --> F;
   proposition-p[first[hlist]] -->
     [hasprop[first[hlist]; glist] --> T;
      otherwise --> have-common-props[rest[hlist]; glist]];
   otherwise --> have-common-props[rest[hlist]; glist]]
```

The function hasprop determines whether a specific proposition p is on a given formula list:

```
hasprop[p; list] =
  [endp[list] --> F;
   proposition-p[first[list]] -->
     [eq[prop-name[p]; prop-name[first[list]]] --> T;
      otherwise --> hasprop[p; rest[list]]];
   otherwise --> hasprop[p; rest[list]]]
```

In addition, the predicate has-composite-formula determines whether a given formula list has a composite formula.

```
has-composite-formula[list] =
  [endp[list] --> F;
   proposition-p[first[list]] --> has-composite-formula[rest[list]];
   otherwise --> T]
```

Given that a formula list, does have composite formulas, the function first-composite-formula returns the first such formula in the list while the corresponding function remove-first-composite-formula returns the original formula list less its first composite formula.

```
first-composite-formula[list] =
  [proposition-p[first[list]] --> first-composite-formula[rest[list]];
   otherwise --> first[list]]

remove-first-composite-formula[list] =
  [proposition-p[first[list]] -->
```

---

[3]Logical formulas are assumed to be represented using the grammar of Figure 4.2.

```
    cons[first[list]; remove-first-composite-formula[rest[list]]];
  otherwise --> rest[list]]
```

Note that these auxiliary functions are chosen based on the logical requirements of the Wang algorithm, without particular concern for efficiency. From an efficiency view-point, these auxiliary functions could be criticized because their use in the Wang algorithm may involve up to four separate traversals of formula lists. An attempt to somehow combine these functions to use only a single traversal is premature, how-ever, since it would result in no more than a small constant factor speedup and would greatly complicate the algorithm.

Using these auxiliary functions, the theorem-p function can be implemented as the basic driver for the Wang algorithm.

```
theorem-p[hlist; glist] =
  [have-common-props[hlist; glist] --> T;
   has-composite-formula[hlist] -->
     apply-hypothesis-reduction
       [first-composite-formula[hlist];
         remove-first-composite-formula[hlist]; glist];
   has-composite-formula[glist] -->
     apply-goal-reduction
       [first-composite-formula[glist]; hlist;
         remove-first-composite-formula[glist]];
   otherwise --> F]
```

The functions apply-hypothesis-reduction and apply-goal-reduction are responsible for applying the individual reduction rules and recursively invoking the theorem-p function on subconjectures.

```
cons2[e1; e2; list] = cons[e1; cons[e2; list]]

apply-hypothesis-reduction[h; newhlist; glist] =
  [negation-p[h] --> theorem-p[newhlist; cons[negend[h]; glist]];
   conjunction-p[h] -->
     theorem-p[cons2[conjunct1[h]; conjunct2[h]; newhlist]; glist];
   disjunction-p[h] -->
     [theorem-p[cons[disjunct1[h]; newhlist]; glist] -->
       theorem-p[cons[disjunct2[h]; newhlist]; glist];
      otherwise --> F];
   implication-p[h] -->
     [theorem-p[newhlist; cons[antecedent[h]; glist]] -->
       theorem-p[cons[consequent[h]; newhlist]; glist];
      otherwise --> F];
   equivalence-p[h] -->
     [theorem-p[cons2[condition1[h]; condition2[h]; newhlist]; glist]
       --> theorem-p
             [newhlist; cons2[condition1[h]; condition2[h]; glist]];
      otherwise --> F]]
```

```
apply-goal-reduction[g; hlist; newglist] =
  [negation-p[g] --> theorem-p[cons[negend[g]; hlist]; newglist];
   disjunction-p[g] -->
     theorem-p[hlist; cons2[disjunct1[g]; disjunct2[g]; newglist]];
   conjunction-p[g] -->
     [theorem-p[hlist; cons[conjunct1[g]; newglist]] -->
        theorem-p[hlist; cons[conjunct2[g]; newglist]];
      otherwise --> F];
   implication-p[g] -->
     theorem-p
       [cons[antecedent[g]; hlist]; cons[consequent[g]; newglist]];
   equivalence-p[g] -->
     [theorem-p
        [cons[condition1[g]; hlist]; cons[condition2[g]; newglist]] -->
      theorem-p
        [cons[condition2[g]; hlist]; cons[condition1[g]; newglist]];
      otherwise --> F]]
```

5.3.3 Proof Generation

The theorem-p function applies the Wang algorithm to determine the validity of a proof conjecture. Unfortunately, its output is not very useful, since it simply yields T for a verified conjecture or F for a refuted one. It would be much more useful if the theorem prover could show why a given conjecture was true or false, producing either a *proof* for a verified conjecture or a *refutation* of a false one.

To provide this additional capability, we now consider how proofs and refutations can be defined as objects of an abstract data type, instances of which can be produced by a modified theorem prover. As an abstract object, a proof consists of a conjecture together with some rationale demonstrating that the conjecture is true. In the case of the Wang algorithm, a rationale typically consists of some application of a Wang reduction rule plus the fact that either one or two subconjectures are true. The truth of each of these subconjectures in turn must be established with proofs of their own which become subproofs of the original proof.

Based on the rationale provided by the choice of Wang reduction rule to apply, proofs and refutations can be classified as belonging to one of five basic types. A *simple proof* is one which succeeds directly by Rule 1a and hence requires no subproofs. Abstractly, its components consist of a proof conjecture and a proposition which occurs in both the hypothesis and goal lists of that conjecture. A *linear proof* is one which succeeds by reduction to a single subproof. Its components consist of a proof conjecture, the number of the reduction rule involved, the hypothesis or goal formula which is reduced, and the subproof of the reduced conjecture. Similarly, a *double proof* is used for the remaining reduction rules which reduce conjectures to two subconjectures. The basic type of refutation is a *simple refutation* which occurs when a proof conjecture consists of propositions only on its hypothesis and goal lists with no common propositions. Finally, a *linear refutation* refutes a conjecture by refuting one of its subconjectures. There is no "double refutation" analogous to a double proof.

Although all the Wang rules which reduce to two subconjectures require that both subconjectures be true to establish the original conjecture, refutation of only one of them is necessary to refute the original; in other words, both conjectures do not need to be refuted.

Given such a characterization of proofs and refutations as abstract data objects, a Lisp representation of such objects can readily be developed using a GRAIL grammar as follows:

⟨proof-or-refutation⟩ ::= ⟨proof⟩ | ⟨refutation⟩

⟨proof⟩ ::= ⟨simple-proof⟩ | ⟨linear-proof⟩ | ⟨double-proof⟩

⟨refutation⟩ ::= ⟨simple-refutation⟩ | ⟨linear-refutation⟩

⟨simple-proof⟩ ::= (⟨proven:conjecture⟩ `verified-by Rule1A`
(⟨common-prop:proposition⟩))

⟨linear-proof⟩ ::= (⟨proven:conjecture⟩ `reduces-by`
⟨reduction:rule⟩ ⟨target:formula⟩
`to` ⟨subproof:proof⟩)

⟨double-proof⟩ ::= (⟨proven:conjecture⟩ `reduces-by`
⟨reduction:rule⟩ ⟨target:formula⟩
`to` ⟨subproof1:proof⟩ `and`
⟨subproof2:proof⟩)

⟨simple-refutation⟩ ::= (⟨refuted:conjecture⟩ `refuted-by Rule1B`)

⟨linear-refutation⟩ ::= (⟨refuted:conjecture⟩ `refuted-by`
⟨reduction:rule⟩ ⟨target:formula⟩
`to` ⟨subrefutation:refutation⟩)

⟨conjecture⟩ ::= (`Assuming` (⟨hypotheses:formula*⟩)
`conclude` (⟨goals:formula*⟩))

⟨rule⟩ ::= ⟨rule2A⟩ | ⟨rule2B⟩ | ⟨rule3A⟩ | ⟨rule3B⟩ |
⟨rule4A⟩ | ⟨rule4B⟩ | ⟨rule5A⟩ | ⟨rule5B⟩ |
⟨rule6A⟩ | ⟨rule6B⟩

⟨rule2A⟩ ::= `Rule2A`

⟨rule2B⟩ ::= `Rule2B`

⟨rule3A⟩ ::= `Rule3A`

⟨rule3B⟩ ::= `Rule3B`

⟨rule4A⟩ ::= `Rule4A`

⟨rule4B⟩ ::= `Rule4B`

⟨rule5A⟩ ::= `Rule5A`

⟨rule5B⟩ ::= `Rule5B`

$$\langle \text{rule6A} \rangle ::= \text{Rule6A}$$

$$\langle \text{rule6B} \rangle ::= \text{Rule6B}$$

Applying the GRAIL method, these grammar rules not only define a Lisp representation for proofs and refutations, but also identify the appropriate data access functions for manipulating that representation. In the case of various types of "rule," data access constants are specified in accordance with the scheme for GRAIL lexical rules described in Section 4.2.4: for example,

$$\text{rule2A} = \text{"Rule2A"}$$

Given the GRAIL characterization of proofs and refutations as data objects, it is now a relatively straightforward matter to construct a theorem prover to return proofs or refutations. The main function is `prove-or-refute`, which returns a list representation of a proof or a refutation (viewed as instances of an abstract data type) for a given proof conjecture. It calls a driver function `prover-aux` which either calls an appropriate reduction function or directly constructs a simple proof or a simple refutation:

```
prove-or-refute[conjecture] =
  {hlist = hypotheses[conjecture];
   glist = goals[conjecture] :
   [have-common-props[hlist; glist] -->
      make-simple-proof[conjecture; first-common-prop[hlist; glist]];
    has-composite-formula[hlist] -->
      apply-hypothesis-reduction
        [conjecture; first-composite-formula[hlist];
         remove-first-composite-formula[hlist]; glist];
    has-composite-formula[glist] -->
      apply-goal-reduction
        [conjecture; first-composite-formula[glist]; hlist;
         remove-first-composite-formula[glist]];
    otherwise --> make-simple-refutation[conjecture]]}

first-common-prop[hlist; glist] =
  [proposition-p[first[hlist]] -->
    [hasprop[first[hlist]; glist] --> first[hlist];
     otherwise --> first-common-prop[rest[hlist]; glist]];
   otherwise --> first-common-prop[rest[hlist]; glist]]
```

Note that the structure of this driver is very similar to that of `theorem-p` given earlier.

The functions for applying hypothesis and goal reductions are reorganized to construct the new proof conjectures for subproofs and then call auxiliary reduction routines `single-reduction` and `double-reduction` to carry out the reductions:

```
apply-hypothesis-reduction[conjecture; h; newhlist; glist] =
  [negation-p[h] -->
```

```
  single-reduction
    [conjecture; h; rule2A;
     make-conjecture[newhlist; cons[negend[h]; glist]]];
conjunction-p[h] -->
  single-reduction
    [conjecture; h; rule3A;
     make-conjecture
       [cons2[conjunct1[h]; conjunct2[h]; newhlist]; glist]];
disjunction-p[h] -->
  double-reduction
    [conjecture; h; rule4A;
     make-conjecture[cons[disjunct1[h]; newhlist]; glist];
     make-conjecture[cons[disjunct2[h]; newhlist]; glist]];
implication-p[h] -->
  double-reduction
    [conjecture; h; rule5A;
     make-conjecture[newhlist; cons[antecedent[h]; glist]];
     make-conjecture[cons[consequent[h]; newhlist]; glist]];
equivalence-p[h] -->
  double-reduction
    [conjecture; h; rule6A;
     make-conjecture
       [cons2[condition1[h]; condition2[h]; newhlist]; glist];
     make-conjecture
       [newhlist; cons2[condition1[h]; condition2[h]; glist]]]]

apply-goal-reduction[conjecture; g; hlist; newglist] =
  [negation-p[g] -->
    single-reduction
      [conjecture; g; rule2B;
       make-conjecture[cons[negend[g]; hlist]; newglist]];
  conjunction-p[g] -->
    double-reduction
      [conjecture; g; rule3B;
       make-conjecture[hlist; cons[conjunct1[g]; newglist]];
       make-conjecture[hlist; cons[conjunct2[g]; newglist]]];
  disjunction-p[g] -->
    single-reduction
      [conjecture; g; rule4B;
       make-conjecture
         [hlist; cons2[disjunct1[g]; disjunct2[g]; newglist]]];
  implication-p[g] -->
    single-reduction
      [conjecture; g; rule5B;
       make-conjecture
         [cons[antecedent[g]; hlist]; cons[consequent[g]; newglist]]];
```

```
equivalence-p[g] -->
  double-reduction
    [conjecture; g; rule6B;
     make-conjecture
       [cons[condition1[g]; hlist]; cons[condition2[g]; newglist]];
     make-conjecture
       [cons[condition2[g]; hlist];
        cons[condition1[g]; newglist]]]]]
```

To apply a reduction involving only one subconjecture, the `single-reduction`
function first of all proves or refutes the subconjecture with a recursive call to `prove-
or-refute`. If the object returned by this recursive call is a proof, the subconjecture
has been verified and a linear proof is constructed using the subproof. Otherwise,
a subrefutation must have been returned, so it is then used in constructing a linear
refutation:

```
single-reduction[conjecture; formula; rule; newconjecture] =
  {subproof-or-refutation = prove-or-refute[newconjecture] :
   [proof-p[subproof-or-refutation] -->
      make-linear-proof
        [conjecture; rule; formula; subproof-or-refutation];
    otherwise -->
      make-linear-refutation
        [conjecture; rule; formula; subproof-or-refutation]]}
```

Double reductions are implemented following a similar pattern. If both subconjectures succeed, a double proof is constructed using the subproofs. If a subconjecture
fails, however, it is used immediately in constructing a linear refutation of the original
conjecture:

```
double-reduction
  [conjecture; formula; rule; newconjecture1; newconjecture2] =
  {subproof-or-refutation1 = prove-or-refute[newconjecture1] :
   [proof-p[subproof-or-refutation1] -->
      {subproof-or-refutation2 = prove-or-refute[newconjecture2] :
       [proof-p[subproof-or-refutation2] -->
          make-double-proof
            [conjecture; rule; formula; subproof-or-refutation1;
             subproof-or-refutation2];
        otherwise -->
          make-linear-refutation
            [conjecture; rule; formula; subproof-or-refutation2]]};
    otherwise -->
      make-linear-refutation
        [conjecture; rule; formula; subproof-or-refutation1]]}
```

We conclude this section with a sample output illustrating the proof generated by the functions we have just defined. Suppose we wish to prove the fairly obvious tautology that

$$((p \wedge q) \vee (\sim p \wedge \sim q)) \rightarrow (p \leftrightarrow q)$$

We first define a driver function for proving a single goal:

```
prove1[goal] =
  prove-or-refute[make-conjecture[(); list1[goal]]]
```

The appropriate call to verify the tautology is

```
prove1[(((P AND Q) OR ((NOT P) AND (NOT Q))) IMPLIES (P EQUIV Q))]
```

and resulting output is as follows:

```
((Assuming () conclude
  (((((P AND Q) OR ((NOT P) AND (NOT Q))) IMPLIES (P EQUIV Q))))
 reduces-by Rule5B
 (((P AND Q) OR ((NOT P) AND (NOT Q))) IMPLIES (P EQUIV Q)) to
 ((Assuming (((P AND Q) OR ((NOT P) AND (NOT Q)))) conclude
   ((P EQUIV Q))) reduces-by Rule4A
  ((P AND Q) OR ((NOT P) AND (NOT Q))) to
  ((Assuming ((P AND Q)) conclude ((P EQUIV Q))) reduces-by Rule3A
   (P AND Q) to
   ((Assuming (P Q) conclude ((P EQUIV Q))) reduces-by Rule6B
    (P EQUIV Q) to
    ((Assuming (P P Q) conclude (Q)) verified-by Rule1A (Q)) and
    ((Assuming (Q P Q) conclude (P)) verified-by Rule1A (P)))) and
  ((Assuming (((NOT P) AND (NOT Q))) conclude ((P EQUIV Q)))
   reduces-by Rule3A ((NOT P) AND (NOT Q)) to
   ((Assuming ((NOT P) (NOT Q)) conclude ((P EQUIV Q))) reduces-by
    Rule2A (NOT P) to
   ((Assuming ((NOT Q)) conclude (P (P EQUIV Q))) reduces-by
    Rule2A (NOT Q) to
    ((Assuming () conclude (Q P (P EQUIV Q))) reduces-by Rule6B
     (P EQUIV Q) to
     ((Assuming (P) conclude (Q Q P)) verified-by Rule1A (P))
     and ((Assuming (Q) conclude (P Q P)) verified-by Rule1A
              (Q)))))))))
```

The discussion of this section should demonstrate strongly not only how but also why "theorem proving" can be automated, at least for the propositional calculus. At the heart of the solution is the ability to interpret the process as a sequence of transformations on symbolic data and to devise a means of controlling or directing the application of those transformations. In Chapter 10, we shall see that this strategy can be employed in developing a theorem prover for a much richer domain, the predicate calculus.

5.4 CANONICAL FORMS

A third type of commonly occurring transformation is conversion to canonical form. A *canonical form* is a designated or "standard" representation for an object chosen from among several different but equivalent symbolic representations. Such transformations may increase or decrease the complexity of a notational phrase, or just simply rearrange subphrases according to some convention. For example, a common mathematical convention for polynomials consists of a series of terms with decreasing exponents, wherein each term is optionally preceded by a numerical coefficient. According to such a convention, the following conversion transformation would be appropriate:

$$x^2 \times 7 - 4 + 2 \times x^4 \;\mapsto\; 2 \times x^4 + 7 \times x^2 - 4$$

As this example illustrates, one use of conversions to canonical form is to improve the readability of notation as presented to human eyes. In addition, however, canonical forms can be useful in simplifying the implementation of subsequent transformations by reducing the number of alternative representations that must be recognized or processed. A third application of canonical forms occurs when two distinct symbolic representations must be compared for "equivalence"; that is, do they both represent the "same" object? Such a circumstance occurs when there is more than one way to represent an object in the input domain with a given notation system. In such cases there exist rules that define the classes of equivalent representations and permit the transformation from one representation to another within a class. However, it is frequently difficult to ascertain the right rules to use and the appropriate order in which to apply them. When a canonical form for a class is carefully defined, transformation to canonical form of two equivalent expressions will produce identical, or nearly identical representations, greatly simplifying the comparison.

5.4.1 Canonical Forms in Algebraic Expression Simplification

In Section 5.2, simplifying transformations were used to improve the readability of algebraic expressions. In addition to applying rules for simplification of expressions, it is also useful to apply rules to put expressions into a canonical form. As indicated, a canonical form is a way of restricting the forms of expression that are allowed; using a canonical form with the inside-out method means that the simplification rules need only deal with a restricted class of expression. For example, there are two ways of representing a negative number, that is, directly as a negative numeric atom (e.g., -3) or as the negation of a positive numeric atom [e.g., (- 3)]. If both possibilities are allowed, the simplification rule for the product of two negatives would require four cases. If the form (- 3) is taken as the canonical form, however, only one case need be analyzed. To use this canonical form for negative numbers, however, the `simplify` function of Section 5.2 must be changed so that the clause for dealing with constants is the following:

```
constant-p[expr] --> make-canonical-constant[expr]
```

The `make-canonical-constant` function required in this clause must convert negative numeric constants into canonical form. This construction can be defined as follows:

```
make-canonical-constant[expr] =
  [greaterp[0; value-of[expr]] -->
    make-negation[make-constant[minus[0; value-of[expr]]]];
  otherwise --> expr]
```

With this change, it can be verified that `simplify` returns expressions in *canonical simplified form* assuming that the `make-simplified-...` functions do so when their arguments are in canonical simplified form.

Now consider the implementation of the `make-simplified-product` function using the following rules from among those provided in Figure 5.3.

$$(0 * e) \longmapsto 0$$
$$(e * 0) \longmapsto 0$$
$$(1 * e) \longmapsto e$$
$$(e * 1) \longmapsto e$$
$$(n_1 * (n_2 * e_1) \longmapsto (n * e_1),$$
$$\text{where } n = n_1 * n_2$$
$$((n_1 * e_1) * n_2) \longmapsto (n * e_1),$$
$$\text{where } n = n_1 * n_2$$

In these rules, e, e_1, and e_2 are, as before, metavariables for arbitrary algebraic expressions, while the metavariables n, n_1, and n_2 denote positive numeric constants. Note that all of the rules involve numeric operands, and that two involve operands which are in turn product expressions with numerical operands. In order to avoid a proliferation of simplification rules, it is useful to define a canonical form for product expressions with numeric operands in which only the first operand may be numeric. This is really just the recognition of when the commutative law for multiplication can be employed, and its applicability can be expressed by the following rule:

$$(e * n) \longmapsto (n * e)$$

Systematic application of this rule can be used to reduce the number of alternative representations for symbolic multiplication. Such a rule can be incorporated into the simplification algorithm by first of all placing the arguments of `make-simplified-product` in canonical order as follows:

```
make-simplified-product[expr1; expr2] =
  [constant-p[expr2] --> canonical-product[expr2; expr1];
  otherwise --> canonical-product[expr1; expr2]]
```

With this transformation, the multiplication rules of Figure 5.3 can be reduced in number since the following can be eliminated:

$$(e * 0) \longmapsto 0$$
$$(e * 1) \longmapsto e$$

$$((n_1 * e_1) * n_2) \;\mapsto\; (n * e_1),$$

$$\text{where } n = n_1 * n_2$$

The implementation of the remaining simplification rules is then carried out in `canonical-product` as follows:

```
canonical-product[expr1; expr2] =
  [and[negation-p[expr1]; negation-p[expr2]] -->
    make-simplified-product[operand[expr1]; operand[expr2]];
   constant-p[expr1] -->
    [eq[value-of[expr1]; 0] --> expr1;
     eq[value-of[expr1]; 1] --> expr2;
     constant-p[expr2] -->
       make-constant[times[value-of[expr1]; value-of[expr2]]];
     numeric-product-p[expr2] -->
       make-simplified-product
         [make-constant
           [times[value-of[expr1]; value-of[operand1[expr2]]]];
          operand2[expr2]];
     otherwise --> make-product[expr1; expr2]];
   and[numeric-product-p[expr1]; numeric-product-p[expr2]] -->
    make-simplified-product
      [make-constant
        [times[value-of[operand1[expr1]];
               value-of[operand1[expr2]]]];
       make-simplified-product[operand2[expr1]; operand2[expr2]]];
   otherwise --> make-product[expr1; expr2]]

numeric-product-p[expr] =
  [product-p[expr] --> constant-p[operand1[expr]];
   otherwise --> F]
```

In a similar fashion, other simplication rules for mathematical expressions can be eliminated by the inclusion of a suitable rule for conversion to canonical form. For example, the commutative law for addition can be employed:

$$(n + e) \;\mapsto\; (e + n)$$

This will eliminate the need for the same types of addition rules (see Figure) as were eliminated from the multiplication rules by implementation of the commutative law for multiplication.

Another example of a canonical conversion rule is the outward propagation of negations. The possibilities are as follows:

$$((- e_1) * e_2) \;\mapsto\; (- (e_1 * e_2))$$
$$(e_1 * (- e_2)) \;\mapsto\; (- (e_1 * e_2))$$
$$((- e_1) / e_2) \;\mapsto\; (- (e_1 / e_2))$$
$$(e_1 / (- e_2)) \;\mapsto\; (- (e_1 / e_2))$$

$$((-\ e_1)\ +\ (-\ e_2))\ \ \mapsto\ \ (-\ (e_1\ +\ e_2))$$

$$((-\ e_1)\ -\ e_2)\ \ \mapsto\ \ (-\ (e_2\ +\ e_1))$$

$$(\sin\ (-\ e))\ \ \mapsto\ \ (-\ (\sin\ e))$$

These rules do not themselves result in simplifications, but may result in simplifications later. For example, if negations within the two operands of a product are propagated outward, the product itself can be simplified to eliminate both negations. Note that the canonical-product function defined earlier in this section must be changed to incorporate outward propagation of negations.

With the inclusion of canonical conversion rules, the set of simplification rules required for the inside-out method can be reduced considerably and yet still yield a very useful simplifier for algebraic expressions. Such a simplifier could then be used to simplify the output of the deriv program. However, if we can assume that the input to deriv is already in canonical simplified form, a better method of producing simplified output from deriv is to perform simplification "on the fly." This can be achieved by modifying deriv to replace each call to make... by a corresponding call to make-simplified..., as follows:

```
deriv[exp; vrbl] =
  [constant-p[exp] --> make-constant[0];
   variable-p[exp] -->
     [eq[name-of[exp]; name-of[vrbl]] --> make-constant[1];
      otherwise --> make-constant[0]];
   negation-p[exp] -->
     make-simplified-negation[deriv[operand[exp]; vrbl]];
   product-p[exp] -->
     make-simplified-sum
       [make-simplified-product
          [operand1[exp]; deriv[operand2[exp]; vrbl]];
        make-simplified-product
          [operand2[exp]; deriv[operand1[exp]; vrbl]]];
   quotient-p[exp] -->
     make-simplified-quotient
       [make-simplified-difference
          [make-simplified-product
             [operand2[exp]; deriv[operand1[exp]; vrbl]];
           make-simplified-product
             [operand1[exp]; deriv[operand2[exp]; vrbl]]];
        make-simplified-power[operand2[exp]; make-constant[2]]];
   sum-p[exp] -->
     make-simplified-sum
       [deriv[operand1[exp]; vrbl]; deriv[operand2[exp]; vrbl]];
   difference-p[exp] -->
     make-simplified-difference
       [deriv[operand1[exp]; vrbl]; deriv[operand2[exp]; vrbl]];
   power-p[exp] -->
```

```
make-simplified-product
  [make-simplified-product
     [exponent[exp]; deriv[base[exp]; vrbl]];
   make-simplified-power
     [base[exp];
      make-simplified-difference
        [exponent[exp]; make-constant[1]]]];
exponential-p[exp] -->
  make-simplified-product[exp; deriv[argument[exp]; vrbl]];
sine-p[exp] -->
  make-simplified-product
    [make-simplified-cosine[argument[exp]];
     deriv[argument[exp]; vrbl]];
cosine-p[exp] -->
  make-simplified-negation
    [make-simplified-product
       [make-simplified-sine[argument[exp]];
        deriv[argument[exp]; vrbl]]]]
```

5.5 SUMMARY

It should be clear from the examples discussed in this chapter that large or complex symbolic computing implementations can be expected to employ all of the transformation types described. Just as conversion to canonical form was used in the inside-out method to achieve simplification, so also can simplification (and reduction) be used to achieve conversion to canonical form. In Chapter 10 such an opportunity will be presented, where the objective will be to prove theorems expressed in the predicate calculus rather than the propositional calculus, as was achieved in Section 5.3.

5.6 EXERCISES

5.1. A logical expression can be reduced to one which contains only the logical operators $\wedge$ (AND), $\vee$ (OR), and $\sim$ (NOT) using the following transformation rules:

$$(x \rightarrow y) \quad \mapsto \quad (\sim x \vee y)$$
$$(x \leftrightarrow y) \quad \mapsto \quad ((\sim x \wedge \sim y) \vee (x \wedge y))$$

Devise a reduction function which implements these transformation rules.

5.2. Simplification rules based on the associativity of conjunction, disjunction, and equivalence can be used to define n-ary versions of these operators (functions of n arguments). Redesign the grammar of Figure 4.2 to obtain representations of given logical expressions as functions of n variables. Write a function to simplify expressions in the new representation according to the rules of associativity.

5.3. A logical expression can be converted to a canonical form by transforming it to a representation called *sum of products*. This representation consists of a disjunction of terms, all of which are conjunctions of propositions or their negations. Such a formula is usually obtained by repeated application of the distributive laws:

$$x \wedge (y \vee z) \quad \mapsto \quad (x \wedge y) \vee (x \wedge z)$$
$$(x \vee y) \wedge z \quad \mapsto \quad (x \wedge z) \vee (y \wedge z)$$

and application of De Morgan's laws:

$$\sim (x \wedge y) \quad \mapsto \quad (\sim x) \vee (\sim y)$$
$$\sim (x \vee y) \quad \mapsto \quad (\sim x) \wedge (\sim y)$$

Assuming the input consists only of formulas which include disjunction, conjunction, and negation, but not implication or equivalence, write a function to convert formulas to sum-of-products form.

5.4. When formulas are in sum-of-products canonical form, as described in Exercise 5.3, a simplified representation is possible which eliminates some parentheses and explicit representation of the logical operators. Propose a grammar for such a representation and write a function to evaluate the truth value of a formula expressed in this notation, given an assignment of truth values to the variables.

5.5. An alternative canonical form for logical expressions is called *product of sums*. Such a representation consists of a conjunction of terms which are disjunctions of literals. The complement of a sum of products can be expressed easily in product of sums form by direct application of De Morgan's law. Devise a grammar for the simplified representation of such logical expressions (as was done in Exercise 5.4) and write a function to obtain the complement of a sum-of-products representation, expressed as a product of sums.

5.6. Canonical representations can often be expressed in a simplified form which can reduce or eliminate the need for keywords to help interpret the structure. Discuss the virtues and weaknesses of such simplified canonical representations of logical formulas versus canonical representations which explicitly include operator representation. Then compare the advantages of canonical representations in general with representations which include the five logical operators $\wedge, \vee, \sim, \rightarrow, \leftrightarrow$ or representations which include the three operators $\wedge, \vee, \sim$.

5.7. Assume logical expressions are defined using only the logical operators $\wedge, \vee, \sim$. It is well known that these operators define a Boolean algebra on the set of truth values. Such a set of operators is called a *universal set* since any Boolean expression can be expressed using only the operators in the set. In fact, only the operators $\wedge, and \sim$ are required to represent any Boolean expression, since disjunction can be expressed in terms of conjunction and negation. Devise and implement a reduction rule for transforming a logical expression which includes disjunction to one in which the disjunction operator does not occur. Then define and implement the inverse of your rule and explain how this implementation is an example of the application of a simplification rule.

5.8. In circuit design, *universal gates* are Boolean functions which permit the representation of any logical expression with a single operator. An example of such a function is the *NAND* operator, often represented by the symbol "↑". This Boolean function of two variables can be defined by the following truth table:

x	y	$x \uparrow y$
0	0	1
0	1	1
1	0	1
1	1	0

Write a function to transform logical expressions which use the conjunction, disjunction, and negation operators to expressions which use only the NAND operator.

5.9. The Boolean function NAND, defined in Exercise 5.8, can be defined as a function of n variables:

$$(\uparrow x_1, x_2, \ldots, x_n) = \sim (\wedge x_1, x_2, \ldots, x_n)$$

where $(\wedge x_1, x_2, \ldots, x_n)$ denotes the conjunction of n elements. Unlike conjunction however, NAND is not associative and:

$$(\uparrow x_1, x_2, \ldots, x_n) \neq (\uparrow x_1, (\uparrow x_2, \ldots, x_n))$$

Design a function to transform an n-ary NAND expression into an equivalent expression consisting only of binary NAND operations.

5.10. If logical constants are permitted as operands, show that the logical operation of implication ($\rightarrow$) is a universal function; that is, all logical expressions can be represented using only the implication operation. Implement a function to transform a logical expression which can include any of the five "standard" operators ($\wedge, \vee, \sim, \rightarrow, \leftrightarrow$) to expressions which include only $\rightarrow$.

6

Environments and Interpretation

A common phenomenon of symbolic notation systems is the existence of different interpretations for a given piece of notation, resulting from the ways the symbols within the notation can be interpreted. For example, the propositional formula "p → q" may have interpretations such as "If queen to king's bishop 7, then checkmate," or "If data abstraction is used, then programming is easy," depending on the meanings assigned to the individual proposition symbols "p" and "q." The assignment of interpretations or meanings to the symbols is often said to provide a *context* for the overall interpretation of the notation.

An important type of interpretation is *evaluation*, in which a value is computed for a notational phrase when given a context specifying values for the symbols within the phrase. For example, by assigning numerical values to the variables within an algebraic expression, a numerical value for the entire expression can be determined. Alternatively, by specifying truth values for the propositions within a logical formula, the truth value of the formula itself may be computed. Such evaluations follow the general pattern of an interpretation application: in each case, the context for interpretation is provided by the set of values specified for the symbols within the notation.

In implementing an interpretation application, the context for the interpretation is usually provided by a data structure called an *environment*. Abstractly, such a data structure is a mapping (function) from the symbols of the notation to the values or meanings associated with them. Simply put, an environment is a way of representing for subsequent retrieval the value associated with each symbol.

Defined as an abstract data type, environments typically require three basic operations and a primitive data element. The key operation is a selector `apply-env[env; symbol]` which determines the appropriate value or meaning associated with a `symbol` in a given environment `env`. The name `apply-env` reflects the view of environments as functions mapping symbols to their values: the value is the result of applying the environment to the symbol. Of course, `apply-env` assumes that the symbol is defined in the given environment; it will report a run-time error if this is not the case. Sometimes, however, an application may need to perform some other action in the case of an undefined symbol. Thus the second operation for environment ADTs is a recognizer `defined-p[env; symbol]`, which determines whether a given `symbol` has been assigned a value.

The third operation of the environment ADT is a constructor `extend-env` to construct environments from existing ones.[1] Given an original environment `env`, `extend-env[env; symbol; value]` returns a new environment which is the same as the original except for an additional mapping between `symbol` and `value`. Any existing value for `symbol` in the original environment is lost (i.e., it can no longer be retrieved by `apply-env`). The `extend-env` operation can be related to the `defined-p` and `apply-env` operations by the following equations:

$$\text{defined-p}[\text{extend-env}[E;\ x;\ a];\ x] = \text{"T"}$$

$$\text{defined-p}[\text{extend-env}[E;\ y;\ a];\ x] = \text{defined-p}[E;\ x] \text{ where } x \neq y$$

$$\text{apply-env}[\text{extend-env}[E;\ x;\ a];\ x] = a$$

$$\text{apply-env}[\text{extend-env}[E;\ y;\ a];\ x] = \text{apply-env}[E;\ x] \text{ where } x \neq y$$

All of these equations are mathematical identities, which hold for all values of E, x, y and a, subject to the constraints given.

Finally, we need a starting point for constructing environments. For this, we will use a symbolic constant `null-env` which specifies an environment in which only default bindings exist. Often, there will be no defaults, and thus `null-env` will specify a completely empty environment, that is, one with no mappings defined. In such a case, the following equation holds:

$$\text{defined-p}[\text{null-env};\ x] = \text{"F"}, \text{ for all } x$$

Whether default bindings are defined or not, however, `null-env` will be used as the basis for constructing arbitrary environments by successive calls to `extend-env`.

This description of environments is quite generic in that it leaves unspecified the nature of symbols and values to be stored in the environments. The values will vary depending on the application; truth values may be stored in an environment used in a propositional calculus application, while numeric values may be stored in an application involving algebraic expressions. Symbols could be stored directly as members of a symbolic data domain or in a more convenient fashion for symbol comparison using a suitable representation of their name. In general, we will take the latter approach, converting symbols from whatever symbolic data domain we are using to the symbolic atoms which name them.

---

[1] Rather than simply using `make-env` as the constructor name, we have used `extend-env` to be somewhat more indicative of the nature of environment construction.

As we shall see, many different physical data models can be used to implement environments as abstract data objects. The choice of a data model is influenced by the type of data value to be associated with symbols in the environment, the need for efficient updating of environments, and the need for efficient access to the values given for the symbols in an environment. It may also be the case that additional properties are required of the environment data type in a given application. In each case, however, the data access functions given above—together with the equations relating them—will characterize the basic properties of environments.

6.1 EVALUATION OF LOGICAL FORMULAS

A simple example of an evaluation application is the determination of the truth of a formula of the propositional calculus in a context specifying the truth of its constituent propositions. To do so, we must develop an environment data structure sufficient to ascertain the truth value of any individual proposition. One possibility is simply to use a list of names of all the propositions which are true and assume that any proposition not named in the list is false. This representation is quite simple and works well for the propositional calculus because there are only two possible truth values for a proposition. However, this representation will not extend well to other notation systems, which will generally involve many possible values for their symbols.

Given this choice of representation, then, implementation of the data access functions is straightforward. The null environment, `null-env`, will be represented by an empty list, corresponding to a default assignment of false for all proposition names.[2] With this interpretation, every proposition has a defined value in the environment, and `defined-p` is given simply by

$$\text{defined-p[env; name]} = T$$

The selector function, `apply-env`, which retrieves the value assigned to a proposition name, is defined as follows:

```
apply-env[env; name] =
  [endp[env] --> F;
    eq[first[env]; name] --> T;
    otherwise --> apply-env[rest[env]; name]]
```

Note that this implementation is unusual for a selector, requiring a search through a data structure rather than simply extracting a list element at a known position. In fact, the value selected is not even contained in the data structure at all, but is implicitly defined by the representation scheme! Nevertheless, we describe data access functions by their abstract behavior, not their implementations, so `apply-env` is truly a selector.

Next consider how our environment representation can be updated to reflect a new truth value for a given proposition, that is, how the constructor

---

[2]Usually, the null environment corresponds to the state where no symbol has been assigned a value. In this case, however, because every symbol in the input domain can have one of only two values, we can infer the value of a symbol from whether it is a member of `env`. We therefore interpret "X is a member of `env`" to mean that X has the value T.

```
                        extend-env[env; prop-name; value]
```

can be implemented. If the new value is T, the proposition name can simply be in-cluded in the env list. If it is F, however, the env list must be modified to ensure that any and all occurrences of the name are removed.

```
        extend-env[env; name; value] =
          [value --> cons[name; env];
           otherwise --> remove-name[env; name]]

        remove-name[env; name] =
          [endp[env] --> ();
           eq[first[env]; name] --> remove-name[rest[env]; name];
           otherwise --> cons[first[env]; remove-name[rest[env]; name]]]
```

Note that a call extend-env[env; "P"; T] will add the symbol P to the env list even if it is already there. Hence, in order to associate the value F with a symbol, we must account for the possibility of multiple instances of the symbol in the env list. Alterna-tively, we could redefine extend-env so that it does not add a symbol to the list if it is already there; this would allow us to simplify remove-name somewhat.

This completes the implementation of our environment ADT for propositions and their truth values. Now we are ready to develop the evaluator for propositional calculus formulas. The evaluator will take two arguments: a propositional formula to be evaluated and an environment specifying the truth values to be used for each proposition in the formula. The result will be the truth value of the formula computed according to the conventional semantics of the various logical formula types. The following examples illustrate typical computations required of the evaluator.

$$\text{evalformula}[(\text{NOT } p); (p)] \Rightarrow F$$
$$\text{evalformula}[(p \text{ EQUIV } q); ()] \Rightarrow T$$
$$\text{evalformula}[((p \text{ AND } q) \text{ AND } r); (p \ q)] \Rightarrow F$$

Design of the evaluator can proceed in a data-driven manner from the GRAIL grammar for the propositional calculus as given in Figure 4.2 and repeated below.

⟨formula⟩   ::= ⟨proposition⟩ | ⟨negation⟩ | ⟨conjunction⟩ |
                    ⟨disjunction⟩ | ⟨implication⟩ | ⟨equivalence⟩
⟨negation⟩   ::= (NOT ⟨negend:formula⟩)
⟨conjunction⟩ ::= (⟨conjunct1:formula⟩ AND ⟨conjunct2:formula⟩)
⟨disjunction⟩ ::= (⟨disjunct1:formula⟩ OR ⟨disjunct2:formula⟩)
⟨implication⟩ ::= (⟨antecedent:formula⟩ IMPLIES ⟨consequent:formula⟩)
⟨equivalence⟩ ::= (⟨condition1:formula⟩ EQUIV ⟨condition2:formula⟩)
⟨proposition⟩ ::= ⟨prop-name:symbolic-atom⟩

For each type of logical formula, a conditional clause is required whose predicate expression contains the recognizer for that formula type and whose result expression implements the corresponding semantics. For example, propositions are evaluated by looking up the name of the proposition in the environment to determine the associated truth value.

```
proposition-p[formula] -->
  apply-env[env; prop-name[formula]]
```

Negations are evaluated by evaluating the negend of the formula and returning F if that evaluation returns T and returning T otherwise.

```
negation-p[formula] -->
  [evalformula[negend[formula]; env] --> F;
   otherwise --> T]
```

A conjunction evaluates to T if both if its conjuncts evaluate to T. That is, if the first conjunct is T, then evaluation of the second conjunct gives the value of the entire conjunction. Otherwise, the conjunction evaluates to F.

```
conjunction-p[formula] -->
  [evalformula[conjunct1[formula]; env] -->
     evalformula[conjunct2[formula]; env];
   otherwise --> F]
```

Similarly, each of the other formula types is handled by implementing the appropriate logic on evaluated subformulas. The complete implementation of evalformula follows easily.

```
evalformula[formula; env] =
  [proposition-p[formula] -->
    [defined-p[env; prop-name[formula]] -->
       apply-env[env; prop-name[formula]];
     otherwise --> error[(Undefined proposition)]];
   negation-p[formula] -->
    [evalformula[negend[formula]; env] --> F;
     otherwise --> T];
   conjunction-p[formula] -->
    [evalformula[conjunct1[formula]; env] -->
       evalformula[conjunct2[formula]; env];
     otherwise --> F];
   disjunction-p[formula] -->
    [evalformula[disjunct1[formula]; env] --> T;
     otherwise --> evalformula[disjunct2[formula]; env]];
   implication-p[formula] -->
    [evalformula[antecedent[formula]; env] -->
       evalformula[consequent[formula]; env];
     otherwise --> T];
   equivalence-p[formula] -->
    [evalformula[condition1[formula]; env] -->
       evalformula[condition2[formula]; env];
     evalformula[condition2[formula]; env] --> F;
     otherwise --> T]]
```

6.2 EVALUATION OF ALGEBRAIC EXPRESSIONS

A second example of an interpretation application is the evaluation of algebraic expressions given an environment of values for its variable names. This application involves the domain of algebraic expressions introduced with the `deriv` example and then summarized using GRAIL notation in Figure 4.1. Since Small Lisp does not include real numbers, however, we will define our variables to range over the domain of integers. This will exclude from further consideration the types of algebraic expression that involve primarily real number computations, namely the exponential, sine, and cosine functions.

In this example, we use a data structure for environments called an *association list*. This data structure consists of a list of symbol-value bindings, each of which is a two-element list containing a symbolic atom and its associated value. To illustrate, an environment specifying the value of 3 for X and 7 for Y could be represented as the list

$$((X\ 3)\ (Y\ 7))$$

The value of a symbol in such an environment will be the value found in the first symbol-value sublist whose first element is the given symbol. Any subsequent bindings for a given symbol are ignored. For example, the binding (X 8) is ignored in

$$((X\ 3)\ (Y\ 7)\ (X\ 8))$$

This approach allows a new binding to be added easily to an environment without the expense of removing old values.

Association lists provide a more general approach to environment representation than the data structure we used for propositions and truth values. The general structure for association lists can be defined by the following GRAIL grammar.

⟨association-list⟩ ::= (⟨binding*⟩)
⟨binding⟩ ::= (⟨bound- sym:symbolic-atom⟩ ⟨assoc-val:arbitrary⟩)

We have specified that the type of values stored in an association list is "arbitrary" to indicate that the kinds of values stored depend on the application.

Given this physical data representation for environments, implementation of the operations required for the environment abstract data type follows directly. First we define an auxiliary funtion `assoc` to find the symbol-value binding for a given symbol. If no such binding exists, `assoc` returns the empty list.

```
bound-sym[binding] = first[binding]

assoc-val[binding] = second[binding]

make-binding[sym; val] = list2[sym; val]

assoc[bindings; sym] =
  [endp[bindings] --> ();
   eq[bound-sym[first[bindings]]; sym] --> first[bindings];
   otherwise --> assoc[rest[bindings]; sym]]
```

This auxiliary function is then used for implementing both defined-p and apply-env.

```
defined-p[env; name] =
  [endp[assoc[env; name]] --> F;
   otherwise --> T]

apply-env[env; name] =
  {binding = assoc[env; name] :
   [endp[binding] --> error2[(Undefined symbol --); name];
    otherwise --> assoc-val[binding]]}

error2[msglist; error-item] = error[append1[msglist; error-item]]

extend-env[env; name; value] = cons[make-binding[name; value]; env]

null-env = ()
```

Note that the apply-env function reports an error if the symbol it is given is not defined in the environment. The error2 auxiliary is defined as a convenient way to call error with both a message and an error value. If some other action is to be taken instead, the defined-p recognizer should first be used to test for undefined symbols.

Now consider the evaluation of an algebraic expression given an environment specifying values for the variables within the expression. This can be implemented as a recursive function whose structure parallels that of evalformula defined in the preceding section:

```
evalmath[expr; env] =
  [constant-p[expr] --> const-val[expr];
   variable-p[expr] --> apply-env[env; var-name[expr]];
   negation-p[expr] --> minus[0; evalmath[operand[expr]; env]];
   otherwise -->
     {op1 = evalmath[operand1[expr]; env];
      op2 = evalmath[operand2[expr]; env] :
      [product-p[expr] --> times[op1; op2];
       quotient-p[expr] --> divide[op1; op2];
       sum-p[expr] --> plus[op1; op2];
       difference-p[expr] --> minus[op1; op2];
       power-p[expr] --> power[op1; op2]]}]

power[x; y] =
  [lessp[y; 0] --> divide[1; power[x; minus[0; y]]];
   eqp[y; 0] --> 1;
   otherwise --> times[x; power[x; minus[y; 1]]]]
```

Note, however, that we have taken advantage of the overloading of the operand1 and operand2 selectors to simplify several of the clauses. Also, we have implemented a power function, since Small Lisp does not provide one.

The evalmath function can now be used to perform sample evaluations as follows:

$$\texttt{evalmath[(X * (Y ** 3)); ((X 7) (Y 2))]} \Rightarrow 56$$
$$\texttt{evalmath[((X - Y) * Z); ((X 7) (Y 9) (Z -3))]} \Rightarrow 6$$

Note that `evalmath` uses only the recognizer and selector data access functions for the composite algebraic expressions. No constructor functions are necessary. The earlier `evalformula` example also follows this pattern, using only recognizers and selectors on the logical formula domain. This is, in fact, a general property of all analysis applications. Such applications were described in Chapter 1 as those which take symbolic input and generate nonsymbolic output. Since no symbolic output is produced in these applications, there is generally no need to use the constructor functions defined for the input data domain. Interpretation and evaluation applications can thus be classified within the analysis application category.

6.3 LISP IN LISP: AN S-LISP INTERPRETER

Now let us consider how the techniques of the preceding two sections apply to a more complex example: the development of an interpreter for Small Lisp programs. Such an interpreter is an example of a *metaprogram*, that is, a program which processes programs. In general, the *target language* of a metaprogram is the language in which the programs to be processed are expressed; in this case the target language is Small Lisp. On the other hand, the *host language* of a metaprogram is the language in which the metaprogram itself is written. Our first interpreter will be a prototype implemented with Small Lisp itself as the host language; thus we will write a Small Lisp program to process Small Lisp programs. The prototype interpreter will actually be processing the S-Lisp representation of Small Lisp programs, as described in Chapter 4. After our prototype interpreter has been constructed, we can consider the implementation of a production version of the interpreter with Pascal as a host language, and the m-Lisp form of Small Lisp as the target language. Appendix C discusses the design of such an interpreter based on the techniques of this chapter and of Chapter 12.

The central problem of a Lisp interpreter implementation is how to provide some means of evaluating expressions in the context of given function and constant definitions and variable bindings. The solution presented here requires the use of two environments. The first maps function names to their definitions, and the second maps constant and variable names to their values. The use of separate environments reflects the fact that Small Lisp has separate "namespaces" for variables and functions, allowing an identifier to be used simultaneously as both a variable name and a function name (see Section B.3.2).

Given function and variable environments called `fn-env` and `value-env`, the heart of the interpreter will be a function

$$\texttt{sl-eval[expr; fn-env; value-env]}$$

which will evaluate a given S-Lisp `expr` in the specified context. The output of `sl-eval` should be the same S-expression that would be computed by a conventional Small Lisp interpreter given the m-Lisp version of `expr` and an equivalent context.

The environments we use will follow the same ADT specification as given in the preceding sections. Thus the constant `null-env` and the functions `defined-p`, `apply-env`, and `extend-env` will be used for both the function and value environments. However, it may be that we will want to have different implementations of each of these environment ADTs. In order to allow this, we will give slightly different names to the environment for functions, namely `null-fn-env`, `defined-fn-p`, `apply-fn-env`, and `extend-fn-env`.

6.3.1 Evaluation

Let us proceed immediately to the design of `sl-eval`, deferring, for the time being, the question of how the function and value environments are initially prepared. Assuming that these environments are available, then, the design can proceed in data-driven fashion working from the GRAIL grammar for Small Lisp expressions as given in Figure 4.3 and repeated below.

⟨expression⟩ ::= ⟨identifier⟩ | ⟨numeric-atom-expr⟩ |
⟨symbolic-atom-expr⟩ | ⟨list-expr⟩ | ⟨fn-call⟩ |
⟨cond-expr⟩ | ⟨let-expr⟩

⟨identifier⟩ ::= ⟨id-name:symbolic atom⟩
⟨numeric-atom-expr⟩ ::= ⟨numeric-val:numeric atom⟩
⟨symbolic-atom-expr⟩ ::= (quote ⟨symbolic-val:symbolic-atom⟩)
⟨list-expr⟩ ::= (quote ⟨list-val:list⟩)
⟨fn-call⟩ ::= (⟨callee:identifier⟩ ⟨arguments:expression⁺⟩)
⟨cond-expr⟩ ::= (cond ⟨clauses:clause⁺⟩)
⟨clause⟩ ::= (⟨predicate:expression⟩ ⟨result:expression⟩)
⟨let-expr⟩ ::= (let (⟨local-defs:local-def⁺⟩)
⟨final-expr:expression⟩)
⟨local-def⟩ ::= (⟨local- var:variable⟩ ⟨local-val:expression⟩)

We expect our evaluator to be a recursive function whose body is a conditional expression with branches implementing the evaluation logic for each of these different expression types.

The first few cases are easy. An identifier represents a variable whose value is determined by lookup from the `value-env`.

```
identifier-p[expr] --> apply-env[value-env; id-name[expr]];
```

Numeric-atom-exprs, symbolic-atom-exprs, and list-exprs are all expressions representing constant data; in each case the value is the represented constant.

```
numeric-atom-expr-p[expr] --> numeric-val[expr];
symbolic-atom-expr-p[expr] --> symbol-val[expr];
list-expr-p[expr] --> list-val[expr]
```

Recall that `sym-val` and `list-val` perform both selection of a `quoted` object and conversion of that object to the S-expression domain.

Before considering function calls, let us first look at conditional expressions and let expressions. A conditional expression requires that its clauses be considered in

order until the predicate of one of them evaluates to T. The result part of this clause is
then evaluated and returned as the value of the entire conditional expression. On the
other hand, if none of the predicates evaluates to T, then a run-time error should be
reported. These actions can be implemented using an auxiliary function sl-evcond.

```
cond-expr-p[expr] -->
  sl-evcond[clauses[expr]; fn-env; value-env];

sl-evcond[condclauses; fn-env; env] =
  [sl-eval[predicate[first[condclauses]]; fn-env; env] -->
     sl-eval[result[first[condclauses]]; fn-env; env];
   single-p[condclauses] -->
     error[(Error in conditional expression -- no true predicate)];
   otherwise --> sl-evcond[rest[condclauses]; fn-env; env]]
```

Note that the GRAIL grammar specifies that clause lists always have at least one
clause; sl-evcond is implemented appropriately.

Evaluation of a let expression is carried out by evaluating its final expression in
the context of a value environment updated by the local definitions. Specifying the
auxiliary function extend-local-env to carry out this updating gives the following
logic for let expressions.

```
let-expr-p[expr] -->
  sl-eval
    [final-expr[expr];
     fn-env;
     extend-local-env
       [fn-env; value-env; local-defs[expr]]];
```

Note that the updated environment which is computed is only made available for evaluation of the final expression; it is not saved or returned in any way for later use. This
reflects the semantics for let expressions as described in Chapter 2.

Updating the local environment must also be carried out carefully to reflect
the proper semantics of Small Lisp. Recall that the assignments to the local variables are conceptually carried out in parallel and become effective only when the final
expression is to be evaluated. Thus each of the expressions in the local-definition
list must be evaluated in the context of the original value environment without any
updates applied. This requirement is reflected in the following implementation of
extend-local-env.

```
extend-local-env[fn-env; value-env; local-defs] =
  {var-name = id-name[local-var[first[local-defs]]];
   val = sl-eval[local-val[first[local-defs]]; fn-env; value-env] :
   [single-p[local-defs] --> extend-env[value-env; var-name; val];
    otherwise -->
      extend-env
        [extend-local-env[fn-env; value-env; rest[local-defs]];
         var-name; val]]}
```

The final type of expression to be handled by sl-eval is the function call. The callee can denote either a built-in Small Lisp primitive or a user-defined function. In either case, however, the argument expressions must first be evaluated before being passed to the function. This evaluation can be handled by an auxiliary sl-evlis, defined as follows:

```
sl-evlis[explist; fn-env; val-env] =
  {val1 = sl-eval[first[explist]; fn-env; val-env] :
   [single-p[explist] --> list1[val1];
    otherwise -->
       cons[val1; sl-evlis[rest[explist]; fn-env; val-env]]]}
```

Since argument lists always have at least one argument, they are analyzed and constructed with single-p and list1.

Once the arguments have been evaluated, we are almost ready to call the specified function. The only remaining requirement is to reset the value environment, removing the bindings for any function parameters and local variables that are currently defined. The only variable bindings that should exist when a function is called are the bindings established by global constant definitions and those predefined for T, F, and otherwise. For the time being, assume that this can be done using an auxiliary function reset-to-global-frame applied to the current value environment. Specifying that the semantics of function application are to be carried out by a further auxiliary sl-apply, the logic of function-call evaluation can now be incorporated into the complete definition of sl-eval as shown in Figure 6.1. Note that this logic reflects the fact that the argument list is evaluated in the context of the current value-env before it is reset to the global frame.

```
sl-eval[expr; fn-env; value-env] =
  [identifier-p[expr] --> apply-env[value-env; id-name[expr]];
   numeric-atom-expr-p[expr] --> numeric-val[expr];
   symbolic-atom-expr-p[expr] --> symbolic-val[expr];
   list-expr-p[expr] --> list-val[expr];
   fn-call-p[expr] -->
     sl-apply
       [callee[expr]; sl-evlis[arguments[expr]; fn-env; value-env];
         fn-env; reset-to-global-frame[value-env]];
   cond-expr-p[expr] --> sl-evcond[clauses[expr]; fn-env; value-env];
   let-expr-p[expr] -->
     sl-eval
       [final-expr[expr]; fn-env;
         extend-local-env[fn-env; value-env; local-defs[expr]]];
   otherwise --> error2[(Bad S-Lisp expression --); expr]]
```

Figure 6.1   Heart of the Small Lisp interpreter: sl-eval.

The implementation of reset-to-global-frame is problematic for our environment ADT as originally formulated. That formulation only provides the operations `defined-p` and `apply-env` for investigating the contents of an environment; there is no way of determining whether or not a given binding is global. This problem can be solved, however, by extending the ADT to include `reset-to-global-frame` as a basic operation together with a complementary operation `mark-global-frame`. The latter function, when applied to a given environment env is defined to return a new environment which is equivalent to env, except that the entire set of current bindings are marked as being in the global frame. New bindings that are subsequently added using `extend-env` will not be in the global frame. If `reset-to-global-frame` is then applied to such an updated environment, it returns the environment which contains only the global frame, discarding all the bindings added after the last call to `mark-global-frame`. For the time being, assume that the implementation of this extended environment ADT is available; we will return to this issue after the discussion of the evaluator has been completed.

Now consider how `sl-apply` can be defined to process function calls in the context of an evaluated argument list and the appropriate global environment frame. To simplify matters, we will assume that functions are always called with the correct number of arguments. Calls to both the built-in Small Lisp primitives and user-defined functions must be handled. For the most part, implementing the semantics of the primitive functions is quite easy, because the primitive functions of our target language (Small Lisp) are already available as primitives in our host language (also Small Lisp)! For example, suppose that we have to evaluate a call to the target language cons function given a list of its evaluated `arguments`. Somehow, we need to implement the semantics of cons in our host language. This is straightforward in the Small Lisp host language, using its built-in cons function.

$$cons[first[arguments]; second[arguments]]$$

The remaining primitives follow a similar pattern, as shown in Figure 6.2. If our host language did not provide these primitives as built-in functions, however, they would have to be implemented. For example, in the Pascal version of the interpreter supplied with this book, the `Primitives` module provides such implementations for each of the Small Lisp primitives; see Section C.3.

The only difficult case in applying the primitives is in dealing with the error "function." If a call to error is made, its argument is printed out and evaluation is terminated. In essence, the value of each outstanding recursive call to `sl-eval` is undefined, as is the value of the highest-level nonrecursive call. If this highest-level call to `sl-eval` is in fact made from the top level, the behavior of the target language error primitive can be simulated by a call to error in the host language. However, the top level of our evaluator may be used within some other function, for example, to perform a series of evaluations returning a list of the results. In this case, it might be more appropriate to return an indication of an "undefined value," together with the error message as the result of the evaluation. This behavior is rather more difficult to simulate and is the subject of Figure 6.7 at the end of the chapter.

In order to evaluate the call of a user-defined function, its definition has to be retrieved and applied. As shown in Figure 6.2, this involves evaluation of the expression comprising the function body in an environment which includes the associations of formal parameters with their corresponding argument values. To add these new

```
sl-apply[callee; args; fn-env; val-env] =
  {fn = id-name[callee] :
   [eq[fn; "first"] --> first[first[args]];
    eq[fn; "rest"] --> rest[first[args]];
    eq[fn; "endp"] --> endp[first[args]];
    eq[fn; "numberp"] --> numberp[first[args]];
    eq[fn; "symbolp"] --> symbolp[first[args]];
    eq[fn; "listp"] --> listp[first[args]];
    eq[fn; "eq"] --> eq[first[args]; second[args]];
    eq[fn; "cons"] --> cons[first[args]; second[args]];
    eq[fn; "plus"] --> plus[first[args]; second[args]];
    eq[fn; "minus"] --> minus[first[args]; second[args]];
    eq[fn; "times"] --> times[first[args]; second[args]];
    eq[fn; "divide"] --> divide[first[args]; second[args]];
    eq[fn; "rem"] --> rem[first[args]; second[args]];
    eq[fn; "eqp"] --> eqp[first[args]; second[args]];
    eq[fn; "lessp"] --> lessp[first[args]; second[args]];
    eq[fn; "greaterp"] --> greaterp[first[args]; second[args]];
    eq[fn; "sym-lessp"] --> sym-lessp[first[args]; second[args]];
    eq[fn; "explode"] --> explode[first[args]];
    eq[fn; "implode"] --> implode[first[args]];
    eq[fn; "error"] --> error[first[args]];
    otherwise -->
      {defn = apply-fn-env[fn-env; fn] :
       sl-eval
         [body[defn]; fn-env;
          add-associations[val-env; parameters[defn]; args]]}]}
```

Figure 6.2   Evaluating function calls: sl-apply.

bindings to the environment, an auxiliary function matches each parameter with its corresponding argument value in a call to extend-env.

```
add-associations[env; parms; args] =
  {new-env = extend-env[env; first[parms]; first[args]] :
   [single-p[parms] --> new-env;
    otherwise --> add-associations[new-env; rest[parms]; rest[args]]]}
```

Thus the bindings available in the evaluation of the body of the function definition are the predefined bindings for T, F, and otherwise, any global bindings that may have been established with constant definitions, and the new parameter bindings set up with the current call.

This completes the definition of sl-eval, the heart of our Small Lisp interpreter. Completion of the interpreter requires only that we provide suitable implementations for our value and function environments and show how the environments are set up initially from the list of constant and function definitions that comprise a Small Lisp program.

6.3.2 Environment Implementation

As a starting point for the representation of both the value and function environments required by our interpreter, we might consider the same kind of representation used previously for algebraic expressions [i.e., association lists (lists of symbol-value pairs)]. In each case, however, this representation turns out to be unsatisfactory, for different reasons. In the case of value environments, we have specified that the ADT provide operations for marking and extracting global frames, requiring an extension to the association list representation. In the case of function environments association lists are semantically adequate but too inefficient for practical application.

The frame processing extensions for value environments introduce a distinction between those identifiers in the global frame and those which are not (local identifiers). An appropriate representation to reflect this distinction is a list of two association lists, one for the global frame and one for the local frame, summarized by the following GRAIL rule:

$$\langle\text{value-env}\rangle ::= (\ \langle\text{local-frame:assoc-list}\rangle\ \langle\text{global-frame:assoc-list}\rangle\ )$$

Lookup operations require that both frames be checked.

```
local-frame[env] = first[env]

global-frame[env] = second[env]

make-value-env[l-frame; g-frame] = list2[l-frame; g-frame]

defined-p[env; name] =
  [endp[assoc[local-frame[env]; name]] -->
    [endp[assoc[global-frame[env]; name]] --> F;
     otherwise --> T];
  otherwise --> T]

apply-env[env; name] =
  {local-binding = assoc[local-frame[env]; name] :
   [endp[local-binding] -->
     {global-binding = assoc[global-frame[env]; name] :
      [endp[global-binding] -->
        error2[(Undefined variable --); name];
       otherwise --> assoc-val[global-binding]]};
    otherwise --> assoc-val[local-binding]]}
```

A null environment consists of two empty frames. Updating the environment adds a binding to the local frame; the local bindings are moved to the global frame when `mark-global-frame` is called. The `reset-to-global-frame` function simply empties the local environment.

```
null-env = (() ())

extend-env[env; name; val] =
  make-value-env
    [cons[make-binding[name; val]; local-frame[env]];
     global-frame[env]]

mark-global-frame[env] = make-value-env[(); local-frame[env]]

reset-to-global-frame[env] = make-value-env[(); global-frame[env]]
```

A new environment representation is also required for function environments. The linear structure of association lists gives rise to a $\Theta(n)$ cost for symbol lookup, where n is the number of symbols stored in the environment. Because large programs may contain very many function definitions (hundreds or even thousands), use of association lists would give rise to an inordinately high cost for every function call.

An improvement in the efficiency of environment access can be achieved by using ordered binary trees for the environment representation. The basic idea here is that each tree node splits the environment into two parts depending on a key symbol. The left half of the environment will contain all bindings of identifiers which are lexicographically less than the key symbol. Conversely, the right half of the environment will contain all bindings of identifiers which are lexicographically greater than the key symbol. The binding for the key symbol itself will be contained in the current tree node. If the number of elements in each half of the representation is relatively well balanced, the cost of symbol look-up will be $\Theta(\log n)$.

We can now design a Lisp environment representation based on this idea. In addition to the interior tree nodes that represent split environments based on a key, we will also need empty nodes for representing subtrees with no bindings. The following GRAIL grammar presents a suitable design.

⟨env-tree⟩ ::= ⟨empty-node⟩ | ⟨tree-node⟩
⟨empty-node⟩ ::= ( )
⟨tree-node⟩ ::= (⟨key:ident⟩ ⟨left-env:env-tree⟩ ⟨right-env:env-tree⟩
                   ⟨key-value:fn-def⟩)

Based on this new representation, the data access functions for environments can be reimplemented as follows.

```
empty-node-p[env-tree] = endp[env-tree]

tree-node-p[env-tree] = not[endp[env-tree]]

empty-node = ()

make-tree-node[key; left-env; right-env; key-val] =
  list4[key; left-env; right-env; key-val]
key[tree-node] = first[tree-node]

left-env[tree-node] = second[tree-node]
```

```
right-env[tree-node] = third[tree-node]

key-value[tree-node] = fourth[tree-node]

defined-fn-p[env; name] =
  [empty-node-p[env] --> F;
   eq[name; key[env]] --> T;
   sym-lessp[name; key[env]] --> defined-fn-p[left-env[env]; name];
   otherwise --> defined-fn-p[right-env[env]; name]]

apply-fn-env[env; name] =
  [empty-node-p[env] --> error2[(Undefined function --); name];
   eq[name; key[env]] --> key-value[env];
   sym-lessp[name; key[env]] --> apply-fn-env[left-env[env]; name];
   otherwise --> apply-fn-env[right-env[env]; name]]

extend-fn-env[env; name; val] =
  [empty-node-p[env] -->
    make-tree-node[name; empty-node; empty-node; val];
   eq[name; key[env]] -->
    make-tree-node[name; left-env[env]; right-env[env]; val];
   sym-lessp[name; key[env]] -->
    make-tree-node
      [key[env]; extend-fn-env[left-env[env]; name; val];
       right-env[env]; key-value[env]];
   otherwise -->
    make-tree-node
      [key[env]; left-env[env];
       extend-fn-env[right-env[env]; name; val]; key-value[env]]]

null-fn-env = empty-node
```

Our environment constructor does not attempt to ensure that the trees it creates are balanced. In the worst case, if we encounter symbols in lexicographic order, the trees constructed will consist of a single branch of length n. However, given random sequences of symbols to be added to the environment, we can expect to see reasonably well-balanced trees [Knu73].

6.3.3 Interpreting a Program

Now consider how we can define an `interpret` function to evaluate an expression in the context of a complete list of Small Lisp function and constant definitions. This requires that we first set up the appropriate environments for functions and values based on the definitions. If we postulate the functions `build-func-env` and `build-const-env` for doing this, we could try to implement our top-level `interpret` function in the following way:

```
interpret[defs; expr] =
  sl-eval[expr; build-func-env[defs]; build-const-env[defs]]
```

This approach is somewhat problematical, however, because it separately builds up the function and constant environments. Thus it does not account for constant definitions which use previously defined functions and constants.

In order to account for the more general form of constant definitions, we need to set up both the function and value environments at the same time. To do this we introduce an auxiliary function

```
setup-envs-then-eval[fn-env; val-env; defs; expr]
```

which successively examines the function and constant definitions (defs), building up the appropriate environments in the accumulating parameters fn-env and val-env. Once all the defs have been processed, expr is evaluated in the context of the established environments. Using this approach, the interpret function can be defined as follows:

```
interpret[defs; expr] =
  setup-envs-then-eval
    [null-fn-env;
     extend-env
       [extend-env[extend-env[null-env; "F"; "F"]; "T"; "T"];
        "otherwise"; "T"];
     defs; expr]
```

The implementation of setup-envs-then-eval is data-driven based on lists of definitions which are either function or constant definitions, previously defined as follows:

⟨fn-def⟩ ::= (defun ⟨fn-name:identifier⟩
               (⟨parameters:identifier$^+$⟩) ⟨body:expression⟩)
⟨const-def⟩ ::= (setc ⟨const-name:identifier⟩ ⟨const-val:expression⟩)

Our setup function can now be defined to process one such definition at a time, adding the appropriate binding to one of the environments.

```
setup-envs-then-eval[fn-env; val-env; defs; expr] =
  [endp[defs] --> sl-eval[expr; fn-env; mark-global-frame[val-env]];
   fn-def-p[first[defs]] -->
     setup-envs-then-eval
       [extend-fn-env[fn-env; fn-name[first[defs]]; first[defs]];
        val-env; rest[defs]; expr];
   const-def-p[first[defs]] -->
     setup-envs-then-eval
       [fn-env;
        extend-env
          [val-env; const-name[first[defs]];
           sl-eval[const-val[first[defs]]; fn-env; val-env]];
        rest[defs]; expr]]
```

This function reflects our design decisions on environment representations and the semantics of Small Lisp. Function environments are set up by associating the entire function definition as the value associated with the function name. The constant definitions are processed using `sl-eval` in the context of the functions and values set up so far. Note that definitions are added to the environment as they are encountered. Thus a function definition later in a list overrides an earlier function definition of the same name, and the same is true for value definitions.

The definitions above provide a complete interpreter for syntactically correct Small Lisp programs written as S-expressions. However, the interpreter is not very robust and may produce unexpected results if given incorrect programs. A better version of an interpreter would include the checks for the following error conditions:

1. The number of arguments passed to a function does not correspond to the number of parameters it has.

2. Incorrect argument types are supplied to built-in functions (e.g., supplying numeric atoms as arguments to `cons`).

3. An attempt is made to redefine a primitive function.

4. An attempt is made to redefine `T` or `F`.

5. The value of a predicate in a conditional clause is neither `T` or `F`.

6.4 INTERPRETATION AND SEMANTICS

In some sense, interpretation applications may be considered the most fundamental applications on a given symbolic computing domain. This is because the interpretation of a notation is generally a direct reflection of the notation's overall meaning, that is, its *semantics*.

In this chapter, we have developed interpretation applications on three symbolic data domains: propositional calculus, algebraic expressions, and Small Lisp programs. In each case, we have relied on an implicit understanding of the application domain's semantics. In general, however, interpretation applications—and indeed all other symbolic computing applications—make sense only when the semantics of the application domain is known and understood.

Without providing a semantics, a symbolic notation system simply defines a set of syntactic objects with no inherit meaning. In the algebraic expression domain, for example, expressions involving operator symbols such as +, -, and * are simply syntactic objects, not necessarily associated with any particular semantics. By convention, however, we do associate a particular meaning with each of these constructs, that is, the mathematical operations of addition, subtraction, and multiplication, respectively. However, it is perfectly possible to associate a different semantics with the syntactic objects, in which case the `evalmath` function of Section 6.2, would be considered incorrect.

Given a specified semantics for an application domain, an interpreter for that domain may be viewed as an implementation of the semantics. By examining the logic of the interpreter, the correspondence is usually directly visible. For example, in the `evalmath` function of Section 6.2, product expressions using the * operator are directly implemented using the Small Lisp `times` function.

Conversely, interpreters for a symbolic data domain can also be used to define its semantics. This approach is known as *operational semantics*. One advantage of the operational approach compared to others is that it provides an executable specification of semantics, which can be subject to testing to remove errors and ensure completeness. On the other hand, operational definitions are often constrained by the expressive power of the particular programming language in which the interpreter is written. The operational approach has often been used in defining the semantics of programming languages. Pagan [Pag81] and Meyer [Mey90] compare the operational approach to several other styles of semantic definition for programming languages.

6.5 EXERCISES

6.1. Consider the environment representation described in Section 6.1 for storing truth values. Reimplement `extend-env` so that it never adds a symbol to the environment list if it is already there. Show how `remove-name` can be simplified if it is assumed that a symbol never occurs more than once on the environment list. Describe the performance trade-offs of this approach versus that given in Section 6.1. Why might this new approach be more prone to error than that given previously?

6.2. Implement the Boolean functions `and`, `or`, and `not` which operate on truth values as follows:

$$\begin{array}{llll}
\text{and}["F"; "F"] & \Rightarrow & F & \qquad \text{or}["F"; "F"] & \Rightarrow & F \\
\text{and}["F"; "T"] & \Rightarrow & F & \qquad \text{or}["F"; "T"] & \Rightarrow & T \\
\text{and}["T"; "F"] & \Rightarrow & F & \qquad \text{or}["T"; "F"] & \Rightarrow & T \\
\text{and}["T"; "T"] & \Rightarrow & T & \qquad \text{or}["T"; "T"] & \Rightarrow & T
\end{array}$$

$$\begin{array}{lll}
\text{not}["F"] & \Rightarrow & T \\
\text{not}["T"] & \Rightarrow & F
\end{array}$$

Reimplement `evalformula` of Section 6.1 using `and`, `or`, and `not` to express the semantics for each of the five types of composite logical formula. Comment on the desirability of your implementation versus that of the implementation given in the text.

6.3. An alternative to using association lists for the implementation of environment data structures is to assign variables to the first, third, fifth, ... (i.e., the odd positions) of a list and to assign the values to which they are bound to the positions immediately following. Thus the variable in the nth position of a list would be bound to the value located at the $(n + 1)$st position. Such a representation is called a *property list* and will be discussed in more detail in Chapter 7. For this exercise define the data access functions `defined-p`, `apply-env`, and `extend-env` for environments implemented using property lists.

6.4. The following grammar defines a representation for rational numbers:

$$\begin{array}{lll}
\langle\text{rational}\rangle & ::= & \langle\text{integer}\rangle \mid \langle\text{ratio}\rangle \\
\langle\text{integer}\rangle & ::= & \langle\text{value:numeric-atom}\rangle \\
\langle\text{ratio}\rangle & ::= & (\ \langle\text{numerator:integer}\rangle\ /\ \langle\text{denominator:integer}\rangle\ )
\end{array}$$

Using Small Lisp, implement the data access functions defined by the grammar and use them to write functions to compute the sum, difference, product and quotient of two rational numbers.

$$\text{(rational-sum 4 (2 / 3))} \Rightarrow \text{(14 / 3)}$$
$$\text{(rational-product 4 (2 / 3))} \Rightarrow \text{(8 / 3)}$$
$$\text{(rational-quotient 14 12)} \Rightarrow \text{(7 / 6)}$$

Note that the results of any evaluation should be a rational number in canonical form. That is, the denominator should be positive and the greatest common divisor of the numerator and denominator should be 1.

6.5. Write a function in Small Lisp to evaluate algebraic expressions over the domain of rational numbers, when those expressions are represented as lists according to the following grammar:

⟨expr⟩	::=	⟨rational⟩ | ⟨variable⟩ | ⟨sum⟩ | ⟨difference⟩ |
		⟨product⟩ | ⟨quotient⟩
⟨variable⟩	::=	⟨name:symbolic-atom⟩
⟨sum⟩	::=	(⟨op1:expr⟩ + ⟨op2:expr⟩)
⟨difference⟩	::=	(⟨op1:expr⟩ - ⟨op2:expr⟩)
⟨product⟩	::=	(⟨op1:expr⟩ * ⟨op2:expr⟩)
⟨quotient⟩	::=	(⟨op1:expr⟩ // ⟨op2:expr⟩)

6.6. Appendix B uses the special value ⊥ (called *bottom*) to indicate the value of an undefined or erroneous computation. Revise the S-Lisp interpreter presented in this chapter so that it calls the `error` function to report an appropriate error message in all the circumstances which result in a value of ⊥ according to Appendix B.

6.7. Modify the S-Lisp interpreter so that it never calls `error`, but instead returns an indication of an "undefined value," together with an appropriate error message, whenever an error occurs or the program being interpreted calls the `error` primitive.

6.8. Most programming languages, including Small Lisp, use *static binding* as the scoping mechanism for variables. Under static binding, the scope of a variable is a static property of the source program. For example, the scope of a parameter in a function definition is restricted to the expression which comprises the body of the function. *Dynamic binding* is an alternative scoping mechanism for variables used by many older dialects of Lisp. Under dynamic binding, the scope of a variable extends to all functions that are called (and all functions that they call, etc.) while the variable is active. For example, consider the following definitions in a variant of Small Lisp using dynamic binding:

```
base = 10

digits[num] =
  [lessp[num; base] --> list1[num];
   otherwise -->
     append1[digits[divide[num; base]]; rem[num; base]]]

binary-digits[num] =
  {base = 2 :
   digits[num]}

base-n-digits[num; base] = digits[num]
```

The `digits` function determines the digit-by-digit representation of a given nonnegative integer. By default, the digits are computed for a `base` 10 representation, for example:

$$\texttt{digits[255]} \;\Rightarrow\; (255)$$

However, using dynamic binding, the digits can be computed to an alternative base:

$$\texttt{binary-digits[255]} \;\Rightarrow\; (1\ 1\ 1\ 1\ 1\ 1\ 1\ 1)$$
$$\texttt{base-n-digits[255;\ 8]} \;\Rightarrow\; (3\ 7\ 7)$$

In the case of `binary-digits`, the scope of its locally defined variable `base` is extended to the definition of the `digits` function when it is called, setting up calculations in base 2. However, when `base-n-digits` is called with the value 8 for its formal parameter `base`, it is the scope of this parameter that is extended into the definition of the `digits` function, allowing base 8 calculations.

(a) Show how the S-Lisp interpreter can be simplified to support dynamic binding instead of static binding. Why do you think that older versions of Lisp used dynamic binding?

(b) Discuss the pros and cons of static and dynamic binding.

6.9. Show how the frame-processing extensions used in the S-Lisp interpreter can be avoided if the interpreter functions are each set up to use three environment parameters instead of two.

7

S-Lisp Programming

7.1 INTRODUCTION

In Chapter 4 (Section 4.5) the *S-Lisp* representation for Small Lisp programs as Lisp data objects was developed. Such a representation was a consequence of specifying the syntax of the language using a GRAIL grammar. In Chapter 6 we demonstrated how an interpreter could be constructed for evaluating Small Lisp programs when presented in the S-Lisp form. We refer to a compiler or interpreter that accepts program definitions written as S-Lisp expressions as an *S-Lisp system*. In this chapter we will examine some of the features of S-Lisp systems, and for the purposes of illustration we shall use a dialect called *Common LISP*. Common LISP is a language which attempts to capture the most useful syntactic features of the many dialects of list languages, collectively referred to as the "Lisp family." The Lisp family includes of course the S-Lisp representation of Small Lisp, which was developed previously. In particular, we will focus on some of those features that make such languages powerful tools for the implementation of symbolic computing applications. A few of these features have already been introduced in our definition and discussion of Small Lisp. They therefore possess an S-Lisp representation and consequently are provided by Common LISP.

There are many S-Lisp languages, and all possess a great deal of similarity with regard to syntax. Nevertheless, until the early 1980s, there was strong resistance to standardization attempts and thus there are different versions of Lisp available all over the world. This resistance, while it has curtailed somewhat the adoption of Lisp as a software development language, has permitted experimentation with features of the language and their implementation. This has resulted in the evolution of Lisp as a language which incorporates powerful, well-motivated language constructs in an efficient implementation.

Lisp programs are not always portable, although Common LISP is being widely adopted as the standard for commercial software development applications. Nevertheless, much of what is described in this chapter using Common LISP for illustration will be useful with, and applicable to, many other Lisp dialects. The exposition in this chapter is not intended to be a programming guide to Common LISP, as there are excellent references on the language.[1] Rather, Common LISP will most often be used to illustrate some of the important aspects of Lisp with respect to symbolic computing that one should expect to find in a commercial S-Lisp implementation.

The reader should therefore focus his or her attention on the implications with respect to symbolic computing of the concept illustrated by a particular S-Lisp example rather than the actual syntax of a form or function as expressed in Common LISP. The reader is encouraged to use either the programmer's manual which accompanies a specific software package or one of the many good Lisp programming guides available, such as Winston and Horn [WH89], for a thorough treatment of the language as well as many tips on programming style.

A common characteristic of virtually all Lisp implementations is that they accept programs in S-Lisp form. This makes it possible to treat Lisp programs as Lisp data objects and to define Lisp interpreters and other program-processing utilities as Lisp programs. In using a typical Lisp system, then, we will deal with Lisp programs only in S-Lisp form, ignoring for the most part the m-Lisp representation introduced in Small Lisp.

Much of what we learned about Small Lisp is applicable to all Lisp implementations. In fact, the S-Lisp representation of Small Lisp is almost immediately acceptable to most Lisp interpreters. Using the `slispify` utility of the Small Lisp system (see Appendix B), the job of translating Small Lisp programs into S-Lisp is generally quite straightforward.

When we simply start an interpreter in interactive mode, the interpreter expects input from a keyboard and sends output to a screen. Prompt characters are used to distinguish input lines from output lines. For the examples in this and succeeding chapters, the character ">" is used to distinguish input (user-entered character sequences) from output (interpreter-generated character sequences). Any line of a sample dialogue that does not begin with ">" is to be interpreted as output. We can enter simple Lisp expressions such as (`numberp 7`) as input and get values such as T as output. We can also enter sets of function definitions using a series of `defun` forms, following which we can enter and have evaluated other Lisp expressions using those functions.

Using the S-Lisp notation, most of the basic functions introduced in Small Lisp are available, as the following dialogue suggests.

---

[1] The definitive reference is generally considered to be Guy Steele's *COMMON LISP: The Language* [Ste90].

```
>(first (quote (A B C)))
   A
>(rest (quote (A B C)))
   (B C)
>(cons (quote (B)) (quote ()))
   ((B))
>(symbolp (quote B))
   T
>(eq (quote A) (quote B))
   NIL
>(numberp 7)
   T
>(- 7 4)
   3
>(/ 9 3)
   3
```

This example also highlights the two main differences between Common LISP and the S-Lisp form of Small Lisp. First of all, arithmetic operations in Common LISP use operator symbols as function names, e.g., "–" and "/" in place of minus and divide. Second, the atom NIL rather than F is used to represent the truth value "false."

However, another observation about this script is the proliferation of expressions of the form (quote S), which identify Lisp constants. Because of their frequency of occurrence, a simplified notation 'S is commonly used. Consider the following dialogue:

```
>(first '(A B C))
   A
>(rest '(A B C))
   (B C)
>(cons '(B) '())
   ((B))
>(symbolp 'B)
   T
>(eq 'A 'B)
   NIL
```

The expressions evaluated here are equivalent to those of the previous script. In fact, whenever an expression of the form 'S is read, it is converted internally into the list structure (quote S).

Function definitions in Common LISP also follow the S-Lisp syntax (using defun) introduced for Small Lisp in Section 4.5:

```
>(defun square (n)
>   (* n n))
   square
```

```
>(square 4)
16
```

A subtle difference is that Common LISP makes no distinction between definitions and expressions; a function definition is treated as an expression and may be entered for evaluation just as any other expression would be. As an expression, the value of a function definition is the name of the function being defined: for example, `square` in the preceding script. Of course, the primary role of `defun` is not the value it computes, but rather the effect that it has: it defines a function and associates it with a given name. In general, we will call an expression that is evaluated for its effects a *form*.[2]

Finally, the reader should review the GRAIL grammar presented in Section 4.5, which defines the S-Lisp representation for Small Lisp. Except for some differences in the choice of identifiers, this grammar defines the appropriate Common LISP representations for the corresponding Small Lisp program definitions and expressions. In particular, the S-Lisp representation of conditional expressions (`cond`) and let expressions (`let`) should be reviewed. The differences between the S-Lisp forms of Common LISP and Small Lisp and can be summarized as follows:

1. The symbolic atom F in Small Lisp is replaced by the symbolic atom NIL in Common LISP.[3]

2. The predefined constant `otherwise`, often used as the predicate of the final clause in a Small Lisp conditional expression, has no such significance in Common LISP. The user can define it as a global constant whose value is T, or simply use T as the predicate of the final clause of a Common LISP conditional expression whenever it is required.

3. The Small Lisp arithmetic functions, whose identifiers are `plus`, `minus`, `times`, and `divide`, are provided in Common LISP by functions whose identifiers are +, -, *, and /, respectively. However, Common LISP includes a numeric data type, *ratio*, which is the data type of the value returned by the division of two integers. Ratios are represented symbolically by a pair of integers separated by the symbol /. Thus in Small Lisp

$$\texttt{divide[32; 6]} \Rightarrow 5$$

while in Common LISP,

$$\texttt{(/ 32 6)} \Rightarrow \texttt{16/3}$$

---

[2] Any construct subject to evaluation, whether for its value or its effects, may be referred to as a "form." However, we will generally continue to use the term "expression" for forms which are evaluated for their value only.

[3] NIL is also used to represent the empty list in Common LISP, so that

$$
\begin{aligned}
\texttt{'()} &\Rightarrow \texttt{NIL} \\
\texttt{(symbolp '())} &\Rightarrow \texttt{T} \\
\texttt{(eq NIL '())} &\Rightarrow \texttt{T}
\end{aligned}
$$

Usually, the distinction between NIL as a truth value and NIL as a list value can be made depending on context. In programs, the preferred style is to use '() to denote the empty list and NIL to denote "false."

4. There are no system functions in Common LISP corresponding to the Small Lisp functions `sym-lessp`, `explode`, or `implode`. However, the effect of these functions is to provide a rudimentary form of string processing in Small Lisp; Common LISP provides a substantially richer set of string processing operations.

5. The keyword `setf` (assignment; see Section 7.5.1) replaces `setc`.

With these exceptions in mind the reader should already be able to read and write many Common LISP programs, as well as translate Small Lisp programs into equivalent Common LISP ones. Table 7.1 summarizes how the various primitive operations of Small Lisp translate into their Common LISP counterparts.

TABLE 7.1   COMMON LISP COUNTER-
PARTS FOR SMALL LISP
PRIMITIVES

	Small Lisp primitive	Common Lisp counterpart
Predefined constants	`T`	`T`
	`F`	`NIL`
	`otherwise`	`T`
Data type predicates	`symbolp`	`symbolp`
	`numberp`	`numberp`
	`listp`	`listp`
List processing	`cons`	`cons`
	`first`	`first`
	`rest`	`rest`
	`endp`	`endp`
Symbol processing	`eq`	`eq`
	`sym-lessp`	none
	`explode`	none
	`implode`	none
Numeric functions	`eqp`	`=`
	`greaterp`	`>`
	`lessp`	`<`
	`plus`	`+`
	`minus`	`−`
	`times`	`*`
	`divide`	`/`
	`rem`	`rem`
Special forms	`quote`	`quote`
	`cond`	`cond`
	`let`	`let`
	`defun`	`defun`
	`setc`	`setf`

7.2 POLYADIC FUNCTIONS

One useful feature of most Lisps is that they provide a variety of functions which take arbitrarily many arguments. Such functions are called *polyadic* functions. As an example, a particularly useful polyadic system function is the function `list`. This function generalizes the `list2` and `list3` functions that were required in earlier Small Lisp implementations, such as `deriv`, by permitting us to construct lists from an arbitrary number of components. As an example, we can construct a list of four components as follows:

```
>(list 'A '(B C) 'D 'E)
 (A (B C) D E)
```

Similarly, the `append` function allows an arbitrary number of lists to be appended together.

```
>(append '(A B) '(C) '() '((D) E))
 (A B C (D) E)
```

The ability to take arbitrarily many arguments is also useful in the numeric functions.

```
>(+ 1 2 3 4 5)
    15
>(* 1 2 3 4)
    24
>(max 7 11 4 8)
    11
>(min 0 8 -2 13)
    -2
```

The `greaterp` and `lessp` functions were defined as binary predicates in Small Lisp. In Common LISP the corresponding functions are ">" and "<". Implemented as polyadic functions, they check whether an arbitrary number of numeric arguments are in, respectively, strictly decreasing or strictly increasing order.

```
>(> 11 10 9 8 7)
    T
>(< 1 1 2 3)
    NIL
```

Common LISP also defines polyadic versions of the logical functions and and or.

```
>(and (eq 'A (first '(A B)))
>      (numberp 3)
>      T
>      (endp (rest '(A))))
       T
```

```
>(or NIL NIL NIL)
 NIL
```

It should be noted that the and and or functions use the McCarthy evaluation scheme; that is, they evaluate arguments in left-to-right order and will not necessarily evaluate all arguments. In the evaluation of an and form, evaluation of the arguments will terminate as soon as one of them evaluates to NIL, and NIL will be returned in that case. Similarly, if an argument to or evaluates to T, the evaluation of the or is terminated immediately with T as the result.[4]

User-defined polyadic functions are achieved in Common LISP by extending the syntax of defun to permit the binding of an indefinite number of arguments to additional locally defined "formal parameters." These identifiers are recognized by the Lisp processor through the use of system-defined keywords. The identifiers of such keywords all begin with "&" and should not be confused with user-defined keywords (these begin with ":"), which will be mentioned later in Section 7.9.

Strictly speaking, polyadic functions are those which have an indefinite number of arguments, with no predefined maximum. However, when the maximum number of arguments that may be supplied by a function call is known, the keyword &optional can be used to specify the additional formal parameters required. For example, suppose that the system function append was not polyadic, but rather binary, that is, a function of two arguments. Then one could generalize the append function to permit it to append two, three, or possibly four lists. A definition for this "new" append could be as follows:

```
(defun append-upto-4 (L1 L2 &optional L3 L4)
  (append L1 (append L2 (append L3 L4))))
```

This definition requires that at least two arguments be supplied when append-upto-4 is called. These are bound to L1 and L2. Up to two additional arguments can be provided in the function call, with the third (if supplied) being bound to L3 and the fourth to L4. The following sample dialogue illustrates the application of this append function:

```
>(append-upto-4 '(A B) '(C D))
  (A B C D)
>
>(append-upto-4 '(A B) '(C D) '(E F))
  (A B C D E F)
```

An important question when using optional parameters is what value is bound to them when an argument is not provided. In Common LISP this value is NIL, a fact that was exploited in our definition of append-upto-4. Suppose, however, that our arguments are numeric rather than lists. In this case it is necessary that "unused" formal

[4]In general, when a truth value is required in Common LISP, it interprets any non-NIL object as "true." Thus an or form will return the value of its first argument that is non-NIL. Similarly, evaluation of an and form continues as long as the arguments evaluate to non-NIL values; if none of them evaluates to NIL, the value of the last argument is returned.

parameters be bound to some default numeric value. The syntax of a function definition using `defun` permits default values to be associated with optional parameters. This is achieved by providing a list pair in place of each optional parameter following the `&optional` keyword. Each pair specifies the identifier of an optional formal parameter and its default value whenever it is not bound to an argument. Thus a function to sum the squares of up to four values can be defined as follows:

```
(defun sumsq4 (x1 &optional (x2 0) (x3 0) (x4 0))
  (+ (* x1 x1) (* x2 x2) (* x3 x3) (* x4 x4)))
```

Note that this implementation uses the fact that "+" is a polyadic function in Common LISP. A sample dialogue is given by

```
>(sumsq4 2 3)
    13

>(sumsq4 1 2 3 4)
    30
```

This latest example illustrates a case where a more "realistic" implementation would not constrain the number of arguments which could be supplied to the function for evaluation.[5] This is the essence of a true polyadic function. To accommodate a function definition where an indefinite number of arguments can be supplied, Common LISP provides the `&rest` keyword. Simply put, `&rest` permits the introduction of *one* additional parameter to the formal parameter specification which will be bound to a list of *all* argument values not yet bound to previous formal parameters, including optional ones.

To illustrate the application of the `&rest` keyword, the calculation of sum of squares given in the previous example can be generalized to accept an indefinite number of arguments as follows:

```
(defun sumsq (x &rest y)
  (cond ((endp y) (* x x))
        (T (+ (* x x) (eval (make-fn-call 'sumsq y))))))
```

The strategy employed is to add the square of the first argument to the result of applying the `sumsq` to the remaining arguments. Since the remaining arguments are in a list bound to the formal parameter Y, we can construct a function call to apply `sumsq` to the remaining values, using the constructor function `make-fn-call`, defined in Section 4.5. The purpose of the `eval` function introduced here is to evaluate the resulting form; `eval` is actually the Common LISP function for evaluating expressions, analogous to the Small Lisp function `sl-eval` defined in Section 6.3.1. The `eval` function will be discussed in more detail in the next section.

Formally, the syntax of `defun` can be extended to include the `&optional` and `&rest` keywords as shown in the following EBNF grammar:

---

[5]The `&optional` keyword is not generally used in this context, occurring more commonly in the definition of functions with optional parameters that require initialization.

⟨function-definition⟩ ::= (defun ⟨function-name⟩ ⟨parameter-list⟩
                                    ⟨function-body⟩)
      ⟨parameter-list⟩ ::= ({ ⟨variable⟩ }
                                    [&optional { ⟨optional-vars⟩ }]
                                    [&rest ⟨variable⟩])
       ⟨optional-vars⟩ ::= { ⟨variable⟩ } | { ⟨default-pair⟩ }
         ⟨default-pair⟩ ::= (⟨variable⟩ ⟨value⟩)
            ⟨variable⟩ ::= ⟨symbolic-atom⟩
               ⟨value⟩ ::= ⟨numeric-atom⟩ | ⟨symbolic-constant⟩
       ⟨function-body⟩ ::= ⟨expression⟩ { ⟨expression⟩ }

Note that this definition permits the use of both &optional and &rest parameters; however, in practice it is more often the case that one or the other is used and depends on whether we wish to define a polyadic function with a maximum number or an undefined number of arguments. This definition also extends the ⟨function-body⟩ syntax to allow more than one ⟨expression⟩; this extension is discussed in Section 7.5.2.

7.3 THE READ-EVAL-PRINT LOOP

Efficient execution of programs is achieved through the application of a compiler to obtain machine-level code in the native language of the processor on which the implementation is being run. Nevertheless, Lisp programs are frequently developed initially using an interpreter because of the interactive opportunities available during source code development and testing. The fact that early Lisp programs could only be executed with interpreters has contributed in part to the misconception that Lisp is not an efficient language in which to program.

The heart of any Lisp interpreter is the process of reading a Lisp expression, evaluating it and then printing the result. This is known as the *read-eval-print* loop. The three parts of this loop are also available as individual Lisp functions read, eval, and print. The read function simply gets the next S-expression from the input stream and returns it. Consider the following example.

```
>(+ (read) 6)
>4
       10
```

The read function is niladic (no formal parameters), so a call to it is denoted (read). Evaluation of such a call requests terminal input as indicated with the > prompt character. After the user enters the numeric atom 4, the evaluation of the + form is completed and the result is printed.

The eval function is the main function used by the interpreter for evaluating Lisp expressions and performs the same task as sl-eval did in Section 6.3. For example, the value of (eval '(cons 'A '(B))) is (A B). Note that '(cons 'A '(B)) represents a symbolic expression constant and does not itself evaluate to (A B). The m-Lisp representation of the form above perhaps makes this more clear:

```
(eval '(cons 'A '(B))) ⟹ eval[(cons (quote A) (quote (B)))]
```

The effect of `eval` then is to take such a symbolic expression constant and interpret it as a Lisp form, that is, evaluate it.

The third function applied in the read-eval-print loop is `print`, whose purpose is to output S-expressions, as the following example illustrates:

```
>(print '(A B C))
    (A B C)
    (A B C)
```

Two copies of the argument to `print` are produced when the `print` form is evaluated! The first copy represents the consequence of executing the `print` function, while the second copy represents the value returned by `print`. The `print` function is an example of a function that produces a *side effect* in addition to returning a value.

A *side effect* is the term generally used to refer to any effect that a subprogram has other than returning a value, that is, any modification of the computer's internal state or external files associated with the program. In fact, `print` is used principally for its side effect; the value returned by `print` is incidental to its main purpose.

Taken all together, one cycle of the read-eval-print loop can be defined by the expression (`print (eval (read))`). An S-expression input by `read` is passed to `eval`, which interprets it as an S-Lisp form. Next, `eval` evaluates the form and returns that result to `print`, which displays it. However, `print` also returns that result as its value. For example, consider the value returned by the expression (`print (eval (read))`) when given to the Lisp interpreter. The interpreter itself is conceptually the same expression, so in effect we want to determine the value of (`print (eval '(print (eval (read))))`). The value of the expression input by `read` is output by the "inner" `print` as a side effect during evaluation of (`print (eval (read))`) by the interpreter. Since this value is the argument of `print`, it is also the value returned to the output step of the interpreter. As a consequence, the effect of entering (`print (eval (read))`) is that the value of the next expression to be entered will be printed twice.

7.4 IMPERATIVE FEATURES OF LISP

A central difference between large S-Lisp systems (such as Common LISP) and Small Lisp is the introduction of functions which have side effects. Small Lisp is a *purely functional* language in which the only semantics that an expression has is the value it denotes, that is, the value returned when the expression is evaluated. Thus there is no possibility of a side effect within a Small Lisp function. In Common LISP, on the other hand, evaluation of expressions may also affect the Lisp global state or cause input/output operations to be performed. Thus functions may have side effects, and this allows Common LISP to support an *imperative* style of programming, as well as the functional style of Small Lisp.

In general, the facilities of S-Lisp systems that support programming with side effects are called *imperative features*. The nomenclature reflects the fact that a call to a function with side effects may be intended more as a command to perform actions rather than as an expression to calculate a value. We have already seen one example of this with `print`. We can paraphrase the expression (`print (eval (read))`) as the command: "*Do* print *the result of* eval*uating the input* read."

A second example is the `defun` facility for function definitions. As a command, it instructs the interpreter to associate a function with a given name. This is its primary role. However, in Common LISP, a call to `defun` is also an expression whose value is the name of the defined function. From this viewpoint, the fact that it defines a function is a side effect of its evaluation.

Although the imperative features of Common LISP, such as `print` and `defun`, have a dual interpretation as both commands and functions, we will generally refer to them only as commands. When using such facilities, it is usually good practice to treat them as pure commands, ignoring any value they return. Conversely, we will reserve the term "function" to describe those facilities which are primarily intended to return results. Indeed, our preference is to avoid side effects in functions, so that they may be interpreted as pure functions in the mathematical sense.

In the following sections, we will examine further imperative features in Common LISP, in particular, features for changing global variables and for modifying data structures. When necessary such facilities can be useful for improving the efficiency of Common LISP programs: for example, by modifying and reusing existing data structures rather than constructing new ones from scratch. Our primary goals will be to show that an imperative programming style is possible and to explain how these facilities work.

The ideal programming style with Lisp is to program without the use of side effects. While side effects make it possible to program some activities conveniently, implementations which employ them extensively are difficult to maintain. Generally, expressions without side effects are more readable than their counterparts which produce side effects, and are said to be *referentially transparent*. Note that useful programs such as our symbolic differentiator can be completely written without the use of side effects. Thus we generally recommend that a purely functional style be used for initial program development. If the functional program proves to be too inefficient, imperative techniques may then be used to improve performance.

7.5 VARIABLE ASSIGNMENT AND SEQUENCING

This section is devoted to a brief examination of a few of the more commonly used commands provided by Common LISP in addition to `print` and `defun` which have already been discussed. In particular, the commands described here are provided to meet the needs of two activities that are common to every program in a procedural language, such as Pascal. These activities are *assignment*, whereby values are bound to identifiers, and *sequencing*, whereby a sequence of commands can be ordered and executed for its effect. Commands similar to the ones described here exist in other dialects of Lisp.

7.5.1 Global Assignment: `setf`

The `setf` form is the basic Common LISP command for globally assigning a value to a variable. In its simplest form, its syntax is similar to the S-Lisp representation of

Small Lisp constant definitions described in Figure 4.4, except that the setf keyword
is used in place of setc:

$$(\text{setf} \ \langle \text{variable} \rangle \ \langle \text{expression} \rangle)$$

For example:

```
>(setf X '(A B))
    (A B)
>(setf Y 'C)
    C
>(cons Y X)
    (C A B)
```

In its more general application, the ⟨variable⟩ within a setf form may denote a component of a data structure using an *access expression*. Examples of setf in this role
are considered in Section 7.8.

The setf operation may modify the Lisp global state, to be described presently,
and should thus be used cautiously. It should be used principally for initializing values
in interactive programming experiments, for assigning values to global flags and parameters, and for updating particular constructs found in Lisp systems, such as *property
lists* and *structures*. It generally should not be used for temporary assignments within
functions. The side-effect-free way to perform such assignments is to use a let expression, based on the corresponding Small Lisp construct and described further in
Section 7.5.3.

7.5.2 Sequential Execution: progn

Programmers who have practiced their craft exclusively with procedural languages
(such as Pascal) frequently find it difficult initially to program in a purely functional
language (such as Small Lisp) because of the lack of any syntax which provides a way
to specify a sequence of instructions. However, the basic element to be "executed" in
a Lisp program is an expression, and therefore a sequence of instructions really only
corresponds to a sequence of expressions. Such sequences occur only when expressions are being evaluated for their side effects. To illustrate how such a sequence can
be evaluated in a purely functional language, we define the following Small Lisp version of progn, which takes a sequence of expressions, evaluates each, and returns the
value obtained from evaluating the final expression:

```
progn[exprlist; fenv; cenv] =
  {result = sl-eval[first[exprlist]; fenv; cenv] :
   [endp[rest[expr-list]] --> result;
    otherwise --> progn[rest[exprlist]; fenv; cenv]}
```

In this example, unless we are at the end of the list, the result of evaluating an expression is simply discarded. Only the result obtained from evaluating the last expression
is kept and returned as the value of the progn call. The other expressions are only
being evaluated for their side effects. Of course, Small Lisp functions do not have
side effects, so this version of progn is not very useful.

Since Common LISP permits the definition and evaluation of functions for their side effects, it provides language primitives for evaluating sequences of expressions. Among these primitives is the command `progn`, whose behavior is analogous to that illustrated by the example above.[6]

In Common LISP the syntax of a `progn` form is as follows:

$$\langle \text{progn-expression} \rangle \ ::= \ (\ \text{progn} \ \{ \ \langle \text{expression} \rangle \ \} \ )$$

Each expression is evaluated in sequence as a command. Then the last expression is evaluated and its value returned as the value of the entire `progn` form. The following sample dialogue illustrates the effect of evaluating `progn`:

```
>(progn (print 1) (print 2) (print 3))
1
2
3
3
```

As each `print` form in the `progn` expression is evaluated, the side effect occurs of displaying the argument of that `print` form. The second occurrence of the value 3 is a consequence of the value of the final `print` form being returned as the value of the `progn`.

A similar concept is used to extend the `cond` and `defun` syntax with what is known as an *implicit progn* feature. In the case of `cond`, each individual clause may have more than one result expression; if the corresponding predicate evaluates to true, all the result expressions are evaluated with the value of the last such expression being returned as the value of the `cond` form. Similarly, in the case of `defun`, the expression comprising the body of the function is replaced by arbitrarily many expressions, as shown in the grammar at the end of Section 7.2.

Use of the implicit progn feature can be illustrated by the following example to solve the well-known (and often cited) Towers of Hanoi puzzle.[7] For N disks, the Towers of Hanoi problem is solved recursively by moving $N - 1$ disks from the start pole to the intermediate pole, moving the Nth disk (the biggest one) from the start pole to the final pole and then moving the other $N - 1$ disks to the final pole. This solution and its application to a stack of two disks is illustrated in the following interactive session:

```
>(defun Hanoi (N pole1 pole2 pole3)
>   (cond ((= N 0) 'Done)
>         (T (Hanoi (- N 1) pole1 pole3 pole2)
>            (print (list 'Move 'top 'disk 'from pole1 'to pole3))
>            (Hanoi (- N 1) pole2 pole1 pole3)))))
```

---

[6]Common LISP provides a number of other primitives for evaluating such sequences; however, only `progn` will be used here. The interested reader should consult [WH89] or [Ste90] for further details.

[7]For those not acquainted with this puzzle, briefly there are three poles and a number of different-sized disks which fit over the poles. Initially, the disks are all on one pole, stacked in order of size with the largest at the bottom. The goal is to move all the disks to another pole (say the third pole), by moving one disk at a time between poles and never placing a larger disk on top of a smaller one.

```
>(Hanoi 2 'P1 'P2 'P3)
    (Move top disk from P1 to P2)
    (Move top disk from P1 to P3)
    (Move top disk from P2 to P3)
    Done
```

The second clause of the conditional expression used the implicit progn feature. In this clause, all three result expressions are primarily being executed for their "side effect," that is, for the messages they print.[8] The results returned as a consequence of evaluating the first two result expressions are ignored, but the result of the third one eventually becomes the value returned by Hanoi. In this example, therefore, the value of Hanoi is always the atom Done.

7.5.3 Local Assignment: let

In Chapter 2, the need for a means of defining local variables resulted in the formulation of a ⟨let-expression⟩. In Common LISP the let form provides the same capability, and for the declaration of local variables within a function body, it is preferred over the setf form wherever possible. The let form "simultaneously" assigns a given set of values to a given set of variables for use in a given set of Lisp expressions. As with the Small Lisp ⟨let-expression⟩, after evaluation of a let form, the variables are reset to the values they had before the evaluation took place. For example, consider the following Small Lisp function definition which employs a ⟨let-expression⟩ in its function body[9]:

```
unit-vector[x; y; z] =
    {d = sqrt[plus[times[x; x]; plus[times[y; y]; times[z; z]]]] :
     list3[divide[x; d]; divide[y; d]; divide[z; d]]}
```

In Common LISP an equivalent function definition can be provided using a let form in place of the ⟨let-expression⟩[10]:

```
(defun unit-vector (x y z)
    (let ((d (sqrt (+ (* x x) (* y y) (* z z)))))
        (list (/ x d) (/ y d) (/ z d))))
```

Any global value of the variable d is unaffected by an application of the unit-vector function. In the nomenclature of functional programming, the let form is sometimes known as an *auxiliary expression*.

In Common LISP the syntax of a let form is as follows:

---

[8]Common LISP provides a format form to provide a more elegant way of generating output messages. Since it is implementation dependent, it will not be discussed here. As always, readers should consult their Lisp reference manual.

[9]For the purposes of illustration we shall assume the existence of a sqrt function and ignore the fact that divide performs integer division.

[10]Note the simplification resulting from the use of the polyadic functions "+" and list.

$$\langle\text{let-expression}\rangle ::= (\ \texttt{let}\ \langle\text{let-list}\rangle\ \langle\text{expression}\rangle\ \{\ \langle\text{expression}\rangle\ \}\ )$$
$$\langle\text{let-list}\rangle ::= (\ \{\ \langle\text{local-definition}\rangle\ \}\ )$$
$$\langle\text{local-definition}\rangle ::= (\ \langle\text{variable}\rangle\ \langle\text{expression}\rangle\ )$$

This syntax extends the S-Lisp form of the Small Lisp ⟨let-expression⟩, incorporating the implicit progn feature. Thus one or more expressions may be included in the body of the let form to be evaluated in the context of the local definitions. The value of the last of these expressions is returned as the value of the entire let form.

An important question about let forms is how do dependencies among the let variables get evaluated. In Common LISP, all ⟨local-definition⟩s are evaluated independently from the others. Thus an earlier binding does not influence a later one in the ⟨let-list⟩. For example, observe the value bound to Y in the following:

```
>(setf X 1)
    1
>(let ((X 2) (Y X)) (+ X Y))
    3
```

The value of X assigned to Y in the second ⟨local-definition⟩ of the let expression is 1, which was originally assigned to X when the setf form was evaluated. Common LISP also provides another "let" command, called let*, where the ⟨local-definition⟩s evaluated left to right in the ⟨let-list⟩, and where earlier bindings can affect later ones. Compare the output in the following example with the result of the previous one:

```
>(setf X 1)
    1
>(let* ((X 2) (Y X)) (+ X Y))
    4
```

7.6 THE LISP GLOBAL STATE

Central to understanding many of the features of Lisp languages is a knowledge of the Lisp global state, that is, an understanding of how S-expressions are stored in memory. The global state essentially provides a context in which the evaluation of expressions is carried out. Since evaluation of certain Lisp forms can result in changes to the global state, this state can serve as a vehicle for both intended and unintended interactions between programs.

Since the representation is implementation dependent, even among different versions of Common LISP, it is necessary to use a model for that representation that hides the actual implementation details. In almost all Lisp systems, the primary building block of the global state is a simple memory structure called a *CONS cell*, so named because the cons function is implemented to construct such structures. In our model the basic CONS cell consists of sufficient memory to hold two addresses which point to other memory structures, and is typically represented graphically by a box partitioned into two regions, as shown in Figure 7.1. The CONS cell actually corresponds to a now little used Lisp data type called a *dotted pair*. While dotted pairs are no longer commonly used in Lisp application programs, the data type is still available in most Lisp languages, and is useful in describing the structures represented by CONS cell diagrams. A dotted pair has the following syntax:

$$\langle\text{dotted-pair}\rangle ::= (\langle\text{S-expression}\rangle . \langle\text{S-expression}\rangle)$$

Examples of dotted pairs which are valid Lisp S-expressions are (A . B) and (A . (B . C)). The first component of a dotted pair corresponds to the "left" region of a CONS cell, and consequently the second component corresponds to the "right" region. A dotted pair is thus a symbolic representation of a CONS cell.

Figure 7.1   Basic CONS cell.

Unfortunately, dotted pairs look like lists whose second element is the symbol ".". This can be confusing because dotted pairs are not lists but are a separate data type of their own.

Since dotted pairs are valid S-expressions in most Lisp dialects, the definition of S-expressions given in Chapter 2 should be extended to include dotted pairs:

$$\langle\text{S-expression}\rangle ::= \langle\text{atom}\rangle \mid \langle\text{list}\rangle \mid \langle\text{dotted-pair}\rangle$$

For example, the dotted pair (A . (B . C)) is represented by a CONS cell which contains pointers to the machine representation of the atom A and to the CONS cell for (B . C). This is illustrated in Figure 7.2. It is important to emphasize the fact that the pointers to A, B, and C are pointing to data structures representing these atoms and are not pointing to the characters themselves. As we shall see shortly, machine representation of the atoms can also be described with CONS cells.

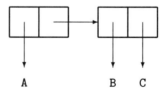

A   B   C

Figure 7.2   Representation of (A . (B . C)).

There are three data access functions for processing dotted pairs. We can give a pseudo-GRAIL definition to specify these functions:

$$\langle\text{dotted-pair}\rangle ::= (\langle\text{car:S-expression}\rangle . \langle\text{cdr:S-expression}\rangle)$$

This definition is not "true" GRAIL because the type being defined is not represented as a Lisp list and GRAIL grammars specifically define list structures. It is perhaps better thought of as a BNF definition in which the R.H.S. nonterminals are augmented with component names. Using a GRAIL-like interpretation of the rule, the car and cdr functions are used to select, respectively, the first and second S-expressions of a dotted pair, as illustrated by the following examples:

$$(\text{car } '(A . (B . C))) \Rightarrow A$$
$$(\text{cdr } '(A . (B . C))) \Rightarrow (B . C)$$

Some of the very first Lisp implementations were developed on the IBM 700 series of processors around 1959 to 1961. These processors included in their hardware architecture an address register and a decrement register which were used to hold the CONS cell pointers. The names CAR and CDR arise from that early Lisp implementation and stand for "Contents of Address Register" and "Contents of Decrement Register," respectively. The functions car and cdr are still found in the function libraries of virtually all Lisp dialects, and because lists are usually implemented using dotted pairs, it is common to see these functions used interchangeably with the list selector functions first and rest, respectively. Contemporary software engineering practice discourages this practice in favor of using the data access functions associated specifically with the data type for which they were implemented.[11]

Following the commonly accepted convention, the constructor function for dotted pairs today would be named make-dotted-pair. However, again for historical reasons, tradition has dictated the name cons instead. The constructor cons constructs a new dotted pair given its two ⟨S-expression⟩ components. For example,

$$(\text{cons } 'A (\text{cons } 'B 'C)) \Rightarrow (A . (B . C))$$

The constructor function provided by Common LISP for both dotted pairs and lists is the same, namely cons, and this is the case for virtually all other Lisp dialects.

As mentioned previously, in S-Lisp systems, lists themselves are not primitives but are implemented in terms of atoms and dotted pairs. By convention, the atom NIL is used to represent the empty list.[12] Nonempty lists are represented as dotted pairs whose CAR field represents the first element of the list and whose CDR field represents the rest of the list. Thus, a list is either NIL or a dotted pair whose CDR is always a list. In particular, a list of one element, say A, is represented by the dotted pair (A . NIL). This is completely equivalent to (A) and both representations are accepted by most Lisp interpreters, although evaluation of the form (print '(A . NIL)) would result in the output being displayed as (A).

As a second example, the list (A (B C) D) has the CONS cell structure given in Figure 7.3. A common practice is to draw a diagonal across a cell field to designate a pointer to the atom NIL; this helps simplify diagrams for lists.

As a final example, we consider the distinction between (A B) and (A . B), a common source of confusion for beginning S-Lisp programmers. A CONS cell diagram of each data object helps to clarify the distinction. The list (A B) is represented

---

[11]This redundancy permits older Lisp programs to be interpreted by contemporary Lisp systems. For our Common LISP illustrations in this text we will refrain from using the selector functions car and cdr on lists.

[12]The atom NIL thus plays a double role, representing both the empty list () and the truth value F. Resolution of this ambiguity generally depends on the context in which NIL occurs. It should also be noted that (symbolp '()) ⇒ T; that is, the empty list is an atom, because '() is synonymous with NIL.

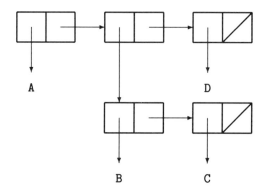

Figure 7.3   Representation of (A (B C) D).

by the CONS cell diagram on the left in Figure 7.4, and the dotted pair (A . B) is represented by the CONS cell diagram on the right. Thus four pointers are required to represent the list (A B), but only two pointers are required to represent the dotted pair (A . B).

Figure 7.4   Representation of lists and dotted pairs.

This last example illustrates the central role of pointers in representing the Lisp global state. In fact, all Lisp objects (atoms and dotted pairs) can be represented by pointers. Thus atoms as well as dotted pairs or lists can be explicitly represented in CONS cell diagrams. The machine representation of atoms is generally more complicated than that of dotted pairs, and consists not only of a CONS cell, but additional structure as well, which provides the representation of an atom with a means of storing its label and indicating its type.

Two ways to distinguish among atom types are by providing additional bytes of memory or by encoding the type as part of the pointer value. With the latter approach, the various types of atom can be distinguished from one another and from dotted pairs by including type information in the most significant bits of the pair of addresses which define the CAR and CDR pointers of a CONS cell. The actual memory organization and method employed is implementation dependent.

A symbolic atom is represented as a structure consisting of a CONS cell plus a variable-length *PNAME* field. The PNAME field identifies the *print name* of the atom, that is, the sequence of characters by which we refer to it. As a consequence, CONS cell diagrams are used to represent the structure of atoms; for example, the atom LONGATOM has the structure given in Figure 7.5. The code "1" is used here to indicate type information for distinguishing a symbolic atom from the other types of atom. The PNAME of the atom is conventionally placed to the right of the CONS cell for the atom. Common LISP provides the function `symbol-name`, which returns the PNAME of a symbolic atom, expressed as a string.

Figure 7.5   CONS cell for an atom.

In the case of symbolic atoms, the fact that their representation includes a CONS cell is very important, for it means that atoms have CAR and CDR fields as well as PNAMEs. In most S-Lisps, the convention is that atoms (representing variables) are given values by placing pointers to those values in their CAR fields. For example, the evaluation of

(setf A 3)

can be viewed conceptually as setting up the structure in Figure 7.6 for the atom A. Note that `setf` does not affect the second field of the CONS cell of an atom. Theoretically, the `car` function could be used to determine the value of a symbolic atom. In some Lisp implementations this is in fact the case, and the following interactive sequence could be observed:

>(car 'A)
3

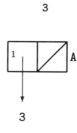

Figure 7.6   CONS cell for atom A with value 3.

However, implementations of Common LISP generally perform type checking on the argument of `car` to ensure that it is a list (or more properly, a dotted pair). In such cases, an error message is generated when the S-expression in the example above is entered.

A similar convention is defined for the CDR field of a symbolic atom. Such an atom can be given other properties (besides a value) by placing a pointer to what is known as the *property list* of an atom in its CDR field. While in some Lisp dialects it is possible to use the `cdr` operation to access the property list of atoms, this is more often provided using the function `get`, to be described shortly.[13]

---

[13]Common LISP actually provides a function `symbol-plist` which returns the entire property list of a symbolic atom. However, `get` is more commonly used since applications generally require access only to specific components on the property list.

While a number of possibilities exist, in our model of memory, numeric atoms will be represented by structures having a CONS cell plus fields for the integer and real representations of the corresponding number. As with symbolic atoms, the CAR field of a numeric atom points to the value of the atom, which is represented symbolically in a CONS cell diagram by its PNAME; that is, the cell points to itself. For example, the numeric atom for 3 is represented as in Figure 7.7. The code "2" denotes here the bit pattern which codes for a numeric atom. The CDR field of numeric atoms is not used. In the case of numeric atoms, the car operation is valid, returning the value of the numeric atom (itself), but the CDR of a numeric atom in most S-Lisps is not valid.

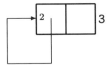

Figure 7.7   CONS cell for the atom 3.

The special symbolic atoms T and NIL, which are reserved to denote the truth value constants, also have CAR and CDR fields. The CAR of each of these atoms points to itself (i.e., (car 'T) ⇒ T and (car 'NIL) ⇒ NIL). We thus say that the value of T is T (denoting "true") and the value of NIL is NIL (denoting "false" or the empty list as appropriate). The structures for T and NIL are represented by CONS cell diagrams in Figure 7.8. By changing the CAR fields, the values of T and NIL can actually be changed in some Lisp dialects, but to do so would hardly be productive and is not permitted in Common LISP.

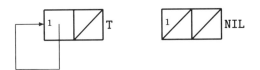

Figure 7.8   CONS cells for T and NIL.

A special atom, which we will represent by *UNDEF*, usually denotes an undefined value in many S-Lisp implementations. When a symbolic atom is first read in, its memory structure is created, a pointer to *UNDEF* is placed in its CAR field and a pointer to NIL is placed in its CDR field. Thus, by default, an atom initially has an undefined value and an empty property list, and can be represented by the CONS cell diagram given in Figure 7.9.

7.7 DESTRUCTIVE MODIFICATION OF LISTS

The basic functions of Lisp do not require a detailed understanding of the structural organization of memory since they do not change the values of pointers. However, some Lisp operations actually modify the pointers of existing CONS cell structures,

UNDEF

Figure 7.9   CONS cell for an atom with undefined value.

and it is in the analysis of these functions that CONS cell diagrams are particularly useful. These operations provide a completeness with respect to CONS cell manipulation that is needed in some applications. Such functions are frequently used to improve the efficiency of Lisp programs by avoiding the creation of unnecessary new structures and instead, modifying existing structures. In such a context, it is convenient to define a fourth class of data access function in addition to constructors, selectors, and recognizers: namely, the *updater*.

An examination of our previous examples reveals the fact that new instances of an abstract data type have always been obtained by constructing them from selected components rather than by replacing components in existing structures. While not essential to the development of most implementations, the ability to update an existing structure provides the opportunity to address problems in a different way, possibly with the added benefit of improved performance or space management.

Modifying existing structures, however, provides the opportunity for unintentionally creating interactions between programs. It is thus bad programming practice to use these operations before the need for improved efficiency has been established. Nevertheless, it is worthwhile to understand their function in order to have a more complete picture of Lisp programming.

The two basic primitives for modifying CONS cells are the `rplaca` and `rplacd` forms. These forms are essentially commands for replacing the CAR and CDR fields, respectively, of any Lisp CONS cell. They thus allow arbitrary changes to be made to the structure of any list or dotted pair.[14] Both `rplaca` and `rplacd` return the newly modified structure as a result of their evaluation. As examples, the lists specified by the first argument in each of the following forms to be evaluated would be modified to correspond to the resulting lists indicated:

$$(\text{rplaca } '((A\ B)\ C\ D)\ '\text{NEW}) \Rightarrow (\text{NEW C D})$$

$$(\text{rplacd } '((A\ B)\ C\ D)\ '(\text{NEW})) \Rightarrow ((A\ B)\ \text{NEW})$$

The `rplaca` and `rplacd` primitives thus allow you to make any arbitrary mutation of S-expression structure. They are often called *destructive* list processing operations because they destroy existing S-expressions in the creation of new ones.

The efficiency of such destructive list processing operations can be seen by considering a function which appends two lists. This function was defined in Chapter 3 (in Small Lisp) and can be written as an S-lisp expression as follows:

---

[14]In some implementations they can also be used to modify the value and property list fields of atoms.

```
(defun append (L1 L2)
  (cond ((endp L1) L2)
        (T (cons (first L1) (append (rest L1) L2)))))
```

Each time the cons operation is used a new CONS cell is created because cons constructs dotted pairs. This function will thus traverse the list L1, creating a new CONS cell for every element. The net effect is to make a copy of L1 with the list L2 attached at the end.[15]

Alternatively, two lists can be appended destructively, as follows:

```
(defun nconc (L1 L2)
  (cond ((eq L1 'NIL) L2)
        ((eq (cdr L1) 'NIL) (rplacd L1 L2))
        (T (nconc (cdr L1) L2) L1)))
```

To emphasize that the pointers of a CONS cell memory structure are being examined and modified, this function is implemented in terms of the representation of lists with dotted pairs, and therefore cdr is used instead of rest. It works by replacing the pointer to NIL in the CDR field of the final CONS cell of L1 with a pointer to the list L2. The modified list L1 is returned as a result. The nconc operation is thus much more efficient than append since it does not create any new CONS cells.[16]

The danger of using destructive operations can be illustrated with the following examples. We start out by defining two lists as follows:

```
(setf L1 '(A B C))
(setf L2 '(D E))
```

Now suppose that we wish to give L1 the value (A B C D E). In this case, nconc can safely be used because we are no longer concerned with the old value of L1:

```
(nconc L1 L2)
```

The resulting structure can be represented by the CONS cell diagram of Figure 7.10. As is evident in the diagram, we now have L1 = (A B C D E) and L2 = (D E). Next we append the list (F G) to the list L1, again using nconc.

```
(nconc L1 '(F G)) ⇒ (A B C D E F G)
```

The resulting structure in memory is now organized as shown in Figure 7.11.

As expected, the value of L1 is now (A B C D E F G). What may be unexpected, however, is that L2's value is now (D E F G). What happened was that the change to L1 also affected L2 since L1 and L2 possessed a *shared structure*. Specifically, in modifying the last CONS cell in the list L1 we also modified the last CONS cell in the list L2. In general, the construction and manipulation of S-expressions can result in a significant amount of shared structure, so that the use of destructive operations can

---

[15]Most S-Lisp implementations provide a version of append that actually copies both lists.

[16]This is essentially how the library function nconc, available in most S-Lisps including Common LISP, works.

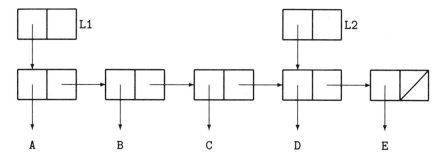

Figure 7.10   CONS cell diagram for (nconc L1 L2).

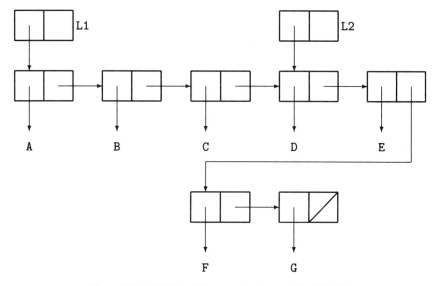

Figure 7.11   CONS cell diagram for (nconc L1 '(F G)).

result in a substantial amount of unintended modification if due care and attention is not exercised. Be warned!

7.8 PROPERTY LISTS

The property list of an atom is used to store global information about the interpretation of that atom in various contexts. It is a list of items which are conceptually (but not actually) grouped into pairs of elements called *indicator-value pairs*. For example, the property list of the atom APPLE might be

```
(color RED food-type FRUIT)
```

This list describes two properties whose indicators are color and food-type and whose corresponding values are RED and FRUIT, respectively. As can be seen from this example, because property indicators and their values are not actual pairs, the mechanism for distinguishing indicators from their values is based on position in the property list. Each indicator occupies an "odd" position, and its associated value immediately follows it in an "even" position of the list.

Although property lists may be implemented using the CDR component of the CONS cells of symbolic atoms, it is preferable to treat them as instances of an abstract data type, with the desired effect of making the actual physical representation described above transparent. Once again, this technique of data abstraction, described previously, requires that access to instances of property lists be provided through data access functions.

As we indicated in our discussion of the implementation of atoms, every atom has a property list which is initially empty. The act of placing an indicator-value pair onto the property list of an existing atom can be viewed as the creation of a new property list for the atom which includes the new pair. Hence a constructor function for property lists should add new pairs. Further, property lists are examples of data structures whose components are likely to be subject to modification. Finally, property lists are usually associated with atoms, and do not stand alone; therefore, a recognizer is generally not required.

In Common LISP (and most other dialects) retrieval of individual properties is done using the system function get. For example, if APPLE has the property list above, then

$$(\text{get 'APPLE 'color}) \Rightarrow \text{RED}$$

$$(\text{get 'APPLE 'food-type}) \Rightarrow \text{FRUIT}$$

Note that get is not strictly a selector function as would be specified by a GRAIL grammar. That is, it is not associated specifically with one component of a property list. One way to define selectors which conform to a GRAIL specification is to use get to implement each selector. This is particularly appropriate when there exist several objects, represented by atoms, which possess the same property. For example, there are many objects which may have a color or a food-type. We can define a selector for the color of an object as follows:

$$(\text{defun color (object) (get object 'color)})$$

To obtain the color of an APPLE we evaluate the form (color 'APPLE). A selector for food-type can be defined similarly.

In Common LISP, properties are added to a property list using an extended form of the setf command, which was introduced previously to assign values to variables.[17] In this case, the first argument of setf, which must specify a location for the value to be placed, consists of a "call" to the function get. The "arguments" of get identify the atom whose property list is to be modified, as well as the indicator to be associated with the value given by the second argument of setf. As an example, the property list for the atom APPLE given previously would result from evaluating the sequence of forms

---

[17]Different Lisp dialects provide separate commands to add indicator-value pairs to property lists, such as putprop and put.

```
(setf (get 'APPLE 'food-type) 'FRUIT)

(setf (get 'APPLE 'color) 'RED)
```

In this example, the apparent calls to get are not evaluated as function calls at all, but are interpreted as *access expressions* denoting memory locations to be updated.[18]

As with get, the function setf is not a constructor as would be specified by a GRAIL rule. However, again it is possible to use the system-provided function to define constructors prescribed by a GRAIL grammar. For example;

```
(defun make-color (object color)
    (setf (get object 'color) color))
```

provides a constructor to "make" the property list of the atom given by the value of object include a new indicator-value pair.[19] The indicator is the atom color, the value of the pair being the value of the formal parameter color.

In some Lisp dialects an important use of property lists is to store the definitions of both system-defined and user-defined Lisp forms. While Common LISP uses a different approach, we describe the approach that employs property lists first.[20]

In those systems that store function definitions on the property list, atoms that represent machine-coded Lisp forms have a pointer to the machine code as the property value associated with particular indicators, such as SUBR or FSUBR. Atoms that represent Lisp forms defined using defun have a representation of the function definition stored after a different indicator, such as EXPR. Most Lisp interpreters actually look up these definitions every time they evaluate a Lisp form, and this makes it possible to redefine the interpretation of any Lisp form during execution, even system-defined ones. This feature provides the programmer with the opportunity to write programs which can generate new functions or modify existing ones during execution. These functions can then be applied during the same execution period. This is a source of great flexibility but requires discipline in application because of the risk of potential disaster.

Property lists provide a mechanism for associating different values or objects with a given identifier. Historically, it has been used not only to capture user-defined properties but also to provide a site for maintaining the Lisp global state, including the global values assigned to variables and the definition of functions. Although the property list is not employed by Common LISP in this manner, it provides a useful conceptual model for the internal representation of function definitions and other information associated with the Lisp global state, where the actual representation is transparent to the user.

---

[18]In Common LISP, the setf command accepts many other forms of access expression as well. In general, if setf is used to store a value in a location specified by an access expression X, the value can be retrieved subsequently by evaluating X as an ordinary expression.

[19]In Common LISP and most other Lisps the setf function (or its equivalent) is also used to change the values of existing pairs as well as to add new ones.

[20]Common LISP provides access to function definitions through the special form function described in Section 7.10.

7.9 DEFINITION OF DATA STRUCTURES

In Chapter 4, the concept of specifying a data structure by a grammar was introduced. In particular, a grammatical formalism was proposed (GRAIL) from which the functions for manipulating the data structure defined by the grammar could be identified. These functions were classified as recognizers, selectors, and constructors. In addition, conventions currently practiced for the naming of data access functions according to their purpose were also identified.

The importance of data abstraction—that is, the hiding of the details of how an abstract data type is actually implemented—is stressed in virtually every textbook on data structures and software engineering today. An examination of some of the previous examples where abstract data types were specified by grammars and implemented as lists shows that there is a considerable degree of similarity in the resulting structure of the function definitions themselves among all selector functions defined, among all constructor functions defined, and to a somewhat lesser extent among all recognizer functions defined. This observation suggests that a useful utility in any Lisp library would be a procedure capable of generating the necessary data access functions from a suitable specification of an abstract data type. In Common LISP such a capability is provided by defstruct.[21]

The construction of a set of data access functions begins with a specification of the abstract data type being implemented. Using defstruct, this consists of a name for the data type and labels for each component of the data structure. For example, we can define an abstract data type for the representation of points in Euclidean space by a triple consisting of the values of the x, y, and z coordinates. This data type can be defined using defstruct as follows:

```
(defstruct point X-coord Y-coord Z-coord)
```

The defstruct form can be viewed as a command; that is, it is evaluated for its side effect, which is to update the Lisp global state to include appropriate definitions for the recognizer, constructor, and selectors of the data type point. As this requires names for the functions, the convention followed by defstruct is as follows:

1. The name of the recognizer function is obtained by appending "-p" onto the data type name.
2. The name of the constructor function is obtained by attaching the prefix "make-" to the data type name.
3. The names of the selector functions are obtained by appending to the data type name, the character "-" followed by each field name.

In the "point" example above, the defstruct would generate the recognizer point-p, the constructor make-point, and the selectors point-X-coord, point-Y-coord, and point-Z-coord.

An instance of an abstract data type is created by the constructor function and can be assigned as the value of an identifier or passed as the argument of a function.

---

[21]defstruct is actually implemented as a macro in Common LISP; however, it is convenient to think of it as a function in the context of this section. (See also Exercise 7.14 at the end of the chapter.)

An important capability in order to make such instances useful is to be able to initialize and update the components. Initialization can be achieved using the update mechanism, which is just another application of the `setf` command described previously. Before illustrating the use of `setf` in this context, we should mention a second method of initialization which is actually provided by `defstruct` itself.

In those situations where we wish to initialize all instances of a particular data type to a predefined set of values upon creation, such default values can be specified as part of the `defstruct` command. In particular, instead of providing a sequence of identifiers for the fields of the data type, a sequence of list pairs is provided. Each list pair specifies the field name and the default value of the field: for example,

```
(defstruct point (X-coord 0) (Y-coord 0) (Z-coord 0))
```

The constructor function, `make-point`, when evaluated will construct an instance of a `point` whose coordinates initially specify the origin of Euclidean space. Thus

```
(setf P1 (make-point))
```

would define P1 to be an instance of a `point`, with its x, y, and z coordinates equal to 0.

To "redefine" or update a component of a structure, the `setf` command can be used. To review, this command requires two arguments; the first specifies the field of some data object to update, and the second specifies the new value. In previous examples, the value fields of atoms and property lists have been updated with `setf`. To update the component of a structure we reference the corresponding field using the selector name. For example, to change the x coordinate of P1 to the value 25 requires the following `setf` command:

```
(setf (point-X-coord P1) 25)
```

This is completely analogous to the mechanism by which property lists were updated, where the indicator of an indicator-value pair on the property list was used to specify the field to be updated rather than the selector function name used in this context. In fact, for Lisp implementations without a `defstruct` command, this analogy suggests a possible approach for the implementation of such a command based on property lists (see Exercise 7.14).

One further enhancement to structured data types defined by `defstruct` and found in contemporary Lisp dialects, including Common LISP, is worthy of mention here. It is possible in Common LISP to modify the default values for the components during the creation of a new instance of some given data type defined with `defstruct`. Using the "point" example as an illustration, it is possible to create a `point`, say P2, whose initial coordinates are not $(0,0,0)$. To do this, we take advantage of the fact that the selector names specified in the `defstruct` command that defined the `point` data type command are also keywords to those fields. Briefly, a *keyword* is a special identifier, which always begins with a ":".[22] The following example serves to illustrate

---

[22] We do not wish to elaborate on the mechanism of implementation or many of the other applications of keywords available in Common LISP in this text. The reader should consult Steele [Ste90] for full details.

how the selector name for a given field can be used to define a keyword for initializing that field. We assume that the defstruct command above for initializing all coordinates to zero has previously been evaluated. The evaluation of the following form will result in the definition of a new point whose initial coordinates do not specify the origin:

$$\text{(setf P2 (make-point :X-coord 10 :Z-coord 25))}$$

P2 is thus defined to be the point $(10, 0, 25)$. Note that any fields not explicitly identified by their corresponding keyword (in this case Y-coord) are initialized to the default value given by the defstruct command.

7.10 LAMBDA EXPRESSIONS

Lambda expressions, which are used to represent functions in Lisp, are an important feature of Lisp systems. First of all, they are pragmatically important because they provide a convenient method for interpretive function definition and application as well as for more general treatment of functions as data objects. Second, lambda expressions are based on the *lambda calculus*, which provides a theoretical model for computable functions [Chu41] and is often used in modeling the semantics of programming languages [Sto77, Mey90]. A more detailed discussion of the relationship between the lambda calculus and lambda expressions may be found in [All78].

A lambda expression represents a function in a manner similar to the definition of a function with the defun command, except that no name is automatically associated with the function. The simplified syntax follows that of defun:

⟨lambda-expression⟩ ::= (lambda ⟨parameter-list⟩ ⟨function-body⟩)
⟨parameter-list⟩ ::= ({ ⟨variable⟩ })
⟨function-body⟩ ::= ⟨expression⟩

For example, a function to square a value may be represented as

```
(lambda (N) (* N N))
```

Using defun, the same function may be defined and associated with the global name square:

```
(defun square (N) (* N N))
```

In fact, the historical means of implementing defun involved storing the lambda expression on the property list of the named atom; however Common LISP uses a different technique.

The parameters and body of a lambda expression can have any of the forms for functions created with defun, including the "implicit progn" extension described previously. The one limitation is the definition of "recursive lambda expressions." Since recursive functions are self-referential, a label is required, in effect naming the lambda expression. A technique for doing this in Common LISP will be described presently.

Otherwise, lambda expressions represent "anonymous" functions, that is, functions that have no name. In Lisp, we can use such anonymous functions wherever named ones could be used. In the basic function application form, for example, we are used to seeing an atom naming the function as the first element of the form. We could equally well use a `lambda` expression in place of a function name in such a context, so that

```
((lambda (N) (* N N)) 4)
```

is a valid Lisp form. In this case all we have done is to substitute the actual function expressed as a lambda expression for the symbolic atom `square` in the following form, which is entirely equivalent:

```
(square 4)
```

In practice, the use of anonymous functions in such direct function applications is rare; they are much more commonly used in situations where functions may be used as arguments to other functions. As we shall see, this occurs in both user-defined and system-defined functions, such as `apply` and `mapcar`. These will be discussed in more detail in Chapter 8. In such instances, advantage is taken of the fact that `lambda` expressions are not restricted to their direct use as Lisp program forms. They can also be used dynamically as Lisp data objects. As we have indicated, we can create `lambda` expressions at run time, pass them around as data objects, and apply them to argument lists as needed.

However, lambda expressions cannot be directly passed to functions which take other functions as arguments. A lambda expression is neither a function itself nor a form which evaluates to a function, but a syntactic object which represents a function. In Common LISP, the special form `function` is used to convert a lambda expression to the function it represents. For example,

```
(function (lambda (N) (* N N)))
```

is a form which evaluates to the square function represented by the lambda expression. Globally defined functions are treated in the same way, so that

```
(function square)
```

also evaluates to the square function.

The power of being able to represent functions as data objects can be illustrated by examining the Lisp approach to sorting. The system function `sort` is a function which takes two arguments: a list to be sorted and a sorting predicate. The sorting predicate must be a function of two arguments which returns any non-NIL value if the arguments are in sorted order, and returns NIL otherwise. Use of the sorting predicate allows a single `sort` function to sort lists according to any sorting criteria whatsoever! For example, suppose that we wanted to sort a list of points, `pt-list`, according to the value of their y-coordinate. Assume that ⟨point⟩ is an abstract data type defined to represent points in Euclidean space. Using the `defstruct` command described previously for implementing abstract data types, we will assume that the selector for the y-coordinate of a ⟨point⟩ is `point-Y-coord`. The ordering of points could be accomplished using `sort` as follows:[23]

```
(sort pt-list
   (function
      (lambda (pt1 pt2)
         (not (> (point-Y-coord pt1) (point-Y-coord pt2))))))
```

Note that in this example we wish to pass the actual function defined by the `lambda` expression, not the data object represented by the corresponding list. This is why `function` has been applied to the `lambda` expression rather than just `quote`.[24] Of course, if we applied neither to the `lambda` expression, the interpreter would try to evaluate the `lambda` expression as an argument, before passing it to `sort`. The `sort` function gains its power from its generality, and this is due entirely to the functional argument it takes as a sorting predicate.

As mentioned earlier, one of the uses of lambda expressions is to provide a "temporary" function definition. This is important if we want to be able to return the space allocated for that function definition to the memory pool after the function has been evaluated. When the definition is to represent a recursive function, `lambda` expressions need to be extended with a naming construct. In Common LISP this can be done using `labels` expressions, which have the following syntax:

$$\text{⟨labels-expr⟩} ::= (\text{ labels } (\{ \text{⟨label-definition⟩} \})$$
$$\text{⟨expression⟩})$$
$$\text{⟨label-definition⟩} ::= (\text{⟨label⟩ ⟨parameter-list⟩ ⟨function-body⟩})$$

The definitions for ⟨parameter-list⟩ and ⟨function-body⟩ remain the same as was given previously in defining `defun`.

The `labels` expression permits the definition of named, locally defined functions. For example,

```
(labels ((subst (X Y L)
            (cond ((endp L) NIL)
                  ((equal (first L) X)
                     (cons Y (subst X Y (rest L))))
                  (T (cons (first L) (subst X Y (rest L)))))))
         (subst OLD-VAL NEW-VAL LST))
```

represents a recursive function which substitutes one item (`NEW-VAL`) for all occurrences of another (`OLD-VAL`) in the given list, `LST`. Such `labels` expressions can be used to represent recursive functions wherever `lambda` expressions can be used to represent nonrecursive ones.

---

[23]The `sort` function we are describing actually sorts the given list destructively. To sort nondestructively, make a copy of the original list before sorting, e.g., (sort (copy-list pt-list) ...).

[24]In order to be compatible with earlier Lisp dialects, Common LISP will also accept a quoted lambda expression. However, the use of `function` more accurately reflects that `sort` expects its (second) argument to be a function rather than a list.

Evaluation of `labels` expressions does not make a permanent change to the Lisp global state; the ⟨label⟩ within such an expression can be used to refer to the given function only during the expression's evaluation. Also, a `labels` expression is obviously not necessary for a recursive function definition using `defun`, since the ⟨function-name⟩ of a ⟨function-definition⟩ can be used for recursive calls.

7.11 EXERCISES

7.1. Suppose that `defun` is not available on your Lisp interpreter. Write a function `define-fn` which creates a `lambda` expression to represent the function definition and stores it under the indicator `EXPR` on the property list of the atom representing the name of the defined function.

7.2. Using `rplaca` and `rplacd`, implement recursive functions `zero-numbers` and `delete-numbers` in Common LISP, which take lists as described and destructively modify them as follows:

(a) `zero-numbers` replaces all numbers in a list of zero or more elements by 0:

$$(\text{zero-numbers } \text{'}(1 \text{ B } 2)) \Rightarrow (0 \text{ B } 0)$$

(b) `delete-numbers` removes all the numbers from a list having at least one nonnumeric element:

$$(\text{delete-numbers } \text{'}(1 \text{ B } 2)) \Rightarrow (B)$$

What problems occur with `delete-numbers` if the list contains only numeric elements?

7.3. Describe the steps that must be performed by an interpreter to evaluate an expression representing a function call. Your description should begin with the expression having been supplied as an argument, and conclude when the value to be returned by the evaluated expression is determined. To illustrate your answer, assume that the expression is `(cons A (rest L))`.

7.4. Write a replacement interpreter in Common LISP for a read/eval/print loop which does the following in each iteration:

1. Read in two Lisp objects, a function and its argument list.
2. Evaluate each argument.
3. Apply the function to the evaluated arguments.
4. Print the result.

Example session transcript:

```
>(interpreter)
>+ (1 2 3 4)
    10
>stop ()
```

7.5. A sparse matrix is one where most of the entries are zero. It is more efficient (in terms of memory usage) to represent such a matrix by a list of values together with their corresponding row and column positions. Write a function to transform a sparse matrix represented as just described into a list of rows. Each row is itself a list of the values of all entries in that row. For example, a matrix whose only non-zero entries are along the diagonals might initially be given by:

$$((10\ 1\ 1)\ (20\ 2\ 2)\ (30\ 3\ 3)\ (40\ 4\ 4)\ (50\ 5\ 5))$$

This representation should be transformed to the following by your function:

$$((10\ 0\ 0\ 0\ 0)\ (0\ 20\ 0\ 0\ 0)\ (0\ 0\ 30\ 0\ 0)\ (0\ 0\ 0\ 40\ 0)\ (0\ 0\ 0\ 0\ 50))$$

7.6. Draw the CONS cell diagram for the structure resulting from the evaluation of the second and third `setf` expressions in each of the following:

(a) `(setf X '(A . B) Y '(A B))`
`(setf P (rplacd X Y))`
`(setf Q (rplacd Y X))`

(b) `(setf X '(A . B) Y '(A B))`
`(setf P (cons (car X) Y))`
`(setf Q (cons (car Y) X))`

7.7. In Common LISP, the `prog1` facility permits the evaluation of a sequence of forms for their side effects in a manner similar to `progn` discussed in Section 7.5.2. However, `prog1` returns the value of the first form evaluated. Suppose that `prog1` is *not* available. Write a function `myprog1` in Common LISP, which takes a list of forms and evaluates them, one at a time, returning the result of evaluating the first form.

7.8. Consider the representation of a modifiable global environment as a property list on the atom `env`.

(a) Define a function `env` of one argument (a variable name) which returns the current value to which the variable is bound in the global environment.

(b) Define the function `update-env` which takes as arguments, a variable name and the value to which it is to be bound, and adds that information to the current environment.

(c) Explain whether there are any restrictions placed on the naming of variables, which are a consequence of your implementation of `env` and `update-env`.

7.9. The following two forms illustrate two different ways of defining a function. Explain the difference by describing what happens as a result of evaluating each form, and show how the function would be called in each case:

```
(setf FN #'(lambda (X)
       (cond ((eq X 'A) T) (T NIL))))
(defun FN (X)
       (cond ((eq X 'A) T) (T NIL))))
```

7.10. Explain what is meant by the statement: "The evaluation of a function generally requires knowledge about the current environment context or global state."

7.11. Show precisely what is evaluated with each iteration of the `read/eval/print` loop in order to process the following input sequence. Without actually running it through a LISP interpreter, show what outputs are produced and then compare your results with those obtained by using the interpreter. Also indicate if and how the environment context is changed in the evaluation of each expression:

```
(setf Z '(A B C))
(defun FN (Y G)
    (let ((Z 10)) (funcall G Z)))
(FN Z #'(lambda (X) (cond ((numberp X) Z) (T 1024))))
```

7.12. A case statement is a selection construct commonly found in procedural languages that permits different sequences of statements to be executed depending on the value of a *key* expression. Common LISP provides a similar construct as the `case` macro.

   (a) The syntax of the `case` macro in Common LISP can be described by a GRAIL grammar. Show how.

   (b) Without using the Common LISP `case` macro, write a function `eval-case` in Common LISP that evaluates `case` expressions as defined by the GRAIL grammar in part (a).

7.13. Suppose that `defstruct` were not available in the Lisp system library. Write an implementation in Common LISP for a function `my-defstruct` which generates the data access functions for the abstract data type named in the argument list. Your implementation should be based on the use of property lists as suggested in Section 7.9.

7.14. A mathematical function f is associative if $f(a, f(b, c)) = f(f(a, b), c)$. What is the relationship between associative mathematical functions and polyadic S-Lisp functions, which were discussed in Section 7.2?

8

Functionals

In this chapter, we explore one of the key characteristics that distinguish Lisp from many other programming languages: the ability to treat functions systematically as data objects. In particular, functions may be passed as arguments, returned as values, assigned to variables, and stored in data structures. Furthermore, functions can be created dynamically by constructing the lambda expressions which represent them and then applying the `function` special form as described in Section 7.10. Alternatively, function definitions (`defun` forms) may be constructed and passed to `eval` to define named functions. Because functions may be used in all the ways you might reasonably expect for data objects, they are often said to be "first-class citizens" in Lisp, in contrast to their second-class status in many other programming languages.

Functions which take functions as arguments or return functions as values are called *functionals*. S-Lisp systems, such as Common LISP, generally provide many important programming tools in the form of *system-defined* functionals. One example is the function `sort` described in Section 7.10. A particularly important class of system-defined functionals are those that provide high-level iteration facilities in Lisp (mapping functions and other iterators); we will examine these in detail in this chapter. We will also see how users may define their own functionals and consider several applications.

8.1 SYSTEM-DEFINED FUNCTIONALS

In this section we describe a few of the more important and commonly used functionals provided by most contemporary Lisp systems, in particular Common LISP.

We begin by considering the basic data access functions necessary for the data type "function". In Common LISP, functions are created as separate data objects by applying the special form `function` either to a lambda expression or to the name of a defined function. Thus `function` serves in the role of a constructor for functions. For recognition, Common LISP provides a predicate `functionp` which distinguishes functions from other types of Lisp data objects. It then only remains to consider selectors to access the "components" of functions. If we consider that a function defines a set of pairs mapping input values to output values, then selection is the process of determining the output value corresponding to a given input value, that is, the process of applying the function to its argument. Common LISP provides two primitives, `apply` and `funcall`, for this purpose.

8.1.1 Function Application: `apply` and `funcall`

To illustrate how a function which has been bound to a formal parameter of a functional can be used, we examine the following attempt to apply such a function in the body of a functional `apply-fn`:

```
(defun apply-fn (f x)
   (f x))


(apply-fn (function rest) '(A B C))
```

There are two reasons why this example fails. First, it is a consequence of the S-Lisp representation of function calls (defined in Figure 4.3) that the identifier `f` occurring in `(f x)` denotes a globally defined function of that name and not the formal parameter `f`. So even though a function is bound to the formal parameter `f`, that value is not retrieved. Assuming that `f` is not the identifier of some function, the function `f` is undefined. Second, even if `f` were evaluated, its value would not be the identifier of the function (which is what we want) but rather the function itself, in this case the function associated with the identifier `rest`. This is equivalent to trying to evaluate the expression

```
((function rest) '(A B C))
```

when what we really want to evaluate is

```
(rest '(A B C))
```

One of the reasons that beginning Lisp programmers may make the mistakes illustrated by this example is a lack of awareness of the distinction the interpreter makes between the first position of an S-Lisp function call and all other positions. The first element must always be either the identifier of a function or an unquoted lambda expression. On the other hand, if these same objects are to be passed as arguments and therefore appear in later positions of a function call, they should evaluate to their functions. Hence `function` should be applied first. This confusion exists only as a result of the S-Lisp representation of function calls and its similarity to the syntax for list constants, where the first element has no special status. However, if we examine the m-Lisp representation as typified by Small Lisp, the difference between a parameter and a function name is more apparent since function calls and list constants have a distinct syntax.

Until now, all our examples have employed the function `function` explicitly in order to make perfectly clear that we are retrieving the function associated with an identifier or lambda expression. However, the frequency with which `function` is required in Common LISP programs is such that it is much more common to use the shorthand symbol `#'`, just as `'` is more commonly used than `quote`. Henceforth, we shall follow common practice and (using a previous example) represent the expression

`(apply-fn (function rest) '(A B C))`

by the expression

`(apply-fn #'rest '(A B C))`

The reader should compare the syntax of the two expressions to be sure that she can easily substitute one for the other. This will generally prove helpful in correctly interpreting how a form will be evaluated, much as using `quote` explicitly often helps to clarify the effect of quoted S-expressions. As a final word of caution, no relation exists between the identifiers, `#'` and `'`, although they share a common character, the single quote or apostrophe.

The solution to the problem of how to apply a parameter whose value is a function to a set of arguments is provided by introducing a functional to perform the task. Common LISP actually provides two: `apply` and `funcall`, and the choice of which one to use depends on how the arguments are supplied.

The Lisp function `apply` is similar to the Small Lisp function `sl-apply` described in Section 6.3, in that it will take the representation of a function and a sequence of arguments embodied in a list and return the result of applying the function to the argument list:[1] for example,

`>(apply #'cons '(A (B C D)))`
`(A B C D)`

Note that `apply` is provided with the arguments of the function to be applied, namely the atom `A`, and the list `(B C D)` in the form of a single Lisp list. The `apply` functional will also accept a `lambda` or `labels` expression representing the function to be applied, so the value of

`(apply fn args)`

might be `(BIG TOP)` if `fn` had the value

---

[1]In the Small Lisp interpreter, functions are directly represented by their names, but in Common LISP we must use `function` or the equivalent shorthand notation `#'`.

```
(lambda (x) (list 'BIG x))
```

and `args` had the value (TOP) (a single-element argument list).

As mentioned previously, there is a second way to apply a function definition to a set of arguments. The `funcall` form can be used as shown in the following examples:

```
>(funcall #'cons 'A '(B C D))
  (A B C D)

>(funcall #'(lambda (x) (list 'BIG x)) 'TOP)
  (BIG TOP)

>(funcall #'(lambda (x11 x12 x21 x22)
>                  (- (* x11 x22)(* x21 x12)))) 1 0 0 1)
   1
```

Note that the arguments of the function to be applied are provided as individual arguments in the `funcall` form rather than in a single list of arguments as was required when using `apply`. Thus `funcall` is an example of a polyadic function, as well as being a functional.

In these examples, the reader should note that we have been careful to use `#'cons` and not `cons` or `'cons`. If `cons` were directly specified as an argument, it would be treated as a variable and evaluated to obtain the value to which it was bound. At the same time, `'cons` denotes the atom `cons` rather than the function of that name.[2] Similarly, a lambda expression must also use the `#'` syntax to be passed as an argument of type "function." Without `#'`, the lambda expression would be interpreted as a function call to `lambda` and would be "evaluated" prior to passing control to the functional. Simply quoting the lambda expression converts it to a list data object, which is what is then passed to the functional rather than the function it represents.

There are two ways in which a function can be associated with an identifier, and the choice affects how the function can be invoked. In the following example, a function is associated with the identifier `fn` using `defun`, and the application of the recognizer `functionp` to the identifier returns T (true). We can therefore retrieve that function with `function` (`#'`) and provide it as the first argument of `apply`:

```
>(defun fn (x)
>   (list 'BIG x))
>
>(functionp #'fn)
    T
>(apply #'fn '(TOP))
    (BIG TOP)
```

As an alternative way of defining a function and associating it with an identifier, consider the following:

---

[2] For compatibility with older Lisp systems, some Common LISP implementations permit `'cons` to be used to specify the function as well as `#'cons`.

```
>(setf fn #'(lambda (x) (list 'BIG x)))
>(functionp #'fn)
   >>Error fn is undefined.
>(functionp fn)
   T
>(apply fn '(TOP))
   (BIG TOP)
```

In this case the function is bound to the global variable fn. Therefore, fn is *not* the identifier of a function, as the application of the recognizer functionp to #'fn shows. Rather it is a variable whose value is a function, and consequently the variable is not quoted when passed as an argument to apply, since it must be evaluated first.

8.1.2 Mapping Functions

A common implementation requirement in symbolic computing is to apply a transformation expressed as a function to each component of a data structure, particularly when the components have a uniform data type. To relieve the programmer from the need to write functions to perform this task, Lisp languages provide an important group of system functionals called *mapping functions* for iteratively applying a given function to the elements or sublists of given lists. A mapping function is so called because it can be viewed as defining a correspondence between two sets of lists. Calls to mapping functions generally have the following syntax (EBNF):

$$\begin{aligned}
\langle\text{mapping-fn-call}\rangle &::= (\ \langle\text{mapping-function}\rangle\ \langle\text{mapped-function}\rangle \\
&\qquad \langle\text{input-lists}\rangle\ ) \\
\langle\text{mapping-function}\rangle &::= \texttt{mapc} \mid \texttt{mapcar} \mid \texttt{mapcan} \mid \\
&\qquad \texttt{mapl} \mid \texttt{maplist} \mid \texttt{mapcon} \\
\langle\text{mapped-function}\rangle &::= \langle\text{function-expression}\rangle \\
\langle\text{input-lists}\rangle &::= \langle\text{list-expression}\rangle\ \{\langle\text{list-expression}\rangle\}
\end{aligned}$$

Here, a ⟨function-expression⟩ is simply an ⟨expression⟩ which evaluates to a function, often an expression using the #' syntax to retrieve the function associated with a given atom. Similarly a ⟨list-expression⟩ is an ⟨expression⟩ which evaluates to a list. In its simplest form, the input consists of a single list which the mapping function transforms into an output list by applying of a *mapped* function having one formal parameter to each component of the input list. This concept can be generalized to permit the mapping of any number of input lists into a single output list. In each case the number of input lists which define a single output list determines the number of formal parameters required of the mapped function. This is because a component of the output list will be obtained by applying the mapped function to a set of values, one value taken from each input list supplied.

Traditional Lisp systems (as well as Common LISP) usually provide six mapping functions. They differ in how they traverse the given lists (two possibilities) and what they do with the results (three possibilities). The mapc, mapcar, and mapcan functionals apply the argument functions to each element in turn of the given input lists. The mapl, maplist, and mapcon functionals, on the other hand, apply functions to all the tail sublists of given lists; that is, those lists obtained by applying the function `rest` to the given lists.

As an illustration of the application of a mapping function, consider the following example. As indicated above, `mapcar` applies its mapped function to a set of values, one from each input list. Since `cons` is a function of two arguments, two input lists are supplied, so

```
>(mapcar #'cons '(A B C) '((1) (3) (5)))
 ((A 1) (B 3) (C 5))
```

applies `cons` successively to A and (1), then B and (3), and finally, C and (5). From this example we can see that `mapcar` is so named because on each iteration it obtains its next set of arguments for the mapped function by taking the CAR of the "unprocessed" remainder of each input list.

As a second example,

```
>(maplist #'cons '(A B C) '((1) (3) (5)))
 (((A B C) (1) (3) (5)) ((B C) (3) (5)) ((C) (5)))
```

supplies as arguments to `cons` (its mapped function) the values (A B C) and ((1) (3) (5)) in the first iteration, (B C) and ((3) (5)) in the second iteration, and finally, (C) and ((5)) in the third iteration.

As shown above, `mapcar` and `maplist` each build a list of the returned results from each individual mapped function application.

The two mapping functions `mapc` and `mapl` supply values to a mapped function in the same way as `mapcar` and `maplist`, respectively. However, they are used less frequently since they apply their argument functions for side effect only. In Common LISP, they return the first input list as a result.

The mapping functions `mapcan` and `mapcon` require that their mapped functions always return lists as values. The value returned by these mapping functions consists of a concatenated list of all the lists returned by the mapped function. The virtue of having the mapped function return a list is that it permits that function to contribute a variable number of components (including none) to the eventual list returned by the mapping function. However, the concatenation is destructive, so caution should be exercised. These forms will be completely safe, however, if the functions they apply build new structures themselves. For example,

```
>(mapcan #'(lambda (n) (list n (* n n))) '(1 2 3 4))
 (1 1 2 4 3 9 4 16)
```

A particularly useful application of `mapcan` and `mapcon` is that they permit the implementation of *filters*. In its simplest form, a *filter* is a function whose purpose is to edit a given list by eliminating those components that do not satisfy some predicate. As an example, a filter can be defined to remove all even numbers from a given list as follows:

```
>(defun odds-only (numbers)
>   (mapcan #'(lambda (x)
>               (cond ((= (rem x 2) 0) '())
```

```
>                              (T (list x))))
>            numbers))
     odds-only

>(odds-only '(1 2 3 4 5 6 7 8 9 10))
   (1 3 5 7 9)
```

This example provides a good illustration of a common use for lambda expressions in Lisp: to specify a function needed only once, in this case to provide a function as the argument to a functional.

8.2 SEQUENCES

A key feature of the iterative process employed by the mapping functions described in the preceding section is the notion that a *sequence* of values are being supplied as arguments to the mapped functions. In the case of mapcar, mapc, and mapcan the sequence was generated by taking the first element from the input list of elements remaining to be used. With respect to maplist, mapl, and mapcon, the rest of the input list remaining was used. It is possible to generalize the concept of mapping since the iteration is related to the control structure for selecting from a sequence of values rather than how the sequence is represented. Consequently, it is possible to define more general mapping functions, as we shall describe in the next section. First, however, it is necessary to describe a native data type found in Common LISP, called a sequence. A *sequence* is an ordered set of elements and can be any finite length, including zero. The sequence of length zero is represented by NIL. Some examples of system-defined sequences include lists, strings, and vectors (depending on the implementation).

The type of a sequence can be determined by using the predicate typep. It is a "generic" data type recognizer, which takes an arbitrary object and compares the data type of its value with a specified data type. The syntax and use of this data access function in recognizing sequences is illustrated in the following sample dialogue:

```
>(typep '(A B C) 'sequence)
   T

>(typep '(A B C) 'list)
   T
```

This example illustrates the "dual" nature of the list data type. In fact, lists are defined as a subtype of the sequence data type.

Since a sequence is a data type, it also has a constructor, namely make-sequence, which permits the specification of user-defined sequences of prescribed length from among the valid sequence types. For example, consider the point data type defined in Section 7.9 using defstruct. An alternative approach is to implement points as sequences of length 3. Furthermore, we can initialize the coordinates to 0 as was done in the defstruct example. The following form constructs a *list type* sequence representation of a point:

```
>(defun make-point ()
>   (make-sequence 'list 3 :initial-element 0))
>(setf P1 (make-point))
    (0 0 0)
```

The first argument of make-sequence is the name of a valid sequence type (implementation dependent), the second argument is the length of the sequence, and the optional third argument, identified by the keyword :initial-element, specifies the value to which all components of the newly created sequence are to be initialized.

Elements of a sequence can be selected using the function elt and specifying an index. For example, elt can be used to define the selector functions for a point, (x, y, z), when implemented as a sequence:

```
>(defun X-coord (pt) (elt pt 0))
>(defun Y-coord (pt) (elt pt 1))
>(defun Z-coord (pt) (elt pt 2))
```

Note that the index of the first position in a sequence is 0.

Finally, sequences can be updated using setf. In this case elt is used to specify the field that is to be updated. So to change the y-coordinate of point P1 to 25:

```
(setf (elt P1 1) 25)
```

The primary reason for introducing sequences in this section is to permit wider application of the mapping concept introduced previously. As we shall see in the next section, there exist mapping functions whose argument definitions extend the range of data types to include any valid sequence.

8.3 GENERALIZED ITERATORS

The mapping functions of Section 8.1 are examples of a general programming concept common to many contemporary functional languages, but not often found in procedural languages. That concept, *high-level iteration*, refers to a construct for programming iteration without requiring that the programmer provide the details of the control structure.

An examination of the kinds of tasks in which iteration is employed suggests that it is possible to classify the application of iteration according to the type of activity required. More explicitly, we can define *generalized iteration* as a computation performed on an abstract sequence of elements for the purpose of performing one of the following:

1. *Side-effect iteration*: a computation on each element of the sequence for side effects only.
2. *Reduction iteration*: an accumulation of the results obtained from applying a computation to each element of the sequence.
3. *Search iteration*: a search for instances which satisfy a given condition among the elements of the sequence.

4. *Filter iteration*: an editing or other transformation of the elements of the sequence.

5. *Merge iteration*: a combining of "parallel" sequences into a single sequence.

In Section 8.1.2, we demonstrated how the six mapping functions `mapl`, `mapc`, `maplist`, `mapcar`, `mapcon`, and `mapcan` can address some of these types of generalized iteration. Because they are historically the first iterators included in early Lisp systems, we shall refer to these functionals as the *traditional map iterators*.

In addition to the traditional map iterators that most Lisp systems provide, additional generalized iterators are often included for even greater flexibility and efficiency. While it is possible to define some of these "newer" constructs using a traditional map iterator, it is usually the case that such an emulation requires extra passes through a list. The new generalized iterators reduce the number of passes required, and also permit their arguments to be sequences other than lists.

It is also the case that the traditional Lisp map iterators are restricted both in the manner arguments are supplied to the function being mapped and in the way results from the successive function applications are used. In applying an n-adic function, the n arguments must either be taken as the successive elements from n given lists (`mapc`, `mapcar`, and `mapcan`) or as successive tail sublists of given lists (`mapl`, `maplist`, and `mapcon`). In some functional languages, generalized map iterators allow the sequence of values for each of the arguments to be specified individually, not only as successive elements of a list or successive tails of a list, but also as possibly infinite sequences such as successive integers, or even arbitrarily through the evaluation of a "sequence" function, whose purpose is to generate the sequence elements. In the remainder of this section, we shall confine our description to those generalized iterators provided by Common LISP, which act on the successive elements of sequences of finite length. To address generalized iteration on infinite sequences requires the notion of *streams*, to be discussed in Section 8.6.

We can classify the traditional map iterators which act on successive elements according to the type of computation performed, by using the scheme defined above. First, the `mapc` functional iteratively applies a mapped function for its effect on the global state, ignoring returned values. Therefore, `mapc` provides a *side-effect iterator* for sequences represented as lists. The `mapcar` iterator provides a means of combining multiple lists into a single one. It also can be viewed as providing a particular instance of accumulation because it builds a list of values obtained from successive applications of the mapped function to the elements of the input lists. The `mapcan` iterator is also a list accumulator, since it builds a concatenated list of result lists (requiring that lists are always returned by the function being mapped). As well, in the preceding section we demonstrated how `mapcan` can also be used as a filter.

Common LISP provides additional iterators which relax the requirement that the input sequence be a list, and which extend the types of accumulation and filtering that can be provided. Another common iterative scheme is missed altogether by the traditional iterators; it is the processing of values in sequence until and only until a certain condition is found to hold. This is the *search iterator* referred to in the classification of generalized iteration above. The remainder of this section is devoted to a description of some of these generalized iterators.

8.3.1 The Functional: `map`

The `mapcar` function is useful when sequences are represented by lists. However, the Common LISP data type ⟨sequence⟩ includes other possible representations besides lists, as indicated previously. Therefore, it is worthwhile to define a functional similar to `mapcar` but which is applicable to any valid ⟨sequence⟩. This capability is provided by the function `map`:

$$⟨\text{map-expr}⟩ ::= (\text{map } ⟨\text{sequence-type}⟩ ⟨\text{mapped-function}⟩$$
$$\{⟨\text{sequence-expression}⟩\})$$
$$⟨\text{sequence-type}⟩ ::= \text{NIL} \mid ⟨\text{valid-sequence-type}⟩$$

The input sequence can be any valid sequence or set of sequences. The number of input sequences determines the number of arguments required by the mapped function. The ⟨sequence-type⟩ determines what specific type of representation is to be used for the output sequence. A NIL ⟨sequence-type⟩ causes `map` to behave like `mapc` does for lists. That is, the mapping function is evaluated only for its side effects. The functionals `mapcar` and `mapc` correspond to special cases of `map` as follows:

$$(\text{mapc } f \ l_1 \ l_2 \ \dots \ l_n) \equiv (\text{map NIL } f \ l_1 \ l_2 \ \dots \ l_n)$$
$$(\text{mapcar } f \ l_1 \ l_2 \ \dots \ l_n) \equiv (\text{map 'list } f \ l_1 \ l_2 \ \dots \ l_n)$$

As an illustration of the use of `map` we consider a variation on the Small Lisp functions `explode` and `implode` described in Chapter 2. The purpose of these functions was to extract the components of a string by "exploding" it into a list of its constituent characters, and to combine ("implode") a list of characters into a string. However neither characters nor strings were data types in Small Lisp, so their representation was achieved using symbolic atoms. Common LISP, however, provides strings as a type of sequence, and therefore the iterators are applicable to their manipulation. The following example illustrates how these functions can be implemented using generalized iterators:

```
(defun explode (char-string)
   (map 'list #'(lambda (x)  x) char-string))

(defun implode (char-list)
   (map 'string #'(lambda (x)  x) char-list))
```

The only role of the mapped function in both `explode` and `implode` is to provide access to each component of the input sequence.

With these two functions it is possible to define a function `concat-strings` to concatenate an arbitrary number of strings to obtain a single one:

```
>(defun concat-strings (&rest string-list)
>   (implode (mapcan #'explode string-list)))
    concat-strings

>(concat-strings "AB" "CD" "DE")
    "ABCDDE"
```

Notice how (in Common LISP) the formal parameter keyword &rest is used to combine an indefinite number of arguments into a list which is then supplied directly as an argument to the map iterator mapcan in the function body.

8.3.2 Accumulation with reduce

The reduce iterator of Common LISP provides a generalized accumulation mechanism which permits a binary function to be used to combine the elements of a sequence. The structure of the reduce form is given by[3]

⟨reduce-expr⟩ ::= (reduce ⟨mapped-function⟩ ⟨sequence-expression⟩
                     [:from-end T] [:initial-value ⟨expression⟩])

Conceptually, when the optional parameters identified in the definition are not included, reduce initializes an accumulating parameter to the first (leftmost) value in the sequence and then applies the binary function with the accumulating parameter and the next value in the sequence as its first and second arguments, respectively. The function is applied repeatedly to the accumulating parameter and subsequent elements until all elements in the sequence have been processed. Inclusion of the :from-end T option causes the finite sequence to be processed from right to left. The :initial-value ⟨expression⟩ option permits the accumulating parameter to be initialized to the value of the ⟨expression⟩ rather than the first element in the sequence.

As an example, consider the application of reduce to the list (A B C) using cons. From the description, reduce initializes the accumulating parameter to the leftmost value in the list, namely A, and since it is an atom, constructs the dotted pair (A . B) in the first iteration. In the second (and final) iteration, (A . B) is "consed" to the atom C. This result is reflected in the following dialogue:

```
>(reduce #'cons  '(A B C))
  ((A . B) . C)
```

To illustrate the effect of the optional parameters, we can reconstruct the original input list (and so provide a rather obscure identity function for lists!) as follows:

```
>(reduce #'cons '(A B C) :from-end T :initial-value NIL)
  (A B C)
```

Note that the :initial-value is required; otherwise, the accumulating parameter would be initialized to the atom C.

The previous examples serve only to illustrate the syntax and effect of the reduce functional. Its practical application is more suitably represented by the archetypal problem used in every introductory programming text as the first illustration of iteration— that of summing a set of numbers. With the set of numbers specified as a list, this task can be defined as follows:[4]

---

[3]Additional options are available with reduce which permit the specification of subsequences. They are not comonly used and are therefore not included in our definition. The interested reader should consult Steele [Ste90].

[4]Of course, since + is a polyadic function in Common LISP, it is simpler and more efficient to sum the numbers just by evaluating (+ 1 4 9 16 25).

```
>(reduce #'+   '(1 4 9 16 25))
55
```

It is important to compare the behavior of `reduce` with that of `mapcar`. The function `mapcar` applies a mapped function to each element of a list and accumulates the
results into a single list. Each element of the original input list can be transformed in
any uniform way, but there is only one method of accumulation. The function `reduce`
provides little opportunity for transforming any of the elements of its input list, but
rather, permits the elements to be accumulated in different ways. Thus these functions
can be combined to provide a general mapping accumulator for lists:

```
(defun mapcar-accum (accum-fn accumulator mapped-fn input-list)
   (reduce accum-fn (mapcar mapped-fn input-list)
                             :initial-value accumulator))
```

The mapping function `mapcar-accum` can be generalized further, in order to
accommodate any type of sequence and not just lists. To do so, recall from Section
8.3.1 that `map` is a generalization of `mapcar`. Therefore, we simply replace the function
call to `mapcar` in `mapcar-accum` by a call to `map` instead:

```
(defun map-accum (accum-fn accumulator mapped-fn input-seq)
   (reduce accum-fn (map (datatype input-seq) mapped-fn input-seq)
                             :initial-value accumulator))
```

To apply `map` correctly it is necessary to identify the data type of the input sequence and
provide this as the first argument of `map`. The function `datatype` returns the data type
of its argument (in this case `input-seq`) and therefore addresses this requirement.[5]
    This user-defined functional captures the generality provided by both `reduce`
and `map` in a map iterator which can be applied to the data type ⟨sequence⟩ and not
just lists. For example, `map-accum` can be used to calculate the sum of the squares of
the first five integers as follows:

```
>(map-accum #'+   0   #'(lambda (x) (* x  x))   '(1 2 3 4 5))
55
```

8.3.3 Search Iteration: `find-if`

An iterative activity not captured by the traditional mapping iterators is that of searching for one or more occurrences of a particular element in a given sequence. In its
simplest form, the iterator simply searches a sequence for an element which satisfies
a given predicate, returning `NIL` if the search fails. Common LISP provides four such
functionals which can be grouped into two complementary pairs. The iterators `some`
and `notany` test for the existence of at least one element satisfying a given predicate,
while the iterators `every` and `notevery` test whether all elements satisfy the given
predicate. We shall refer to these four functionals as the *predicate iterators*. The syntax of a predicate iterator expression is as follows:

---

[5]`datatype` is implementation dependent and may require user definition, depending on the implementation of the system function `type-of`.

⟨predicate-iterator⟩ ::= (⟨predicate-functional⟩ ⟨mapped-predicate⟩
                             {⟨sequence-expression⟩})
⟨predicate-functional⟩ ::= some | notany | every | notevery
⟨mapped-predicate⟩ ::= ⟨mapped-function⟩

Note that in predicate functionals the mapped function must be a predicate.

In each case the predicate functional should be viewed as a true predicate, although the implementation of these functionals, like many other system-defined Lisp predicates, may in fact return some non-NIL value other than T whenever the predicate is true. Functions which possess this property—returning NIL for false, and some non-NIL expression to represent true—are called Lisp *semipredicates*. Such functions provide the properties of a predicate and at the same time permit the non-NIL value to be used in some other way than simply as a truth value. Semipredicates are very convenient in Lisp programming, and occasionally necessary, as in the case of providing a mapped function to the functional find-if, as we shall now see.

The system functional find-if is provided in Common LISP to find an element of the input which satisfies a given predicate. In its simplest form (without optional keywords), find-if requires only two arguments: a sequence and a semipredicate with one formal parameter which is to be applied to each element in the sequence. For example, the first numeric element of a given sequence seq can be determined as follows:

```
(find-if #'(lambda (elem) (cond ((numberp elem) elem)
                                (T NIL)))
    seq)
```

The sequence is examined from left to right and the first element which satisfies the semipredicate is returned.[6]

As with the predicate iterators, Common LISP provides a complementary functional to find-if, specifically find-if-not, which finds the first element that does *not* satisfy the given semipredicate. Also provided are functionals to count the number of elements which do or do not satisfy a given semipredicate (called count-if and count-if-not respectively). In all instances, the basic syntax of the appropriate S-expressions corresponds to that illustrated for find-if in the example above.

8.3.4 Filters

The final class of iterator types to mention is that of filters. As was illustrated in the preceding section, mapcan can be used to define filters. In order to do so, however, it is necessary to define the mapped function in a clever way by providing it with the dual role of acting as a predicate which performs the test for inclusion, and at the same time generating a suitable list representation which can then be concatenated onto the previously filtered elements of the original input list. Therefore, Common LISP provides two pairs of functionals for removing elements from sequences (including lists). As with the other generalized iterators, each pair of functions provides a function to

---

[6]Like reduce, find-if possesses an optional parameter, :from-end T, which causes the search to proceed from right to left when included.

remove all elements satisfying a given predicate, and a complementary function to re-move all elements not satisfying the predicate. The `remove-if` and `remove-if-not` functionals take a predicate and sequence as arguments and return a new sequence with the appropriate elements removed. The `delete-if` and `delete-if-not` func-tionals destructively modify the input sequence to obtain the appropriately modified result.[7] The example given in the preceding section of using `mapcan` to filter the odd numbers from a given set can be achieved using `remove-if` as follows:

```
>(defun odds-only (numbers)
>   (remove-if #'(lambda (x) (= (rem x 2) 0)) numbers))
    odds-only

>(odds-only '(1 2 3 4 5 6 7 8 9 10))
    (1 3 5 7 9)
```

Note the simpler predicate required, as compared with the version of this function given previously. This is because it is no longer necessary for the mapped function to return lists.[8]

The `remove-if` filter and its companion functions are examples of one of a class of tasks which collectively are often referred to as *editing*. Common LISP provides a number of other useful "editing" iterators, of which we shall describe only one com-plementary pair: `substitute-if` and `substitute-if-not`. As the name implies, `substitute-if` replaces all elements in a sequence which satisfy a given predicate by a new element. The syntax for a `substitute-if` form is

$$\langle\text{substitute-if-expr}\rangle ::= (\text{ substitute-if }\langle\text{replacement}\rangle$$
$$\langle\text{mapped-predicate}\rangle$$
$$\langle\text{sequence-expression}\rangle \text{)}$$
$$\langle\text{replacement}\rangle ::= \langle\text{expression}\rangle$$

In conjunction with `find-if` the filter iterators provide a suite of powerful, widely used functionals for editing sequences. They are particularly important in sym-bolic computing, where they can be used to simplify the representation of abstract objects.

8.4 USER-DEFINED FUNCTIONALS

In the preceding sections, system functionals were described which demonstrate the treatment of functions as data objects, usually for the purpose of passing them as argu-ments and applying them selectively or iteratively. In addition, an example of a user-defined functional was provided—that being the definition of `map-accum`. It should be clear from these examples how functions are specified in Lisp as data objects. In this section, we will examine in more detail how user-defined functionals are specified.

---

[7]Common LISP also provides a useful special case of `remove-if` called `remove-duplicates`. When applied to a sequence, this function removes all multiple copies of elements in the sequence.

[8]Common LISP actually includes a predicate `evenp` which could be used in place of the lambda expression given.

In particular, some interesting examples of user-defined functionals will be examined which not only pass functions as arguments but also return them as values.

We begin with a brief summary of what has been discussed in the preceding sections, particularly as it pertains to the implementation of user-defined functionals. We have stressed that the first element of the S-Lisp representation of a function call has special significance as the identifier of the function being called, and therefore it is not evaluated by the Lisp interpreter. Consequently, a formal parameter to which a function is bound cannot be used as the first element of a form since it must be evaluated first. Instead, as described earlier, Lisp provides the system functionals `apply` and `funcall` to retrieve these functions and then apply them to a set of arguments. Therefore, it follows that in a typical user-defined functional, whenever the programmer desires to call the function bound to a formal parameter, an `apply` or `funcall` form should be used. On the other hand, if the function definition is to be treated as a data object, it can be passed around directly as the value of the formal parameter. This was illustrated in the example of the preceding section where the user-defined mapping functional `map-accum` was given. In the remainder of this section, we will focus on the actual construction of functions as data objects within the body of a functional, that is, the construction of functions during run time.

An important consequence of the representation of a function as a data object is the opportunity it provides the programmer to write functions which can, during the course of execution, create other functions dynamically, that is, program generation of functions which can themselves be evaluated during the run time of the program that created them. This capability has many applications. For example, the sequence of steps required by a robot to traverse a room containing obstacles can be viewed as a program which the robot is to execute. The structure of such a program depends on the current position and nature of the hazards in the room. Such a program can be thought of as a plan, and its construction can be carried out by the robot itself, using input about the room's environment.

A less ambitious example is the construction of a data access function (DAF) generator. The following example illustrates a user-defined alternative to the system-defined function provided in Common LISP for this purpose, namely `defstruct`.

A common way to characterize many "object-oriented" abstract data types is to associate a set of properties with that type. Any instance of the defined type will then consist of an assignment of values to some or all of the properties. One way to represent abstract objects which can be defined in this way is by using the property lists of symbolic atoms, described in Section 7.8. A second way of representing an abstract data object is with association lists, described in Section 6.2, with each ⟨binding⟩ corresponding to a property and its value. From the grammar for association lists given in that section, it should be clear that any specific example we choose to implement in this way will have the same general structure and therefore the data access functions— the recognizer, selectors, constructor, and updaters—will be implemented in the same way. This observation suggests that we can write a function to generate the necessary data access functions if we provide as arguments the properties that characterize our abstract data type.

Association lists are so frequently used in Lisp programming that many Lisp interpreters include system functions for accessing them. For example, in Common LISP the function `assoc` retrieves pairs from association lists as follows:[9]

```
>(setf APPLE '((color RED) (shape ROUND)))
 ((color RED) (shape ROUND))


>(assoc 'shape APPLE)
 (shape ROUND)
```

With the aid of this function we can proceed to the definition of a simple DAF generator.

The DAF generator is to define all the data access functions required to provide an implementation for any given abstract data type, when characterized by a set of properties. In keeping with the naming conventions we have described previously, the recognizer will have -p as a suffix, and the constructor will have `make-` as a prefix. The names for the selectors will correspond to the property names given since these names determine which component of the association list is to be retrieved. In order to allow different abstract data types to possess the same property names, the name of the actual data type will be used as a prefix to each property name. The updater function names will then be obtained by adding the prefix `set-` to the selector names.

Since we have described the system DAF generator `defstruct` previously in Section 7.9, we will use it as a model for the implementation of our user-defined DAF generator. In particular, the syntax of a call to our DAF generator, to be called `define-ADT`, will be as follows:

$$\langle\text{DAF-expr}\rangle ::= (\text{define-ADT } \langle\text{data-type}\rangle \{ \langle\text{indicator}\rangle \})$$
$$\langle\text{data-type}\rangle ::= \langle\text{symbolic atom}\rangle$$
$$\langle\text{indicator}\rangle ::= \langle\text{symbolic atom}\rangle$$

The primary purpose of the DAF generator will be to construct function definitions. In each case the definition will then be evaluated for the purpose of producing the side effect of associating an identifier with the function. A function, `mkatom`, will be required to construct the name of each function. This is achieved by concatenating strings (using `concat-strings` as defined in Section 8.3.1) and then converting the resulting string to a symbol using the Common LISP function `intern`.[10]

The implementation also requires constructor functions to build function definitions, function calls, and unevaluated S-expressions. In Section 4.5, a GRAIL grammar was provided which defined these objects, and from which suitable constructors were defined in Small Lisp. For convenience we provide these definitions again, this time in Common LISP, together with the definition of `mkatom`:

---

[9]This function is analogous to the Small Lisp function `assoc` defined in Section 6.2.

[10]Common LISP provides two types of symbol: *interned* and *uninterned*. Interned symbols are the "usual" kind; they are created automatically whenever a symbolic atom is used in an S- expression for the first time. The function `intern` ensures that a *constructed* symbolic atom is interned. For further details, consult Steele [Ste90].

```
(defun make-fn-def (name parms body)
   (list 'defun name parms body))

(defun make-fn-call (fn args)
   (cons fn args))

(defun make-list-expr (lst)
   (list 'quote lst))

(defun make-symbolic-atom-expr (sym)
   (list 'quote sym))

(defun mkatom (&rest strings)
   (intern (apply #'concat-strings strings)))
```

We also define the following auxiliary function for more concisely building function
calls.

```
(defun build-fn-call (fn &rest args)
   (cons fn args))
```

This allows us to use

```
(build-fn-call name arg1 ... argn)
```

instead of

```
(make-fn-call name (list arg1 ... argn))
```

We can now proceed to the implementation of the actual DAF generator itself.

To begin with, a function is required to build the initial association list each time
an instance of a given data type is constructed. In addition, a function is required to
modify the existing value of an association pair. These general utilities will be used by
the constructor and updaters for each data type subsequently defined:

```
(defun build-assoc-list (indics)

  (cond ((endp indics) nil)
        (T (cons (list (first indics) '?)
                 (build-assoc-list (rest indics))))))

(defun update-assoc-list (lst indic value)

 (cond ((endp lst) (list (list indic value)))
       ((eq indic (first (first lst)))
            (cons (list indic value) (rest lst)))
       (T (cons (first lst)
               (update-assoc-list (rest lst) indic value)))))
```

For each type of data access function (recognizer, selector, constructor, and updater) a function is defined which constructs a DAF function of a given type. We begin
with the generation of selectors. Before actually writing a function to construct a selector it is useful to prepare a template which reflects the structure of the function
we wish to build. Within the template we revert to the use of quote rather than ' to
make apparent the actual list structure and to help identify the appropriate constructor functions for building such expressions. For the example at hand, a typical selector
function will retrieve the value of a particular component using an association list:

```
(defun Type-Indic (x)
  (second (assoc (quote Indic) x)))
```

In this case, the values of the meta-variables *Type* and *Indic* are used to construct the actual name of the selector and to specify what indicator is to be used to
retrieve the appropriate pair from the association list of x. The value to which the
formal parameter x is bound must therefore be an association list with some pair possessing the indicator *Indic*. The second element of the selected pair is then returned
as the value of the function call. The value of the meta-variable *Indic* is quoted because it is a constant in the selector function.

As a consequence of this analysis, the function selector which is to be designed
to construct selector functions must possess two formal parameters, type and indic
corresponding to the meta-variables in the template. The body of the function will
consist of a function call to make-fn-def to build the defun suggested by the template,
which is then evaluated immediately (using eval) to place the function definition on
the Lisp global state. Thus we have

```
(defun selector (type indic)
  (eval
    (make-fn-def
      (mkatom (symbol-name type) "-" (symbol-name indic))
      '(x)
      (build-fn-call
        'second
        (build-fn-call 'assoc (make-symbolic-atom-expr indic) 'x)))))
```

The reader should remember that the value of indic is determined at the time
the selector is constructed, so the selector function generated is specific to that particular indicator. So make-symbolic-atom-expr is used to make the value of indic
a constant, that is, a quoted atom. Consequently, a selector function will need to be
constructed for every indicator associated with the abstract data type and specified in
the argument list of define-ADT.

Instances of an abstract data type are to be represented by association lists. The
association list initially assigned to each instance will consist of a list of pairs whose
first elements are the indicators corresponding to the selectors defined, and whose
second elements are set to "?". An additional pair is added to the association list to

facilitate recognition of the data type being defined. From these design considerations
a template for a typical constructor function is

```
(defun make-Type ()
    (update-assoc-list
        (build-assoc-list
            (quote (ADT I₁...Iₙ)))
        (quote ADT)
        (quote Type))))
```

The constructor function to be generated will therefore be a function of no arguments, returning as its value an association list with an initialized pair for each indicator $I_j, 1 \le j \le n$, from the set of indicators which collectively specify the components
of the data type. Consequently, the arguments required to build a constructor function are type, to provide a value for $Type$, and a list indics to provide the values for
the indicators The body of the constructor function will be assembled using the previously defined function build-assoc-list, to build an association list which includes
the constant ADT as an indicator, and update-assoc-list to modify the value of the
association pair (ADT ?) to be (ADT $Type$). The result is

```
(defun constructor (type indics)
    (eval
        (make-fn-def
            (mkatom "make-" (symbol-name type))
            '()
            (build-fn-call
                'update-assoc-list
                (build-fn-call
                    'build-assoc-list (make-list-expr (cons 'ADT indics)))
                (make-list-expr 'ADT)
                (make-symbolic-atom-expr type)))))
```

Particular note should be made of the expression (make-list-expr 'ADT) included in the definition of constructor. Inspection of the template for a constructor reveals the need to include the expression (quote ADT) as an argument of the
function call to build-assoc-list, and not just ADT, which would be treated as an
identifier and evaluated if the constructor function were ever called.

In the design of constructor, an additional association pair was introduced,
distinguished by the indicator ADT. Recognition will be based on sampling the association list of an arbitrary data object for that indicator and comparing its associated value
with a prescribed value for the recognized data type. The data type to be recognized
is represented in the template by $Type$:

```
(defun Type-p (item)
    (eq Type (second (assoc (quote ADT) item))))
```

At the time a data type is defined (and therefore all its data access functions),
the function to construct the recognizer requires a value for $Type$:

```
(defun recognizer (type)
  (eval
    (make-fn-def
      (mkatom (symbol-name type) "-p")
      '(item)
      (build-fn-call
        'eq
        (make-symbolic-atom-expr type)
        (build-fn-call
          'second
          (build-fn-call 'assoc (make-list-expr 'ADT) 'item))))))
```

It should be noted that the recognizer created only distinguishes one association list representation of an abstract data type from another. It is not a validater and may produce an error if applied to a data object that cannot be interpreted as an association list, that is, a list of pairs.

The final type of data access function to define is the updater for each component of an abstract data object. A template specifying the structure of a typical updater is given by

$$\text{(defun set-}Type\text{-}Indic \text{ (item value)}$$
$$\text{(update-assoc-list item (quote } Indic \text{) value))}$$

Thus a typical updater modifies the association list that is bound to the formal parameter item, replacing the existing value of an association pair whose indicator is *Indic* by the value bound to value. The particular indicator for which this updater is defined is specified at the time the function is constructed, that is, when define-ADT is called. The function to construct updaters typified by the template is

```
(defun updater (type indic)
  (eval
    (make-fn-def
      (mkatom "set-" (symbol-name type) "-" (symbol-name indic))
      '(item value)
      (build-fn-call
        'update-assoc-list
        'item
        (make-symbolic-atom-expr indic)
        'value))))
```

With these functions defined, we can implement the function define-ADT:

```
(defun define-ADT (type &rest indics)
       (mapc #'(lambda (x) (selector type x)) indics)
       (mapc #'(lambda (x) (updater type x)) indics)
       (constructor type indics)
       (recognizer type)
```

```
(concat-strings
   "data type: " (symbol-name type) " defined."))
```

As was indicated in the description of `selector`, the function definitions constructed by `constructor`, `recognizer`, and `updater` are immediately evaluated by `eval`. This results in each `defun` form being evaluated for its side effect—the association of each function with its identifier. Thus the values returned by `selector`, `recognizer`, `constructor`, and `updater` are the results of that evaluation, namely, the identifiers of the functions defined.

As an example use of `define-ADT`, suppose that we wish to construct an abstract data type for shipping orders from a warehouse. A simple way to describe a shipment is to characterize it in terms of four components: the content of the order, the quantity of goods in the order, the destination address, and the cost.[11] Based on this interpretation, a GRAIL grammar could be defined:

⟨shipment⟩ ::= (⟨content:S-expression⟩ ⟨quantity:S-expression⟩
                  ⟨address:S-expression⟩ ⟨cost:S-expression⟩)

From this grammar we could proceed to implement the necessary data access functions to manipulate ⟨shipment⟩s represented as lists of four elements. However, rather than implement the data access functions ourselves from the grammar, we let the DAF generator do it for us. In doing so, notice that a ⟨shipment⟩ is now implemented as an association list of four pairs. The following sample trace illustrates how the DAF generator creates the necessary data access functions:

```
>(define-ADT 'shipment 'content 'quantity 'address 'cost))
   (Data Type shipment defined)

>(setf ORDER1 (make-shipment))
   ((content ?) (quantity ?) (address ?) (cost ?))

>(setf ORDER1 (set-shipment-content 'ORDER1 'WIDGETS))
   ((content WIDGETS) (quantity ?) (address ?) (cost ?))

>(setf ORDER1 (set-shipment-quantity 'ORDER1 1500))
   ((content WIDGETS) (quantity 1500) (address ?) (cost ?))

>(setf ORDER1 (set-shipment-address 'ORDER1
> '(24 Sussex Drive OTTAWA)))
   ((content WIDGETS) (quantity 1500) (address (24 Sussex Drive
      OTTAWA)) (cost ?))

>(setf ORDER1 (set-shipment-cost 'ORDER1 '$25000))
   ((content WIDGETS) (quantity 1500) (address (24 Sussex Drive
      OTTAWA)) (cost $25000))
```

---

[11]A more realistic example would obviously include other important data, such as the purchaser's address, expected delivery date, and so on.

```
>(shipment-content ORDER1)
   WIDGETS


>(shipment-p 'ORDER1)
   T
```

It should be noted that the grammar was "conveniently" defined to reflect the true nature of the data access functions defined by the DAF generator. In particular, no type checking was required of any of the values used to update an instance of a ⟨shipment⟩. Obviously, there are inappropriate values which would be accepted in an update. This suggests a possible modification to the DAF generator implementation, that is, determine an appropriate component recognizer and apply this, within the generated updater function, to any potential value prior to modifying the association list.

One final comment should be made concerning this example. Common LISP employs a "call by value" mechanism for parameter passing, and this is why `setf` is used each time a value is returned following the call to an updater function. Although it might seem reasonable to embed the `setf` assignment inside the updater function, applying it to the formal parameter would not have any effect on the argument that was bound to the formal parameter.

8.5 REPRESENTING SETS WITH FUNCTIONS

As a second example of functions defining functions, we consider the representation of sets by functions rather than the more common approach of representing sets by lists. One of the disadvantages of the latter, more popular approach, is the difficulty of representing infinite sets, such as the set of all numeric atoms. From another point of view, however, representing the set of all numeric atoms can be viewed as just the set of elements for which the `numberp` function returns T. Thus, in some sense, the `numberp` function itself represents the set of all numeric atoms by distinguishing those elements that belong to the set from those that do not.

In general, then, we can represent sets by suitable *membership* predicates, that is, by functions which return a Boolean value indicating whether or not a given item is a member of the set. For example, if the function $S(x)$ represents the set $\{a, b, c\}$, then $S(a)$, $S(b)$, and $S(c)$ should evaluate to true, with $S(x)$ evaluating to false for any other value of x. With this method of set representation, the problem is how to construct and manipulate the objects of the set abstract data type (ADT) in terms of this membership function.

First consider how we might specify a set ADT in Lisp, regardless of how we implement it. The fundamental property of sets is that they have members, so we specify the function (`member-p S elem`) to return T if `elem` is a member of `S`, NIL otherwise. We also need methods for constructing sets. Let the constant `empty-set` denote the set with no members. To construct sets with a single element in them, we specify the function (`make-singleton-set elem`) which returns such a set given its element `elem`. Finally, we specify the `make-union` constructor to construct a new set comprising all the elements that are in either of two given sets, and the `make-intersect` constructor which returns the set of all elements existing in both of two given sets. We thus require any implementation of the set ADT to provide functions implementing all these properties.

Now consider how the basic operations of our ADT can be implemented using membership predicates to represent sets. In Lisp, these membership predicates will just be Lisp functions that return T or NIL, indicating whether or not a given item is a member of the represented set. Thus implementation of the member-p function is straightforward: we apply the membership predicate representing the set to the given element and return the result:

```
(defun member-p (S elem)
    (funcall S elem))
```

Observe that member-p is a functional, since the argument S is a function.

Our set ADT must also provide constructor functions to provide the appropriate membership predicates representing the desired sets. These predicates will generally be represented by lambda expressions. Recall that the syntax for lambda expressions is as follows:

⟨anon-fn⟩ ::= (lambda ({ ⟨variable⟩ }) ⟨expression⟩)

From this definition we can implement a constructor function to build a lambda expression, given a list of formal parameters and an expression representing the body of the "anonymous" function:

```
(defun make-anon-fn (params body)
    (list 'lambda params body))
```

This constructor can be used in the body of all our functions whenever we wish to construct a lambda expression. While we could obviously construct the lists to provide S-Lisp representations of lambda expressions within the functions as required, the use of a constructor function hides the actual representation, which is in keeping with the data abstraction approach.

For example, the membership predicate which represents the empty set should return NIL when applied to any element, since no element is ever a member of the empty set. Therefore, the empty-set constant can be defined as follows:

```
(setf empty-set (make-anon-fn '(elem) 'NIL))
```

Note that empty-set is not the identifier of the function. What we wish to assign as values to variables, such as empty-set, are lambda expressions, so that the values of these identifiers can subsequently be used as the first element of a form. As we shall see presently, the constructor functions for making new sets will build forms inside lambda expressions, and the first element of these forms will be the value bound to a formal parameter of a constructor function.

To represent a set consisting of a single element, we need to construct a lambda expression of the form

```
(lambda (elem) (equal elem (quote Singleton)))
```

where ***Singleton*** is the data item corresponding to the single object that is in fact a member of the particular singleton set represented by the lambda expression.

To generate membership functions which represent singleton sets, we will define the constructor function `make-singleton-set`, which will return the appropriate lambda expression.[12]

```
(defun make-singleton-set (the-elem)
  (make-anon-fn
     '(elem)
     (build-fn-call 'equal 'elem (make-list-expr the-elem))))
```

To illustrate the effect of this constructor, we can use `make-singleton-set` to construct the appropriate representation for the set whose only element is the number 1:

```
(make-singleton-set 1) ⇒ (lambda (elem) (equal elem '1))
```

To construct sets with more than one member, we can define functionals which build new functions representing sets in terms of existing functions. For example, given the membership predicates for two sets, how does one describe the membership predicate which represents their union? To answer this, observe that any element in the union must be in one of the two sets. Therefore, we can apply the membership predicates for the two original sets to a given element. If either of the results is T, the element is in their union. In this case, the membership predicate representing the union must also return T; otherwise, it returns NIL.

The implementation of a `make-union` functional can use this logic to construct membership predicates which represent the union of two sets as follows:

```
(defun make-union (set-fn1 set-fn2)
  (make-anon-fn '(elem)
    (build-fn-call
       'or
       (build-fn-call set-fn1 'elem)
       (build-fn-call set-fn2 'elem))))
```

Here we see why lambda expressions were assigned as the values of identifiers, such as `empty-set`. The expression

```
(build-fn-call set-fn1 'elem)
```

constructs a form (*F* elem), where *F* is replaced by whatever lambda expression is bound to the formal parameter `set-fn1` when the function `make-union` is called. Later, if the lambda expression constructed by `make-union` is ever evaluated, then the form (*F* elem) will be evaluated, and whatever lambda-expression was used for *F* when the form was constructed will be applied to the value bound to `elem`.

---

[12]`make-singleton-set` uses the functions `make-fn-call` and `make-list-expr` defined in the preceding section (as well as Section 4.5) for constructing S-Lisp representations of ⟨fn-call⟩s and ⟨list-expr⟩s, respectively.

New sets can also be constructed using set intersection. A `make-intersect` functional can be constructed in a manner similar to that of `make-union`. In this case an element must be in both the original sets to be in their intersection:

```
(defun make-intersect (set-fn1 set-fn2)
  (make-anon-fn '(elem)
    (build-fn-call
      'and
      (build-fn-call set-fn1 'elem)
      (build-fn-call set-fn2 'elem)))))
```

The examples above illustrate the basic method for defining different operations on sets represented by membership predicates. A particular advantage of this representation is that infinite sets can be defined. Such sets cannot be explicitly represented by lists because lists are implemented as finite sequences. For example, it is not possible to represent the set of positive and negative integers by a list of integers. However, the system function `numberp` is in fact a membership predicate and therefore provides a function representation of the set.

A second limitation of the list representation of sets is the difficulty of defining the complement of a set explicitly. This is possible only when the universal set, U, is finite and known. The complement of a set, A, is the set of all elements in U that are not also members of A. The complement can be computed by determining the set difference: $U - A$. Such a set operation can be defined when sets are represented as functions in the following way:

```
(defun make-set-diff (fa fb)
  (make-anon-fn '(elem)
    (build-fn-call
      'and
      (build-fn-call fa 'elem)
      (build-fn-call 'not (build-fn-call fb 'elem)))))
```

In order to define set complement, we require a representation of the universal set:

```
(setf universal-set (make-anon-fn '(elem) 'T))
```

Since this function returns true for every argument, every element is a member of the universal set. With this constant defined we can construct the complement of any set using the following functional:

```
(defun make-complement (set-fn)
  (make-set-diff universal-set set-fn))
```

For example, the complement of the singleton set { 1 } can be assigned as the value of the identifier `not-one` as follows:

```
>(setf not-one (make-complement (make-singleton-set 1)))
(lambda (elem)
```

```
        (and ((lambda (elem) T) elem)
             (not ((lambda (elem) (equal elem '1)) elem)))))

>(funcall not-one 2)
   T
```

While these examples illustrate the power of a set representation based on membership predicates, there are other useful ways of extending the set ADT which cannot be implemented easily on a functional representation, but which do admit of straightforward implementation on a list representation. For example, if we specify a `subset` function to determine whether one set is a subset of another, we will not be able to implement it with a functional representation. In terms of the list representation, however, the implementation is straightforward.

In a sense, both the functional and the list representations provide only a partial implementation of an ideal fully extended set ADT. We can choose between the representations depending on the facilities actually needed in a given application, or we can develop an implementation based on more than one method of representation.

With multiple representation strategies, we will require functions which are able to provide transformations between representations when possible. For example, if one representation is based on the functional approach described in this section, we may want a way of constructing sets in a different representation by specifying their membership predicates. Without knowing what our exact representation for sets is, we could specify that the function (`functional-set fn`) returns an alternative representation of the set whose membership predicate is `fn`. For example, the call

(functional-set 'numberp)

specifies construction of the infinite set of all numeric atoms. While we can manipulate expressions such as (`functional-set fn`) symbolically, we must of course eventually define the function `functional-set` according to how the alternate set representation is implemented. Thus a fully robust set ADT is but another example of a symbolic computing problem.

8.6 STREAMS

We conclude this chapter by returning to the problem of generalized iteration, in particular, a means of performing iteration on infinite sequences. To extend the capabilities described previously to such sequences requires that a new data structure be defined to represent sequences, called a *stream*.

The motivation for streams comes from the observation that sequences implicitly impose an ordering on their elements. When we "scan" a sequence we begin by examining the first element, in effect partitioning the sequence into two components—the first element and the rest of the sequence. Having processed or otherwise examined the first element, we go on to process a new sequence consisting of all the elements left from the original sequence. Thus the first element of the new sequence is really the second element of the old sequence. We repeatedly define new sequences and examine their first elements in order to examine sequentially the elements of the original sequence.

This way of accessing elements of sequences is reflected in the functions provided to handle a particular type of sequence—the list. In this case we have functions `first` and `rest`, which provide precisely the type of access described. In particular, `rest` always returns a list, so we can apply it successively to a list removing more and more elements until the list is empty. If `rest` were applied to an infinite list repeatedly, new elements would be endlessly available.

The problem of representing an infinite number of objects was addressed in the preceding section by exploiting the fact that although we might need to represent an infinite set, only a finite number of elements from that set would ever be accessed. Put another way, we will only ever evaluate a membership function a finite number of times. Therefore, all the elements of a set need not be generated; all we really need to do is to generate the ones we require when we need them. It is this idea that can be employed in the representation of infinite sequences.

We begin first with the definition and implementation of a particular type of function called a *generator*. A generator is a function which returns a "new" value every time it is called. A trivial example is the function

```
(defun one () 1)
```

which tirelessly generates a "1" each time it is called. Thus the function `one` can be viewed as a generator of the sequence $1, 1, 1, \ldots$, and as we did with membership predicates, we can use a function to represent an infinite sequence. A more interesting generator is the system function found in many Lisp systems called `gensym`. In Common LISP this function produces new (uninterned) symbolic atoms each time it is called and is often used in programs as a way of introducing new identifiers during run time.

To describe how to define a "more interesting" user-defined generator, we consider the problem of constructing a generator for the positive integers. The obvious approach is to implement in the body of a function the basic increment statement `x := x + 1`. In Common LISP this statement can be expressed by

```
(setf x (+ x 1))
```

If `x` has been initialized, then each time the `setf` form is evaluated, the value of `x` will be increased by 1. Consequently, it is merely a matter of making this statement the body of a function to generate the integers:

```
(defun pos-integers ()
   (setf x (+ x 1)))
```

Each time the form (`pos-integers`) is evaluated, the next integer in the sequence $1, 2, 3, \ldots$ is returned, providing that x was initially set to 1. The disadvantage of this simple solution is that the identifier x is global to the function `pos-integers`. This means that it must be initialized externally, and it can be altered by some other, presumably inadvertent, reference to it made in some other context. The solution is to *encapsulate* x by defining the function corresponding to pos-integers inside a let form:[13]

```
(setf pos-integers
      (let ((x 0))
           #'(lambda ()
                (setf x (+ x 1)))))
```

Now, each time we evaluate the form (funcall pos-integers) we generate another positive integer. Notice that the functional funcall is required since pos-integers is not the identifier of a function, but rather evaluates to the function.

We can now proceed with a formal definition of the abstract data type *stream*. A stream is defined to be a pair consisting of a value, called the *first element of the stream*, and another stream, called the *rest of the stream*. The data access functions consist of selectors to access these two components, and a constructor to make new streams from existing ones by adding elements to the front of an existing stream. When streams are finite, a recognizer for the empty stream is required. Streams may also be updated by adding elements to the end of a stream. Obviously, the implementation of the data access functions depends on the actual representation of a stream. Streams provide the data model for the processing of input and output in Common LISP.

To implement generalized mapping functions for infinite sequences, we will represent these sequences by an appropriately defined stream data type. In particular, a stream will be a list pair consisting of the first element and an encapsulated generating function for producing the next element. The data access functions for this representation are as follows:

```
(defun make-stream (init-val gen-fn)
   (list init-val gen-fn))

(defun first-stream (stream)
   (first stream))

(defun rest-stream (stream)
   (make-stream (funcall (second stream)) (second stream)))
```

Observe how rest-stream, when called, evaluates the generator and constructs a new stream which corresponds to the rest of the original stream. In other words, the next element need not be calculated until it is actually needed. This technique of deferring the evaluation of a given expression until necessary is called *lazy* or *delayed evaluation*.

Using these functions, the positive integers can be implemented as a stream:

```
>(setf s1 (make-stream (funcall pos-integers) pos-integers))
```

---

[13]*Encapsulation* is the technique of limiting the scope of definition of a symbol, so that any value assigned within a particular context is not accessible outside it. Winston and Horn [WH89] give a very good treatment of encapsulation techniques for Common LISP programming.

```
>(first-stream s1)
1

>(setf s2 (rest-stream s1))

>(first-stream s2)
2

>(setf s3 (rest-stream s2))

>(first-stream s3)
3
```

To implement a mapping function equivalent to mapcar, it is important that we do not evaluate the sequence, nor attempt to apply the mapped function to each element, since it is infinite. Instead, our mapping function should construct a new stream with only the first element defined. With this in mind, the implementation is as follows:

```
(defun map-stream (fn stream)
  (make-stream
     (funcall fn (first-stream stream))
        #'(lambda ()
              (map-stream  fn (rest-stream stream))))))
```

As an example of its application, mapstream can be used to construct a stream representation of all the positive even integers from all the positiveintegers by applying the mapped function

```
#'(lambda (x) (* x 2))
```

to each element in the stream S1:

```
>(setf pos-integers (let ((x 0))
>                            #'(lambda () (setf x (+ x 1))))))

>(setf s1 (make-stream (funcall pos-integers) pos-integers))

>(first s1)
1

>(setf s2 (map-stream #'(lambda (x) (* x 2)) s1))

>(first s2)
2

>(setf s2 (rest-stream s2))

>(first s2)
4
```

8.7 EXERCISES

8.1. Write a function `my-map` which takes two arguments, a list and a function, and applies the function to each element of the list, returning a list of the results. Do *not* use any of the mapping functions defined in Common LISP.

8.2. Write a function `treemap` which takes a function and tree and applies the function to every leaf in the tree.

8.3. Using `find-if`, write a functional `exists` which takes a predicate and a list as arguments and returns T (true) if at least one of the elements in the list satisfies the predicate specified in the first argument. For example,

$$(\text{exists } \text{\#'numberp } \text{'(A B 3 C))} \Rightarrow T$$

since 3 is a numeric atom. What constraint on the predicate is required?

8.4. Using `find-if` and `funcall`, write a function `all` which takes two arguments, a function of one variable, and a list. The function `all` returns T (true) if its first argument, interpreted as a predicate, is true for every element in the second argument (the list). For example,

$$(\text{all } \text{\#'numberp } \text{'(1 2 3 4 5))} \Rightarrow T$$

since 1, 2, 3, 4, and 5 are all numeric atoms. Need the predicate be constrained?

8.5. In this chapter it was demonstrated how it is possible to represent a set of elements without repetition by a function P, where the expression (P X) evaluates to T if X is a member of the set. Define a function `set-delete` which takes a set and an atom, and deletes that atom from the set. Your implementation should use the data access functions for S-Lisp defined in Sections 4.5 and 8.4.

8.6. When their arguments are identifiers or lambda expressions, the `apply` and `funcall` functions are redundant in that each can be defined in terms of `eval`. Nevertheless, circumstances often make one or the other preferable to `eval`. Construct simple examples to illustrate when `apply` or `funcall` are more convenient. Write implementations of `apply` and `funcall`, called `My-apply` and `My-funcall`, in terms of `eval`.

8.7. Without using the function `remove-duplicates`, write a function (`mapunion fn lst`) which applies the function specified by `fn` to each element in `lst`, and then computes the set union of the results, eliminating duplicate elements. For simplicity, you may assume that the `fn` when applied to each element of the `lst` returns a list. The following example illustrates how `mapunion` works:

```
>(mapunion #'rest '((1 B) (2 D B) (3 C D)))
  (B D C)
```

8.8. In "game-playing" programs, the consequences of alternative moves can be reflected by a data structure described in Section 3.10, called an AND/OR tree. Initially, only the leaves of the tree are assigned values. These values identify which leaves correspond to winning positions and which positions are losing ones. To recognize which is which, a test predicate is applied to the value of the node.

To determine if a winning move exists, a function `winner` is applied to the root of the tree. This function takes two arguments, an AND/OR tree and the test predicate for evaluating leaves, and evaluates the internal nodes (nonleaves) of a tree as follows:

- If the current node is a leaf, return the result of applying the test predicate to the leaf.
- If the node is on an even-numbered level of the tree (the root is on level 0, its descendents on level 1), return T if one of its successors returns T.
- If the node is on an odd level, return T if all its successors return T.
- Otherwise, return NIL.

Implement the function winner in Common LISP, and test it on a tree whose leaves are labeled by numeric and nonnumeric atoms. To represent the AND/OR tree, define with a GRAIL grammar a suitable list representation. Note that a node may have any number of descendents. Your test predicate should return true only if the value of the leaf label is WIN.

8.9. Some programming languages provide a feature called *partial application*, which permits some of the formal parameters to be assigned values without actually evaluating the function. The result of partial application is to produce a new function similar to the one from which it was defined, but with fewer free parameters since some have been constrained. For example, a function (add10 X) that always adds 10 to its parameter X could be obtained from the more general function (+ X Y) by constraining X always to have the value 10.

(a) Let FN be a function with n formal parameters expressed as a lambda expression. Write a Common LISP function (partial-apply FN Z) that returns as its value a function that is like FN but with one less parameter. The first parameter of FN is replaced in the new function by the fixed value Z.

(b) Suppose that FN was the name of a user-defined function, rather than a lambda expression. Define an implementation for partial-apply to accommodate this possibility.

8.10. Write a function (finite-list lst) that returns a generator function for the argument lst, which specifies a particular finite list. As an illustration, the following example defines the value of AB to be a generator function for the list (A B). Successive calls to the function generate successive elements of the list. When all elements have been generated the function returns NIL:

```
>(setf AB (finite-list '(A B))

>(funcall AB)
 A

>(funcall AB)
 B

>(funcall AB)
 NIL
```

8.11. Write a function copy-stream that makes a copy of a given stream. The copy should be a "genuine" one; that is, modifications to one copy should not affect the structure of the other.

8.12. In Exercise 2.10, the reader explored the representation of sets by lists, while Section 8.5 described their representation using membership functions. A third possibility, which captures some of the flavor of the list representation, is to use streams.

    (a) Determine which of the set operations of *union*, *intersection*, *complement* and *set membership* can be implemented with streams as operands, if only finite sets are considered.

    (b) Which operations are possible when the operands are streams representing infinite sets?

    (c) Discuss the strengths and weaknesses of using streams to represent sets.

8.13. The auxiliary function `update-assoc-list` was defined in Section 8.4 to support maker and updater functions generated by `define-ADT`. Given an association list which is some instance of an ADT, `update-assoc-list` is used to update the value associated with a given indicator. In performing this operation, it makes a new copy of the association list up to the point of the indicator. Show how `update-assoc-list` can be programmed to avoid this copying using destructive list processing operations. Comment on the safety of the destructive list processing operations in this application.

9

Metaprogramming

As introduced in Chapter 1, *metaprogramming* refers to the application of symbolic computing techniques to programs as data objects, that is, the development of programs about programs. The Small Lisp interpreter of Section 6.3 is an example of such a metaprogram, based on the S-Lisp representation of Small Lisp programs described in Section 4.5. The ability to manipulate programs as data objects makes many other interesting applications possible, as well. In fact, this is why Lisp systems routinely use the S-Lisp form; the ease of manipulating Lisp programs as Lisp data objects means that Lisp systems can provide a large number of useful metaprograms not commonly available in other programming environments.

Just as symbolic computing applications in general can be classified according to their input/output characteristics, so can metaprograms. The analyzer category consists of metaprograms which take programs as input and produce nonprogram output. This includes the Small Lisp interpreter of Section 6.3, metaprograms to produce cross-reference listings of a given source program, *checker* metaprograms to look for programming errors, and others. The generator category includes utilities for automatically generating programs or program components from nonprogram input. For example, the data access function (DAF) generator described in Section 8.4 is in this category. The manipulation category consists of metaprograms which process programs to produce modified versions thereof. In Section 9.2 we shall examine *program transformation* metaprograms which modify programs to change their performance characteristics without changing their semantics. Finally, the translator category in-

200

cludes compilers which translate programs into a lower-level language for efficient execution, as well as tools for source-to-source translation between high-level languages.

In this chapter, we will consider metaprograms written in Common LISP to process Small Lisp programs as data objects. Common LISP is thus said to be the *host language* of the metaprograms, while Small Lisp is the *target language*. We will illustrate example inputs and outputs for our metaprograms in the m-Lisp syntax of Small Lisp, in order to clearly distinguish between the programs being manipulated and the metaprograms that do so. Of course, our metaprograms will actually be written to process the S-Lisp form of Small Lisp as defined in Section 4.5.[1] We could also use Small Lisp as the host language, just as we did in the implementation of the Small Lisp interpreter in Section 6.3. In employing Common LISP as a host language, however, we will be taking advantage of some of the programming features described in the preceding two chapters—in particular, features for high-level iteration.

9.1 PROGRAM CHECKING TOOLS

Program checking tools are analysis metaprograms designed to find errors or anomalies in programs. For example, a tool could be defined to check Small Lisp programs for function calls which have an incorrect number of arguments according to the function definition. Such a condition is always an indication of an error. Other tools can check for situations which are not necessarily in error, but seem anomalous. For example, a programmer might define a temporary variable in a let expression, but never get around to using it.

Program checkers may be found as integral components of compilers or as stand-alone tools. In general, the checking facilities found in compilers tend to be very cost-effective, so that they are worth using every time a program is compiled. For example, the type analysis performed by a Pascal compiler is quite straightforward (since the types of all Pascal variables must be declared) and is useful for both type checking and the generation of efficient code using type information. Furthermore, many kinds of common programming error result in type violations, so that type checking is a very effective tool for program debugging.

Stand-alone program checkers can be useful in various situations. First of all, a given compiler may not implement the checking facilities desired. For example, many compilers for the C programming language do very little checking, relying on programmers to make use of a stand-alone program checker called "lint." More important, certain kinds of program checking are inappropriate for use every time a program is compiled. For example, type analysis is expensive for weakly typed languages such as Small Lisp and cannot always yield definitive results. Rather than paying for this every time a program is compiled, a stand-alone tool allows the programmer to perform this checking as and when desired. Other types of checking may only occasionally give rise to useful error reports, but can be worth trying when a particularly nefarious bug needs to be isolated. A software development shop may also find it useful to develop its own program checkers in-house to enforce local programming standards or to per-

---

[1]However, we can convert from m-Lisp to S-Lisp and back again with the `slispify` and `mlispify` programs described in Appendix B.

form *program-specific* checks (i.e., checks that are only relevant to a given (presumably large) application program or system).

9.1.1 Type Checking for Small Lisp

Small Lisp programs often fail due to type errors encountered at run time; for example, supplying an atom as the second argument to `cons`. If it were possible to find all occurrences of such errors by analysis of a program before its execution, debugging could be simplified considerably. In general, however, this is not possible. For example, consider the following program, consisting solely of the function `sqrfirst`.

$$\text{sqrfirst}[x] = \text{times}[\text{first}[x]; \text{first}[x]]$$

Without knowing what data is to be supplied to `sqrfirst`, it is impossible to know whether or not a run-time error will occur.

Nevertheless, it is possible to detect many situations in which run-time errors will definitely occur. For example, the expression `plus[cons[x; y]; z]` is erroneous because `cons` always yields a list as its result, while `plus` requires a numeric atom as its first argument.[2] In other cases, it may be possible to definitely rule out run-time type errors; for example, the type of the first argument to `plus` is always correct in `plus[times[x; y]; z]`.

Now consider the design of a type checker for Small Lisp. Its main goal is to find all situations which would definitely lead to type errors at run time and report them as such. A secondary goal is to find potential run-time errors—situations in which an error cannot be ruled out—and report them as warnings. However, since this may lead to many spurious messages, a production version of the checker should implement it as an option under user control.

Types in Small Lisp. Our type checker will work with the native data types of Small Lisp, classified according to the hierarchy shown in Figure 9.1. In this diagram, branches indicate a subtype relationship—specifically that the lower type along a branch is a subtype of the upper type. This is significant in Small Lisp, because any object of a subtype may be used wherever an object of its supertype, or its super-supertype, and so on, may be required. For example, the numeric atom which results from a `plus` operation may be quite legally supplied as the S-expression required as the first argument to `cons`. On the other hand, the list resulting from `cons` may not be supplied as an argument to `plus` because the list type is not a subtype of the numeric atom type.

In addition to the standard types of Small Lisp, the type hierarchy also introduces the special type "void" to represent the "type" of the `error` primitive. In fact, `error` never returns a value, so void is actually the *empty type* (i.e., the type containing no values). Hence void is a subtype of every other type, making the `error` primitive acceptable in any context.

We can represent the possible types of Small Lisp expressions in Lisp according to the GRAIL rules given in Figure 9.2.

----

[2] We ignore degenerate examples such as `F --> plus[cons[x; y]; z]`, in which case a run-time error never arises because the erroneous expression is never evaluated.

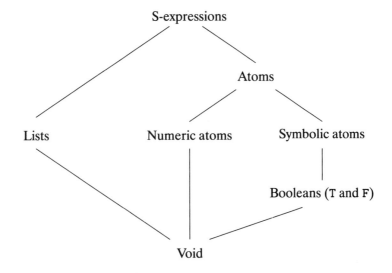

Figure 9.1   Hierarchy of Small Lisp types.

```
        ⟨type⟩ ::= ⟨arbitrary-type⟩ | ⟨list-type⟩ | ⟨atom-type⟩ |
                   ⟨symbol-type⟩ | ⟨numeric-type⟩ | ⟨boolean-type⟩ |
                   ⟨void-type⟩
⟨arbitrary-type⟩ ::= S-EXP
     ⟨list-type⟩ ::= LIST
     ⟨atom-type⟩ ::= ATOM
   ⟨symbol-type⟩ ::= SYM
  ⟨numeric-type⟩ ::= NUM
  ⟨boolean-type⟩ ::= BOOL
     ⟨void-type⟩ ::= VOID
```

Figure 9.2   GRAIL grammar for Small Lisp types

The last seven rules shown are lexical rules whose R.H.S. consists of an atom. As described in Section 4.2.4, such rules specify the definition of data access "constants," such as

```
(setf arbitrary-type (quote S-EXP))
```

Of course, the recognizers `arbitrary-type-p`, and so on, are also specified by virtue of the alternation rule.

We can now implement our type compatibility relation on this representation for types. An actual type is compatible with an expected type if it is the same as the expected type or a subtype of it, that is, if it is *included* within the expected type. The function `included-type-p` checks whether `type1` is included in `type2`:

```
(defun included-type-p (type1 type2)
  (cond ((void-type-p type1) T) ((void-type-p type2) NIL)
        ((boolean-type-p type2) (boolean-type-p type1))
        ((numeric-type-p type2) (numeric-type-p type1))
        ((symbol-type-p type2)
          (cond ((symbol-type-p type1) T)
                (T (boolean-type-p type1))))
        ((atom-type-p type2)
          (cond ((atom-type-p type1) T)
                ((included-type-p type1 symbol-type) T)
                (T (numeric-type-p type1))))
        ((list-type-p type2) (list-type-p type1))
        ((arbitrary-type-p type2) T)))
```

Whenever the type of an expression is compatible with its context, we can be certain
that no run-time type error will occur.

Type signatures.   The *type signature* of a function specifies the types of objects taken and returned by that function. For example, using mathematical notation,
we might specify the type signatures of cons and plus as follows:

cons : S-expression × List → List

plus : Numeric atom × Numeric atom → Numeric atom

Alternatively, type signatures may be represented as Lisp data objects according to
the following GRAIL rule:

⟨signature⟩ ::= ((⟨argument-types:type⁺⟩) ⟨result-type:type⟩)

Using this specification, we can now represent the type signatures of cons and plus
as follows:

```
((S-EXP LIST) LIST)
((NUM NUM) NUM)
```

The type signatures for the other Small Lisp primitives can be specified similarly.

Our type checker can be defined to use these signatures to verify that the expressions supplied in any given context match the type of expression expected. Assume that the type signatures of all the functions in our program, both primitive and
user-defined, are made available in a *signature environment*, which provides the operations apply-signature-env and extend-signature-env defined on a suitable
representation following the techniques of Chapter 6. Also assume that the types of
all the global constants are supplied in a *variable-type environment* with the operations
apply-var-type-env and extend-var-type-env. This provides all the information
necessary to check systematically all the expressions in a Small Lisp program.

Reporting type errors.   The only issue that remains is what the output of
the type-checking program should be. The goal is to report the errors and warnings
that occur in a manner which correlates them with the original source program. One
approach would be to define the concept of "annotated source programs" as a data

type for program listings containing error messages. However, we will take a more
expedient approach which simply returns a modified copy of the source program as
output. The idea is that erroneous expressions will be embedded in function calls to
the TYPE-ERROR and POTENTIAL-TYPE-ERROR "functions." However, these are not
functions at all, merely devices to mark the errors in the source text. For example, in
the m-Lisp notation,the expression

$$plus[cons[x; ()]; 2]$$

would be returned as

$$plus[TYPE-ERROR[cons[x; ()]]; 2]$$

indicating that the cons function-call did not have the type expected of it The annota-
tion process can be implemented with the following function check-expr, assuming
the existence of an appropriate function type-of-expr to return the type of an expression in the context of given signature and variable-type environments.

```
(defun check-expr-type (expr expected-type signatures var-types)
   (let ((expr-type (type-of-expr expr signatures var-types)))
      (cond ((included-type-p expr-type expected-type) expr)
            ((included-type-p expected-type expr-type)
             (make-fn-call
               (make-identifier 'POTENTIAL-TYPE-ERROR)
               (list expr)))
            (T (make-fn-call
               (make-identifier 'TYPE-ERROR)
               (list expr)))))))
```

Note that a potential type error is reported if the type of an expression is a proper
supertype of the expected type; in this case, we do not know whether the actual value
of the expression at run time will be of the expected type.
   The type-of-expr function is defined as follows:

```
(defun type-of-expr (expr signatures var-types)
   (cond ((numeric-expr-p expr) numeric-type)
         ((symbol-expr-p expr) symbol-type)
         ((list-expr-p expr) list-type)
         ((identifier-p expr)
          (apply-var-type-env var-types (id-name expr)))
         ((fn-call-p expr)
          (result-type
            (apply-signature-env signatures (id-name (callee expr)))))
         ((cond-expr-p expr)
          (union-of-clause-types (clauses expr) signatures var-types))
         ((let-expr-p expr)
          (type-of-expr (final-expr expr) signatures
            (add-local-var-types
              (local-defs expr) signatures var-types)))))
```

The appropriate type is returned immediately for numeric atoms, symbolic atoms, or lists. The type of variables and function calls is determined by application of the appropriate environment. In the case of conditional expressions, note that an object returned may result from *any* one of the conditional clauses. Thus the type of a conditional expression is the *union* of the types of the result parts of each conditional clause. The type of a let expression is simply the type of its final expression, but determined in the context of an extended environment of variable types.

Determining the union of two types simply means returning the smallest type that includes all the values of both types.

```
(defun union-types (type1 type2)
  (cond ((included-type-p type1 type2) type2)
        ((included-type-p type2 type1) type1)
        ((list-type-p type1) arbitrary-type)
        ((list-type-p type2) arbitrary-type)
        (T atom-type)))
```

Given this function, the union of all the clause types can be determined using two high-level loops. First of all, mapcar is used to produce a list of the result types for each clause, and then reduce is used to accumulate these successively into a union.[3]

```
(defun union-of-clause-types (clauses sigs types)
  (reduce #'union-types
          (mapcar #'(lambda (clause)
                      (type-of-expr (result clause) sigs types))
                  clauses)))
```

Turning to let expressions, the function add-local-var-types is used to extend the environment of variable-types to include types for the local variables of a let expression. This operation is conceptually similar to the environment updating within the Small Lisp interpreter's extend-local-env function described in Section 6.3.1. Rather than the recursive approach taken there, however, we can use reduce to process each local definition (def) in turn and accumulate the successively extended environment:

```
(defun add-local-var-types (defs sigs var-type-env)
  (reduce #'(lambda (extended-env-so-far def)
              (extend-var-type-env
                extended-env-so-far
                (id-name (local-var def))
                (type-of-expr (local-val def) sigs var-type-env)))
          defs
          :initial-value var-type-env))
```

Note that the initial-value of the environment being accumulated is the original var-type-env passed in.

---

[3]Note that this could be expressed more directly using the map-accum functional described in Section 8.4.

The functions above allow us to check a single expression in the context of its expected type. Now consider how we can systematically type check all the subexpressions of an expression, as well as the expression itself. The general strategy is to work inside-out, checking and returning annotated copies of the subexpression. The expression is then rebuilt and type-checked as appropriate. For example, in typechecking a function call, the first step is to type- check the arguments. The following type-check-args function does this, given the arguments and their expected types (which can be determined from the function's signature).

```
(defun type-check-args (args e-types sigs types)
  (mapcar #'(lambda (arg e-type)
              (type-check arg e-type sigs types))
          args
          e-types))
```

The mapcar iteration processes each argument in turn, returning a rebuilt list of possibly annotated arguments.

Similarly, the first step in checking a conditional expression is to check each of the clauses.

```
(defun type-check-clauses (clauses e-type sigs types)
  (mapcar #'(lambda (clause)
              (make-clause
                (type-check (predicate clause) boolean-type sigs types)
                (type-check (result clause) e-type sigs types)))
          clauses)
```

Note that the predicate of each clause is checked with boolean-type as its expected type, while each result part is checked in the context of the expected type of the conditional expression.

Now consider how the subexpressions within the local definitions of a let expression are checked. Each local value expression should be type-checked in the context of an arbitrary expected-type, because there is no restriction placed on the types of local variables.

```
(defun type-check-local-defs (defs sigs types)
  (mapcar #'(lambda (def)
              (make-local-def
                (local-var def)
                (type-check (local-val defs) arbitrary-type sigs types)))
          defs))
```

With these procedures to type-check subexpressions of the structured expression types, we can now implement the recursive driver of our expression-checking algorithm.

```
(defun type-check (expr expected-type signatures var-types)
  (cond ((fn-call-p expr)
```

```
              (let ((arg-types
                        (argument-types
                          (apply-signature-env signatures
                             (id-name (callee expr)))))))
                 (check-expr-type
                   (make-fn-call (callee expr)
                      (type-check-args
                         (arguments expr) arg-types signatures var-types))
                      expected-type signatures var-types)))
             ((cond-expr-p expr)
               (make-cond-expr
                 (type-check-clauses
                    (clauses expr) expected-type signatures var-types)))
             ((let-expr-p expr)
               (make-let-expr
                 (type-check-local-defs
                    (local-defs expr) signatures var-types)
                 (type-check
                    (final-expr expr) expected-type signatures
                    (add-local-var-types
                       (local-defs expr) signatures var-types))))
             (T (check-expr-type expr expected-type signatures var-types))))
```

In the case of function calls, note that the types of the arguments are determined from the function signature and used in checking the arguments. The function call is then rebuilt and is itself checked by check-expr-type described previously. Conditional expressions are rebuilt similarly from the checked conditional clauses. However, there is no point in checking the type of the entire expression; any type error here would already have been more precisely indicated in the type-checking of the result parts of one or more clauses. Similarly, a reconstructed let expression does not have to be itself checked once its final expression has been checked.

Given this expression checker, it is then possible to construct routines to check function and constant definitions. For example, the body of a function definition is checked in the context of an expected type which is the result type specified by the function's signature. The only wrinkle is that the variable-type environment used in checking the function body must be updated from the global environment to include the appropriate bindings between the function parameter names and their associated types as specified by the function signature.

The type-checking algorithm described here assumes that appropriate variable-type and signature information is available for all the global constants and functions that will be encountered. In some languages, such information is made readily available through type declarations. Unfortunately, this is not the case in Small Lisp or other Lisp languages. However, the equivalent effect can be achieved by requiring the user to specify the appropriate types and signatures separately. In this case, the driver routine for the type checker would have to provide a convenient form of input for such type and signature information and a way of converting such information to the appropriate variable-type and signature environments.

9.1.2 Type Inference

Rather than requiring the user to specify types and signatures as input to the type-checking algorithm, it is possible to work them out automatically. Such a process is called *type inference*. Often, the types and signatures determined by automatic type inference will be exactly those that the user would have specified. Sometimes, however, the typing may be reasonable but not reflect the programmer's intent. For example, the type signature inferred for a function

$$\texttt{extend-numlist[n; nums] = cons[n; nums]}$$

will be

$$\text{S-expression} \times \text{List} \to \text{List}$$

although the user might have intended

$$\text{Numeric atom} \times \text{List} \to \text{List}$$

Furthermore, if the program is erroneous, the inferred typing may be incorrect. Nevertheless, the information determined can be useful in finding type errors and makes the type checker considerably more convenient to use.

The basis for type inference in Small Lisp can be illustrated by the following example function to count the number of elements of a list which are themselves lists.

```
count-sublists[lst] =
  [endp[lst] --> 0;
   listp[first[lst]] --> plus[count-sublists[rest[lst]]; 1];
   otherwise --> count-sublists[rest[lst]]]
```

We can work out the type signature for `count-sublists` by examining the ways in which its parameter `lst` is used and the types of values that may be returned. The parameter `lst` is used as an argument to the functions `endp`, `first`, and `rest`, which have the following type signatures:

$$\texttt{endp} : \text{List} \to \text{Boolean}$$
$$\texttt{first} : \text{List} \to \text{S-expression}$$
$$\texttt{rest} : \text{List} \to \text{List}$$

Thus `lst` is always treated as an object of type "List," so it is reasonable to infer that that is its type.

Now consider the possible types of returned values. The returned type will be the union of the types returned by each clause of the conditional expression. Clearly, the first two clauses each return an object of type "Numeric atom." The third clause is a recursive call, whose type is the type of object returned by the lower-level call to `count-sublists`, which may in turn be the type of a yet lower-level call, and so on. Eventually, the recursion must terminate with one of the first two clauses, however. The type of object returned at that point and hence at all recursive levels is "Numeric atom." In this way, we infer that the signature of `count-sublists` should be

$$\text{List} \to \text{Numeric atom.}$$

Inferring the types of arguments is generally more complex than illustrated in the analysis of count-sublists. Consider for example, the following function:

$$\text{n-and-its-square[n]} = \text{cons[n; times[n; n]]}$$

Here the parameter n is used as the "S-expression" required as the first argument of cons and as the "Numeric atom" arguments required by times. Since the parameter must be acceptable in both these contexts, its type should be the *intersection* of the corresponding types (i.e., the type whose values consist of the intersection of the sets of values of the two given types). In this case, the argument type should be "Numeric atom," since it is a proper subtype of "S-expression."

Further complications in argument-type inference arise in analyzing conditional expressions. Consider the following function to determine the last character of an atom.

```
last-char[a] =
  [numberp[a] --> rem[a; 10];
   otherwise --> last[explode[a]]]
```

The parameter a is used as an S-expression, a numeric atom, and a symbolic atom, respectively, by numberp, rem, and explode. If we simply take the intersection of all these types, we end up with void, because there are no numeric atoms which are also symbolic atoms. However, individual arguments passed to last-char are never used in both numeric and symbolic atom contexts. Rather, they may be used in *either* of these contexts, depending on the control flow.

In general, the type of an argument should be determined as the union of the types established for it along each *control flow path*. Along any given path, the type of the argument must be the intersection of the type contexts in which it is used. In the example, the type along the path involving the rem function is numeric atom, while that along the path involving the explode function is symbolic atom. Hence the type of the argument to last-char is "atom."

These rules for inferring the signature of a function from its definition assume that the types and signatures of all other constants and functions are given. In general, however, user-defined constants and functions will depend on other user-defined constants and functions, perhaps even recursively. How is it be possible, then, to work out appropriate types and signatures for a complete set of such constant and function definitions that comprise a Small Lisp program?

In general, the rules for type inference can be thought of as equations specifying the relevant types associated with one definition in terms of the types associated with other definitions. For example, consider the following functions to take a list of numbers and, respectively, add either the odd ones or the even ones to a given accumulator value.

```
add-odd-nums[nums; accum] =
  [endp[nums] --> accum;
   otherwise --> add-even-nums[rest[nums];  plus[first[nums];accum]]]

add-even-nums[nums; accum] =
```

```
            [endp[nums] --> accum;
             otherwise --> add-odd-nums[rest[nums]; accum]]
```

Let $\mathcal{R}(f)$ denote the result type of a function f and $\mathcal{A}_i(f)$ denote the type of the ith argument of f. Then the type inference equations for our example are as follows:

$$\mathcal{R}(\texttt{add-odd-nums}) = \mathcal{A}_2(\texttt{add-odd-nums}) \cup \mathcal{R}(\texttt{add-even-nums})$$
$$\mathcal{R}(\texttt{add-even-nums}) = \mathcal{A}_2(\texttt{add-even-nums}) \cup \mathcal{R}(\texttt{add-odd-nums})$$
$$\mathcal{A}_1(\texttt{add-odd-nums}) = \mathcal{A}_1(\texttt{endp}) \cup (\mathcal{A}_1(\texttt{endp}) \cap \mathcal{A}_1(\texttt{rest}) \cap \mathcal{A}_1(\texttt{first}))$$
$$\mathcal{A}_2(\texttt{add-odd-nums}) = \mathcal{R}(\texttt{add-odd-nums}) \cup \mathcal{A}_2(\texttt{plus})$$
$$\mathcal{A}_1(\texttt{add-even-nums}) = \mathcal{A}_1(\texttt{endp}) \cup (\mathcal{A}_1(\texttt{endp}) \cap \mathcal{A}_1(\texttt{rest}))$$
$$\mathcal{A}_2(\texttt{add-even-nums}) = \mathcal{R}(\texttt{add-even-nums}) \cup \mathcal{A}_2(\texttt{add-odd-nums})$$

Substituting in the known types for the primitive functions, the latter four equations become

$$\mathcal{A}_1(\texttt{add-odd-nums}) = \text{List} \cup (\text{List} \cap \text{List} \cap \text{List})$$
$$\mathcal{A}_2(\texttt{add-odd-nums}) = \mathcal{R}(\texttt{add-odd-nums}) \cup \text{Numeric atom}$$
$$\mathcal{A}_1(\texttt{add-even-nums}) = \text{List} \cup (\text{List} \cap \text{List})$$
$$\mathcal{A}_2(\texttt{add-even-nums}) = \mathcal{R}(\texttt{add-even-nums}) \cup \mathcal{A}_2(\texttt{add-odd-nums})$$

In this example, the equations are satisfied with the following type assignments:

$$\mathcal{R}(\texttt{add-odd-nums}) = \mathcal{R}(\texttt{add-even-nums}) = \text{Numeric atom}$$
$$\mathcal{A}_1(\texttt{add-odd-nums}) = \mathcal{A}_1(\texttt{add-even-nums}) = \text{List}$$
$$\mathcal{A}_2(\texttt{add-odd-nums}) = \mathcal{A}_2(\texttt{add-even-nums}) = \text{Numeric atom}$$

These assignments correspond to add-odd-nums and add-even-nums each having the following type signature, as desired:

$$\text{List} \times \text{Numeric atom} \to \text{Numeric atom}$$

Unfortunately, however, there are other solutions to this set of equations, resulting in the signatures

$$\text{List} \times \text{Atom} \to \text{Atom}$$

and

$$\text{List} \times \text{S-expression} \to \text{S-expression}$$

These solutions are inferior because they give unnecessarily general result and argument types to the functions. The goal, then, is to find a *minimal* solution, that is, one which yields the most restrictive types possible.

In general, the minimal solution to a type inference problem can be determined using an iterative technique involving converging "approximations." Initially, we start with an approximation of "void" for each of the unknown types. At each iteration we compute a new set of approximations by substituting the current approximations into the R.H.S. of each of the equations. As the iteration proceeds, the types determined will gradually converge, moving up the hierarchy of Figure 9. The iterative process terminates when the new set of approximations is the same as the previous set; at this point the approximations are no longer approximate, but represent a valid solution to the type inference equations. Because the approximations start with "void" and add specific type information only as actually required by the equations, the solution determined will also be minimal.

The type inference problem considered here is an instance of a general class of *data flow analysis* problems that can arise in metaprogramming applications. Many other interesting data flow problems arise in the construction of optimizing compilers and can be solved using techniques similar to that shown here for type inference [ASU86].

9.2 PROGRAM TRANSFORMATION

Program transformation is an important metaprogramming application which allows for the structured development of efficient software. In program transformation, automated rules are used to transform working programs into more efficient equivalents. This allows a two-stage strategy to be used for the development of efficient software: an initial high-level programming stage in which programs are developed without any premature concern for efficiency, followed if necessary, by a performance improvement stage in which transformations are applied to increase efficiency.

There are many kinds of program transformation which can be applied to improve efficiency. We consider a few examples only in the following sections.

9.2.1 In-Line Coding

One important program transformation is *in-line coding*, the replacement of a function call by a modified copy of the function body. This transformation is very useful for improving the efficiency of programs written using data abstraction, by systematically replacing calls to data access functions by equivalent in-line code. It can also be the starting point for a more intensive program transformation process: Once a function has been coded in-line, its detailed implementation can be optimized in the context of the particular way it is used.

In Small Lisp, functions can usually be coded in-line using a simple macro expansion process. Given a function call with arguments $a_1, a_2, \ldots, a_n$ and a corresponding function definition with parameter-names $p_1, p_2, \ldots, p_n$, a function call may be replaced by a copy of the body of the function definition, in which each occurrence of a parameter p_i is replaced by the corresponding argument a_i. For example, given the definition

$$\texttt{list2[x; y] = cons[x; cons[y; ()]]}$$

one can code the expression `list2["-"; x]` in-line to get the equivalent expression

$$\texttt{cons["-"; cons[x; ()]]}$$

Often, however, macro expansion yields less efficient code due to duplicated subexpressions. For example, suppose that the expression `abs[costly-calc[x]]` were to be coded in-line using the following definition of the absolute value function.

```
abs[n] =
 [lessp[n; 0] --> minus[0; n];
  otherwise --> n]
```

The result would be the expression

```
[lessp[costly-calc[x]; 0] --> minus[0; costly-calc[x]];
 otherwise --> costly-calc[x]]
```

which doubles the cost of a costly calculation.

Another problem with in-line coding by substitution is that name conflicts may arise if the function body contains a let expression. For example, consider how the function

```
max-of-3[x; y; z] =
 {w = [greaterp[x; y] --> x;
          otherwise --> y] :
  [greaterp[w; z] --> w;
   otherwise --> z]}
```

might be in-line coded in the expression max-of-3[u; v; w]. Using straightforward substitution of the parameters would yield

```
{w = [greaterp[u; v] --> u;
         otherwise --> v] :
 [greaterp[w; w] --> w;
  otherwise --> w]}
```

which is clearly incorrect. Such name conflicts can be resolved, however, by appropriately renaming let-expression variables.

There is also a second approach to in-line coding which avoids the code duplication and name conflict problems. Instead of substituting parameters into the function body, the idea is to enclose it in a let expression to bind each parameter to its associated argument. In the absolute value example, the in-line equivalent to abs[costly-calc[x]] becomes

```
{n = costly-calc[x] :
 [lessp[n; 0] --> minus[0; n];
  otherwise --> n]}
```

This improves on the previous version by avoiding the repeated calculation of costly-calc[x]. In the case of max-of-3[u; v; w], the in-line coded result is

```
{x = u; y = v; z = w :
 {w = [greaterp[x; y] --> x;
          otherwise --> y] :
  [greaterp[w; z] --> w;
   otherwise --> z]}}
```

which is correct but awkward. Although in-line coding with let expressions always works, direct substitution is preferable if follow-up optimizations are to be applied.

9.2.2 Accumulator Introduction

An example of a higher-level transformation is that of *accumulator introduction*, the transformation of a function to use a recursive auxiliary with an accumulating parameter. As described in Section 3.6, the use of accumulating parameters often allows nested linear recursions to be transformed into tail recursions, which can in turn be compiled to efficient iterative code. The following schematic pattern or *schema* illustrates a general form of accumulator introduction.

$$f[x] =$$
$$[p_1[x] \rightarrow a;$$
$$p_2[x] \rightarrow g[f[d[x]]; e[x]]]$$

$$\longmapsto$$

$$f[x] = f\text{-aux}[x; a]$$

$$f\text{-aux}[x; \text{accum}] =$$
$$[p_1[x] \rightarrow \text{accum};$$
$$p_2[x] \rightarrow f\text{-aux}[d[x]; g'[e[x]; \text{accum}]]]$$

The idea of this schematic pattern is that it is applicable for an arbitrary constant a and for arbitrary functions p_1, p_2, d, e, g given the existence of an appropriate function g'. In many cases g and g' will be the same function, for example, if g is plus, times, or append.

Consider how accumulator introduction can be applied to the factorial function.

```
fact[n] =
  [eq[n; 0] --> 1;
   otherwise --> times[fact[minus[n; 1]]; n]
```

This implementation of factorial is not in the schematic form given above, but it can be placed in such a form by simple rearrangements.

```
fact[n] =
  [iszero[n] --> 1;
   alwaystrue[n] --> times[fact[sub1[n]]; identity[n]]]

iszero[n] = eq[n; 0]

alwaystrue[n] = true

sub1[n] = minus[n; 1]

identity[n] = n
```

This directly matches the schema above, giving the following implementation of `fact` using accumulating parameters.

```
fact[n] = fact-aux[n; 1]

fact-aux[n; accum] =
  [iszero[n] --> accum;
   alwaystrue[n] --> fact-aux[sub1[n]; times[identity[n]; accum]]]
```

Rather than introducing these extra functions, however, it is simpler to allow a more general interpretation of $p_1[x]$, $p_2[x]$, $d[x]$, and $e[x]$, namely that each of them may stand for an arbitrary term involving x, rather than just a monadic function applied to x. Following this approach, the original definition of the factorial function can immediately be transformed to its accumulating-parameter version.

```
fact[n] = fact-aux[n; 1]

fact-aux[n; accum] =
  [eq[n; 0] --> accum;
   otherwise --> fact-aux[minus[n; 1]; times[n; accum]]]
```

The only restriction on the application of accumulator introduction to any program which matches the schema is that an "appropriate" function g' must exist. In particular, the function g' must form an *associative pair* with g with respect to the constant a; that is, the following must hold:

$$g[a; y] = g'[y; a]$$
$$g[g[a; y]; z] = g'[y; g'[z; a]]$$
$$g[g[g[a; y]; z]; w] = g'[y; g'[z; g'[w; a]]]$$

etc.

Any function which is both associative and commutative (e.g., plus, times, and, or, union, and intersection) will form an associative pair with itself and any constant. Functions such as append, which are associative but not commutative, may still form an associative pair with itself, given a suitable constant (() in the case of append). Finally, a function which is itself neither associative nor commutative may be paired with a different function to form an associative pair. For example, append1 and cons form an associative pair with respect to the constant (), because

$$append1[(); y] = cons[y; ()]$$
$$append1[append1[(); y]; z] = cons[y; cons[z; ()]]$$

etc.

Now consider accumulator introduction applied to the reverse function

```
reverse[list] =
  [endp[list] --> ();
   otherwise --> append1[reverse[rest[list]]; first[list]]]
```

Since append1 and cons form an associative pair with respect to (), this can be transformed immediately to the following version using accumulating parameters:

```
reverse[list] = reverse-aux[list; ()]

reverse-aux[list; accum] =
  [endp[list] --> accum;
   otherwise --> reverse-aux[rest[list]; cons[first[list]; accum]]]
```

Note that efficiency is improved in this case, not only by the replacement of nested linear recursion with tail recursion, but also by the replacement of the expensive append1 operation with the inexpensive cons primitive.

The accumulator introduction schema can be extended to incorporate additional recursive clauses. In fact, there may be arbitrarily many additional clauses involving the g function with a nested recursion.

$$p_3[x] \; \text{-->} \; g[f[d_2[x]]; \; e_2[x]]$$

Each such clause is separately transformed to a tail-recursive call using the complementary g' function and the accumulating parameter.

$$p_3[x] \; \text{-->} \; f\text{-aux}[d_2[x]; \; g'[e_2[x]; \; \text{accum}]]$$

There may also be tail-recursive clauses in a function to be transformed. Each clause of the form

$$p_4[x] \; \text{-->} \; f[e_3[x]]$$

simply results in an a corresponding tail recursion with an unchanged accumulating parameter.

$$p_4[x] \; \text{-->} \; f\text{-aux}[e_3[x]; \; \text{accum}]$$

To illustrate accumulator introduction in the presence of additional recursive clauses, consider the count-symbols function which counts the number of atomic elements in a list.

```
count-symbols[list] =
  [endp[list] --> 0;
   symbolp[first[list]] --> plus⌊count-symbols[rest[list]]; 1];
   otherwise --> count-symbols[rest[list]]]
```

This function matches the basic schema for accumulator introduction but has an additional tail-recursive clause. The extra clause is handled easily using the p_4 transformation described above:

```
count-symbols[list] = count-syms-aux[list; 0]

count-syms-aux[list; accum] =
  [endp[list] --> accum;
   symbolp[first[list]] -->
     count-syms-aux[rest[list]; plus[1; accum]];
   otherwise --> count-syms-aux[rest[list]; accum]]
```

9.3 TRANSLATION

Translator metaprograms are those which perform translation of computer programs from one programming language to another. Depending on the purpose of the translation, such metaprograms can be divided into two major subtypes. The first—and by far the most common—is the *compiler*. Compilers are designed to arrange for the execution of a source program written in a high-level language by translation to an appropriate lower-level language. Often, the lower-level language is the actual *machine language* understood by a computer, or an equivalent *assembly language* form thereof. It is also common to translate to an *intermediate language*, which can be characterized as the machine language of an *abstract machine*. The execution of programs in such a language can then be achieved by an interpreter for the abstract machine which executes on the target computer. A third form of compilation translates from one high-level language to another, relying on an preexisting compiler for the second language to arrange for the program's execution.

In contrast to the compiler category, the second subtype of translator metaprogram is designed for *source-to-source* translation between high-level languages. Rather than arranging for execution, the goal here is to obtain a version of the original program in a new language for further development and maintenance by human programmers. There are various reasons for performing such translations, such as "porting" the software to a new system, integrating the software with other software already written in the second language and translating to a production language such as Pascal from a prototyping language such as Small Lisp. In each case, the goal is to provide a "quality" translation which preserves, to the extent possible, the readability and maintainability of the original source code.

In this section, we will focus on the construction of a source-to-source translator taking Small Lisp programs as input and producing Pascal programs as output. The main goal for this tool will be to assist in the development of production Pascal versions of symbolic computing applications prototyped in Small Lisp. In particular, we will concentrate on a translator for the main algorithms of an application. As described in Chapter 4, when such algorithms are programmed abstractly, we can expect that they will be relatively easy to translate because they rely on no special language features for data manipulation. However, we should not expect to produce good-quality translations of ADT implementations. Such implementations are heavily dependent on the data structuring facilities provided by the language and should be carefully handwritten in a style appropriate to the language.

It will also be possible to use the source-to-source translator as a rudimentary compiler. This can be achieved by providing an appropriate run-time library implementing the Small Lisp primitive functions. Fortunately, the same library developed for the Pascal version of the Small Lisp interpreter is suitable for this purpose (see Section C.3). Nevertheless, it should be realized that a compiler developed in this fashion is an expedient solution only; a production compiler generally uses a variety of techniques to produce much more efficient code on a particular machine architecture. For example, see [ASU86] for an introduction to classical compiler design techniques and [AS85] for compilation in Lisp-like languages.

9.3.1 Translation from Small Lisp to Pascal

Now let us analyze the requirements for a source-to-source translator for translating from Small Lisp to Pascal. For example, consider the translation of the `sl-evlis` function from Section 6.3.1.

```
sl-evlis[explist; fn-env; val-env] =
  {val1 = sl-eval[first[explist]; fn-env; val-env] :
   [single-p[explist] --> list1[val1];
    otherwise -->

        cons[val1; sl-evlis[rest[explist]; fn-env; val-env]]]}
```

This example illustrates many of the important features of Small Lisp, including recursive function definitions, function calls, let expressions, and conditional expressions. Fortunately, this example translates quite easily to the following Pascal function definition, which actually comprises part of the Small Lisp interpreter described in Appendix C:

```
FUNCTION slEvlis
           (explist : ExpressionListType; fnEnv : FnEnvType;
            valEnv : ValueEnvType) : GenericListType;
  VAR val1 : sExpressionType;
BEGIN
  val1 := slEval(First(explist), fnEnv, valEnv);
  IF SingleP(explist) THEN slEvlis := Cons(val1, EmptyList)
  ELSE slEvlis := Cons(val1, slEvlis(Rest(explist), fnEnv, valEnv))
END;
```

The similarity of these two definitions arises largely from the fact that both languages support recursive function definitions and have similar syntaxes for function calls and variable names. However, there are a number of differences as well. First of all, Pascal requires that all its variables, parameters, and function results be given explicit types. Second, the let expression of Small Lisp must be simulated using assignment statements for the local variables and an appropriate action to process the final expression. Similarly, the conditional expression of Small Lisp cannot be translated directly to a Pascal expression, but must somehow be implemented as an if-statement. In the example, translation of the expressions to statements works out fairly well because the method of returning a function result in Pascal is to "assign" it to the function name. Thus the result expressions of the Small Lisp conditional can be replaced by corresponding assignments to the function name.

In this section, we will work through the details of translating Small Lisp expressions to appropriate Pascal statements and expressions. This will allow us to translate the body of a Small Lisp function definition into the series of statements that comprise the body of corresponding Pascal function definition. Construction of the full Pascal function definition, including declaration of the parameters and the local variables of a function, will be left as an exercise. Note, however, that the use of user-specified type signatures and the type inference techniques of Section 9.1.1 may be useful in constructing such declarations.

As the previous example illustrates, our general approach to translation will involve one-to-one mappings of Small Lisp variables and functions to corresponding entities in Pascal. The correspondence will not be exact, however, because the type structures of the languages differ. In general, the goal will be to specify the types for the Pascal entities that would "naturally" be used. Consider, for example, the translation of Small Lisp predicates, such as the function `single-p`. In Small Lisp these functions return a symbolic atom `T` or `F` to denote true or false. A literal translation would attempt to simulate this behavior by returning some sort of Pascal representation of a symbolic atom. However, the natural approach is to translate Small Lisp predicates to Pascal predicates; that is, to functions which return objects of Pascal's built-in `BOOLEAN` type. In this way, we attempt to maintain the quality of the translated programs by preserving the intent of the original code.

A key issue in translation from Lisp to Pascal is how to deal with lists. In many cases, lists are a natural data structure for the problem at hand, regardless of whether the problem is to be solved in Small Lisp or Pascal. Since Pascal does not include any special facilities for lists, a reasonable solution in this case is to provide Pascal implementations of Lisp's list-processing primitives. Section C.1.3 describes an appropriate Turbo Pascal module implementing the operations `EndP`, `SingleP`, `First`, `Rest`, `Cons`, and `List1` to correspond to the similarly named Lisp primitives together with the symbolic constant `EmptyList`, to correspond to the Lisp empty list `()`. This module is generic, allowing objects of any type representable in one unit of computer memory (i.e., the size of a pointer) to be stored as the elements of a list. Thus lists of integers, Booleans, or any type implemented using pointers can be handled.

Of course, lists are also used in Small Lisp as the implementation type for other types of data structure. In such cases, the natural representation in Pascal might involve some other data-structuring mechanism, such as records or arrays. However, it is unrealistic to expect a translator to make such data structure selections automatically, so a good-quality translation may require reimplementation of the data structure by hand. Nevertheless, the hand translation will be minimized if data abstraction is used, because it will be confined to the implementations of the relevant data access functions. Thus our translator will always use the strategy of translating list-processing operations to the corresponding routines of Section C.1.3, leaving it up to the "translation engineer" to make any appropriate substitutions.

Now consider how Small Lisp expressions can in general be translated to Pascal. Recall that there are seven basic types of Small Lisp expression:

$$\langle expression \rangle ::= \langle value \rangle \mid \langle variable \rangle \mid \langle function\text{-}call \rangle \mid$$
$$\langle conditional\text{-}expression \rangle \mid \langle let\text{-}expression \rangle$$
$$\langle value \rangle ::= \langle numeric\text{-}atom \rangle \mid " \langle symbolic\text{-}atom \rangle " \mid \langle list \rangle$$

The natural choice for numeric atoms is to translate them to Pascal numeric constants of the `INTEGER` data type. In the case of the symbolic atoms `T` and `F`, we will assume that they denote truth values and translate to the corresponding values of Pascal's `BOOLEAN` type, namely `TRUE` and `FALSE`. Other symbolic atoms will generally be translated to string literals (e.g., the symbolic atom R2D2 translates to the Pascal character string 'R2D2'). This allows tests for equality and lexicographic ordering to be implemented easily. Such a translation will not always be appropriate but is the choice likely to reflect the natural Pascal approach in most cases.

In general, list constants cannot be translated in any elegant fashion into Pascal. As mentioned above, the empty list () will translate to the Pascal symbolic constant EmptyList. Our strategy for other list constants, such as (A B C), will be to simulate them using List... constructors [e.g., List3('A', 'B', 'C')]. Often these translations will be inappropriate, however. Fortunately, the use of such literal list constants is generally rare within Small Lisp programs. When they do occur, they are often found within the data access functions of an ADT, which will probably have to be hand implemented anyway.

Small Lisp variables can generally be translated to Pascal variables with similar names. However, hyphens must be eliminated; our strategy will be to capitalize the letter following the hyphen in an effort to maintain the readability of the identifier. Also, the special variables T, F, and otherwise, which are treated like predefined constants in Small Lisp, will be translated to the corresponding Pascal constants TRUE, FALSE, and TRUE, respectively.

The translation of function calls is relatively straightforward because the syntax of function calls is directly parallel in the two languages. In the case of Small Lisp's arithmetic primitives, however, the appropriate Pascal operator expression will be used (e.g., plus[x; y] will be translated to x + y). Note also that the eq function for comparing either numeric or symbolic atoms can be translated to operator expressions with = for comparing integers or string values. Similarly, the < operator will be used for lexicographic string comparison corresponding to the sym-lessp function.

The translation of let expressions involves two entities. The first is a list of Pascal assignment statements to emulate the local definitions of the let expression. The second is the Pascal expression that results from translation of the final expression of the let expression. Furthermore, translation of the final expression can lead to more statements to be included. For example, consider the following nested let expressions.

```
{n1 = first[numlist];
 n2 = first[rest[numlist]] :
{sum = plus[n1; n2];
 diff = minus[n1; n2] :
 plus[times[sum; sum]; times[diff; diff]]}}
```

This can be translated into the four Pascal assignment statements

```
n1 := First(numlist);
n2 := First(Rest(numlist));
sum := n1 + n2;
diff := n1 - n2;
```

and the Pascal expression sum * sum + diff * diff. The latter expression represents the value of the original Small Lisp let expression; before it is evaluated the assignments must be executed to set up the appropriate values of sum and diff. Of course, the variables introduced by these statements also have to be declared in the enclosing Pascal block. A further complication is that nested let expressions introduce new scopes in Small Lisp and hence can redefine a variable name which is already in use. Such situations will lead to name conflicts in translation to Pascal. However, we will ignore this possibility in our prototype translator.

The translation of conditional expressions is somewhat more complex. In general, a conditional expression involving several clauses will translate to a series of nested if-statements for each clause. However, we will also need a variable to represent the result of the conditional expression. Consider, for example, the following conditional expression:

```
[endp[x] --> 0;
 numberp[first[x]] --> times[first[x]; length[x]];
 otherwise --> -1]
```

Suppose that we create a variable CondResult to stand for the value of the expression. The result expression of each clause can then be translated to an assignment to this variable. This assignment is embedded in the THEN part of an if-statement whose IF part contains the translation of the corresponding predicate. Each such if-statement is then embedded as the ELSE part of the preceding one:

```
IF Null(x) THEN CondResult := 0
ELSE IF Numberp(First(x)) THEN
  CondResult := First(x) * Length(x)
ELSE IF TRUE THEN CondResult := -1
```

Note, however, that this general translation scheme produces a statement of the form IF TRUE THEN ⟨assignment⟩ whenever a clause with an otherwise is translated. In such cases, it is more appropriate to drop the trivial condition to obtain

```
IF Null(x) THEN CondResult := 0
ELSE IF Numberp(First(x)) THEN
  CondResult := First(x) * Length(x)
ELSE CondResult := -1
```

This results in a higher-quality translation. Since the use of otherwise as the last predicate in a Small Lisp conditional is very common, it is important to include this special case as part of a source-to-source translator.

Another low-quality aspect of this scheme for translating conditionals is the introduction of the artificial CondResult variable—it is not what you would expect a Pascal programmer to produce. Fortunately, in most cases it is possible to identify a preexisting target variable which is to receive the value of the conditional expression. In particular, whenever a conditional expression is used as the body of a function, the name of that function becomes a suitable target variable in Pascal, because function results are returned by assigning them to the function name: for example, translation of the absolute value function

```
abs[n] =
   [lessp[n; 0] --> minus[0; n];
    otherwise --> n]
```

uses Abs as the target variable:

```
FUNCTION Abs(n : INTEGER) : INTEGER;
BEGIN
   IF n < 0 THEN Abs := 0 - n
   ELSE Abs := n
END;
```

Similarly, if a conditional expression appears on the R.H.S. of a local or global variable definition, the variable being defined provides the appropriate target. This strategy also applies recursively to conditional expressions nested as the result parts of conditional clauses or the final expressions of let expressions. For example, in the translation of sl-evlis given previously, slEvlis is used as the target in a conditional expression embedded within a let expression. In fact, the only cases for which this strategy cannot be employed are when the conditional expression is found as the predicate of a conditional clause, the argument of a function call, or a subexpression of one of these. In such cases, a temporary variable such as CondResult will have to be introduced. However, these cases rarely occur in practice.

9.3.2 Translator Construction

The analysis of the preceding section has shown how each type of Small Lisp expression can be translated using appropriate Pascal expressions and statements. Now consider how we can build a prototype of such a translator. Rather than generating Pascal code directly, however, our prototype will generate a suitable Lisp representation of the Pascal code. Thus the output of our prototype translator will not be directly available in Pascal form. Nevertheless, once the output is in this Lisp representation of Pascal, it is relatively simple to produce proper Pascal code using the facilities of an S-Lisp system such as Common LISP. Alternatively, if a production Small Lisp to Pascal translator were to be developed, there are techniques to be described in Chapter 12 that could be employed to provide neatly formatted (*pretty-printed*) Pascal output.

In fact, we need only develop a Lisp representation for a small subset of the possible Pascal statements and expressions. The GRAIL grammar of Figure 9.3 presents a suitable Lisp representation of this subset.

For example, the body of the Abs function would be represented as

```
(IF (n < 0) THEN (Abs := (0 - n))
ELSE (Abs := n))
```

In our Lisp representation of Pascal, note that we have included the concept of compound statements enclosing lists of statements in BEGIN-END keywords. Unfortunately, one rather awkward aspect of the Pascal syntax is that lists of more than one statement cannot be directly included as the THEN or ELSE parts of an if-statement. Instead, such lists must first be made into a compound statement. Since our translation algorithms will often be creating lists of statements to be included in such contexts, it would always be expedient to embed them in compound statements. However, this would often result in redundant BEGIN-END keywords encapsulating a single statement. Instead, we will use the following function to encapsulate multielement lists while avoiding unnecessary keywords:

```
(defun build-unit-stmt (stmts)
    (cond ((single-p stmts) (first stmts))
          (T (make-compound stmts))))
```

⟨statement-list⟩ ::= ⟨statement*⟩
⟨statement⟩ ::= ⟨assignment⟩ | ⟨if-then⟩ | ⟨if-then-else⟩ | ⟨compound⟩
⟨assignment⟩ ::= (⟨variable:pasc-ident⟩ := ⟨value:pasc-expr⟩)
⟨if-then⟩ ::= (IF ⟨predicate:pasc-expr⟩ THEN ⟨result:statement⟩)
⟨if-then-else⟩ ::= (IF ⟨predicate:pasc-expr⟩ THEN ⟨result:statement⟩
                    ELSE ⟨alternate:statement⟩)
⟨compound⟩ ::= (BEGIN ⟨body:statement-list⟩ END)
⟨pasc-expr⟩ ::= ⟨integer⟩ | ⟨string⟩ | ⟨pasc-ident⟩ | ⟨pasc-call⟩ |
               ⟨operation⟩
⟨integer⟩ ::= ⟨int-val:numeric-atom⟩
⟨string⟩ ::= (QUOTE ⟨string-val:symbolic-atom⟩)
⟨pasc-ident⟩ ::= ⟨pasc-name:symbolic-atom⟩
⟨pasc-call⟩ ::= (⟨pasc-fn:pasc-ident⟩ ⟨args:pasc-expr$^+$⟩)
⟨operation⟩ ::= (⟨pasc-op1:pasc-expr⟩ ⟨operator:operator⟩
               ⟨pasc-op2:pasc-expr⟩)
⟨operator⟩ ::= ⟨op-name:symbolic-atom⟩

Figure 9.3   GRAIL grammar for Pascal statements and expressions.

Again, recognizing and handling such frequently occurring special cases is important to quality translation.

Now consider the input/output characteristics of our expression translator. Given a Small Lisp expression as input, there are three possible results of the translation. Sometimes the result is simply a Pascal expression (e.g., in translating variables and symbolic constants). In other cases, such as the translation of let expressions, the result is a list of statements and an expression to be evaluated after the statements are executed. The third possibility is illustrated by the translation of conditional expressions when a target variable is specified to receive the value of the expression. In this case, the result of a translation is simply a series of statements which will effect the appropriate assignment to the target variable.

In order to handle these cases, we will construct a translator that operates in two different modes. In the first mode, the translator will produce the Pascal expression corresponding to a given Small Lisp expression and an auxiliary list of statements to be executed before this expression, if needed. Let us specify that (pasc-expr sl-expr) be the function to determine the Pascal expression resulting from translation of a given

Small Lisp expression sl-expr, while (aux-stmts sl-expr) will return the corresponding list of auxiliary statements, if any. In the second mode of translation, a target variable will be specified for the expression value, and the translator will produce the list of Pascal statements that ensures that the variable receives this value. This will be achieved by the function

(xlate-with-target sl-expr pasc-var)

to translate the Small Lisp expression sl-expr, where pasc-var is the Pascal variable which is to receive the expression value.

    In fact, the xlate-with-target function is really the top-level function to be used in translating the body of a function definition from Small Lisp to Pascal. Regardless of what type of expression is found as the body of a Small Lisp function, the body of the corresponding Pascal function must be a statement list which passes the return value back by assigning it to the function name. In most cases, this is achieved by translating in the first mode (i.e., to a Pascal expression) and then assigning the expression determined to the target variable. Any auxiliary statements necessary are inserted before the assignment. This is reflected by the default clause in xlate-with-target:

```
(defun xlate-with-target (sl-expr pasc-var)
  (cond ((let-expr-p sl-expr)
          (append (xlate-local-defs (local-defs sl-expr))
                  (xlate-with-target (final-expr sl-expr) pasc-var)))
        ((cond-expr-p sl-expr)
          (xlate-clauses (clauses sl-expr) pasc-var))
        (T (append1 (aux-stmts sl-expr)
                  (make-assignment pasc-var (pasc-expr sl-expr))))))
```

Let expressions and conditional expressions could be handled in this fashion as well. As described above, however, it is preferable to pass the target variable down to the lower levels of the translation in order to avoid creation of artificial variables like CondResult. In the case of let expressions, for example, the target variable is made available in the translation of the final expression. In the translation of conditional expressions, the target variable will be made available to each clause.

    The local definitions of a let expression translate to a series of assignment statements. Rather than constructing these assignments directly, however, it is again preferable to pass the target variable down so that it is available in the translation of each value expression:

```
(defun xlate-local-defs (defs)
  (reduce #'append
          (mapcar #'(lambda (def)
                      (xlate-with-target
                        (local-val def)
                        (xlate-var-name (local-var def))))
                  defs)))
```

Once the individual statement lists for each definition have been determined, they are all appended together using the reduce functional.

Translation of conditional clauses also passes the target variable down for translation of the result part of each clause:

```
(defun xlate-clauses (clauses pasc-var)
  (let ((pred1 (predicate (first clauses)))
        (result1 (result (first clauses))))
    (let ((pred-expr (pasc-expr pred1)) (pred-stmts (aux-stmts pred1))
          (result-stmts (xlate-with-target result1 pasc-var)))
      (cond ((true-p pred-expr) result-stmts)
            ((single-p clauses)
             (append1 pred-stmts
               (make-if-then
                 pred-expr (build-unit-stmt result-stmts))))
            (T (append1 pred-stmts
               (make-if-then-else
                 pred-expr
                 (build-unit-stmt result-stmts)
                 (build-unit-stmt
                   (xlate-clauses (rest clauses) pasc-var)))))))))

(defun true-p (pasc-id)
  (eq (pasc-name pasc-id) 'TRUE))
```

No target variable can be made available for translation of the predicate, however, so it is directly translated to a Pascal expression. Any auxiliary statements needed for the predicate are inserted before the actions for the clause. Note that the true-p catches the special case of an otherwise predicate; it also catches the equivalent cases where T or "T" is the predicate.

Now consider the implementation of the pasc-expr and aux-stmts functions which translate a Small Lisp expression to a Pascal expression and its associated auxiliary statements. The implementation of pasc-expr follows the requirements identified in the preceding section:

```
(defun pasc-expr (sl-expr)
  (cond ((numeric-atom-expr-p sl-expr)
         (make-integer (numeric-val sl-expr)))
        ((symbolic-atom-expr-p sl-expr)
         (make-string (symbolic-val sl-expr)))
        ((list-expr-p sl-expr)
         (make-pasc-call
           (make-pasc-ident
             (implode 'List (length (list-val sl-expr))))
           (pasc-expr-list (list-val sl-expr))))
        ((identifier-p sl-expr)
```

```
              (let ((the-name (id-name sl-expr)))
                (cond ((eq id-name 'T) (make-pasc-ident 'TRUE))
                      ((eq id-name 'F) (make-pasc-ident 'FALSE))
                      ((eq id-name 'otherwise)) (make-pasc-ident 'TRUE))
                      (T (make-pasc-ident (dehyphenize id-name))))))
            ((fn-call-p sl-expr)
             (let ((the-fn-name (id-name (callee sl-expr)))
                   (pasc-args (pasc-expr-list (arguments expr))))
               (cond ((operator-fn-p the-fn-name)
                      (make-operation (first pasc-args)
                        (pasc-operator the-fn-name) (second pasc-args)))
                     (T (make-pasc-call
                          (capitalize (dehyphenize the-fn-name))
                          pasc-args)))))
            ((let-expr-p sl-expr) (pasc-expr (final-expr sl-expr)))
            ((cond-expr-p sl-expr) (make-pasc-ident 'CondResult))))
```

Note that the translation of function calls may produce operation expressions through the appropriately defined auxiliary functions `operator-fn-p` and `pasc-operator`. Also note that the translation of a conditional expression will yield the temporary variable `CondResult`; however, this will occur only if a conditional expression is found within a function call or a conditional predicate.

Auxiliary statements to go along with the expression determined by `pasc-expr` may be needed in the translation of function calls, let expressions, and conditional expressions. These are produced by the `aux-stmts` function:

```
(defun aux-stmts (sl-expr)
  (cond ((numeric-atom-expr-p sl-expr) '())
        ((symbolic-atom-expr-p sl-expr) '())
        ((list-expr-p sl-expr) '())
        ((identifier-p sl-expr) '())
        ((fn-call-p sl-expr) (stmts-for-args (arguments sl-expr)))
        ((let-expr-p sl-expr)
         (append (xlate-local-defs (local-defs sl-expr))
                 (aux-stmts (final-expr sl-expr))))
        ((cond-expr-p sl-expr)
         (xlate-clauses (clauses sl-expr)
           (make-pasc-ident 'CondResult)))))
```

In the case of function calls, these auxiliary statements are just those that may be needed for the function's argument expressions, and are provided by the `argstmts` function:

```
(defun stmts-for-args (args)
  (cond ((single-p args) (aux-stmts (first args)))
        (T (append (aux-stmts (first args))
                   (stmts-for-args (rest args))))))
```

In the case of a let expression, the auxiliaries consist of all the assignments which result from translating the local definitions, together with any auxiliaries needed for the final expression. In the case of a conditional expression, the auxiliary statements are all those which result from translation of the conditional clauses with a target variable of `CondResult`.

9.4 EXERCISES

9.1. Design and implement a checker for the following errors and anomalies in a Small Lisp program.

  (a) Undefined functions
  (b) Undefined variables
  (c) Incorrect number of arguments in a function call

  Hint: See Section 9.1.1 on type checking for a suitable way to report errors or anomalies.

9.2. Specify appropriate type signatures for the functions `symbolp`, `eq`, `first`, `greaterp`, `sym-lessp`, `implode`, `explode`, and `error`.

9.3. Provide a GRAIL grammar for a simple programming language, based on the S-Lisp version of Small Lisp given in Section 4.5, which is extended to permit the explicit typing of functions and variables. That is, when a programmer writes a program in your language, information on the data type of variables and the values returned by functions must be provided. Use the same nonterminal, terminal, and component names for the various types of expression as were used in defining the GRAIL grammar of Small Lisp wherever possible. Since type information will be included, use the GRAIL rules given in Figure 9.2 to define the possible types. Implement the data access functions defined by your grammar.

9.4. Consider user programs written in the language defined in Exercise 9.3. Using the type checking functions given in Section 9.1.1, write a function `type-check-defns` that takes as input a list of function and constant definitions in this language and type-checks those definitions. Make sure to account for the fact that some functions may call other functions which are also defined in this list of definitions.

9.5. Extend the Small Lisp type-checking system with a notion of user-defined abstract data types. Each abstract data type should be given a name to be used in declaring variables of that type and specifying signatures of functions which take or return objects of that type. Furthermore, each abstract data type should also have an associated implementation type, which is acceptable for the purposes of type checking as equivalent to the ADT name within the implementation of its data access functions. For example, `AlgExprType` might be specified as the type name of algebraic expressions, with an implementation type of `S-EXP`. Data access functions on algebraic expressions would be allowed to treat such objects using arbitrary operations on S-expressions. However, client programs of the algebraic expression ADT, such as `deriv` and `simplify`, would only be able to use the data access functions supplied by the ADT.

9.6. Define the function `intersection-types` which returns the type intersection of two given types. If the two types have no values in common, their intersection is "void."

9.7. The control flow path through a given clause of conditional expression involves both the predicate and the result of that clause as well as the predicates of all previous clauses.

Show that this definition is necessary in correctly inferring the argument type for the following function.

```
signify[n] =
    [lessp[n; 0] --> list2["-"; minus[0; n]];
     otherwise --> list2["+"; n]]
```

9.8. Design and implement an algorithm to infer the argument types of a nonrecursive function given its definition and assuming that type signatures are available for all other functions. *Hint*: Analyze each subexpression in the context of an expected type for the expression. When an occurrence of a given argument is found, the expected type of the expression provides a context type for the argument that may be intersected with other such types along the control flow path. Initially, assume that the expected type of the body of the function definition is void. When processing an argument of a function call, the expected type becomes the type of that argument as specified by the signature of the called function. When processing the predicate of a conditional expression, the expected type is Boolean.

9.9. It is not actually necessary to set up the type inference equations to apply the iterative-convergent technique. Instead, initial environments of variable types and function signatures can be set up with VOID supplied as the approximation for all unknown types. The rules described previously for computing argument and result type information can then be applied to all the definitions in the program. This will result in a new set of types and signatures. The process can then be repeated until convergence is achieved. Implement the type inference algorithm using this approach.

9.10. Implement an in-line coder for Small Lisp which generally uses let expressions to establish argument to parameter bindings but uses direct substitution in the following cases.

(a) The argument is a literal constant (i.e., an atom or a list).
(b) The argument is a variable name and no name conflict arises from its substitution.
(c) The formal parameter occurs only once in the function body, and no name conflict arises from substitution of the corresponding argument expression.

Assume that the function being coded in-line does not access any global variables. Experiment with the systematic replacement of data access functions with equivalent in-line code. What improvements in efficiency do you get? Comment on the maintainability of the resultant code.

9.11. A program transformation system for Small Lisp might include a simplifier for Small Lisp expressions analogous to the algebraic expression simplifier studied in Chapter 5. Clearly, many of the arithmetic simplifications that apply for algebraic expressions also carry over to Small Lisp expressions. What other types of simplifications are possible? Describe simplification rules for as many of the primitive functions of Small Lisp as you can and at least two rules for the simplification of conditional expressions. Construct a Small Lisp expression simplifier implementing your rules.

9.12. Design and implement a transformation tool that performs accumulator introduction.

9.13. How can the mapcan functional be used to improve the efficiency of xlate-local-defs? Recall that mapcan destructively appends the lists returned by the mapped function. Prove that its use in xlate-local-defs is safe.

9.14. Complete the Small Lisp to Pascal expression translator by developing the routines necessary for translating identifiers and for recognizing and translating operator functions.

Using the features of an appropriate S-Lisp system such as Common LISP, modify the translator to produce Pascal code directly rather than the Lisp representation defined.

9.15. Develop a complete Small Lisp to Pascal translator building on the expression translator given. Use the type inference techniques of Section 9.1.1 together with user-supplied type signatures to produce the appropriate type declarations for the Pascal variables and functions.

10

Predicate Calculus and Resolution

This chapter brings together many of the concepts and techniques which have been introduced previously in order to tackle a significant problem for symbolic computing: the automation of mathematical theorem proving. Besides being an interesting problem in its own right, the implementation of an automated theorem prover provides a significant component in the retrieval of information from a "knowledge base," that is, a data base whose contents consist of abstract representations of "beliefs" that a computer system possesses about some problem domain. In such a system, deduction is used as the method for obtaining (or more specifically, inferring) "new" facts from the existing data base. The formal language for the representation of facts in the data base is the predicate calculus. Like the propositional calculus discussed in Chapter 5, the predicate calculus is a language for specifying logical statements, together with a set of rules for making inferences (i.e., deriving new statements) and for determining the truth of such statements.

In this chapter, the following issues related to the design of an automated theorem prover will be addressed:

1. Development of a grammar for the representation of propositional statements in the predicate calculus.

2. Analysis and formulation of a canonical form for the representation of inputs to the theorem prover.

3. Description of the resolution principle on which the theorem prover will be based.

The purpose of this chapter is to show how a range of topics introduced earlier—including environments, grammars, transformations—are brought to bear on a particularly significant symbolic computing problem and influence the structure of its solution. For a discussion of the history of the development of the resolution principle, and to examine its merits or to explore alternative proof strategies, the interested reader should consult any of a number of excellent books which address the topic of *knowledge representation*. This topic is a major area of artificial intelligence and a rich source of problems in symbolic computing.[1]

10.1 REPRESENTATION IN THE PREDICATE CALCULUS

What are the virtues of the predicate calculus as a language for the representation of information symbolically? After all, the propositional calculus which was introduced in Chapter 5 also provides a formal language for such representation. Furthermore, strategies exist, such as the method of Wang, for proving theorems about facts expressed in such a language. The answer lies in the fact that the predicate calculus is a more expressive language than the propositional calculus. This greater expressiveness is provided in a variety of ways.

First, predicate calculus is a more powerful logical formalism than the propositional calculus because it incorporates variables and functions. The basic idea is to replace propositions representing simple statements with predicate expressions representing parameterized statements. For example, a generalization of the statement: "If Fred teaches symbolic computing, then symbolic computing is easy" might be "If Fred teaches x, then x is easy" which is a parameterized statement using the variable x. Note that the latter form of statement cannot be represented by a single expression in the propositional calculus, but can, in some cases, be expressed using several separate statements, one per value of x. More specifically, the domain of x must be finite; otherwise, an infinite number of statements would be required. The predicate expression is a more general way of making a statement because it permits the representation of expressions whose truth value is not constant, but rather depends on the values assigned to variables. As the example suggests, for each subject that Fred may teach, it may or may not be the case than students will find that particular subject easy.

In the predicate calculus, then, predicate expressions replace propositions (of the propositional calculus) as the atomic logical formulas. Formally, a *predicate expression* is the application of an n-ary predicate to n *terms* ($n \geq 0$). That is, it is a function which is applied to n terms and which evaluates to a truth value. Each term is either a *variable* or a *function expression*. A function expression is the application of an m-ary function to m terms ($m \geq 0$). For example, suppose that P denotes a predicate meaning "greater than" and f denotes a function meaning "sum of." The

---

[1]See, for example, Charniak and McDermott [CM84] for further details on the use of predicate calculus as a formal language for representation, as well as a discussion of the resolution principle and other inference strategies.

logical statement "x is greater than the sum of y and z" can then be represented by $P(x, f(y, z))$.

Second, the predicate calculus provides greater expressiveness in the number of ways that atomic formulas can be combined to provide composite expressions. To begin with, using predicate expressions as the atomic logical formula type, composite logical formulas may be formed in the same five ways as in propositional calculus (negation, conjunction, disjunction, implication, and equivalence). In addition, two further ways are also provided using *quantifiers*. These two new formula types each have two components, namely a *bound variable* and a *quantified formula*.

The first of these new formula types is the *universally quantified formula*, which asserts that for all possible values of its bound variable, the quantified formula is true. Such formulas are often written using an upside-down "A" as a universal quantifier symbol meaning "for all." For example, asserting $\forall x P(x)$ means that for all values of x, the predicate expression $P(x)$ is true.

The second new formula type is the *existentially quantified formula*, which asserts that for at least one value of its bound variable, the quantified formula is true. These formulas are often written using a backwards "E" as the quantifier symbol meaning "there exists." For example, asserting $\exists x P(x)$ means that there exists at least one value of x such that $P(x)$ is true.

The advantage of extending the allowable types of logical formulas to include quantified expressions is that it provides a way of representing symbolically propositions about classes of objects, rather than just propositions about specific objects. This is particularly valuable if we want to be able to express a set of useful (nontrivial) axioms and from them derive some "interesting" inferences. In fact, it can be argued that all the really useful logical formulas are those which express universal or existential quantification. Empirically, in the context of their use as a language for knowledge representation, this is usually the case—the important facts, for the purpose of inference, generally are quantified formulas.

Now consider a GRAIL grammar describing formulas of the predicate calculus as Lisp data objects. Such a grammar is defined in Figure 10.1. This grammar introduces ⟨pred-expr⟩, ⟨universal⟩, and ⟨existential⟩ as new types of ⟨formula⟩ beyond those given for the propositional calculus. In addition, the syntax of predicate expressions incorporates the new type ⟨term⟩, which can be either a ⟨func-expr⟩ or a ⟨variable⟩. In addition to these new types of object, note that the nature of conjunctions and disjunctions as data objects has changed to allow arbitrarily many conjuncts and disjuncts, respectively. In the remainder of the chapter we shall refer to this grammar whenever we wish to represent logical formulas of the predicate calculus. In particular, we will use the "names" of the data access functions specified by the grammar to refer to the components of logical formulas of the predicate calculus, whether or not we are referring to the list representation of those formulas.

10.2 INTERPRETATION OF PREDICATE CALCULUS

At the beginning of this chapter, we stated that one of the motivations for examining the predicate calculus was its role as a formal language for knowledge representation, and we concluded the preceding section with a grammar for defining instances from

⟨formula⟩	::=	⟨pred-expr⟩ | ⟨negation⟩ | ⟨conjunction⟩ | ⟨disjunction⟩ | ⟨implication⟩ | ⟨equivalence⟩ | ⟨universal⟩ | ⟨existential⟩
⟨pred-expr⟩	::=	(⟨pred-name:pred-id⟩ ⟨terms:term*⟩)
⟨term⟩	::=	⟨func-expr⟩ | ⟨variable⟩
⟨func-expr⟩	::=	(⟨func-name:func-id⟩ ⟨arguments:term*⟩)
⟨negation⟩	::=	(NOT ⟨negend:formula⟩)
⟨conjunction⟩	::=	(AND ⟨conjuncts:formula*⟩)
⟨disjunction⟩	::=	(OR ⟨disjuncts:formula*⟩)
⟨implication⟩	::=	(⟨antecedent:formula⟩ IMPLIES ⟨consequent:formula⟩)
⟨equivalence⟩	::=	(⟨condition1:formula⟩ EQUIV ⟨condition2:formula⟩)
⟨universal⟩	::=	(FORALL ⟨bound-var:variable⟩ ⟨quantified-form:formula⟩)
⟨existential⟩	::=	(EXISTS ⟨bound-var:variable⟩ ⟨quantified-form:formula⟩)
⟨pred-id⟩	::=	⟨p-name:symbolic-atom⟩
⟨func-id⟩	::=	⟨f-name:symbolic-atom⟩
⟨variable⟩	::=	⟨v-name:symbolic-atom⟩

Figure 10.1   GRAIL grammar for formulas of the predicate calculus.

the input domain of logical formulas of the predicate calculus. The strength as well as the weakness of this representation is that it ignores the interpretation or meaning associated with the terms, functions, and predicates that make up an expression. The truth of a logical formula in the predicate calculus is determined solely by the logical structure of the expression, as was the case with propositional calculus.

When the predicate calculus is used to represent a body of knowledge about a given subject, that knowledge is expressed as a set of logical formulas called assertions. *Assertions* are statements which are placed in a data base on the basis that they can be true by virtue of their interpretation, if not their logical structure. Assertions are thus formulas which represent true statements about the items of concern.

Implicit in the formulation of this representation is that proper interpretations be assigned to the variables, function names, and predicates of the set of logical formulas. First of all, the universe D of values that the variables may represent must be defined. Second, each m-ary function must be given an interpretation by defining its mapping from m-tuples of values from D into a single such value.[2] Finally, similar interpretations must be given for each n-ary predicate—those mappings from n-tuples of values in D into truth values.

---

[2]This is generally given as an *intensional* description of the nature of the function rather than as an *extensional* listing of all input tuples and their corresponding values.

Note that for both functions and predicates, a special case exists when the number of arguments is zero (i.e., m or n equals 0). A function with no arguments is a function whose value is constant and can in fact be used to represent a particular constant from the domain D. Similarly, a predicate with no arguments represents a statement whose truth value is independent of the values of any variables—in other words, a proposition.

In general, then, to use a set of formulas to represent some body of knowledge, a complete interpretation of its variables, functions, and predicates must be given. Conversely, a set of formulas by itself may be used to represent many possible worlds, depending on the interpretation. Given a set of formulas and an interpretation, if all of the formulas represent true statements about the interpretation (i.e., about the world being represented), the interpretation is said to be a *model* of the set of formulas.[3] In particular, a set of assertions which represent a knowledge base should be consistent; that is, there should be no contradictions among the set of assertions, nor should any contradiction be deducible from them. In the next section, we shall see that consistency is a necessary property of a data base whose contents are represented by logical formulas if we are to be able to make useful inferences.

In the formal context, logical inferences are established from a set of logical formulas called premises by applying allowable rules of inference for the predicate calculus. Initially, these rules are applied to the premises, but they can then also be applied to the derived formulas. Thus theorem proving, when viewed as the derivation of new formulas from an initial set of formulas, becomes the derivation of new facts about a body of knowledge when applied to a set of formulas representing that knowledge. Note, however, that any derivable fact from a given set of formulas is true in all possible models of the set of formulas. A true statement about a model, then, may not always be derivable and in particular will not be derivable if it is not also true of all other models of the formula set. If a true statement about a model is not derivable, then the set of formulas only partially represents the model.

It is interesting to compare the notion of a set of formulas representing a body of knowledge with the more conventional notion of knowledge represented in a data base. In a conventional data base environment, user queries are answered simply by retrieving information that is stored in an interconnection network of usually linear data structures. If knowledge is represented using logical formulas, however, queries can be answered, not only by retrieval of simple facts, but also by making logical deductions. This means that all the information contained in the data base need not be explicitly represented. Retrieval through inference proceeds in the following manner. To determine from the data base an object satisfying certain constraints, a logical assertion is made that such an object exists, and a proof of that assertion is attempted. If the theorem prover is constructive in nature, successful completion of the proof will also find a particular object satisfying the given constraints.

Now, since a knowledge base includes assertions whose truth is a consequence of the interpretation, it follows that knowledge bases are generally incomplete in the sense that there will usually be "facts" which may be true for the given interpretation,

---

[3]This may be a rather counterintuitive definition of "model"; it reflects the logician's point of view, however, emphasizing the formulas themselves over any particular body of knowledge they might represent.

but cannot be obtained using the "rules of transformation" of the predicate calculus, since these rules can only produce inferences which are true for all possible models. In other words, logical inference does not take "meaning" into account. This is the weakness of the predicate calculus representation that we alluded to earlier.

Theorem proving can also serve as a general-purpose computational technique. This is the basis for an area of research called *logic programming* and is embodied in the programming language PROLOG (PROgramming in LOGic).[4] PROLOG is an example of a class of programming languages which are called *declarative*. This means that the sequencing of steps to perform a computation is not explicitly specified by the programmer. Rather, the sequencing is determined by the requirements of a "theorem prover" to derive a result from a set of statements corresponding to the body of the program. In order to be acceptable to a theorem prover, the syntax of PROLOG provides a means of expressing program statements as assertions. Thus a PROLOG program can be viewed as a data base whose contents are reflected by the assertions that define its body, and the inferences that can be derived from those assertions. PROLOG is an important language for the implementation of symbolic computing applications. For details on PROLOG, the interested reader should consult *Programming in PROLOG* by Clocksin and Mellish [CM81].

10.3 RESOLUTION THEOREM PROVING

Theorem proving is very much more difficult in the predicate calculus than in the propositional calculus, but practical first-order theorem provers have been developed using what is known as the *resolution* principle. Resolution theorem provers can be designed to be complete in the sense that given a formula F and a set of formulas S, such a theorem prover will find a proof that F logically follows from S if such a proof exists. Unfortunately, it is possible that a resolution theorem prover may never terminate in dealing with a purported theorem that actually has no proof. In fact, it is a result in general that no theorem prover can be guaranteed to terminate in such a situation; resolution theorem provers therefore provide us with as much as can be expected.

In proving that a given formula F logically follows from a set of formulas S the strategy of a resolution theorem prover is to show that the negation of F ($\sim F$) is *inconsistent* with S. This means that there are no models for the set of formulas S', where S' is the union of S and $\{\sim F\}$. The models of S' are just the models of S in which $\sim F$ is also true. However, if F logically follows from S, then F is true in all models of S, and $\sim F$ is false in all models of S, so there are no models of S'. In this case S' is said to be *unsatisfiable*. Conversely, if S' is unsatisfiable but S is satisfiable, then for all models of S, $\sim F$ must be false and F must be true. This in turn means that S logically implies F by a form of deduction analogous to the truth table method of the propositional calculus. To show that F logically follows from a satisfiable set of formulas S, then, it is sufficient to show that S' is unsatisfiable.

---

[4]Logic programming has become a very rich topic for research from which a number of specific languages besides PROLOG have been developed. A well-respected treatment of the topic of logic programming can be found in *Logic for Problem Solving* by R.A. Kowalski [Kow79].

The resolution theorem proving process basically consists of four steps. The first step is to reduce every formula H in S' to a canonical form called its *conjunctive normal form*. The conjunctive normal form is essentially a "product of sums"; that is, it is the conjunction (i.e., product) of terms called *clauses*, each clause being a disjunction (i.e., sum) of literals. In the predicate calculus, terms can be either predicate expressions or negations of predicate expressions.

The second step is to transform each conjunctive normal form into a different representation called the *clause-form equivalent*. This is a very simple form to work with, containing no implications, equivalences, or explicitly quantified formulas. It can conveniently be represented by a set of clauses. Then the union of two such sets is again a set of clauses and corresponds to the clause-form equivalent of the conjunction of the two formulas represented by the sets.

Once the clause-form equivalent of each formula H in S' is found, the second step is completed by taking the union of all the clauses to form the clause-form equivalent of the entire set of formulas S'. The assertion of this conjunction simply reflects the assumption that all the formulas are true; that is, the entire set of formulas S' is satisfiable. This set provides the initial input to the next step (the application of the resolution principle) by providing a representation of S' as a collection of clauses.

The third step of resolution theorem proving is to use the resolution inference rule (to be defined presently) to derive more clauses which follow from pairs of clauses of S'. For each pair of clauses which belong to S', and for which the rule can be applied, a new clause is defined and added to the set S'. This process is carried out repeatedly until a null disjunct (i.e., null clause) is created. This corresponds to the discovery of a contradiction.

The final step is the recognition of a null disjunct. A *null disjunct* is a disjunction whose set of terms is the empty set. Since a disjunction is true if and only if at least one of its disjuncts are true, a null disjunct is always false. When a null disjunct is found, S' has then been proven to be unsatisfiable and hence we can conclude that F is proven to logically follow from S. This is because the original set S was assumed to be satisfiable. As $S' = S \cup \{\sim F\}$ is unsatisfiable, therefore, $\sim F$ must be inconsistent with S. Since this result is true of all models, it is the case that $S \cup \{F\}$ is satisfiable; that is, F follows logically from S.

In the following sections each of these steps is described in more detail.

10.4 CONVERSION TO CONJUNCTIVE NORMAL FORM

This section addresses the first step of the theorem-proving process just described. The activity required is an example of the symbolic computing technique of transformation to canonical form; in this case, the transformation of a set of logical formulas defined by the GRAIL grammar given previously, into a set of clauses—the conjunctive normal form of the input set. The output set is thus a subset of the input set, and therefore the grammar which defines the valid inputs can also be used to define the outputs.

Conversion of a formula to a conjunctive normal form is a multistep process, and each step is addressed separately in the remainder of this section.

10.4.1 Elimination of Implications and Equivalences

The first step is to eliminate all implications and equivalences using the following rules, expressed in terms of the GRAIL grammar for inputs:

$$(f1 \ \text{IMPLIES} \ f2) \mapsto (\text{OR} \ (\text{NOT} \ f1) \ f2)$$

$$(f1 \ \text{EQUIV} \ f2) \mapsto (\text{AND} \ (\text{OR} \ (\text{NOT} \ f1) \ f2) \ (\text{OR} \ (\text{NOT} \ f2) \ f1))$$

The transformation of a logical formula to an equivalent expression that is free of the operations of implication and equivalence can be described by the following recursive definition:

1. If the logical formula is a predicate expression, it contains no implications or equivalences; therefore, return the formula.
2. If the logical formula is a negation, transform its negend.
3. If the logical formula is a disjunction or conjunction, transform the operands (disjuncts or conjuncts).
4. If the logical formula is a quantified expression, transform its quantified form.
5. Otherwise, transform the operands of the logical formula (it is either an implication or an equivalence) and construct a new formula by applying the appropriate one of the two rules given above.

This replacement process can be implemented as a recursive program defined on the domain of predicate calculus formulas as follows. The prior implementation of the data access functions for the abstract data type ⟨formula⟩, based on the grammar of Figure 10.1, is assumed:

```
(defun eliminate1 (WFF)
  (cond ((pred-expr-p WFF) WFF)
        ((negation-p WFF)
         (make-negation (eliminate1 (negend WFF))))
        ((conjunction-p WFF)
         (make-conjunction
           (mapcar #'eliminate1 (conjuncts WFF))))
        ((disjunction-p WFF)
         (make-disjunction
           (mapcar #'eliminate1 (disjuncts WFF))))
        ((implication-p WFF)
         (make-disjunction
           (list
             (make-negation (eliminate1 (antecedent WFF)))
             (eliminate1 (consequent WFF)))))
        ((equivalence-p WFF)
         (let ((F1 (eliminate1 (condition1 WFF)))
               (F2 (eliminate1 (condition2 WFF))))
           (make-conjunction
             (list
```

```
                    (make-disjunction
                      (list (make-negation F1) F2))
                    (make-disjunction
                      (list (make-negation F2) F1))))))
           ((universal-p WFF)
             (make-universal
               (bound-var WFF)
               (eliminate1 (quantified-form WFF))))
           ((existential-p WFF)
             (make-existential
               (bound-var WFF)
               (eliminate1 (quantified-form WFF))))))
```

Observe the role of the functional mapcar in the implementation of eliminate1. The actual mapping that we require (and that is conveniently provided by mapcar) is as follows. Given a mapped function which both takes a formula as an argument and returns a formula, the mapping function should apply that mapped function to all elements of a formula list and return the new formula list comprising the result formulas. In this case we want to eliminate the implications and equivalences from the conjuncts and disjuncts of the formula bound to WFF,[5] and then construct an equivalent formula from the transformed conjuncts and disjuncts.

10.4.2 Inward Propagation of Negations

The second step of conversion to conjunctive normal form is to propagate the negations inward so that only predicate expressions are negated. Again, it is possible to characterize the possible transformations by a set of rules:

$$(\text{NOT (NOT } f)) \mapsto f$$
$$(\text{NOT (AND } f1\ f2 \ldots fn)) \mapsto (\text{OR (NOT } f1)\ (\text{NOT } f2) \ldots (\text{NOT } fn))$$
$$(\text{NOT (OR } f1\ f2 \ldots fn)) \mapsto (\text{AND (NOT } f1)\ (\text{NOT } f2) \ldots (\text{NOT } fn))$$
$$(\text{NOT (FORALL } x\ f)) \mapsto (\text{EXISTS } x\ (\text{NOT } f))$$
$$(\text{NOT (EXISTS } x\ f)) \mapsto (\text{FORALL } x\ (\text{NOT } f))$$

A recursive definition for the required transformation is given by:

1. If the logical formula is a predicate expression, negate it.
2. If the logical formula is a negation, transform the negend.
3. Otherwise, apply the appropriate rule as given above, depending on whether the logical formula is a conjunction, disjunction, or quantified expression (universal or existential).

---

[5]WFF (pronounced "woof") is short for *well-formed formula*, a commonly used term synonymous with "logical formula." Its use in the function emphasizes the fact that there is an assumption that the formal parameter will only be bound to valid representations of logical formulas, and therefore no validity checking is performed.

In order to implement the inward propagation of negations, it is most convenient to define two mutually recursive procedures. The first, `propagate`, processes formulas recursively looking for negations:

```
(defun propagate (WFF)
   (cond ((pred-expr-p WFF) WFF)
         ((negation-p WFF) (negate (negend WFF)))
         ((conjunction-p WFF)
            (make-conjunction
               (mapcar #'propagate (conjuncts WFF))))

         ((disjunction-p WFF)
            (make-disjunction
               (mapcar #'propagate (disjuncts WFF))))

         ((universal-p WFF)
            (make-universal
               (bound-var WFF)
               (propagate (quantified-form WFF))))

         ((existential-p WFF)
            (make-existential
               (bound-var WFF)
               (propagate (quantified-form WFF))))))
```

When `propagate` finds a negation, it calls the second procedure, `negate`, to form the replacement formula and continue the negation process. In directly applying the rules above, `negate` would form subexpressions that are negations themselves and which would have to be simplified recursively by a call to `propagate`. Instead of doing this, however, formation of the negated subexpressions are skipped by having `negate` call itself directly:

```
(defun negate (WFF)
   (cond ((predexpr-p WFF) (make-negation WFF))
         ((negation-p WFF) (propagate (negend WFF)))
         ((conjunction-p WFF)
            (make-disjunction
               (mapcar #'negate (conjuncts WFF))))

         ((disjunction-p WFF)
            (make-conjunction
               (mapcar #'negate (disjuncts WFF))))

         ((universal-p WFF)
            (make-existential
               (boundvar WFF)
               (negate (quantifiedform WFF))))
```

```
((existential-p WFF)
 (make-universal
  (boundvar WFF)
  (negate (quantifiedform WFF))))))
```

Once again mapcar has been used to permit the application of a mapped function (propagate and negate) to the operands of a disjunction or conjunction.

10.4.3 Variable Standardization

The third step in conversion to conjunctive normal form is to standardize variables. The purpose of this step is to rename the quantified variables of every quantified expression so that each quantifier binds a unique variable name. This will pave the way for the eventual elimination of quantifiers.

First of all, a function is needed to generate a new unique variable name every time it is called. There are several ways that such a function could be implemented, such as by keeping track of names already supplied in the Lisp global state, or by interactively asking the user for new unique names. We shall not concern ourselves with the actual implementation of such a function since it is commonly provided in Lisp systems. For our purposes we shall use the function provided in Common LISP, called gensym. In its simplest form, gensym can be treated as a function of no arguments, in which case it returns a different symbol of the form G-nnn each time it is called, where nnn denotes a sequence of digits.[6]

The second requirement for the implementation of variable standardization is the need to provide an environment which maps the old names for variables to their newly generated names. When a universal or existential formula is encountered, a new unique name is generated for, and replaces, its bound variable. The new name must also be used to replace all occurrences of the original bound variable in the formula which is quantified; the environment is thus used to define which replacements must occur in the recursive analysis of formulas.

A function to standardize the variables of a formula may now be implemented as follows:

```
(defun WFF-rename (WFF)
  (ren-aux WFF null-env))

(defun ren-aux (WFF env)
  (cond ((pred-expr-p WFF)
         (make-pred-expr
          (pred-name WFF)
          (mapcar #'term-rename (terms WFF))))

        ((negation-p WFF)
         (make-negation (ren-aux (negend WFF) env)))
```

---

[6]The number of digits is implementation dependent.

```
      ((conjunction-p WFF)
        (make-conjunction
          (mapcar
            #'(lambda (conj) (ren-aux conj env))
            (conjuncts WFF))))

      ((disjunction-p WFF)
        (make-disjunction
          (mapcar
            #'(lambda (disj) (ren-aux disj env))
            (disjuncts WFF))))

      ((universal-p WFF)
        (let ((newvar (gensym)))
          (make-universal
            newvar
            (ren-aux
              (quantified-form WFF)
              (add-env env (bound-var WFF) newvar)))))

      ((existential-p WFF)
        (let ((newvar (gensym)))
          (make-existential
            newvar
            (ren-aux
              (quantified-form WFF)
              (add-env env (bound-var WFF) newvar)))))))))

(defun term-rename (term)
  (cond ((variable-p term) (apply-env env term))
        ((func-expr-p term)
          (make-func-expr
            (func-name term)
            (mapcar #'term-rename (arguments term))))))
```

10.4.4 Elimination of Existential Quantifiers

The fourth step in conversion to conjunctive normal form is to eliminate existential quantifiers by a process known as *Skolemization*. Consider, for example, the formula

$$\forall x \forall y \exists z P(x, y, z) \qquad (10.1)$$

which asserts that, for all values of x and y, there is a z (dependent on x and y), such that $P(x, y, z)$ is true. If this is in fact true, then a function g will exist such that the values of z which make $P(x, y, z)$ true are given by $z = g(x, y)$. The function g is called a *Skolem function* and allows formula (10.1) to be replaced by the following formula:

$$\forall x \forall y P(x, y, g(x, y)) \qquad (10.2)$$

The validity of this Skolemization substitution can be seen as follows. If formula (10.1) is true, at least one Skolem function g exists for each model of (10.1), so all models of (10.1) are also models of (10.2) with some additional interpretation for g. This in turn means that (10.2) is true in all models of (10.1) (with an additional interpretation for g). On the other hand, if formula (10.1) is false, no function g can exist and hence there are no models of (10.2). Formula (10.2) is thus unsatisfiable, that is, false in all possible interpretations.

Skolemization is applicable to any well-formed formula obtained as a result of the first three steps in the conversion of a logical expression to conjunctive normal form. Each existentially quantified subformula of such a well-formed formula is replaced by a corresponding subformula possessing a unique Skolem function. As illustrated by the example above, the terms of such a function depend on the universally quantified variables within whose scope the subformula lies.

Now consider how a function, skolemize, can be defined to recursively introduce Skolem functions and replace existentially quantified variables. Whenever a Skolem function is to be introduced it must have argument terms for each of the currently visible universally quantified variables. Thus we introduce an auxiliary function SK-AUX as the recursive workhorse, having a parameter uvars which is a list of these currently visible universally quantified variables. A form (make-func-expr (gensym) uvars) can then be used to generate the Skolem term. A second parameter evars now becomes necessary to specify the environment mapping existential variables encountered so far to the Skolem terms that will be used to replace them.

The Skolemization process can be implemented as follows:

```
(defun skolemize (WFF)
  (sk-aux WFF '() null-env))

(defun sk-aux (WFF uvars evars)
  (cond ((pred-expr-p WFF)
            (make-pred-expr
              (pred-name WFF)
              (mapcar #'(lambda (trm) (sk-term trm uvars evars))
                (terms WFF))))

         ((negation-p WFF)
            (make-negation (sk-aux (negend WFF) uvars evars)))

         ((conjunction-p WFF)
            (make-conjunction
              (mapcar
                #'(lambda (conj) (sk-aux conj uvars evars))
                (conjuncts WFF))))

         ((disjunction-p WFF)
            (make-disjunction
              (mapcar
```

```
                    #'(lambda (disj) (sk-aux disj uvars evars))
                    (disjuncts WFF))))

          ((universal-p WFF)
            (make-universal
              (bound-var WFF)
              (sk-aux (quantified-form WFF)
                      (cons (bound-var WFF) uvars)
                      evars)))

          ((existential-p WFF)
            (sk-aux
              (quantified-form WFF)
              uvars
              (add-env evars
                       (bound-var WFF)
                       (make-func-expr (gensym) uvars))))))

  (defun sk-term (term uvars evars)
    (cond ((variable-p term)
           (cond ((member term uvars) term)
                 (T (apply-env evars term))))
          (T (make-func-expr
               (func-name term)
               (mapcar #'(lambda (trm) (sk-term trm uvars evars))
                       (arguments term)))))))
```

10.4.5 Elimination of Universal Quantifiers

At this point, a logical formula has been transformed into an expression devoid of implications and equivalences, and possessing distinct labels for each quantified variable. In addition, no existentially quantified expressions remain as a result of Skolemization. The fifth step in transforming the representation of the original logical formula to conjunctive normal form is the "elimination" of the explicit representation of universal quantification. In actual fact universally quantified formulas are neither eliminated nor replaced by an alternative formula. Rather, this step serves only to simplify the symbolic representations of the universally quantified expressions obtained upon completion of the previous four steps. More important, this representation is only applicable to expressions which have been assigned unique quantified variable labels and for which existential quantification has been eliminated.

The simplification is achieved by representing the formula as the *matrix* of its *prenex* form. The prenex form of a formula is that obtained by propagating all its universal quantifiers outward, a step which is valid given that all variables have unique names. After conversion to prenex form, a formula will typically look like $\forall x \forall y \forall z \ldots$, where $\ldots$ denotes a formula containing no quantifiers and is the matrix of the prenex formula. Since all existentially quantified variables have been eliminated from the formula, the matrix can be used to represent the entire formula using the assumption that all its variables are implicitly universally quantified. The implementation of functions to perform this task is left as an exercise for the reader (see Exercise 10.3).

10.4.6 Conjunctive Normal Form

The matrix obtained in the preceding step now serves as the representation of our formula. It can be viewed as a formula recursively constructed using conjunction and disjunction with predicate expressions and their negations as "atomic" entities. To convert to conjunctive normal form, the formula must now be transformed to a single conjunction of a set of clauses, each of which is a disjunction of literals (i.e., predicate expressions and their negations).

This transformation can be achieved by recursively applying the following rules:

$$(\text{OR } f1 \ (\text{AND } f2 \ f3)) \mapsto (\text{AND } (\text{OR } f1 \ f2) \ (\text{OR } f1 \ f3))$$
$$(\text{OR } f1 \ (\text{OR } f2 \ f3)) \mapsto (\text{OR } f1 \ f2 \ f3)$$
$$(\text{AND } f1 \ (\text{AND } f2 \ f3)) \mapsto (\text{AND } f1 \ f2 \ f3)$$

The first of these rules is applied first and in effect "propagates" all conjunctions outward. Conjunctions and disjunctions can then be "flattened out"; that is, expressed as a single polyadic disjunction or conjunction using the second and third rules. Finally, if the entire formula involves no conjunctions—in other words, it is a single disjunction or literal—it is made into a conjunction with a single conjunct. Similarly, if any conjunct is a single literal rather than a disjunction of literals, it is made into the disjunction of a single literal.

The following example summarizes this section by illustrating the transformation of a set of logical formulas, specifying a set of assertions and an inference, to conjunctive canonical form.

We begin with the following assertions:

```
(FORALL X ((R X) IMPLIES (L X)))
(FORALL X ((D X) IMPLIES (NOT (L X))))
(EXISTS X (AND (D X) (I X)))
```

These three formulas constitute the set S. Now suppose that we wish to determine whether

```
(EXISTS X (AND (I X) (NOT (R X))))
```

can be inferred from these premises. This expression defines F. The set of formulas $S' = S \cup \{\sim F\}$ thus consists of

```
(FORALL X ((R X) IMPLIES (L X)))
(FORALL X ((D X) IMPLIES (NOT (L X))))
(EXISTS X (AND (D X) (I X)))
(NOT (EXISTS X (AND (I X) (NOT (R X)))))
```

To convert the formulas to clause-form equivalent, we first eliminate implications and equivalences. This transforms the set S to the following:

```
(FORALL X (OR (NOT (R X)) (L X)))
(FORALL X (OR (NOT (D X)) (NOT (L X))))
(EXISTS X (AND (D X) (I X)))
(NOT (EXISTS X (AND (I X) (NOT (R X)))))
```

Next we propagate negations inward:

```
(FORALL X (OR (NOT (R X)) (L X)))
(FORALL X (OR (NOT (D X)) (NOT (L X))))
(EXISTS X (AND (D X) (I X)))
(FORALL X (OR (NOT (I X)) (R X)))
```

At this point it is necessary to standardize quantified variables. While it is self-evident that the four quantified variables each called X in the four formulas refers to four different variables, this must be made explicit:

```
(FORALL G1 (OR (NOT (R G1)) (L G1)))
(FORALL G2 (OR (NOT (D G2)) (NOT (L G2))))
(EXISTS G3 (AND (D G3) (I G3)))
(FORALL G4 (OR (NOT (I G4)) (R G4)))
```

Thus G1, G2, G3, and G4 are four distinct quantified variables, replacing X. Skolemization can now be performed to eliminate existential quantifiers:

```
(FORALL G1 (OR (NOT (R G1)) (L G1)))
(FORALL G2 (OR (NOT (D G2)) (NOT (L G2))))
(AND (D (A1)) (I (A1))))
(FORALL G4 (OR (NOT (I G4)) (R G4)))
```

Here (A1) is the list representation (as defined by the grammar of Figure 10.1) of a Skolem function of no variables (i.e., a Skolem "constant"). In this instance, we assume that (EXISTS G3 (AND (D G3) (I G3))) is true when G3 = (A1). Of course, the formula may be true for other values of G3 as well.

Universal quantifiers can now be made implicit:

```
(OR (NOT (R G1)) (L G1))
(OR (NOT (D G2)) (NOT (L G2)))
(AND (D (A1)) (I (A1))))
(OR (NOT (I G4)) (R G4))
```

Note that quantification is still implied by the appearance of otherwise free variables G1, G2, and G4 in the formulas.

In this example, we now have four formulas in conjunctive normal form. Except for (AND (D (A1)) (I (A1)))) each formula consists of a single conjunct which is a disjunction. The formula (AND (D (A1)) (I (A1)))), on the other hand, possesses two conjuncts, which are, in effect disjunctions with one disjunct. The conjunctive normal form of the set S' is given by

```
(AND
  (OR (NOT (R G1)) (L G1))
  (OR (NOT (D G2)) (NOT (L G2)))
  (OR (D (A1)))
  (OR (I (A1)))
  (OR (NOT (I G4)) (R G4)))
```

10.5 CLAUSE-FORM EQUIVALENT REPRESENTATION

Once each formula in the set S' of formulas has been converted to conjunctive normal form, the representation of each by its clause-form equivalent and the determination of the clause-form equivalent of the entire set of formulas is straightforward. In conjunctive normal form each formula consists of a single conjunction; its clause-form equivalent is simply the set of all its conjuncts, which now consist only of clauses (disjunctions of literals). Since each clause can only be a disjunction, it can be represented by a set of literals (predicate expressions or their negations). This set can be implemented as a list and is obtained by applying the selector function disjuncts to the list representation of the disjunction, as defined by the grammar of Figure 10.1.

The clause-form equivalent of a formula can be obtained from the list representation by applying the selector conjuncts to the conjunctive normal form. This returns a list of the conjuncts. Since the set S' is an implicit conjunction of formulas, the clause-form equivalent of the entire set is simply the union of the sets of clauses for each formula. Using a list representation for sets, the Lisp function append can be used to define set union; in particular, the clause-form equivalent of S' is obtained by appending the lists corresponding to the clause-form equivalents. Thus the entire set of formulas may be represented as a list of clauses, which in turn are just lists of literals. Each list of literals is implicitly a disjunction, and the list of disjunctions is implicitly a conjunction.

As a consequence of this analysis, it is useful to adopt a different, simpler representation for the clause-form equivalent from that specified by the grammar of Figure 10.1. The grammar for clause-form equivalent representation is given in Figure 10.2.

Continuing the example of Section 10.4, the conjunctive normal form obtained there can be represented, using the grammar of Figure 10.2, by the following clause-form equivalent set:

```
(
  (  (NOT (R G1))   (L G1)    )
  (  (NOT (D G2))   (NOT (L G2))    )
  (  (D (A1))   )
  (  (I (A1))   )
  (  (NOT (I G4))   (R G4)   )
)
```

It is clear from this representation that what remains is a list of five clauses. Each clause is in turn a list of predicate expressions or the complement of predicate expressions.

⟨clause-form-equiv⟩ ::= (⟨clause*⟩)

⟨clause⟩ ::= (⟨predicate*⟩)

⟨predicate⟩ ::= ⟨pred-expr⟩ | ⟨negation⟩

⟨pred-expr⟩ ::= (⟨pred-name:pred-id⟩ ⟨terms:term*⟩)

⟨term⟩ ::= ⟨func-expr⟩ | ⟨variable⟩

⟨func-expr⟩ ::= (⟨func-name:func-id⟩ ⟨arguments:term*⟩)

⟨negation⟩ ::= (NOT ⟨negend:pred-expr⟩)

⟨pred-id⟩ ::= ⟨p-name:symbolic-atom⟩

⟨func-id⟩ ::= ⟨f-name:symbolic atom⟩

⟨variable⟩ ::= ⟨v-name:symbolic atom⟩

Figure 10.2   GRAIL grammar for the representation of clause-form equivalents.

10.6 RESOLUTION INFERENCE RULE

Given a set of formulas represented by their clause-form equivalent, the resolution inference rule can be applied repeatedly to derive any fact which logically follows from the set of formulas. The basic idea is to find conflicting literals in a pair of clauses and construct a new clause which is the union of the literals of both clauses, less the conflicting literals. For example, let a, b, c, d, and e be metavariables denoting literals (predicate expressions or their negations). Using our list representation for clauses, given the clauses (a b c) and ($\sim c$ d e), the literals c and $\sim c$ conflict. This means that either $\sim c$ or c is true, which in turn means that either (a b) is true or (d e) is true, further implying that the clause (a b d e) is true. By the resolution inference rule, a clause has been derived whose literals comprise the union of the literals of the two original clauses less the conflicting literals.

In resolution theorem proving, recall that the basic goal is to show that the set of formulas S' is unsatisfiable. This is typically done by showing that for some literal a, both it and its negation must be true. This situation is reflected in the clause-form equivalent of S' by having two clauses, (a) and ($\sim a$). By the resolution inference rule, the two clauses have conflicting literals, so a new clause may be inferred whose literals are the union of the literals of the first two clauses less the conflicting literals. In this case, the result is a clause with no literals at all, represented as ( ) and called the *null disjunct* or *null clause*. Whenever the null disjunct is derived in resolution theorem proving, the original set of formulas S' is proven to be unsatisfiable, completing the proof.

In general, the notion of conflicting literals does not require that the literals contradict each other in all cases, but only that there exist substitutions for their (universally quantified) variables which generate such contradictions. For example, in the pair of clauses ($P(x)$ $Q(x,y)$) and ($\sim P(a)$ $R(b)$), the literals $P(x)$ and $\sim P(a)$ conflict for $x = a$. Either $\sim P(a)$ is true or $P(a)$ is true, which in turn means that either $Q(a, y)$ is true or $R(b)$ is true. Thus the new clause $(Q(a, y)\ R(b))$ can be inferred from the two given ones by the resolution inference rule.

The resolution inference rule is not restricted to dealing with pairs of conflicting literals, but may find a substitution under which several literals conflict. Consider, for example, the clauses $(P(x, f(x))\ P(a, y)\ Q(y))$ and $(\sim P(z, f(a))\ Q(f(z)))$. Both $P(x, f(x))$ and $P(a, y)$ conflict with $\sim P(z, f(a))$ under the substitutions $x = a, y = f(a), z = a$. In this case, either $\sim P(a, f(a))$ is true or $P(a, f(a))$ is true, in turn implying that $Q(f(a))$ is true from the first clause or $Q(f(a))$ is true from the second clause. Since these are both the same, by the resolution inference rule we can infer the simple, single-literal clause $(Q(f(a)))$ from the original two complicated clauses.

In general, resolution inference consists of matching the literals of one clause with the negated literals of a second clause, by finding a suitable substitution for variables. This matching process is called *unification* and the substitutions that permit such a match to occur are called *unifying substitutions*, or simply *unifiers*. If such a match is found, the two clauses are said to *resolve*. The literal eliminated from each clause is said to be *resolved out* and the remaining, inferred clause is called the *resolvent*. The resolvent is produced by eliminating the matched literals and applying the unifying substitution to the remaining literals.

This section has attempted to explain the concept behind the inference rule that will be the "driver" for the theorem prover. From a symbolic computing viewpoint the important issues are those of representation of the input and implementation of the resolution rule itself. The input consists of a set of clauses which collectively define the clause-form equivalent of the set $S' = S \cup \{\sim F\}$, where we wish to show that F can be inferred from the set of formulas S. To implement the resolution principle requires a strategy for deciding how to examine subsets of clauses from both the clause-form equivalent and the set of resolvents that will accumulate with each unifying substitution that is made. Theorem proving is thus transformed into a problem of searching for a sequence of transformations from a set of assertions to a "goal" formula; in the case of resolution theorem proving, it is the search for a sequence of unifiers that results in obtaining the null clause as a resolvent.

10.7 UNIFICATION

Unification is the process by which new resolvents are created and added to the initial set of clauses in the search for the null clause.[7] From the examples given in the preceding section, a unifying substitution can be specified by a set of pairs, each pair specifying a universally quantified variable and a value bound to it. This is characteristic of the environment data types described in Chapter 6, and this observation suggests that environments can be applied in this context.

The process of unification on clauses may be formally described as follows. Let θ denote an environment mapping variables to terms for substitution. For a given clause C, let $C[\theta]$ denote the clause obtained from C by performing the substitution

---

[7]The concept of unification can in fact be applied to logical formulas in general. For the purposes of this chapter, however, it will be applied only to disjunctions of literals (clauses).

defined by θ. The substitution θ is called a unifier for a set of literals $\{L_i\}$ if there exists a literal L such that $L_i[\theta] = L$ for each L_i, in which case L is called a *unification* for $\{L_i\}$. Thus under the substitution θ all occurrences of the literals L_i are replaced by the literal L.

For any given set of literals $\{L_i\}$, there may in fact be several unifiers. For example, for the pair of predicate expressions

$$P(x, f(y), b)$$
$$P(x, f(b), b)$$

two possible unifiers are

$$\theta_1 = [x = a, \; y = b]$$
$$\theta_2 = [y = b]$$

θ_1 produces the unification $L_1 = P(a, f(b), b)$, while θ_2 produces the unification $L_2 = P(x, f(b), b)$. The unifier θ_2 is said to be *more general* than θ_1 since it does not require a substitution for the variable x. The use of θ_2 instead of θ_1 will keep x free to be instantiated in some other way in further resolution steps, and hence is to be preferred.

In performing unification, then, it is desirable to find a most general unifier for a given set of literals. A unifier θ producing a unification L for a set of literals $\{L_i\}$ is *a most general unifier* if, for any other unifier θ_1 producing L_1, there is a further substitution θ_2 such that $L[\theta_2] = L_1$.

It is also possible that for a given set of literals no unifier exists. In this case, the set of literals is said to be *not unifiable*.

A *unification algorithm* is a procedure for determining whether a given set of literals is unifiable, and if so, a most general unifier for them. This algorithm can be implemented using a technique called pattern matching, a topic discussed in the next chapter. Since each predicate expression is to be represented by a list of constants, variables, and function expressions in our implementation, the following observations can be employed in such an algorithm, which in effect compares the structure and components of two lists:

1. If both objects are variables, they are replaced in the unification by a new unique variable.

2. If both objects are function expressions, the function names must be identical and corresponding components of their argument lists must be recursively compared. Constants are but special cases of function expressions and correspond to functions of no variables.

3. If one object is a variable, the corresponding component in the unification is a copy of the other object.

4. If none of the above is satisfied, no unifier exists.

In an actual implementation, these observations are embodied in a recursive algorithm to construct the unifier θ rather than the unification L. This is preferable to returning the unification since it provides us with an environment which defines the bindings of the same variables in other predicate expressions of a clause. The unification algorithm is used to obtain resolvents by applying it to an unnegated predicate expression from one clause and the negend of a negated predicate expression from a second clause. This process is described in the next section.

10.8 THE RESOLUTION PROCESS

Unification is the basis for defining the inference rule that is employed in a resolution theorem prover. Formally, the resolution inference rule is specified as follows. Let $\{L_i\}$ and $\{M_i\}$ be the sets of literals of two clauses $C1$ and $C2$. Then let $\{l_i\}$ be a subset of $\{L_i\}$ and $\{m_i\}$ be a subset of $\{M_i\}$, such that a most general unifier θ exists for the union: $\{l_i\} \cup \{\sim m_i\}$. The resolution inference rule then states that clauses $C1$ and $C2$ logically imply clause $C3$, whose literals are given as follows:

$$(\{L_i\} - \{l_i\})[\theta] \cup (\{M_i\} - \{m_i\})[\theta]$$

That is, the literals of $C3$ are obtained by applying the unifier θ to two sets of literals: the literals of $C1$ except for $\{l_i\}$ and the literals of $C2$ except for $\{m_i\}$. The union of the two resulting sets provides the literals of $C3$. As defined previously, the clause $C3$ is said to be a *resolvent* of $C1$ and $C2$.

For every pair of clauses $C1$ and $C2$, the *complete resolution process* determines all resolvents of the two clauses by applying the resolution inference rule to all combinations of subsets of literals $\{l_i\}$ and $\{m_i\}$. Note that certain combinations can be eliminated immediately as not unifiable:

1. When not all the literals have the same predicate name
2. When $\{l_i\} \cup \{\sim m_i\}$ does not consist of either all negative or all positive literals

The *resolution procedure* for showing the unsatisfiability of a set of clauses S' can now be described as follows:

1. Using the unification algorithm to obtain most general unifiers, apply the resolution process to all pairs of clauses in S' yielding a set of resolvents $R(S')$.
2. If any resolvent is the null disjunct, the proof is complete. Otherwise, augment the set S' with the additional formulas $R(S')$ and repeat the procedure.

This procedure is essentially a breadth-first search for a refutation of the satisfiability of S'.

Given that S' is formed by the union of S and $\{\sim F\}$, the resolution procedure can also be used to construct a proof by contradiction that S implies F.[8] This is done by associating with each resolvent generated, the parent clauses from which it was derived. When the null disjunct is obtained, a proof can be constructed by tracing the sequence of applications of resolution backward to the original clauses in S'. This trace is equivalent to constructing a tree whose root is the null clause, whose internal nodes are resolvents, and whose leaves are the initial set of clauses which were obtained in the transformation of $S \cup \{\sim F\}$ to clause equivalent form.

We can now apply the resolution principle, via the unification algorithm, to obtain resolvents from the initial set of clauses obtained in the example of Section 10.4:

$$C1 = (\ (\text{NOT } (\text{R G1}))\ (\text{L G1})\ )$$

---

[8]This is also referred to as a *refutation* proof.

$$C2 = (\ (\text{NOT } (D \ G2)) \ (\text{NOT } (L \ G2))\ )$$
$$C3 = (\ (D \ (A1))\ )$$
$$C4 = (\ (I \ (A1))\ )$$
$$C5 = (\ (\text{NOT } (I \ G4)) \ (R \ G4)\ )$$

From this set, the following resolvents are obtained:

1. ((NOT (R G5)) (NOT (D G5))) from $C1$ and $C2$ using the unifier [G1 = G2]. Since both G1 and G2 are both variables, the resolvent contains a new variable G5.
2. ((NOT (L (A1)))) from $C2$ and $C3$ using the unifier [G2 = (A1)].
3. ((NOT (I G6)) (L G6)) from $C1$ and $C5$ using the unifier [G1 = G4]. Again, the matching of two variables results in a new variable, G6, being introduced into the resolvent.
4. ((R (A1))) from $C4$ and $C5$ using the unifier [G4 = (A1)].

None of the resolvents is the null clause, so they are added to the initial set, providing a total of nine clauses. For convenience of reference, the four new ones are labeled as follows:

$$C6 = (\ (\text{NOT } (R \ G5)) \ (\text{NOT } (D \ G5))\ )$$
$$C7 = (\ (\text{NOT } (L \ (A1)))\ )$$
$$C8 = (\ (\text{NOT } (I \ G6)) \ (L \ G6)\ )$$
$$C9 = (\ (R \ (A1))\ )$$

In the second iteration, four more clauses can be obtained. However, the first of these is ((NOT (R (A1)))) from $C1$ and $C7$ using the unifier [G1 = (A1)]. At this point, we observe that this resolvent is the negation of clause $C9$ and therefore when resolved with it will yield the null clause as a new resolvent using unifier [(A1) = (A1)]. In a breadth-first search, of course, all possible resolvents (there are three more) would be generated from the nine clauses, and it would not be until the third iteration, on the resulting set of thirteen clauses, that the null clause would be obtained as a resolvent.

As with any search, efficiency is an important issue for automated theorem proving, and two important questions arise:

1. What is the "best" way to obtain new resolvents?
2. What happens if no proof exists?

Attempting to answer the first question has resulted in the formulation of a number of different strategies, each of which restricts which clauses can be used to obtain resolvents. Such restrictions generally result in strategies which are incomplete; that is, they are not always guaranteed to find a proof whenever one exists. Practical theorem provers may combine strategies in order to provide completeness or at least to reduce the number of cases in which they will fail. For example, PROLOG permits assertions only in the form of *Horn clauses*. Horn clauses are clauses with at most one positive literal, and this restriction simplifies the search for potential candidates for unification.

The second question actually expresses a more serious problem. Predicate calculus is not *decidable*; that is, there is no general way to evaluate quantified formulas to determine their validity. In the propositional calculus this could always be determined by constructing a truth table. As a consequence, it will not always be possible to determine the validity of any logical formula. In the context of the resolution inference principle, this means that it will not always be possible to show unsatisfiability of a given clause-form equivalent. It is, however, the case that if a formula is valid, a proof exists, and therefore, if our theorem prover is complete, it will (eventually) find a proof given a valid clause-form equivalent. For practical reasons, implementation of complete resolution theorem provers should suspend execution after a predetermined time has passed or a number of resolvents have been produced without obtaining the null clause.

10.9 EXERCISES

10.1. Use resolution to establish that (EXISTS X (H X)) can be inferred from the following assertions:

```
(FORALL X ((L X) IMPLIES (OR (P X) (A X))))
(EXISTS X (AND (L X) (NOT (P X))))
(FORALL X ((A X) IMPLIES (H X)))
```

10.2. Define in Common LISP a function which returns the value T if a given S-expression defines a valid clause-form equivalent according to the GRAIL grammar given in Figure 10.2.

10.3. In Section 10.4.5 a representation called the *matrix of the prenex formula* was described. Implement a function which eliminates universal quantifiers, returning its result in this representation. Define grammars which describe the symbolic input and output domains of the function.

10.4. Among the methods for proving theorems of the propositional calculus are the truth-table method and the method based on Wang's rules. Another proof method is called *natural deduction*. A system called LCF [GMW81] has been developed which implements natural deduction proofs. The system employs what are referred to as *rewrite rules*. After reading the article, describe the primary purpose of the rewrite rules, and how they extend the expressiveness of propositional logic as a formal language for the representation of knowledge.

10.5. Under what circumstances do Horn clauses (as defined in Section 10.8) arise? That is, show what kinds of logical formulas give rise to Horn clauses in their transformation to conjunctive normal form.

10.6. Propose a representation of the clause-form equivalent if one assumes that it includes only Horn clauses and show how such a representation permits a more efficient search for pairs of clauses which can be unified. Rewrite the clauses $C1$ through $C5$, given in Section 10.8, using the representation proposed. Compare the effort required with that of searching for unifiers among a set of arbitrary clauses.

10.7. Write a function that recognizes whether a given logical formula becomes a Horn clause when transformed to conjunctive normal form.

10.8. Consider a restricted form of clause-form equivalent consisting only of Horn clauses in which no variable occurs more than once in any predicate or function.

    (a) Write a resolution theorem prover for such restricted clause-form equivalents.

    (b) What implementation difficulties arise if multiple occurrences of variables are permitted in predicates or functions?

    (c) Why is the restriction prohibiting multiple occurrences unrealistic?

10.9. Logics can be used to represent knowledge and language. Certain kinds of knowledge cannot be appropriately represented with propositional calculus. Predicate calculus (first-order logic) extends propositional calculus by adding a universal quantifier and an existential quantifier. There has been much debate about whether first-order logic is sufficient to handle all kinds of knowledge. Some solutions look at extending first-order logic (to second-order, for example), while others add new operators to first-order logic which result in different classes of logics. Cushing [Cus87] and Delgrande [Del87] have taken two different approaches to handling this problem. Read the articles cited and discuss their respective approaches and the kind of knowledge or language constructs their approaches are designed to deal with.

11

Symbolic Pattern Matching

Pattern matching is the process of comparing notational phrases to see if one is similar to another. One well-known example where pattern matching occurs is in the implementation of operating system command languages to provide a "wild card" capability for selecting file names. Anyone who has ever used MS-DOS is familiar with the notation used in the following command:

```
DIR *.TMP
```

to selectively obtain a listing of all files with the file name extension TMP. In the example the sequence of characters *.TMP is often referred to as the *pattern*, while each file name and extension provides a *target* to which an attempt is made to match the pattern. A common variant is illustrated by

```
DIR FILE??.DAT
```

which selectively lists all files possessing a six-character name beginning FILE and the extension DAT. Such an example illustrates an application of *string pattern matching* where the matching is performed on a character-by-character basis. In addition to such file name patterns, string pattern matching is often used in text editors for powerful find-and-replace commands. Taken even further, string pattern matching has also been used as a programming technique underlying the SNOBOL4 programming language [GPP71].

From the symbolic computing viewpoint, however, it is more interesting to define pattern matching in terms of arbitrary symbolic data structures and their components. In effect, the constraint that the data structure be a string and the components be characters is relaxed. This form of matching, called *structural pattern matching*, can often be used to produce some very elegant solutions to complex symbolic computing problems. For example, the unification process in resolution theorem proving is an instance of pattern matching. There are many other uses of structural pattern matching in artificial intelligence, particularly where knowledge representation and retrieval are an integral part of the application. Furthermore, structural pattern matching can be used in programming languages to control the application of procedures to structured data objects. Called *pattern-directed invocation*, it is a technique employed by logic programming languages such as PROLOG and functional languages such as Miranda[1] [Tur85], Haskell [HWe90], and Standard ML [Tof89]. In this chapter, we shall explore the implementation of structural pattern matching and some of its applications, including unification and pattern-directed invocation.

11.1 PATTERN VARIABLES

Consider, for example, the representation of library data, with each citation being represented by a list according to the following (GRAIL) grammar:

$$
\begin{aligned}
\langle citation \rangle &::= (\ \langle author:names \rangle \ \langle title:id\text{-}expr \rangle \ \langle publisher:id\text{-}expr \rangle \\
&\qquad \langle date:year \rangle \ \langle area:id\text{-}expr \rangle \ ) \\
\langle names \rangle &::= (\ \langle id\text{-}expr^{+} \rangle \ ) \\
\langle id\text{-}expr \rangle &::= (\ \langle atom^{+} \rangle \ ) \\
\langle year \rangle &::= \langle year\text{-}val:numeric\text{-}atom \rangle
\end{aligned}
$$

Thus a typical citation might be

```
( ((R Cameron) (A Dixon))
  (Symbolic Computing)
  (Prentice Hall)
  1992
  (Computer Science)
)
```

Alternatively, we might embed indicators in the list representation to produce an association list:

```
( (AUTHOR ((R Cameron) (A Dixon)))
  (TITLE (Symbolic Computing))
  (PUBLISHER (Prentice Hall))
  (DATE 1992)
  (AREA (Computer Science))
)
```

---

[1]Miranda is a trademark of Research Software Ltd.

A query made to a data base of assertions consisting of citations represented by lists can be characterized by a suitable *pattern* list which can be likened to a template. For example, the question: "Is there a book entitled *Symbolic Computing*" could be represented by the template list

```
(? (Symbolic Computing) ?  ?  ?)
```

if the citations are stored according to the grammar given above. Alternatively, if the citations are represented by association lists, an appropriate pattern that corresponds to the query is

```
( (AUTHOR ?)
  (TITLE (Symbolic Computing))
  (PUBLISHER ?)
  (DATE ?)
  (AREA ?)
)
```

In each case a special symbolic atom, ?, has been used to identify those components of the structure of a citation which are not required to answer the query. In effect, ? serves as a placeholder which preserves the structure of the list representation by identifying the existence of a component without actually requiring a specific value. In comparing the pattern to entries in the data base of library citations, the symbol ? matches any S-expression. Clearly, either template would match the corresponding example citations given previously.

As indicated, the use of ? eliminates the need to know the actual values of certain components but requires explicit knowledge of the citation representation. As well, it is desirable that all citations adopt a uniform representation; otherwise, different templates will be required. Such an assumption is unrealistic since it is frequently the case that citations may require a different number of components, journal citations being one such example. Therefore, a simpler template for characterizing the request might be the following:

```
( * (Symbolic Computing) *)
```

using the grammar representation, or

```
( * (TITLE (Symbolic Computing)) *)
```

using the association list representation. No longer must the number of components be identified in the structure of the pattern. In this case the symbol * is being used to match an indefinite number (zero or more occurrences) of S-expressions. In effect we are looking for a match to any list that includes (Symbolic Computing) or (TITLE (Symbolic Computing)) as a sublist somewhere among its components!

A *matching* algorithm is one which compares two lists in a fashion similar to the list function `equal`, except whenever either of the pair of components being compared is a *pattern variable*. The symbolic atoms ? and * are examples of pattern variables.

A simple matching algorithm can be formulated to perform the match illustrated by the requirements of the citation example. We begin with an EBNF grammar for patterns:

$$\begin{aligned}
\langle\text{pattern}\rangle &::= \langle\text{literal}\rangle \mid \langle\text{segment-var}\rangle \mid \langle\text{element-var}\rangle \mid \\
&\qquad \langle\text{segment}\rangle \\
\langle\text{literal}\rangle &::= \langle\text{atom}\rangle \\
\langle\text{element-var}\rangle &::= \text{?} \\
\langle\text{segment-var}\rangle &::= \text{*} \\
\langle\text{segment}\rangle &::= (\ \{\ \langle\text{pattern}\rangle\ \}\ )
\end{aligned}$$

It is apparent that there are two types of symbolic atom in a template list: literals, which match only images of themselves, and pattern variables, which can match to arbitrary S-expressions. So far, two types of pattern variable have been introduced: *element variables*, such as ?, which match to any single S-expression, and *segment variables*, which match to any number of S-expressions, collectively called a *segment*.

The data access functions, specifically the recognizers, are easily defined from the grammar and are therefore not given here. Instead, we proceed directly to the implementation of a matching algorithm to compare two objects. For simplicity, we assume that only pattern can contain pattern variables:

```
(defun simple-match (pattern target)
 (cond
    ((literal-p pattern) (eq pattern target))
    ((element-var-p pattern) T)
    ((segment-var-p pattern) T)
    ((segment-p pattern)
       (cond
          ((endp pattern) (endp target))
          ((literal-p target) NIL)
          ((segment-var-p (first pattern))
             (segment-match (rest pattern) target))
          ((endp target) NIL)
          ((simple-match (first pattern) (first target))
             (simple-match (rest pattern) (rest target)))
          (T NIL))))))
```

The matching algorithm is quite straightforward, except when a pattern whose first element is a segment variable must be matched to a segment of target. The matching of segment variables to sequences of zero or more S-expressions requires that the following cases be examined. Assume that target has length N:

1. Match the segment variable to "nothing." Then the rest of the pattern must be matched to the entire target.

2. Match the segment variable to (first target). In this case we then attempt to match the rest of the pattern to the rest of the target.

3. Match the segment variable to the first n ($1 < n < N$) elements of the target. In this case we then attempt to match the rest of pattern to the $N - n$ remaining elements of target.

4. Match the segment variable to all elements in target. This match succeeds only when there are no elements other than segment variables following the segment variable of the pattern currently under consideration. Any remaining segment variables can be matched to the null segment.

Since step 2 is really the same as step 3 for $n = 1$, and step 4 the same as step 3 for $n = N$, segment matching is an iterative process and can be defined recursively with the segment variable initially matched to the segment (). The segment variable is then matched to larger and larger segments constructed from the target list: This process is provided by the function segment-match, which is called by simple-match when the first component of pattern is a segment variable:

```
(defun segment-match (pattern target)
  (cond
    ((simple-match pattern target) T)
    ((endp target) NIL)
    (T (segment-match pattern (rest target)))))
```

For the purposes of exposition we have chosen to implement segment-match using recursion as the method of iteration. However, as we have seen in Chapter 8, Common LISP also includes high-level iterators which often provide a simpler and more efficient alternative. Their suitability depends on how easily the mapped function and the input set can be defined. In this case, a closer examination of the implementation of segment-match reveals that segments are being constructed from target in a particular way. In effect, simple-match is being applied iteratively to the sequence: target, (rest target), (rest (rest target)), ..., and finally (), an observation which suggests that segment-match can indeed be implemented conveniently with iterators (see Exercise 11.2).

11.2 NAMED PATTERN VARIABLES

The simplicity of this approach for specifying a retrieval is apparent. In addition, the approach hints at a possible way to implement the processing of queries using a "natural language-like" syntax, without the implementation of an elaborate front-end processor to transform query statements into suitable internal representations. Such an implementation requires only that the queries be expressed as Lisp lists. The interpretation of queries expressed in this manner consists of matching the inputs with a large "dictionary" of patterns and then formulating responses by identifying the components that match the pattern variables. In fact, this is the approach taken in some implementations of "advice-giver" programs modeled after Joseph Weizenbaum's ELIZA [Wei65].

However, the matching capability provided in the preceding section is unsuitable for addressing the requirements of query processing as described because it limits the types of retrieval that can be performed: in particular, the type of response that can be generated when a match succeeds. In effect, only queries about the existence of lists which match a query pattern can be answered, with the possible additional result of providing the actual list which permitted the match to return T.

To extend the capabilities, the role of the pattern variables ? and * must be extended. As suggested in the introduction to this section, a useful extension is to be able to extract relevant components from the target list as another result of the matching process. To achieve this it is necessary to label pattern variables, and then bind values to them. Such pattern variables are called *named pattern variables*.

The EBNF grammar given previously for ⟨pattern⟩s can be extended to include named pattern variables by just modifying the definitions of ⟨segment-var⟩ and ⟨element-var⟩:

$$
\begin{aligned}
\langle\text{segment-var}\rangle &::= \ *\langle\text{identifier}\rangle \\
\langle\text{element-var}\rangle &::= \ ?\langle\text{identifier}\rangle \\
\langle\text{identifier}\rangle &::= \ \langle\text{alpha}\rangle \ \{ \ \langle\text{alpha-numeric}\rangle \ \} \\
\langle\text{alpha-numeric}\rangle &::= \ \langle\text{alpha}\rangle \ | \ \langle\text{numeric}\rangle \\
\langle\text{alpha}\rangle &::= \ \text{A} \ | \ \text{B} \ | \ \ldots \ | \ \text{z} \\
\langle\text{numeric}\rangle &::= \ \text{0} \ | \ \text{1} \ | \ \ldots \ | \ \text{9}
\end{aligned}
$$

With this definition, all pattern variables are named pattern variables.[2]

11.2.1 Data Retrieval Through Pattern Matching

The advantage of labeling pattern variables is that it allows one to retrieve the individual components of a pattern list. To capture the intent of an input query as an information retrieval activity, we can represent it with a pattern which can be matched to a data base of target patterns. Using the example citation data base of the preceding section, we can construct a pattern to represent a question such as "Who wrote *Symbolic Computing?*" This could be represented by

```
( ?X   (Symbolic Computing) ?T0 ?T1 ?T2)
```

or more simply by:

```
( ?X   (Symbolic Computing) *T0)
```

Furthermore, the second pattern has the virtue of not requiring a knowledge of the exact number of elements in the representation of a citation; all that is required is knowing that the author is the first component of a citation and precedes the title. This permits us to adopt a more flexible representation for citations, reflecting the reality that there are usually a variable number of components.

Therefore, let us assume that a citation can have fewer or more than five components, and furthermore that no component must appear in every citation. The question "When was *Symbolic Computing* published?" cannot be represented by

```
( ?T1 (Symbolic Computing) ?T2 ?Y ?T3)
```

---

[2]While it is a useful feature to employ both named and unnamed pattern variables, for the purposes of exposition the latter have been excluded from the examples which follow. It is left as an exercise for the reader to incorporate this feature in the subsequent functions.

since this representation is based on prior knowledge of the position of the components in a citation and its length. Instead, the question can be represented as a pattern using segment variables:

```
( *T1 (Symbolic Computing) *T2 ?Y *T3)
```

In this case the only assumption we are making about how citations are represented is that the date of publication follows the title. The role of *T1 is to address the possibility that some component will precede the title. Similarly, *T2 provides for the case that there is some number of components between the title and the date. Finally, *T3 is needed to reflect the possibility that the date is not the last component of the citation.

However, it is at this point that a weakness in this choice of representation for citations can be observed. For, since *T2 and *T3 are segment variables, they can match zero or more components in a citation, and therefore the element pattern variable ?Y could be matched to (Prentice Hall) with *T2 matched to () and *T3 matched to (1992 (Computer Science)). Alternatively, it could also match 1992 with *T2 matching (Prentice Hall) and *T3 matching (Computer Science). A third possibility also exists, for *T2 can match ((Prentice Hall) 1992), when ?Y matches (Computer Science) and *T3 matches (). The choice of which pattern variables are matched to which structures is determined by the order in which the bindings are made. To obtain the alternative assignments, a more complex control technique is usually used.[3]

For the library citation example, at least, the problem of multiple assignments can be avoided by adopting the previously described association list representation for citations. The patterns for the queries given in the examples above become

```
((AUTHOR ?X) (TITLE (Symbolic Computing)) *T0)
( *T1 (TITLE (Symbolic Computing)) *T2 (DATE ?Y) *T3)
```

When the element variables ?X and ?Y are matched against the contents of the data base, ?X is bound to ((R Cameron) (A Dixon)) and ?Y is bound to 1992. In both examples the segment variables *T0, *T1, *T2, and *T3 serve only to match other components of the citation list that do not actually have to be retrieved. They provide an illustration of where unnamed pattern variables could also be used, since the answers to the queries do not require the values to which the segment variables are bound.

11.2.2 Invoking Transformations Through Pattern Matching

Information retrieval is but one application of pattern matching. As a second example of how pattern matching with named variables is applicable, we return briefly to the topic of transformations. In Chapter 5 the simplification of expressions was performed according to the applicability of a prescribed set of rules. These rules can be defined using the results of pattern matching. For example, suppose that we wish to simplify

---

[3]Called *backtrack programming*, this technique requires that the state of the computation that produced the match be saved, so that if the match produced by that computation is not the desired one, the state can be restored and an alternative match generated. See Henderson [Hen80] for a description of the implementation of backtrack programming in functional programming languages.

Boolean conjunctions of an indefinite number of conjuncts represented in prefix form. Among our set of rules might be the following:

$$\text{(AND *C1 (AND *C2) *C3)} \mapsto \text{(AND *C1 *C2 *C3)}$$

$$\text{(AND *C1 T *C2)} \mapsto \text{(AND *C1 *C2)}$$

$$\text{(AND *C1 NIL *C2)} \mapsto \text{NIL}$$

Here we have used pattern variables to express the templates which correspond to the applicability of certain rules of simplification. When a match to any of these patterns occurs, the named pattern variables are bound to a suitable sequence of S-expressions. These values are then used to compose the resulting simplified object. This example illustrates the value of pattern representation, particularly the simplicity with which rules expressed as lists can be represented. Each of the three rules captures in a single expression all possible variants of that rule. In this context, one can imagine a procedure for constructing the desired output list being associated with the corresponding pattern from which the output is derived. Section 11.5 will discuss how pattern matching can be used to invoke such a procedure whose associated pattern has been matched.

11.2.3 Retrieval of Bound Pattern Variables

The preceding two examples motivate the need to modify the pattern-matching function `simple-match` to accommodate the binding of pattern variables during the matching process. Therefore, we need to redefine `simple-match` so that it returns the bindings obtained during a successful match rather than just the truth value T. It is therefore appropriate to define a representation for the output domain of the revised function, which we shall call `match`.

A "successful" match will result in the environment of bindings obtained during the match process. A "failed" match will return the value of FAILURE. One complication is that it is possible for a pattern to have no pattern variables in which case no bindings will be produced in a successful match. This situation can be accounted for simply by returning the "empty" environment. It is evident that the value of FAILURE should distinguish between a valid environment and a failure to complete a match. Since NIL is a valid environment, it is not suitable. Instead, a simple alternative is to use a distinguishing atom such as FAIL. These output requirements are formalized in the following GRAIL grammar:

$$\langle\text{match}\rangle ::= \langle\text{success}\rangle \mid \langle\text{failure}\rangle$$
$$\langle\text{success}\rangle ::= (\langle\text{environ:environment}\rangle)$$
$$\langle\text{failure}\rangle ::= \text{FAIL}$$

If the match succeeds, the ⟨environment⟩ returned will specify the bindings of pattern variables to the specific items they match in the target. An element variable will be bound to the single object it matches. A segment variable matches zero or more objects; it will therefore be bound to the list of these objects. As discussed in Chapter 6, many different data structures can be used to implement environments. For the present, we will assume that an association list representation is used in order to make our matching examples concrete.

Some examples of the values returned by `match` serve to illustrate the structure of a ⟨match⟩ output:

1. Successful match with no pattern variables:

$$(\texttt{match '(A B C) '(A B C))} \Rightarrow \texttt{(())}$$

2. Unsuccessful match:

$$(\texttt{match '(?A B ?C) '(X Y Z))} \Rightarrow \texttt{FAIL}$$

3. Element variables bound to atoms:

$$(\texttt{match '(?A B ?C) '(X B Z))} \Rightarrow \texttt{(((?C Z)(?A X)))}$$

4. An element variable bound to a list:

$$(\texttt{match '(?A B C) '((X) B C))} \Rightarrow \texttt{(((?A (X))))}$$

5. A segment variable bound to an atom:

$$(\texttt{match '(*A B C) '(X B C))} \Rightarrow \texttt{(((*A (X))))}$$

6. A segment variable bound to a list:

$$(\texttt{match '(*A B C) '((X) B C))} \Rightarrow \texttt{(((*A ((X)))))}$$

In each case corresponding to a successful match, the value returned is a ⟨match⟩ containing an environment of binding pairs. Note that in example 4 the value associated with `?A` is `(X)`, while in example 5 the value associated with `*A` is `X`. Although the list representations of the binding pairs are the same, in example 5 the list `(X)` is interpreted as the segment consisting of one element, namely `X`.

The function to be defined, `match`, therefore should return a ⟨match⟩ in order to provide the bindings which permit the match to succeed.[4] In the case where no pattern variables exist, or the match does not succeed, no binding pairs are returned. A call to an auxiliary function, `match1`, is used to initialize the environment of binding pairs to the empty list. The function `simple-match`, defined in the preceding section, could have been used as a predicate to test for the existence of a match, before performing `match1`, which adds bindings to `env`. However, this is an inefficient way to implement `match` because it requires that the matching be "performed" twice.

Instead, the implementation employs the commonly accepted strategy of partitioning the matching problem into specific cases based on the type of matching to be performed. To guide the design of `match`, the previously implemented function `simple-match` can be used to identify the matching types. Specifically, there are four possibilities:

---

[4]For the purposes of this example we continue to assume the constraint adopted in the definition of `simple-match` that only the value bound to the formal parameter `pattern` may contain pattern variables. In addition, we will also assume that no pattern variable occurs more than once in a pattern.

1. *Equality matching*, where the `pattern` contains no pattern variables.
2. *Element variable matching*, where an element variable is matched to the entire `target`.
3. *Segment variable matching*, where a segment variable is matched to the entire `target`.
4. *Segment matching*, where a segment variable is matched to some subset of elements of `target`.

For each of these types of matches, a function is defined to perform the match when a recognizer identifies that function's applicability to the `pattern` in question.

With these considerations in mind, the desired functions can be implemented in Common LISP as follows:

```
(defun match (pattern target)
  (match1 pattern target null-env))


(defun match1 (pattern target env)
  (cond
    ((literal-p pattern) (equality-match pattern target env))
    ((element-var-p pattern) (pattern-var-match pattern target env))
    ((segment-var-p pattern) (pattern-var-match pattern target env))
    ((segment-p pattern)
         (cond
           ((endp pattern)
             (cond
               ((endp target) (make-success env))
               (T failure)))
           ((literal-p target) failure)
           ((segment-var-p (first pattern))
                (segment-match pattern target env null-seg))
           ((endp target) failure)
           ((equal (first pattern) (first target))
                (match1 (rest pattern) (rest target) env))
           (T (let ((new-match (match1 (first pattern)
                                       (first target)
                                       env)))
                (cond
                  ((failure-p new-match) failure)
                  (T (match1 (rest pattern)
                             (rest target)
                             (environ new-match)))))))))))

(defun equality-match (pattern target env)
  (cond
    ((equal pattern target) (make-success env))
    (T failure)))
```

```
(defun pattern-var-match (pattern target env)
 (make-success (extend-env env pattern target)))


(defun segment-match (pattern target env segment)
 (let ((new-match (match1 (rest pattern)
                          target
                          (extend-env env (first pattern) segment))))
    (cond
       ((endp target) new-match)
       ((failure-p new-match)
                (segment-match pattern
                               (rest target)
                               env
                               (extend-segment segment
                                               (first target))))
       (T new-match)))))
```

To retrieve the values to which an element variable is bound, the environment on the returned ⟨match⟩ data structure can be scanned, using apply-env, for the variable and the single value to which it has been bound. In the case of a segment variable, it will be bound to a sequence of zero or more values, and the entire sequence (represented as a list) defines the value retrieved.

It is an interesting exercise to implement pattern matching by using side effects to save and recover the pattern variable bindings.

11.3 REPLICATION IN PATTERNS

To provide a more general pattern-matching mechanism, it would be useful to represent the replication of elements or segments in some way. As a simple example, we might be interested in defining a pattern that would match all lists that have the same value (an atom or a list) in their first and last positions. This situation corresponds to a replication of elements. Using the named pattern variables defined so far, we could permit a pattern variable to occur more than once in a pattern. Thus

(?X *Y ?X)

captures the structure of a pattern that would meet the requirement. To provide such a capability requires that the clause in match which recognizes element variables be modified to determine whether a given element variable is already bound to a value. If so, that value must be matched with the target pattern. Otherwise, the element variable can be bound to the target pattern. Therefore, it is necessary to define a new function elem-var-match to replace the call to pattern-var-match when an element variable is recognized. The function elem-var-match is similar to pattern-var-match except that an additional clause is added to the conditional expression. This clause checks whether the element variable is already defined on env.

If so, that value is compared with the target for a match. The affected function body is revised as follows:

```
(defun elem-var-match (pattern target env)
(cond
    ((defined-p env pattern)
            (cond
                ((equal (apply-env env pattern) target)
                                        (make-success env))
                (T failure)))
    (T (make-success (extend-env env pattern target)))))
```

The proposed pattern will match targets such as (A B A), (A A), and (A B C A), as well as those where the first and last elements are lists, such as ((A B) C (A B)). However, the identification of pattern replication needs to be generalized to include the matching of segments, that is, the recognition of the repetition of a sequence of S-expressions.

For example, (?X ?Y ?X) would not match (A B C A B), since the replication that we observe in this example is a segment, namely the S-expression A followed by the S-expression B. The pattern that comes to mind follows from the approach suggested by the case for element variables, specifically

$$(*X *Y *X)$$

To match such patterns requires that we modify the functions `pattern-var-match` and `segment-match` so that they too check to see whether the pattern variable (in this case a segment pattern variable) is already bound, as was done in the implementation of `elem-var-match`. However, this check is more complex than that for element pattern variables since it is necessary to "delay" abandoning a match if a segment variable is already defined until it has been determined that the segment cannot be reconstructed again from the remainder of the target to be matched.

Therefore, when a segment variable is found on the environment of bound pattern variables, we first check whether the segment which is bound to that variable is embedded in the segment, `target`, which we are now trying to match to the same variable. If it is, the matching process can continue by trying to match `pattern`, "minus" the segment variable, to the remainder of `target`, after removing the segment to which the variable is already bound. Otherwise, the match must be abandoned and a different segment variable binding attempted. This is why `segment-match` is recursively called with the original environment and a segment to be bound tentatively to the segment variable. It permits different segments to be bound to the variable, in an attempt to obtain a match.

Thus, to accommodate the multiple occurrence of segment pattern variables in a pattern, `seg-var-match` is defined to replace `pattern-var-match`, and `segment-match` is revised and reimplemented as follows:

```
(defun seg-var-match (pattern target env)
(cond
```

```
      ((defined-p env pattern)
            (cond ((equal-seg (apply-env env pattern) target)
                                              (make-success env))
                  (T failure)))
      (T (make-success (extend-env env pattern target)))))

  (defun segment-match (pattern target env segment)
  (cond
    ((defined-p env (first pattern))
          (let ((seg-var-binding (apply-env env (first pattern))))
               (cond
                 ((equal-seg seg-var-binding target)
                         (match1 (rest pattern)
                                 (match-rest seg-var-binding
                                             target)
                                 env))
                 (T failure))))
    (T (let ((new-match (match1 (rest pattern)
                          target
                          (extend-env env (first pattern)
                                      segment))))
          (cond
            ((endp target) new-match)
            ((failure-p new-match)
                  (segment-match pattern
                                 (rest target)
                                 env
                                 (extend-segment segment
                                                 (first target))))
            (T new-match))))))
```

Unfortunately, the function match as now defined is still deficient. Consider, for example, the following two match attempts using match and noting the ⟨match⟩ returned:

```
>(match '((*X ?Y *Z) ?Y) '((A B C) A))
   ((((*Z (B C)) (?Y A) (*X ()))))

>(match '((*X ?Y *Z) ?Y) '((A B C) B))
    FAIL
```

Thus match fails to find a match for the second example. However, a match in fact exists, for *X can match A, ?Y can match B, and *Z can match C. A closer inspection of the sequence of bindings that are made during the attempted match reveals that the subpattern (*X ?Y *Z) has been matched to (A B C) with the resulting ⟨match⟩ given by

```
      (((*Z (B C)) (?Y A) (*X ())))
```

Now, to complete the match, ?Y must be matched to B. But ?Y is already bound to A, so it is necessary to "back up" to the point which resulted in ?Y being bound to A. That point occurs with *X, whose binding must therefore be a different segment from (). Such a transfer of control is possible in the current implementation only when the segment variable which must be redefined is at the same level in the list structure of the pattern; otherwise, the procedure that created the segment binding will have been exited, and it will subsequently be impossible to undo that binding.

This problem arises because at the time of binding *X there are several alternatives possible, and it is not possible to determine in advance which alternatives will lead to matches. One way to solve this problem is to employ backtrack programming, mentioned in Section 11.2 (footnote 2). It is also possible to generate all possible matches that can be achieved at any stage of the matching process. Such an approach requires that we retain all possible binding alternatives whenever the function segment-match is applied. The list of bindings can subsequently be filtered by elem-var-match or seg-var-match whenever the pattern variable has previously been bound. While such an approach avoids the need to implement backtrack programming, it is likely to be very inefficient, because of the potential for an exponential growth in the number of alternatives which must subsequently be searched. The details of such an implementation are left as an exercise (see Exercise 11.10).

In the next section, the effect of pattern variables matching each other will be discussed, a possibility that also contributes to the complexity and potential inefficiency of a pattern matcher. Therefore, a third possibility for implementing matching which improves its efficiency is to restrict the structure of the allowable patterns. One particular instance where this is done is in PROLOG, which permits only patterns which represent Horn clauses.

11.4 MATCHING BETWEEN PATTERN VARIABLES

When pattern variables are permitted in the target of a match, then the generality of pattern matching is further extended. However, the complexity of the matching algorithm is also affected, particularly when dealing with segment variables, which can now match segments which may contain pattern variables (bound or unbound). Therefore, in this section we will examine this extension in the context of patterns which contain only element variables.

Another reason for considering this case is that it is applicable to an activity described in Chapter 10, namely unification. Therefore, the technique of pattern matching can be employed to implement a unification algorithm, and it is in conjunction with this application that the problem of matching two patterns, each of which can contain element variables, will be discussed.

As we saw in Chapter 10, the purpose of unification is to construct a new clause (the resolvent) from a pair of previously defined clauses. The new clause is obtained from the old ones by eliminating a predicate expression from one clause when its negation occurs in the second clause. That negation is also eliminated from the second clause. Since predicate expressions may contain universally quantified variables, such variables are bound to values chosen so that a predicate expression and its negation occur in the pair of clauses simultaneously. Such a set of bindings is called a unifier and, as was shown previously, can be represented with an environment data structure.

When viewed as a pattern-matching problem, unification consists of comparing two clauses, each represented by a list of patterns, and obtaining a unifier, represented as an environment. This unifier can then be used to construct a resolvent by substituting the values to which the universally quantified variables (represented as element pattern variables) have been bound for each occurrence of those variables in the literals of the clauses. Eliminating the patterns corresponding to the predicate expression and its negation, the union of the remaining patterns define the resolvent.

To illustrate the idea and also provide insight into the implementation of a suitable matching algorithm, we begin with the set of clauses given in Section 10.7 from which resolvents were obtained. The universally quantified variables are now replaced by element pattern variables:[5]

$$C1 = (\ (\text{NOT } (R \text{ ?G1})) \ (L \text{ ?G1}) \ )$$
$$C2 = (\ (\text{NOT } (D \text{ ?G2})) \ (\text{NOT } (L \text{ ?G2})) \ )$$
$$C3 = (\ (D \text{ (A1)}) \ )$$
$$C4 = (\ (I \text{ (A1)}) \ )$$
$$C5 = (\ (\text{NOT } (I \text{ ?G4})) \ (R \text{ ?G4}) \ )$$

Notice that each clause-form equivalent is essentially a list of patterns corresponding to predicate expressions and the negation of predicate expressions. To find a unifier, a matching function, (`unify clause1 clause2`), takes patterns one at a time from `clause1` and "compares" that pattern with each of the patterns in `clause2`. Comparison consists of determining that exactly one of the two clauses is a negation, and if so, attempting to match the negend of the negation with the other pattern. Each time a match is found, another unifier is obtained for the pair of clauses.

For example, from clause $C5$ we can select the negend of the predicate (NOT (I ?G4)) as the pattern and and try to match it to the lone predicate expression from clause $C4$, namely (I (A1)), using the function `match`:

$$(\text{match } \text{'}(I \text{ ?G4}) \text{ '}(I \text{ (A1)})) \quad \Rightarrow \quad (((\text{?G4 (A1)})))$$

Obviously, `match` can be used to obtain unifiers which bind constants to quantified variables. It would also appear that `match` can solve the problem of resolving upon $C1$ and $C5$ to obtain the unifier ((?G1 ?G4)). Since no distinction is made with regard to symbolic atoms in the representation of the `target`, names such as ?G4 are treated as if they were constants. Of course, the function which takes this unifier and constructs a resolvent must now recognize that the value to which ?G1 is bound is itself a universally quantified variable and construct a new unique label for substitution. However, there is a more serious problem with this approach that is illustrated by applying it to the following clauses:

---

[5]The syntax for the representation of clause-form equivalents does not actually require a special notation for pattern variables. Constants are represented by Skolem functions of no arguments (i.e., lists), so the universally quantified variables are the only variables in such expressions, and can be used directly. However, to illustrate more clearly the role of pattern variables and pattern matching in this context, we continue to use the notation defined earlier in this chapter.

$$C1 = (\ (\text{P ?X ?X}) \ )$$
$$C2 = (\ (\text{NOT (P ?Y (A))}) \ )$$

`match` can be applied to the corresponding patterns in two ways. First, patterns can be selected from clause $C1$ and matches attempted with targets obtained from $C2$:

`(match '(P ?X ?X) '(P ?Y (A)))`   ⇒   `FAIL`

In this case, no match occurs since ?X cannot be bound to both ?Y and A at the same time, because ?Y is not recognized as an element pattern variable. Alternatively, patterns can be selected from $C2$ and matches attempted with targets from $C1$:

`(match '(P ?Y (A)) '(P ?X ?X))`   ⇒   `(((?Y ?X)))`

In this case, the environment is incomplete since ?X should be bound to (A) and, in effect, ?Y should be as well. Clearly, this example suggests that `match` must be augmented to recognize the occurrence of element variables in `target` and permit them to be matched against components of `pattern`. Using `match` as a model, then, a new matching function called `unify-match` is defined to permit the matching of element variables in either the `pattern` or the `target`. Since segment variables are not required for this application, they have not been included in the implementation:

```
(defun unify (clause1 clause2)
  (cond
    ((endp clause1) failure)
    (T (let ((unifier (unify1 (first clause1) clause2)))
         (cond
           ((failure-p unifier) (unify (rest clause1) clause2))
           (T unifier))))))

(defun unify1 (pattern clause)
  (cond
    ((endp clause) failure)
    ((negation-p pattern) (unify2 (negend pattern) clause))
    (T (unify2 (make-negation pattern) clause))))

(defun unify2 (pattern clause)
  (cond
    ((endp clause) failure)
    (T (let ((unifier (unify-match pattern (first clause) null-env)))
         (cond
           ((failure-p unifier) (unify2 pattern (rest clause)))
           (T unifier))))))

(defun unify-match (pattern target env)
  (cond
    ((literal-p pattern) (equality-match pattern target env))
```

```
((element-var-p pattern) (elem-var-match pattern target env))
((endp pattern)
        (cond
          ((endp target) (make-success env))
          (T failure)))
((literal-p target) failure)
((endp target) failure)
((equal (first pattern) (first target))
        (unify-match (rest pattern) (rest target) env))
(T (let ((new-match (unify-match (first pattern)
                                 (first target)
                                 env)))
      (cond
        ((failure-p new-match) failure)
        (T (unify-match (rest pattern)
                        (rest target)
                        (environ new-match)))))))))))

(defun equality-match (pattern target env)
 (cond
   ((equal pattern target) (make-success env))
   ((element-var-p target) (elem-var-match target pattern env))
   (T failure)))

(defun elem-var-match (pattern target env)
 (cond
   ((endp target) failure)
   ((defined-p env pattern)
   (let ((value (apply-env env pattern)))
        (cond
          ((element-var-p value) (extend-env env value target))
          ((equal value target) (make-success env))
          (T failure))))
   (T (extend-env env pattern target))))
```

The purpose of the auxiliary functions unify1 and unify2 is to select the appropriate arguments for the formal parameters pattern and target in a systematic manner. For efficiency, the pattern is converted to the negation of a predicate expression if it is to be matched with negations from clause2. This avoids having to construct the negation (or select the negend) of each predicate expression in clause2 before looking for a unifying match. As with the previous matching functions unify returns an environment embedded in a ⟨match⟩. For example,

```
(unify ( (P ?X ?X) ) ( (NOT (P ?Y (A))) ))   ⇒   (((?Y (A)) (?X ?Y)))
```

Note that although this environment does not explicitly specify that ?X is bound to (A), it can be obtained from the binding pairs since "bound to" is a transitive relation with respect to element variables; that is, if Y is bound to C and X is bound to Y, then X is bound to C, where X and Y are element variables and C can be either an element variable or a constant.

11.5 PATTERN-DIRECTED INVOCATION

Section 11.3 suggested that patterns could be associated with procedures and used to determined when those procedures would be evaluated. This technique is called *pattern-directed invocation* and is employed in a number of advanced programming languages. In the early 1970s pattern matching was first used to control the invocation of procedures in programs. One of the objectives was to develop goal-directed programming languages and was motivated by efforts to implement planning strategies in programs. Such goal-oriented languages were collectively referred to as *planner-type languages*, and some specific examples include Sussman, Winograd, and Charniak's MICRO-PLANNER [SWC71], Sussman and McDermott's CONNIVER [SM72], Hewitt's PLANNER [Hew72], and Davies' POPLER [Dav73]. All of these systems used the idea of invoking procedures through pattern matching.

The basic idea is to associate a pattern with each procedure, called the *procedure pattern*. This pattern might include pattern variables, and the procedure body would be evaluated only when it was possible to match the procedure pattern. The test for matches would occur when certain activities were attempted, such as asserting (i.e., putting) some object into a data base, or trying to infer something from a data base. The body of such a procedure would be expressed in terms of the pattern variables within the procedure pattern which would be bound to values as a consequence of a match. In this manner, values could be passed to the procedure in a manner different from the more usual binding of formal parameters using the positional notation of traditional function calls. To illustrate the flow of control during execution of a series of data base requests, we examine how a program designed to construct "high-level" descriptions from "low-level" assertions might be organized.

We begin with a formal definition for procedures, which will be represented using an S-Lisp notation. A *procedure* is a program module that can be invoked by matching its associated pattern. The syntax for a ⟨procedure⟩ is given by the following grammar:

> ⟨procedure⟩ ::= (PROCEDURE ⟨pattern:procedure-pattern⟩
>   ⟨proc-body:expression⟩)
> ⟨procedure-pattern⟩ ::= ⟨pattern⟩

where the ⟨expression⟩ comprising the body of the procedure specifies a calculation in terms of the pattern variables bound by the ⟨procedure-pattern⟩. Although for the purposes of this example we have provided a grammar which defines a ⟨procedure⟩, the actual syntax is not important, only that the structure of each procedure should include certain features, the most significant being the procedure pattern. We have therefore adopted a greatly simplified representation for procedures that will be sufficient for the purposes of exposition but does not reflect their full capabilities. For such details, the reader should consult one of the references on planner-type languages cited above.

The problem to be examined is that of recognizing the existence of triangles given that assertions have been made about the existence of line segments. One can imagine this problem arising if one attempts to construct a description of the image of a scene. The image is represented by a matrix of integers called pixels, which specify the light intensity at particular points in the image. Many techniques exist for identifying the edges in a scene from an examination of this matrix.

To illustrate the basic idea behind pattern-directed invocation of procedures in the context of the problem above, we shall assume the existence of an environment "data base" called `assertions` on which patterns, represented as lists, can be stored. We also assume the existence of some special system functions whose purpose is to initiate and control the evaluation of procedures and the modification of the data base. Specifically, these functions are `assert`, `infer`, and `delete`. The function `assert` places its argument (a pattern) in the system-defined data base, and then uses the pattern to invoke procedures. The function `infer` invokes procedures without modifying the data base (except possibly as a side effect), while `delete` removes patterns from the data base. In addition, the function `asserted-p` is a predicate that determines whether a given pattern matches anything in the data base.

We begin with the following assertions:

```
(assert (A 0 0))
(assert (B 0 10))
(assert (C 10 0))
```

The intent of these assertions is to store the coordinates of three points and associate with each a label. A convenient place to put this information is on the property lists of the labels, so the following procedure is designed to do this:

```
(procedure (?P ?X ?Y)
  (cond
    ((and (numberp ?X) (numberp ?Y) (symbolp ?P))
            (setf ?P (quote X) ?X)
            (setf ?P (quote Y) ?Y)
            (delete (list ?P ?X ?Y)))
    (T NIL)))
```

This procedure is to be invoked through an interpreter whenever any pattern of three components is asserted, that is, stored on `assertions`. However, unless the first component is an atom and the second and third components are numbers, the procedure returns false. Otherwise, the property list of the symbolic atom bound to the pattern variable ?P is updated to include the indicators X and Y, with corresponding values equal to the values to which the pattern variables ?X and ?Y are bound. Finally, the list matching the pattern which invoked the procedure is removed from the data base.

Obviously, the role of the interpreter is central to the implementation of pattern invocation of procedures. The sequence of steps that are performed is as follows:

1. An attempt is made to place a pattern in the data base. The function `assert` checks for the pattern's prior existence in the data base and updates `assertions` if necessary.

2. `assert` attempts to find among all previously defined procedures those whose procedure patterns match the newly asserted pattern. For each such match, a list of the bindings for the pattern variables together with the procedure body is supplied to an interpreter for evaluation of the procedure body.[6]

3. Each procedure whose pattern matches the assertion is evaluated for its side effects, which may consist of further assertions, inferences, deletions, or other modifications of the global state.

The functions `infer` and `delete` behave in a similar manner to `assert`, modifying the data base, searching for procedures with matching patterns, and evaluating the procedure bodies of procedures where matches occur.

As described then, the evaluation of an S-expression such as

```
(assert (A 0 0))
```

begins by recognizing that a call to `assert` is a request to place the argument pattern (A 0 0) in the data base. Following this task, the interpreter would then look for procedures to which the asserted pattern can match. In this case the procedure defined above would be invoked, the pairs (X 0), and (Y 0) would be placed on the property list of A, and the pattern (A 0 0) would be deleted from the data base. A similar result would follow the assertion of patterns (B 0 10) and (C 10 0).

It is important to note a distinction being made in the role of ?X and ?Y as symbolic atoms in the procedure pattern and in the procedure body of the example procedure above. Although the same symbol is used, the occurrence of the element variables in the procedure body will have been bound to values determined at the time the procedure pattern was matched. This does not, however preclude the possibility of an unbound element variable occurring inside a procedure body. Such a situation could occur if a matching was to be performed. Such a situation will be illustrated shortly.

This ambiguity has prompted the definition of a third type of named pattern variable, sometimes referred to as a *given pattern variable*, suggesting that its value is assumed to have already been defined. In the example above, all occurrences of element variables in the procedure body would be replaced by the appropriate symbols to indicate given variables. With the simplified notation used for this example, however, the introduction of a third pattern variable will not be required, although the reader should be aware of this alternative method of representation.

The definition of procedures is often characterized by the objective of continuously sampling additions made to the data base for the purpose of recognizing when certain inferences can be drawn from those assertions. For this reason, such procedures are sometimes called "experts" or "demons," to reflect the fact that they are activated when the "appropriate" set of circumstances occurs.

Consider now the introduction of a second procedure, a "triangle expert," so called because it recognizes when it is possible to infer a triangle from the assertions made to the data base. The "expertise" employed is that three points can define the vertices of a triangle, provided that the lengths of the sides satisfy the triangle inequality. This definition is captured in the following procedure definition:

---

[6]The interpreter can be modeled after `sl-eval`, defined in Chapter 6.

```
(procedure (TRIANGLE ?X ?Y ?Z)
(cond
  ((and (> (+ (len ?X ?Y) (len ?X ?Z)) (len ?Y ?Z))
        (> (+ (len ?X ?Z) (len ?Y ?Z)) (len ?Y ?X))
        (> (+ (len ?Y ?Z) (len ?X ?Y)) (len ?X ?Z)) )
              (assert (list (quote TRIANGLE) ?X ?Y ?Z)))
    (T NIL)))
```

In effect, this procedure verifies that the sum of the lengths of any two sides of the proposed triangle is greater than the length of the third. If so, the triangle is asserted into the data base.

A design consideration that must be included in the design of the interpreter is reflected in this example: that is, what prevents this procedure from invoking itself infinitely often as a consequence of asserting (TRIANGLE ?X ?Y ?Z)? The immediate answer is "nothing" unless the interpreter keeps track of what patterns have previously invoked this procedure in the current calling sequence. A simpler solution is not to permit recursive calls of these procedures. In practice, both techniques have been employed.

When invoked, this procedure will place the pattern (TRIANGLE ?X ?Y ?Z) in the data base, with ?X, ?Y, and ?Z replaced by the values to which they are bound. It would be inappropriate, however, to invoke the procedure before the three line segments making up the sides were known to exist. Their existence can be provided by the following assertions to update the data base:

```
(assert (LINE A B))
(assert (LINE A C))
(assert (LINE C B))
```

Clearly, when enough lines are asserted, it is possible that they define a triangle. Therefore, following each assertion of a line it seems reasonable to check to see if it can be used to form a triangle. This test is captured in the following procedure:

```
(procedure (LINE ?X ?Y)
(cond
  ((and
      (or (infer (list (quote LINE) ?X ?Z))
          (infer (list (quote LINE) ?Z ?X)))
      (or (infer (list (quote LINE) ?Y ?Z))
          (infer (list (quote LINE) ?Z ?Y))))
            (infer( list (quote TRIANGLE) ?X ?Y ?Z)))
    (T NIL)))
```

This procedure attempts to find two line segments with endpoints equal to the value of ?X and ?Y and sharing a common endpoint. If this condition can be satisfied, the value to which ?Z is bound will be the label of the common endpoint. In effect, this procedure searches for three connected points, and if they can be found, it tries to determine if the line segments connecting the points define a triangle. This procedure is also an example of one which includes an element variable that is not bound to any value as the result of matching the procedure pattern. Note that it occurs within a list which will be used as a pattern for the purpose of performing another match. That is, infer will invoke a pattern matcher that attempts to match the argument of infer to the procedure patterns of previously defined procedures.

Now, since no pattern containing the atom TRIANGLE is currently in the data base, the interpreter looks for procedures whose patterns match the list (TRIANGLE ?X ?Y ?Z), where ?X, ?Y, and ?Z have been bound to values as a consequence of matching the procedure pattern. This of course matches a previously defined procedure, so it is invoked. Using our previous assertions about lines, following the inference of (LINE C A), an attempt would be made to infer (TRIANGLE C A B). Since the coordinates of C, A, and B satisfy the triangle inequalities as expressed in a previous procedure, (TRIANGLE C A B) would be asserted into the data base.

One final procedure illustrates how the data base can be "cleaned up" to reduce or eliminate redundant information. Since it is now possible to infer the lines which make up the sides of (TRIANGLE C A B) with the definition of an appropriate procedure, we can remove these assertions from the data base:

```
(procedure (TRIANGLE ?X ?Y ?Z)
(cond
    ((asserted-p (list (quote TRIANGLE) ?X ?Y ?Z))
            (delete (list (quote LINE) ?X ?Y))
            (delete (list (quote LINE) ?X ?Z))
            (delete (list (quote LINE) ?Y ?X))
            (delete (list (quote LINE) ?Y ?Z))
            (delete (list (quote LINE) ?Z ?X))
            (delete (list (quote LINE) ?Z ?Y)))
    (T NIL)))
```

The following dialogue summarizes the manipulation of the data base that has occurred with this example. The procedures described are assumed to have been entered previously. The global variable assertions contains a set of lists which reflect assertions made by either the user or the system. After each assertion, the contents of the data base assertions are displayed:

```
> assertions
()
>       (assert (A 0 0))
()
>       (assert (B 0 10))
()
>       (assert (C 10 0))
()
>       (assert (LINE A B))
((LINE A B))
>       (assert (LINE A C))
((LINE A C) (LINE A B))
```

```
>    (assert (LINE C B))
((TRIANGLE C A B))
```

Notice that nothing is in `assertions` following the first three assertions. This is because the procedure that was invoked as a result of pattern matching deleted the corresponding patterns after the coordinate information was internalized on the property
lists of the point labels. Furthermore, following the assertion of (LINE C B), the specified line segment is placed only temporarily in the data base. It is removed almost
immediately following execution of the "cleanup expert," leaving only the assertion
about the triangle. Now even though the line segments that form the three sides of
the triangle have been removed, it should still be possible to infer them from the current contents of the data base. Therefore, we require one further expert, a procedure
that infers line segments. Assuming, for the purposes of this example, that triangles
are the only "high-level" objects composed of lines, the following procedure suffices:

```
(procedure (LINE ?X ?Y)
       (or (asserted-p (list (quote TRIANGLE) ?X ?Y ?Z))
           (asserted-p (list (quote TRIANGLE) ?Z ?X ?Y))
           (asserted-p (list (quote TRIANGLE) ?Y ?Z ?X))
           (asserted-p (list (quote TRIANGLE) ?X ?Z ?Y))
           (asserted-p (list (quote TRIANGLE) ?Y ?X ?Z))
           (asserted-p (list (quote TRIANGLE) ?Z ?Y ?X))))
```

In this example, then, the result has been to arrive at a single assertion in the
data base as a consequence of six previous assertions. To illustrate the usefulness of
pattern matching, many important implementation details for the interpreter have
not been addressed explicitly in this explanation. Nevertheless, the example gives the
flavor and hints at the complex problems associated with planner-type languages.

An important issue raised by the notion of pattern directed invocation is that it
conflicts with the principle of data abstraction. With traditional function calls based on
positional notation, it is possible to pass arguments to function bodies without explicit
knowledge of the representation, and this is what permits us to employ this important software engineering principle. However, this is not the case when designing a
procedure to be invoked by pattern matching, where it is necessary to know the representation of the "argument" that will invoke it. This conflict is recognized by the
programming language community, and there is considerable interest in the possibility of developing pattern-directed invocation which can "coexist" with data abstraction
[Wad87].

The original planner-type languages are now primarily of historical interest.
However, as indicated in the introduction to this chapter, pattern matching still finds
application in contemporary languages. As well as the pattern-directed invocation
found in PROLOG, pattern matching is used to retrieve components from data structures and to control sequencing in programs written in functional languages, such as
Miranda, Haskell, and Standard ML, cited in the introduction to this chapter. While
much of the documentation of these languages is available mainly in journal publications or technical reports, the use of Standard ML and Miranda in some commercial
applications has resulted in more readily available publications being produced for

the professional and the casual user (see, for example, *The Definition of Standard ML* [MTH90]). It is expected that this trend will continue for such languages as they are adopted for software product development.

11.6 Exercises

11.1. In pattern matching, segment variables are defined to provide a means of matching zero or more elements in a target pattern. Describe, using examples, the alternatives to be accounted for and what is matched when the first component of a pattern is an unnamed segment variable, and that pattern is to be compared to a target pattern. Assume that no pattern variables are present in the target pattern.

11.2. Implement the function `segment-match` of Section 11.1 using high-level iterators, described in Chapter 8.

11.3. Modify the function `match`, defined in Section 11.2, to permit both named and unnamed pattern variables to be included in a pattern.

11.4. You are given a Common LISP function (`match pattern target`) which tries to match `pattern` to `target` and returns NIL if no match can be made. Otherwise, it returns an environment `env` binding all pattern variable identifiers with the corresponding S-expressions in `target` to which they matched. A function (`eval-body expr env`) exists to evaluate `expr` with the values of identifiers given on `env`.

Write a function (`eval-proc target proc-env-lst`) which will evaluate the body of the first ⟨procedure⟩ on `proc-env-lst`, whose ⟨procedure-pattern⟩ matches `target`. A ⟨procedure⟩ is defined by the grammar of Section 11.5. You may assume that a pattern can be any S-expression and can include only named pattern variables.

11.5. The following GRAIL grammar defines a simple programming language.

$$
\begin{aligned}
\langle\text{program}\rangle \ &::=\ (\ (\ \langle\text{fn-defs:fn-def*}\rangle\ )\\
&\qquad \langle\text{final-expr:expr}\rangle\ )\\
\langle\text{expr}\rangle \ &::=\ \langle\text{id}\rangle\ |\ \langle\text{truth-val}\rangle\ |\ \langle\text{constant}\rangle\\
&\qquad |\ \langle\text{cond-expr}\rangle\ |\ \langle\text{fn-call}\rangle\\
\langle\text{fn-def}\rangle \ &::=\ (\ \text{FN}\ \langle\text{fn-name:id}\rangle\ (\ \langle\text{params:id*}\rangle\ )\\
&\qquad \langle\text{body:expr}\rangle\ )\\
\langle\text{cond-expr}\rangle \ &::=\ (\ \text{COND}\ \langle\text{clauses:clause*}\rangle\ )\\
\langle\text{clause}\rangle \ &::=\ (\ \langle\text{pred:expr}\rangle\ \langle\text{result:expr}\rangle\ )\\
\langle\text{fn-call}\rangle \ &::=\ (\ \langle\text{callee:id}\rangle\ \langle\text{args:expr*}\rangle\ )\\
\langle\text{id}\rangle \ &::=\ \langle\text{id-name:symbolic-atom}\rangle\\
\langle\text{truth-val}\rangle \ &::=\ \langle\text{true}\rangle\ |\ \langle\text{false}\rangle\\
\langle\text{true}\rangle \ &::=\ \text{T}\\
\langle\text{false}\rangle \ &::=\ \text{F}\\
\langle\text{constant}\rangle \ &::=\ (\ \text{QUOTE}\ \langle\text{S-expression}\rangle\ )
\end{aligned}
$$

In pattern-directed invocation of procedures, a pattern must be associated with an expression, and a mechanism must be provided to identify those procedure patterns which match the input pattern. Suppose that all procedure patterns are constrained to exclude segment variables. Extend the grammar to include ⟨procedure⟩s in addition to ⟨fn-def⟩s, if the body of a ⟨procedure⟩ can be any ⟨expr⟩ as defined by the grammar, and ⟨procedure⟩s have *no* names; that is, they are unnamed and identifiable only by their procedure patterns.

11.6. Describe a data structure that can be used to keep track of and retrieve ⟨procedure⟩s as defined in Exercise 11.5. How does it differ from an environment data structure?

11.7. For procedures whose syntax is defined by the extensions requested to the grammar of Exercise 11.5, define a function (`invoke target-pattern proc-env`) that finds all procedures on the environment `proc-env` whose procedure patterns match `target-pattern`. As each one is found, it is evaluated by a function `proc-eval` whose arguments consist of an environment of bound identifiers and an expression, namely the procedure body. You may assume the existence of `proc-eval`. Your implementation should include the construction of a variable environment for binding the element variables of a procedure pattern to the corresponding values in `target-pattern`.

11.8. Show how the the function `sl-eval`, defined in Section 6.3, could be modified to provide an evaluator that could process ⟨procedure⟩s as defined in Exercise 11.5. Discuss the circumstances under which element variables would be encountered by the evaluator.

11.9. Let P be a list of n segment variables, and suppose it is to be matched to a target, T, of k elements, none of which are pattern variables. Devise a formula which expresses in terms of n and k how many possible alternative matches can be made of the pattern P to the target T.

11.10. Modify the implementation of `match` described in Section 11.3 so that the function `match` returns a list of all possible ⟨match⟩es of `pattern` to `target`: for example,

```
(match '(*X *Y) '(A B))  ⇒
   (((*Y ())(*X (A B)))((*Y (B))(*X (A)))((*Y (A B))(*X ())))
```

That is, three ⟨match⟩es are returned, each ⟨match⟩ being a list of one element specifying a set of bindings.

Hint: This will require that functions such as `match1` and `segment-match` be modified to return ⟨match⟩es rather than environments. Furthermore, `segment-match` must test all possible segments that can be constructed from `target`, rather than terminating when the first successful match is encountered.

12

Textual Notation

In previous chapters, we have represented symbolic data domains using Lisp lists. As discussed in Chapter 2, however, this use of list notation compromises the readability of symbolic input and output in order to rapidly develop application prototypes. Once such a prototype has been developed, it may be desirable to construct a production version of it which uses a more readable form of notation. For example, consider a symbolic differentiation program taking input such as

```
(x * (sin (x ** 2)))
```

and generating the corresponding output:

```
((2 * ((x ** 2) * (cos (x ** 2)))) + (sin (x ** 2)))
```

The production version could be set up to deal with more readable forms of input and output, such as the following:

```
x * sin (x ** 2)
```

```
2 * x**2 * cos(x**2) + sin(x**2)
```

It may be considerably easier for the user of a symbolic computing application to work with such improved input and output forms. We will refer to such improved notations as *textual* notations to emphasize that they are not constrained by the requirements of the list-based notations we have used previously. Note, however, that even further improvements to readability of the notation could be achieved using typeset notations.

$$x \sin x^2$$

$$2x^2 \cos x^2 + \sin x^2$$

However, these latter notations are probably impractical for symbolic computing applications, because of the difficulty of specifying and displaying them with commonly available computing equipment.[1]

Given a Lisp-based prototype for a symbolic computing application, there are three basic problems to be solved in developing versions which work with improved textual notations. The first is to define the new notation representing the symbolic data. A reasonable way to do this is to develop an EBNF grammar for the notation, working from the GRAIL grammar of its list-based prototype. Although this is a reasonably straightforward task, there are some pitfalls to be avoided, such as the possibility of defining an ambiguous grammar.

The second problem in converting to a textual notation is to construct input routines which convert this notation into the internal representation used by the symbolic data type. The input process generally consists of two phases: *lexical analysis* and *parsing*. In lexical analysis, individual characters from the input stream are formed into *tokens* (i.e., basic elements of the notation). For example, the input characters

```
sin(x**2)
```

might first be formed into the tokens sin, (, x, **, 2, and). Parsing hierarchically then groups the input tokens to determine the appropriate symbolic data structures. For example, x, ** and 2 might first be grouped together to form a power expression whose base is the variable x and whose exponent is the constant 2. The power expresson would then be grouped together with the sin and parenthesis tokens to form the appropriate sine expression.

The third requirement in dealing with textual notations is to invert the parsing process, providing output routines which convert symbolic data objects back into a textual form. It is relatively straightforward to reproduce the textual representation as a stream of tokens. Often, however, this output stream will not fit within the margins of a single line; it then becomes important to format the output in a readable fashion. For example, the readability of

```
4 * x**3 * cos(2 * x)
+ 11 * x**2 * sin(x)
- 5 * cos(x) * sin(x)
```

is severely compromised if it is formatted in an inappropriate fashion such as the following.

```
4 * x**3 * cos(2 * x) + 11 * x
**2 * sin(x) - 5 * cos(x) * sin
(x)
```

----

[1]As a secondary form of output, it may nevertheless be quite useful to produce typeset notation (in a suitable typesetting language) for inclusion in printed documents.

The process of generating neatly formatted output representations is known as *pretty-printing*.

12.1 DEFINING NOTATIONS USING EBNF

The first step in upgrading a symbolic computing application to use a textual notation is to make sure that the notation is well defined. In general, we will use EBNF grammars to specify textual notations. We will also relate these grammars to the original GRAIL grammars to ensure that the mapping from the textual notation to the abstract structure of the symbolic data domain is clear. In some cases, we may have an existing EBNF description which is suitable. Otherwise, we will work from GRAIL grammars to develop textual notations, incorporating operators, punctuation, and keywords as appropriate.

The major constraint in developing textual notations is to ensure that the notation is easy to parse; that is, it is easy to determine what symbolic data structure is represented by any given item of notation. This is important for both human readability of the notation and to allow parsing routines to be constructed in a straightforward fashion. The most severe problem in this regard is that grammars may be *ambiguous*, in which case two different symbolic data structures may have the same textual representation.

12.1.1 Ambiguity in Infix Grammars

Unfortunately, ambiguity is a common problem for symbolic notation systems which use infix operators. For example, consider the development of a textual notation for the domain of algebraic expressions. Working from the GRAIL grammar of Figure 4.1 and following common conventions, we might first develop an EBNF grammar for algebraic expressions as shown in Figure 12.1. This grammar eliminates the systematic use of parentheses that characterize the Lisp representations we have previously used for algebraic expressions. In so doing, however, the grammar has introduced ambiguities—for example, x + y * z might correspond to either ((x + y) * z) or (x + (y * z)) in list notation.

Ambiguity in interpreting notational phrases can be illustrated by examining possible *derivation trees* (also called *parse trees*) for the phrases. A derivation tree shows how the start symbol for the grammar (⟨expression⟩ for algebraic expressions) can be successively expanded to generate a given phrase. For example, Figure 12.2 shows the derivation tree for cos(x + 14). Derivation trees are drawn in an upside-down fashion, with the start symbol at the top (the root). At each step, a nonterminal symbol is "expanded" by placing its definition or one of its alternative definitions below it; branches are then drawn connecting the initial nonterminal symbol to each terminal and nonterminal symbol in its definition. This process continues until all nonterminal symbols have been expanded and only terminal symbols remain. As shown in Figure 12.2, however, the breakdown of basic tokens into individual characters is usually omitted.

In general, a phrase is ambiguous if there are two or more derivation trees for it. Each derivation tree corresponds to a valid way of parsing the phrase. Given an

⟨expression⟩ ::= ⟨constant⟩ | ⟨variable⟩ | ⟨negation⟩ | ⟨product⟩ |
                   ⟨quotient⟩ | ⟨sum⟩ | ⟨difference⟩ | ⟨power⟩ |
                   ⟨exponential⟩ | ⟨sine⟩ | ⟨cosine⟩
  ⟨negation⟩ ::= - ⟨expression⟩
   ⟨product⟩ ::= ⟨expression⟩ * ⟨expression⟩
  ⟨quotient⟩ ::= ⟨expression⟩ / ⟨expression⟩
       ⟨sum⟩ ::= ⟨expression⟩ + ⟨expression⟩
⟨difference⟩ ::= ⟨expression⟩ - ⟨expression⟩
     ⟨power⟩ ::= ⟨expression⟩ ** ⟨expression⟩
⟨exponential⟩ ::= exp (⟨expression⟩)
      ⟨sine⟩ ::= sin (⟨expression⟩)
    ⟨cosine⟩ ::= cos (⟨expression⟩)
  ⟨constant⟩ ::= ⟨digit⟩ { ⟨digit⟩ }
  ⟨variable⟩ ::= ⟨letter⟩ { ⟨letter⟩ }

Figure 12.1 Ambiguous EBNF grammar for algebraic expressions.

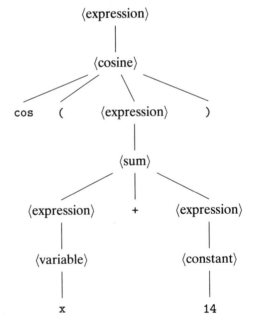

Figure 12.2 Derivation tree for cos(x + 14).

ambiguous phrase, then, it is impossible to determine its abstract structure uniquely. For example, Figure 12.3 shows the two possible derivation trees for the expression x + y * z according to the grammar of Figure 12.1. The two ways of parsing the phrase yield the two different symbolic data structures representing (x + (y * z)) and ((x + y) * z).

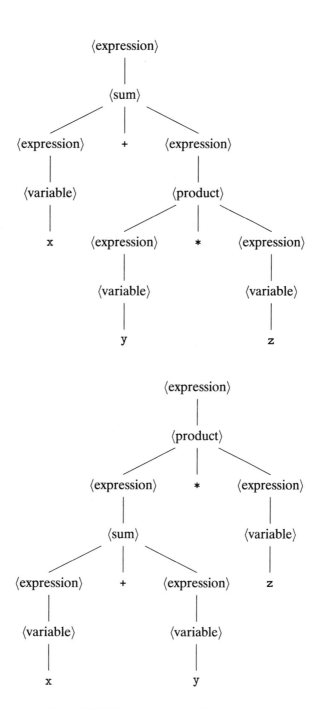

Figure 12.3   Two derivation trees for x + y * z.

The grammar of Figure 12.1 is ambiguous in many other ways as well. Note that the derivation trees of Figure 12.3 do not depend on which particular infix operators are involved. Thus expressions such as x - y - z and x * y * z are also ambiguous according to this grammar. In each case the expression has two distinct derivation trees, representing two different abstract structures. In the latter case, however, the grammatical ambiguity does not give rise to semantic ambiguity, because ((x * y) * z) and (x * (y * z)) are equivalent by the associativity of multiplication.

Proper definition of a textual notation requires that all grammatical ambiguities be resolved. In the case of algebraic expressions, we can resolve the ambiguities using standard mathematical conventions for *precedence* and *associativity*. According to these conventions, we try to form product and quotient subexpressions before sums or differences (i.e., the * and / operators take precedence over + and -). Thus the expression x + y * z should always be parsed to produce (x + (y * z)), while x / y - z should yield ((x / y) - z). The unary negation operator also enters the picture, having higher precedence than addition or subtraction, but lower precedence than multiplication or division. Thus - x / y + z is interpreted ((- (x / y)) + z). The power operator has the highest precedence of all, so that parsing x * y ** 3 produces (x * (y ** 3)).

Within precedence levels, associativity rules are used to resolve the remaining ambiguities. Most of the operators are *left-to-right* associative, meaning that we try to form subexpressions with the leftmost operator first. Thus x - y + z is parsed as ((x - y) + z) rather than as (x - (y + z)). However, the power operator is *right-to-left* associative, so that x ** y ** z is parsed as (x ** (y ** z)).

In essence, the precedence and associativity rules can be used to disambiguate the grammar of Figure 12.1 by restricting how subexpressions may be formed. For example, a product expression may never be formed with a sum as an operand. This is because the multiplication operation always takes precedence and would be formed as a subexpression before the sum. These restrictions may actually be incorporated into the grammar as shown in Figure 12.4. Note that several nonterminals have been introduced to stand for restricted classes of ⟨expression⟩ and used to replace it in the appropriate subexpression contexts. According to this grammar, then, every expression has an unambiguous derivation, such as that for x + y * z shown in Figure 12.5.

The grammar of Figure 12.4 also introduces a rule for parenthesized expressions in order to allow any type of symbolic expression data structure to be represented in the textual notation. Without parentheses, there would be no way of representing in the textual notation various types of expression that are perfectly acceptable in list notation [e.g., (x * (y + z))]. With parenthesized expressions allowed in the grammar, however, this example can now be represented as x * (y + z). By selectively using parentheses only when necessary to make the meaning clear, our textual notation improves on the "Lots of Irritating, Silly Parentheses" that characterize Lisp list notation.

12.1.2 Design for Readability

Although the design of notations and their grammars can be frought with ambiguity and parsing problems if approached in an ad hoc way, these problems can be avoided if

$$
\begin{aligned}
\langle\text{expression}\rangle &::= \langle\text{negation}\rangle \mid \langle\text{sum}\rangle \mid \langle\text{difference}\rangle \mid \langle\text{term}\rangle \\
\langle\text{term}\rangle &::= \langle\text{product}\rangle \mid \langle\text{quotient}\rangle \mid \langle\text{factor}\rangle \\
\langle\text{factor}\rangle &::= \langle\text{power}\rangle \mid \langle\text{primary}\rangle \\
\langle\text{primary}\rangle &::= \langle\text{constant}\rangle \mid \langle\text{variable}\rangle \mid \langle\text{exponential}\rangle \mid \langle\text{sine}\rangle \mid \\
&\qquad \langle\text{cosine}\rangle \mid \langle\text{parentheses}\rangle \\
\langle\text{negation}\rangle &::= \text{-} \langle\text{term}\rangle \\
\langle\text{product}\rangle &::= \langle\text{term}\rangle * \langle\text{factor}\rangle \\
\langle\text{quotient}\rangle &::= \langle\text{term}\rangle / \langle\text{factor}\rangle \\
\langle\text{sum}\rangle &::= \langle\text{expression}\rangle + \langle\text{term}\rangle \\
\langle\text{difference}\rangle &::= \langle\text{expression}\rangle - \langle\text{term}\rangle \\
\langle\text{power}\rangle &::= \langle\text{primary}\rangle ** \langle\text{factor}\rangle \\
\langle\text{exponential}\rangle &::= \text{exp} (\langle\text{expression}\rangle) \\
\langle\text{sine}\rangle &::= \text{sin} (\langle\text{expression}\rangle) \\
\langle\text{cosine}\rangle &::= \text{cos} (\langle\text{expression}\rangle) \\
\langle\text{constant}\rangle &::= \langle\text{digit}\rangle \{ \langle\text{digit}\rangle \} \\
\langle\text{variable}\rangle &::= \langle\text{letter}\rangle \{ \langle\text{letter}\rangle \} \\
\langle\text{parenthesis}\rangle &::= (\langle\text{expression}\rangle)
\end{aligned}
$$

Figure 12.4   Unambiguous EBNF grammar for algebraic expressions.

appropriate design guidelines for readable notations are followed. In fact, a systematic design approach is very important if grammatical ambiguity is to be avoided, because there is no general way to decide whether or not an arbitrary grammar is ambiguous [AU72, pp. 203–204].

One approach to grammar design is to use marker tokens systematically to distinguish among the different ways of expanding the grammatical rules. Thus wherever alternative forms are specified using the alternation (|) metasymbol, a distinct marker should be introduced for each alternative. Ideally, a marker should be the first token in an alternative to identify it as clearly as possible. Marker tokens should also be used with repeated phrases (designated with { } metasymbols). In this case, the tokens are needed to indicate when repetition of the phrase stops. Furthermore, if there are any optional phrases (designated with [ ] metasymbols), markers should be introduced to indicate the presence or absence of the option. In this way, the markers allow an unambiguous and easily parsed grammar to be constructed. The marker tokens should also be chosen to be distinctive yet unobtrusive in order to enhance readability for the human eye.

Consider, for example, the use of marker tokens in the EBNF grammar of Small Lisp expressions as shown in Figure 12.6. Note the use of the marker tokens ", (, [, and { to identify four of the alternative expression types. The only other tokens that may begin an expression are numeric-atom tokens or identifier tokens. Numeric atoms essentially serve as their own marker tokens. In the case of identifiers, however, further analysis is required to distinguish between variables and function calls as expressions.

Variables and function calls thus do not follow the pattern of having a marker as their first token. Examining the next possible token, it would appear that a "[" token following an identifier should serve as the marker for function calls. However,

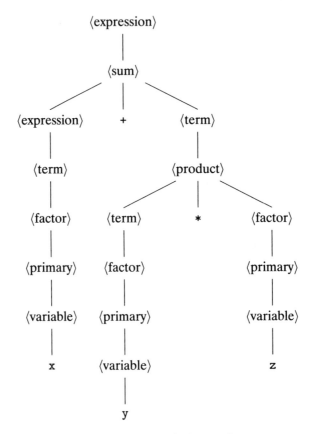

Figure 12.5 Unambiguous derivation tree for x + y * z.

```
            ⟨expression⟩ ::=  ⟨value⟩ | ⟨variable⟩ | ⟨function-call⟩ |
                              ⟨conditional-expression⟩ | ⟨let- expression⟩
                  ⟨value⟩ ::=  ⟨numeric-atom⟩ | " ⟨symbolic-atom⟩ " | ⟨list⟩
               ⟨variable⟩ ::=  ⟨identifier⟩
                   ⟨list⟩ ::=  ( { ⟨S-expression⟩ } )
          ⟨function-call⟩ ::=  ⟨function-name⟩ [ ⟨argument-list⟩ ]
          ⟨function-name⟩ ::=  ⟨identifier⟩
          ⟨argument-list⟩ ::=  ⟨expression⟩ { ; ⟨expression⟩ }
 ⟨conditional-expression⟩ ::=  [ ⟨clause-list⟩ ]
            ⟨clause-list⟩ ::=  ⟨clause⟩ { ; ⟨clause⟩ }
                 ⟨clause⟩ ::=  ⟨expression⟩ --> ⟨expression⟩
         ⟨let-expression⟩ ::=  { ⟨let-list⟩ : ⟨expression⟩ }
               ⟨let-list⟩ ::=  ⟨local-definition⟩ { ; ⟨local-definition⟩ }
       ⟨local-definition⟩ ::=  ⟨variable⟩ = ⟨expression⟩
```

Figure 12.6 EBNF grammar of Small Lisp expressions.

this must be verified by considering the possible markers for variables. Since there is no second token within a variable, we must consider any token which might follow the variable as an expression (i.e., any token which might follow ⟨expression⟩ in the grammar). The possible tokens are

  ;   ]   -->   :   }   ⟨identifier⟩   ⟨comment-line⟩

considering the full grammar of Small Lisp as shown in Appendix B. Any token in this set following an identifier hence serves as a marker for variables. Since variables and function calls can thus be distinguished by looking ahead to the token following an identifier, there is no need to introduce distinct markers preceding the identifier. Indeed, if this were done it would only serve to clutter the notation, detracting from its readability.

The grammar of Small Lisp expressions also illustrates the use of marker tokens with repeated phrases. For example, in the arguments of a function call, the " ; " token is the marker indicating that there are more arguments in the list, while the "]" token marks the end of the list. The same markers are also used for the clauses of a conditional expression. The local definitions of a let-expression follow a similar pattern except that the " : " token serves as the end-of-list marker.

As the example of Small Lisp illustrates, it is relatively straightforward to develop readable notations with unambiguous grammars through the use of appropriate marker tokens. If an application requires it, constructs using infix operators can be accommodated as well, provided that care is taken in the grammar formulation to reflect appropriate precedence and associativity rules.

12.2 LEXICAL ANALYSIS

In preparation for parsing, a *lexical analyzer* is commonly used to group together characters from an input stream to form the basic tokens of a notation. Consider, for example, a lexical analyzer for algebraic expressions in the textual notation of Figure 12.4. The basic tokens it should produce are the operators +, -, *, /, and **, the keywords sin, cos, and exp, the grouping tokens (and), and ⟨variable⟩ and ⟨constant⟩ tokens, such as x and 213. Essentially, the role of the lexical analyzer is to transform a stream of characters into a stream of such tokens. In doing so, it provides an important service to the parser, considerably simplifying its implementation.

12.2.1 Lexical Structure of a Notation

Complete specification of a lexical analyzer also requires that certain issues with respect to the lexical structure of a notation be addressed. First of all, there must be a way to resolve any ambiguities in the way an input stream is divided up into tokens. For example, the algebraic expression

                                          x**12

might be divided into the five tokens x, *, *, 1, and 2, or alternatively, into the three tokens x, **, and 12. A reasonable solution is to specify that the next token at any point is the one which matches the longest sequence of following input characters. This is the approach taken by most modern programming languages and the one that we will use here, but is not the approach used by some older languages such as FORTRAN.

A second issue is the role of *white space*—sequences of blank, newline, and possibly other nonprintable characters—in the notation. In this case, we again follow a commonly used rule of modern programming languages: any number of white space characters can appear between two tokens, but no white space may appear within a token unless it is explicitly permitted for that token type.[2] This approach allows a notation to be freely formatted for readability.

A third issue that arises in some notation systems is how keywords are treated. The basic question is whether the keywords should be reserved for use as keywords or whether they are also allowable as instances of other token types. For example, in the algebraic expression notation of Figure 12.4, the keywords sin, cos, and exp are also syntactically acceptable as ⟨variable⟩ tokens. Again, we will generally take the approach followed by modern programming languages, which is that keywords are treated as reserved words. This has the advantage of avoiding confusion and also simplifies lexical analysis and parsing by allowing each lexical token to be given a unique type.

Although we have discussed each of these issues in the context of requirements for lexical analysis, they are in fact aspects of the notation system itself and should be addressed as part of its definition.

12.2.2 A Lexical Analyzer for Algebraic Expressions

Now let us consider the implementation of a lexical analyzer for the algebraic expression notation of Figure 12.4. First we build a prototype in Small Lisp. The prototype will accept a list of input characters and return a list of tokens to be passed to the parser. Let us represent input characters according to the GRAIL grammar of Figure 12.7 and the tokens to be produced according to that of Figure 12.8. Although these representations may not be entirely practical, they allow us to demonstrate the principles of lexical analysis in a straightforward prototype.

```
     ⟨character⟩  ::=  ⟨plus⟩ | ⟨hyphen⟩ | ⟨asterisk⟩ | ⟨slash⟩ |
                       ⟨left-paren⟩ | ⟨right-paren⟩ | ⟨letter⟩ | ⟨digit⟩ |
                       ⟨blank⟩ | ⟨newline⟩
          ⟨plus⟩  ::=  +
        ⟨hyphen⟩  ::=  -
       ⟨asterisk⟩  ::=  *
         ⟨slash⟩  ::=  /
    ⟨left-paren⟩  ::=  lParen
   ⟨right-paren⟩  ::=  rParen
         ⟨blank⟩  ::=  blank
       ⟨newline⟩  ::=  newline
        ⟨letter⟩  ::=  ⟨letter-val:symbolic-atom⟩
         ⟨digit⟩  ::=  ⟨digit-val:numeric-atom⟩
```

Figure 12.7 Representation of input characters.

---

[2]Blanks are typically permitted within "character string" tokens in programming languages.

$$
\begin{aligned}
\langle\text{algebraic-token}\rangle &::= \langle\text{plus-op}\rangle \mid \langle\text{minus-op}\rangle \mid \langle\text{times-op}\rangle \mid \langle\text{divide-op}\rangle \mid \\
&\qquad \langle\text{expon-op}\rangle \mid \langle\text{sin-word}\rangle \mid \langle\text{cos-word}\rangle \mid \langle\text{exp-word}\rangle \mid \\
&\qquad \langle\text{left-paren-token}\rangle \mid \langle\text{right-paren-token}\rangle \mid \\
&\qquad \langle\text{variable-sym}\rangle \mid \langle\text{constant-sym}\rangle
\end{aligned}
$$

```
          ⟨plus-op⟩ ::= +
         ⟨minus-op⟩ ::= -
         ⟨times-op⟩ ::= *
        ⟨divide-op⟩ ::= /
         ⟨expon-op⟩ ::= **
  ⟨left-paren-token⟩ ::= lParen
 ⟨right-paren-token⟩ ::= rParen
         ⟨sin-word⟩ ::= sin
         ⟨cos-word⟩ ::= cos
         ⟨exp-word⟩ ::= exp
      ⟨variable-sym⟩ ::= ( var ⟨sym-val:symbolic-atom⟩ )
      ⟨constant-sym⟩ ::= ( const ⟨num-val:numeric-atom⟩ )
```

Figure 12.8   Representation of algebraic tokens.

The lexical analysis for algebraic expressions proceeds by case analysis on the first character in the input stream. When a token is recognized, it is concatenated to the result of lexically analyzing the rest of the input stream.

```
algebraic-lexer[char-list] =
  [endp[char-list] --> ();
   otherwise -->
     {ch1 = first[char-list];
      more-chars = rest[char-list] :
      [plus-p[ch1] --> cons[plus-op; algebraic-lexer[more-chars]];
       hyphen-p[ch1] --> cons[minus-op; algebraic-lexer[more-chars]];
       asterisk-p[ch1] -->
         [endp[more-chars] --> list1[times-op];
          asterisk-p[first[more-chars]] -->
             cons[expon-op; algebraic-lexer[rest[more-chars]]];
           otherwise --> cons[times-op; algebraic-lexer[more-chars]]];
        slash-p[ch1] --> cons[divide-op; algebraic-lexer[more-chars]];
        left-paren-p[ch1] -->
          cons[left-paren-token; algebraic-lexer[more-chars]];
        right-paren-p[ch1] -->
          cons[right-paren-token; algebraic-lexer[more-chars]];
        blank-p[ch1] --> algebraic-lexer[more-chars];
        newline-p[ch1] --> algebraic-lexer[more-chars];
        digit-p[ch1] --> get-constant[digit-val[ch1]; more-chars];
        letter-p[ch1] --> get-word[list1[letter-val[ch1]]; more-chars];
        otherwise --> error2[(Invalid character in input); ch1]]}]
```

In several cases, single characters are immediately recognized as tokens. In the case of the ∗ character, however, we must check for an ⟨expon-op⟩ by looking ahead to see if the next character is also a ∗. Blanks and newline characters are simply discarded. If the first character is a digit or a letter, we call auxiliary procedures to find all the characters of the appropriate constant, variable, or keyword token.

```
get-constant[num; more-chars] =
  [endp[more-chars] --> list1[make-constant-sym[num]];
   digit-p[first[more-chars]] -->
     get-constant
       [plus[times[num; 10]; digit-val[first[more-chars]]];
        rest[more-chars]];
   otherwise -->
     cons[make-constant-sym[num]; algebraic-lexer[more-chars]]]

get-word[letters; more-chars] =
  [endp[more-chars] --> list1[make-the-word[letters]];
   letter-p[first[more-chars]] -->
     get-variable
       [append1[letters; letter-val[first[more-chars]]];
        rest[more-chars]];
   otherwise -->
     cons[make-the-word[letters]; algebraic-lexer[more-chars]]]


make-the-word[letters] =
  {the-word = implode[letters] :
   [eq[the-word; sin] --> sin-word;
    eq[the-word; cos] --> cos-word;
    eq[the-word; exp] --> exp-word;
    otherwise --> make-variable-sym[the-word]]}
```

Essentially, these procedures each represent a separate state of the lexical analyzer, scanning through the characters of a word or a numeral until the end of it is found.

Now consider the development of a production version of the lexical analyzer in Pascal. Note that the Small Lisp version uses list data structures to represent both the stream of input characters and the stream of output tokens. Corresponding data structures in a production version would impose considerable overhead on the system. In fact, the use of such data structures can make the cost of lexical analysis a dominant factor in symbolic computing applications. This is because the number of characters in the input stream may well be several times greater than the number of tokens represented (depending on the amount of white space and the average size of words and numerals). Furthermore, there may be up to twice as many lexical tokens as symbolic data objects, depending on the number of keywords and punctuation marks. Thus, even if the main algorithms of a symbolic computing application are conceptually more complex than lexical analysis, they may require considerably fewer resources because they may be processing an order-of-magnitude fewer data elements.

Fortunately, there is no need to maintain the input character stream as a physical list. As indicated by the Small Lisp prototype, determination of a given token requires no more than examination of a single character beyond the end of the token. Furthermore, once a character is examined, no previous character in the input stream need be examined again. Thus the input stream in our production lexical analyzer can be maintained using a single-character buffer `CurrentChar` and a routine `AdvanceCharStream` which reads the next input character into this buffer. For convenience, `AdvanceCharStream` is specified to indicate the end of the input stream by assigning a special value `EOFchar` to `CurrentChar`. With the inclusion of an appropriate routine to initialize the input source, these facilities provide a suitable abstraction of the input character stream for use by the lexical analyzer.

The interface that the lexical analyzer provides to the parser can be specified similarly. A buffer variable `CurrentToken` will hold the currently pending token, and a routine `AdvanceTokenStream` will advance to the next token in the input stream. A special token `EOStoken` will mark the end of the token stream. This approach avoids the construction of a physical list of tokens, which—as we shall see in the following section on parser construction—is not needed in the parser implementation. Even if this were not the case, however, this abstraction could still be used to construct the token stream.

The basic Pascal implementation of the lexical analyzer follows directly from these decisions:

```
TYPE TokenKind = (PlusOp, MinusOp, TimesOp, DivideOp, ExponOp,
                  LeftParenToken, RightParenToken, SinWord, CosWord,
                  ExpWord, ConstantSym, VariableSym, EOStoken);
     TokenType =
       RECORD
         CASE kind : TokenKind OF
           ConstantSym : (NumVal : INTEGER);
           VariableSym : (SymVal : STRING)
       END;

VAR CurrentToken : TokenType;

PROCEDURE AdvanceTokenStream;
  PROCEDURE SetTokenAndAdvance(theKind : TokenKind);
  BEGIN
    CurrentToken.kind := theKind;
    AdvanceCharStream
  END;

BEGIN
  CASE CurrentChar OF
```

```
          EOFchar: CurrentToken.kind := EOStoken;
          '+' : SetTokenAndAdvance(PlusOp);
          '-' : SetTokenAndAdvance(MinusOp);
          '*' : BEGIN
                  GetNextCh;
                  IF CurrentChar = '*' THEN SetTokenAndAdvance (ExponOp)
                  ELSE CurrentToken.kind := TimesOp
                END;
          '/' : SetTokenAndAdvance(DivideOp)
          '(' : SetTokenAndAdvance(LeftParenToken);
          ')' : SetTokenAndAdvance(RightParenToken);
          ' ', NewLine : BEGIN AdvanceCharStream; AdvanceTokenStream END
          '0'..'9': GetConstant
          'A'..'Z', 'a'..'z': GetVariable
        ELSE Error2('Illegal character in input', CurrentChar)
        END
      END;
```

Note that the implementation always assumes that the next character is available in
CurrentChar. If a symbol is determined without examining the following character,
AdvanceCharStream must nevertheless be called to update CurrentChar. Variables
are constructed as String objects using the string concatenation operator (+) of Extended Pascal.

```
      PROCEDURE GetConstant;
      BEGIN
        CurrentToken.kind := ConstantSym;
        CurrentToken.NumVal := ORD(CurrentChar) - ORD('0');
        AdvanceCharStream;
        WHILE CurrentChar IN ['0'..'9'] DO BEGIN
          CurrentToken.NumVal :=
            CurrentToken.NumVal * 10 + ORD(CurrentChar) - ORD('0');
          AdvanceCharStream
        END
      END;

      PROCEDURE GetVariable;
        theWord : String;
      BEGIN
        CurrentToken.kind := VariableSym;
        theWord := CurrentChar;
        AdvanceCharStream;
        WHILE CurrentChar IN ['A'..'Z', 'a'..'z'] DO BEGIN
          theWord := theWord + CurrentChar;
          AdvanceCharStream
        END;
        IF theWord = 'sin' THEN CurrentToken.kind := SinWord
```

```
      ELSE IF theWord = 'cos' THEN CurrentToken.kind := CosWord
      ELSE IF theWord = 'exp' THEN CurrentToken.kind := ExpWord
      ELSE BEGIN
        CurrentToken.kind := VariableSym;
        CurrentToken.SymVal := theWord
      END
    END;
```

As a further example of this lexical analysis strategy, the design of a lexical analyzer for Small Lisp is described in Section C.4.1 and its corresponding implementation may be found in the source code supplied with this book. It illustrates a number of additional details, including appropriate initialization and error-handling code. It also illustrates how object-oriented programming techniques allow slightly different versions of the lexical analyzer to be set up for interactive input versus file input.

12.2.3 Lexical Analyzers In General

Lexical analysis for a well-designed notation can often follow the straightforward pattern of the algebraic expression example. In many cases, the single-character lookahead illustrated by the example is sufficient. This is to be expected with a good notation, because the ability to break down the input stream easily into tokens also enhances readability. Other cases are only slightly more complex. For example, the Pascal programming language requires two-character lookahead to distinguish between the real numeral 1.5 and the integer numeral 1 in the subrange 1..5. In such cases, lexical analyzers can be implemented with relatively simple modifications to the approach illustrated by `algebraic-lexer`.

Some notations, however, such as the FORTRAN programming language, require considerably more complicated lexical analysis. For example, the FORTRAN looping statement

```
                 DO 3 I = 1,3
```

consists of the keyword DO, the statement label 3, the variable I, the operator =, and the loop bounds 1 and 3 separated by a comma. On the other hand, the FORTRAN statement

```
                 DO 3 I = 1.3
```

is parsed as an assignment statement, consisting of a variable DO3I, the assignment operator =, and a real numeral 1.3.[3] Lexical analysis to distinguish these cases is quite complicated. It is of course, quite easy to type a "." instead of a "," and not catch the mistake when reading over the program later. In fact, this very mistake is reported to have been made in a program controlling the *Mariner I* spacecraft, resulting in its loss [Neu86].

If a notation requires complicated lexical analysis, or if it is simply a notation with a large number of different token types, it is reasonable to consider techniques to automate the generation of the lexical analyzer. This can be done using *regular ex-*

---

[3]FORTRAN allows blanks within tokens.

pressions as a notation for describing the lexical structure of tokens. A lexical-analyzer generator can then be formulated as a symbolic computing application on regular expressions as a symbolic data domain. For example, see [ASU86] for a discussion of this approach.

12.3 PARSING

Given the token stream for a notational phrase as determined by a lexical analyzer, a *parser* is used to discover how the tokens can be grouped hierarchically to reflect the grammar of the notation. In principle, the parser could be designed to construct and return the actual derivation trees for the notational phrases. However, we shall instead consider parsers which construct and return the symbolic data structures that represent the notation. For example, given the algebraic expression x + y * z, its parser would return the data structure resulting from a make-sum operation on the variable x and the result of a make-product operation on the variables y and z. Such a data structure might be drawn as an *abstract syntax tree*, as shown in Figure 12.9. In this diagram, x, y, and z each represent variables as symbolic data objects, while ⟨sum⟩ and ⟨product⟩ represent sum and product data objects, respectively. Note that the abstract syntax tree is a considerably simplified representation in comparison to the corresponding derivation tree shown in Figure 12.5. Nevertheless, it contains all the information necessary to fully describe the symbolic data object.

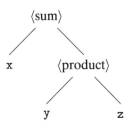

Figure 12.9   Abstract syntax tree for x + y * z.

For notations and grammars developed according to the readability principles of Section 12.1.2, a form of parsing known as *recursive-descent* parsing is appropriate. In this approach, a set of mutually recursive parsing procedures is written—in general, one per grammar rule. Decisions about which way parsing is to proceed are made on the basis of the marker tokens within the grammar.

Consider the development of a recursive descent parser for algebraic expressions in the notation of Figure 12.4. It is organized as a collection of parsing procedures ParseExpression, ParseTerm, ParseSine, ParseVariable, and so on. Each procedure accepts tokens from the input stream until the construct it deals with is recognized. It then arranges to return the appropriate symbolic data object to its caller, constructing it if necessary. First consider the parsing procedure for the ParsePrimary procedure. The grammar rule for ⟨primary⟩ defines it as one of six different types of construct. Fortunately, the grammar rules for each of these expression types each begin with a distinct marker token, making implementation of ParsePrimary easy.

```
FUNCTION ParsePrimary : AlgExprType;
BEGIN
  CASE CurrentToken.kind OF
    ConstantSym : ParsePrimary := ParseConstant;
    VariableSym : ParsePrimary := ParseVariable;
    ExpWord : ParsePrimary := ParseExponential
    SinWord : ParsePrimary := ParseSine;
    CosWord : ParsePrimary := ParseCosine;
    LeftParenToken : ParsePrimary := ParseParenthesis
  ELSE Error('Expecting <primary>.')
  END
END;
```

Once one of the alternatives has been parsed successfully, it is immediately returned by ParsePrimary to its caller.

Implementation of the parsing procedures called by ParsePrimary is also straightforward. The ParseConstant procedure converts the string representation of the constant into a symbolic data object using the MakeConstant converter specified by the GRAIL grammar for algebraic expressions in Figure 4.1.

```
FUNCTION ParseConstant : AlgExprType;
BEGIN
  IF CurrentToken.kind = ConstantSym THEN BEGIN
    ParseConstant := MakeConstant(CurrentToken.NumVal);
    GetNextToken
  END
  ELSE Error('Expecting constant.')
END;
```

The ParseVariable procedure is similar. The ParseSine procedure is a typical example of a parsing procedure derived from a construction rule.

```
PROCEDURE AcceptToken(theKind : TokenKind);
BEGIN
  IF CurrentToken.kind = theKind THEN GetNextToken
  ELSE ExpectingTokenError(theKind)
END;

FUNCTION ParseSine : AlgExprType;
  VAR arg : AlgExprType;
BEGIN
  AcceptToken(SinWord);
  AcceptToken(LeftParenToken);
  arg := ParseExpression;
  AcceptToken(RightParenToken);
  ParseSine := MakeSine(arg)
END;
```

The auxiliary `AcceptToken` procedure is used to advance the input stream if the currently pending token is of a specified kind; otherwise, it reports an error. Within `ParseSine`, if the `sin` and `(` tokens are accepted, the argument to the sine expression is parsed as an expression. Once the final `)` is accepted, the symbolic data object representing the sine expression is constructed and returned. The `ParseCosine` and `ParseExponential` procedures are similar.

The `ParseParenthesis` procedure involves a slight wrinkle.

```
FUNCTION ParseParenthesis : AlgExprType;
   VAR arg : AlgExprType;
BEGIN
   AcceptToken(LeftParenToken);
   arg := ParseExpression;
   AcceptToken(RightParenToken);
   ParseParenthesis := arg
END;
```

Note that the component expression is returned as the result of `ParseParenthesis` without being incorporated into another symbolic data object. This is because parenthesized expressions occur, not as part of the symbolic data domain defined by the original GRAIL grammar for algebraic expressions Figure 4.1), but because they were introduced in the textual notation to allow the grouping of an expression to be indicated unambiguously.

Now consider implementation of the `ParseFactor` procedure. Referring to Figure 12.4, note that the rule for ⟨factor⟩ defines it as either a ⟨primary⟩ or as a ⟨power⟩ whose first element is a ⟨primary⟩. In this case, the two alternatives are said to have ⟨primary⟩ as a common *left factor*. Following the left factor, a marker token ** indicates that the ⟨factor⟩ is indeed a ⟨power⟩ expression; any other token indicates that it is simply a ⟨primary⟩. This leads to the following implementation:

```
FUNCTION ParseFactor : AlgExprType;
   VAR e1, e2 : AlgExprType;
BEGIN
   e1 := ParsePrimary;
   IF CurrentToken.kind = ExponOp DO BEGIN
      GetNextToken;
      e2 := ParseFactor;
      ParseFactor := MakePower(e1, e2)
   END
   ELSE ParseFactor := e1
END;
```

A separate parsing procedure `ParsePower` is not needed because the ⟨power⟩ symbol occurs only within the rule for ⟨factor⟩.

Perhaps the most difficult problem for recursive-descent parsers is to deal with *left-recursive* grammar rules. The implementation of `ParseTerm` illustrates the problem. Again referring to Figure 12.4, note that two of the alternatives for ⟨term⟩, namely ⟨product⟩ and ⟨quotient⟩, are defined by rules which each recursively begin with a ⟨term⟩ in the leftmost position. Thus to parse a ⟨term⟩ which appears to be a ⟨product⟩, we must first parse the ⟨term⟩ which is its first component. But without having advanced the input stream at all, this ⟨term⟩ may also appear to be a ⟨product⟩, leading to an infinite loop.

The solution to this problem is to recognize that while a ⟨product⟩ or ⟨quotient⟩ may have a first operand which is in turn a ⟨product⟩ or ⟨quotient⟩, the recursion must eventually terminate with a ⟨factor⟩ as the first operand at some level. Thus, in parsing a ⟨term⟩, we first parse a ⟨factor⟩. This gives us the ⟨term⟩ at the lowest level of the recursion. If the following token is either * or /, we complete the parsing of the ⟨product⟩ or ⟨quotient⟩. This gives us the ⟨term⟩ at the next level up in the recursion. We repeat this process as long as the next token in the input stream is either a * or /. This strategy is reflected in the following implementation of ParseTerm.[4]

```
FUNCTION ParseTerm : AlgExprType;
  VAR e1, e2 : AlgExprType;
BEGIN
  e1 := ParseFactor;
  WHILE CurrentToken.kind IN [TimesOp, DivideOp]  DO
    IF CurrentToken.kind = TimesOp THEN BEGIN
      GetNextToken;
      e2 := ParseFactor;
      e1 := MakeProduct(e1, e2)
    END
    ELSE BEGIN
      GetNextToken;
      e2 := ParseFactor;
      e1 := MakeQuotient(e1, e2)
    END;
  ParseTerm := e1
END;
```

Separate ParseProduct and ParseQuotient procedures are not needed.

Left recursion also occurs in the ⟨expression⟩ domain with the ⟨sum⟩ and ⟨difference⟩ rules. With the incorporation of appropriate logic for recognizing ⟨negation⟩ expressions, the implementation can be developed in a straightforward fashion following the pattern of ParseTerm. This would then complete the implementation of the recursive parsing procedures for algebraic expressions.

A further example of recursive-descent parsing, giving additional implementation details, is provided by the parser for Small Lisp described in Section C.4.2. In particular, that parser illustrates a straightforward approach to handling parsing errors without terminating the execution of the calling program.

---

[4]Dealing with left recursion in a top-down parser is more commonly described using transformations of the grammar rules which eliminate left recursion [ASU86, pp. 176–178]. Our approach leaves the grammar rules untransformed so that they more closely reflect the abstract structure of the symbolic objects being parsed.

12.3.1 Parsing in General

The recursive-descent parsing technique is generally appropriate for well-designed notations following the readability principles of Section 12.1.2. In the most straightforward cases, the notation and its grammar will include marker symbols so that the decision about which alternative to use in parsing a production can always be made by considering the first token of the production. In the terminology of formal parsing theory, grammars which exhibit this property are called LL(1).[5] Even if this is not true, however, a grammar may be sufficiently close to LL(1) form that a recursive-descent parser can easily be constructed with some left-factor and left-recursion analysis. For example, programming languages such as Pascal and its descendents generally fall within this category.

There are grammars and notations for which recursive-descent parsing is inappropriate. Fortunately, there are practical parsing techniques which can handle many such cases. In particular, a grammar which is not in LL(1), or convertible to LL(1), may still be within a wider class of LR grammars that can be parsed using bottom-up methods. See [ASU86] for further information on LL and LR grammars and descriptions of various practical parsing techniques.

It is also possible to automate the construction of parsers. A *parser-generator* is a symbolic computing application which takes a grammar as input and produces a corresponding parser as output. Many parser-generators exist, including the popular "yacc" program on Unix systems. Most such parser-generators do not actually generate parsers as programs, however, but generate parsing tables which are used by general-purpose table-driven parsers. However, there is no particular reason why a parser-generator for LL(1) grammars, for example, could not produce recursive-descent parsing routines as output directly.

12.4 PRETTY-PRINTING

Pretty-printing is the process of displaying symbolic notation with suitable spacing, indentation, and line breaks to make it easy to read. One of the advantages of Lisp systems (including Small Lisp) for symbolic computing is that they provide built-in pretty-printers for Lisp lists. Although such pretty-printers are necessarily generic (i.e., independent of any particular symbolic computing application), they generally do a pretty good job of making symbolic output readable. Some Lisp environments provide user-programmable pretty-printers to tailor the output to a particular symbolic notation [Wat83]. However, when the production version of a symbolic computing application is to be developed using a textual notation, readable symbolic output will almost certainly require a specialized pretty-printer to be developed for the notation.

The major issue in pretty-printing is how to print a symbolic data object when it will not fit on a single line. For example, consider the following Small Lisp conditional expression as an item of notation to be pretty-printed.

```
[greaterp[x; 0] --> x; otherwise --> minus[0; x]]
```

---

[5]LL(k) grammars allow such decisions to be made on the basis of the first k symbols of the remaining input stream.

If the line width is 40 characters, it could be printed as

```
[greaterp[x; 0] --> x; otherwise -->
minus[0; x]]
```

but this is definitely not pretty. Instead, it is preferable to keep each clause together on a single line and line them up:

```
[greaterp[x; 0] --> x;
 otherwise --> minus[0; x]]
```

In general, the main objectives are to avoid breaking up subobjects and to use indentation to indicate the level of nesting.

Sometimes, however, it becomes necessary to break a subobject over two lines. For example, suppose that our conditional expression was to be printed within a line width of 26 characters. It could be printed without breaking up the second clause, but we would get a dangling bracket for the conditional expression.

```
[greaterp[x; 0] --> x;
 otherwise --> minus[0; x]
                          ]
```

Instead, it is preferable to break the clause and pretty-print the expression as follows.

```
[greaterp[x; 0] --> x;
 otherwise -->
   minus[0; x]]
```

In essence, when printing the final clause, we want to reserve some right-margin space for the] of the conditional expression, leaving an effective line width of only 25 characters. Note also that thc result part of the clause is indented with respect to the predicate part at the beginning of the clause. This makes it clear that the last line does not start a new clause but is part of the one started on the preceding line.

These examples illustrate typical decisions that are involved in defining a pretty-printed form of a notation. In many cases, however, the decisions will be a matter of personal preference.

12.4.1 Unparsing

As a first step in the development of a pretty-printer, let us initially consider how a printer of symbolic objects can be developed without any special formatting actions. Such a printing program is often called an *unparser*, reflecting the fact that it inverts the parsing process. Like a parser, an unparser can be organized as a series of mutually recursive procedures. For example, consider an unparser for Small Lisp expressions. The main routine would simply call the appropriate unparser for a particular expression type, as follows:

```
PROCEDURE UnparseExpression(x : LispExprType);
BEGIN
```

```
        IF NumAtomQ(x) THEN UnparseNumAtom(x)
        ELSE IF SymAtomQ(x) THEN UnparseSymAtom(x)
        ELSE IF ListExprQ(x) THEN UnparseListExpr(x)
        ELSE IF IdentifierQ(x) THEN UnparseIdentifier(x)
        ELSE IF FnCallQ(x) THEN UnparseFnCall(x)
        ELSE IF CondExprQ(x) THEN UnparseCondExpr(x)
        ELSE IF LetExprQ(x) THEN UnparseLetExpr(x)
      END;
```

Routines for the various expression types are then responsible for emitting the appropriate tokens and recursively printing any subcomponents, as illustrated by the following routines for conditional expressions:

```
      PROCEDURE UnparseCondExpr(x : LispExprType);
      BEGIN
        Emit(LeftBracketToken);
        UnparseClauseList(Clauses(x));
        Emit(RightBracketToken)
      END;


      PROCEDURE UnparseClauses(clauses : ClauseListType);
      BEGIN
        UnparseClause(First(clauses));
        WHILE NOT SingleP(clauses) DO BEGIN
          Emit(';') ;
          clauses := Rest(clauses);
          UnparseClause(First(clauses))
        END
      END;


      PROCEDURE UnparseClause(clause : ClauseType);
      BEGIN
        UnparseExpression(Predicate(clause));
        Emit('-->');
        UnparseExpression(Result(clause))
      END;
```

In these routines, the Emit procedure is the interface to the output stream, specifying a new string to be produced on that stream.

To ensure that the output produced by the unparser can be correctly processed as a Small Lisp program, the Emit procedure must add white space (one or more blanks or newlines) between consecutive tokens. In Small Lisp, it is always safe to have such white space, and sometimes necessary. The usual case is that Emit will add a single blank between tokens. However, to conveniently break the output stream into lines, Emit will insert a newline character instead of a blank if a globally specified LineWidth would be exceeded by printing the next string on the current line. Defined in this way, Emit is the only output primitive needed by the unparser. As we shall see, however, it must be used in conjunction with other output routines in definition of a pretty-printer.

12.4.2 Format Control

A pretty-printer has the same basic structure as an unparser, but with additional logic to control output formatting. This can be achieved by including additional formatting facilities within the output stream abstraction and modifying the unparser procedures to use these formatting routines in the desired ways. We present here the design for a Small Lisp pretty-printer, used in conjunction with the Small Lisp interpreter of Appendix C.

Our pretty-printer uses an output stream abstraction which provides three groups of formatting facilities. The first of these groups consists of the Emit procedure described above together with a SuppressBlank procedure for suppressing the blank normally inserted between tokens. For example, after the [character beginning a conditional expression, there is no need for a blank before the predicate expression of the first clause; this blank can be suppressed by calling SuppressBlank sometime after the Emit(' [') and before the next token is emitted.

The second group of formatting facilities, consisting of the procedures NewBlock, Indent, and EndBlock, is used to control the indentation during pretty- printing. The parameterless NewBlock and EndBlock procedures are used to delimit the printing of a "block" with a particular level of indentation. The indentation is established by the current printing column when NewBlock is called. During the printing of the block, its indentation may be changed by calling the Indent procedure, specifying a relative offset. For example, in printing a global constant definition, it is reasonable to indent two spaces after printing out the constant name:

```
PROCEDURE PrintConstDef(def : LispDefnType);
BEGIN
  NewBlock;
  PrintCommentList(Comments(def));
  PrintIdentifier(ConstName(def), 0);
  Indent(2);
  Emit('=');
  PrintExpression(ConstVal(def), 0);
  EndBlock
END;
```

The EndBlock procedure terminates the block, resetting the indentation to that which existed before the block began.

The third group of formatting facilities provided by the output stream abstraction provide for the insertion of line breaks at appropriate spots. It includes the procedure LineBreak and the functions AvailableSpace and SpaceGainedByLineBreak. The LineBreak procedure is used to force an immediate line break in the output stream and insert a specified number of blank lines. For example, each function and constant definition in a Small Lisp program might be separated by a blank line:

```
PROCEDURE PrintDefinitionList(defs : DefinitionListType);
BEGIN
  WHILE NOT EndP(defs) DO
    BEGIN
      PrintDefinition(First(defs));
      defs := Rest(defs);
      IF NOT EndP(defs) THEN LineBreak(1)
    END
END;
```

Such line breaks are *unconditional*, because they do not depend on current formatting parameters.

The `AvailableSpace` and `SpaceGainedByLineBreak` functions are used in calculations to determine whether or not *conditional* line breaks should be inserted. The `AvailableSpace` function determines the amount of space remaining on the current output line; if this is less than the space required to print an object, a line break may be inserted. However, if the line break would not result in a sufficient space gain, it may be inappropriate. For example, the line break after `foo` in

```
foo
  [list1; (A long list of symbolic atoms);
   list3]
```

does not help, so it should be omitted:

```
foo[list1; (A long list of symbolic atoms);
   list3]
```

Such calculations can be made by the `SpaceGainedByLineBreak` function, which returns the amount of space that would be available on the next line if a line break were issued immediately.

Calculations to determine whether an object fits in the available space can be made by a set of recursive functions `SpaceAfterExpression`, `SpaceAfterFnCall`, and so on. These functions take an object to be printed and an available amount of space and return one of the following:

1. The amount of space that would be left if the object can be successfully printed in the given space.

2. An arbitrary negative number if it cannot.

For example, the calculations for lists are implemented by the following procedure.

```
FUNCTION SpaceAfterList
           (x : sExpressionType; initialSpace : INTEGER) : INTEGER;

VAR remainingSpace : INTEGER;

BEGIN
  remainingSpace := initialSpace - 2;
  IF EmptyListP(x) THEN SpaceAfterList := remainingSpace
```

```
    ELSE BEGIN
      remainingSpace := SpaceAfterSexpr(FirstOf(x), remainingSpace);
      x := RestOf(x);
      WHILE NOT EmptyListP(x) AND (remainingSpace >= 0) DO
        BEGIN
          remainingSpace := SpaceAfterSexpr(FirstOf(x), remainingSpace - 1);
          x := RestOf(x)
        END;
      SpaceAfterList := remainingSpace
    END
END;
```

The initial amount of space is immediately decreased by two to account for the parentheses around the list. The space is then decreased by that required for each list element. After the first element of the list, an additional decrement of one is used for each element because of the blank that must be inserted between list elements. If the amount of space remaining ever becomes less than zero, the calculation is terminated immediately to return this negative value as an indication that the list will not fit.

The final technique required for the prettyprinter implementation is the use of a MarginReserve parameter to each of the recursive pretty-printing procedures. This parameter is used to specify that the last line printed for a construct should leave sufficient right-margin space to print out trailing delimiters of higher-level constructs. Consider, for example, the following procedure for pretty-printing lists.

```
PROCEDURE PrettyList(x : sExpressionType; MarginReserve : INTEGER);

BEGIN
  IF (SpaceGainedByLineBreak >= SpaceGainNeededForLineBreak) AND
     (SpaceAfterList(x, AvailableSpace - MarginReserve) <= 0) THEN
    LineBreak(0);
  NewBlock;
  Emit('(');
  SuppressBlank;
  Indent(2);
  IF NOT EmptyListP(x) THEN
    BEGIN
      WHILE NOT EmptyListP(RestOf(x)) DO
        BEGIN
          PrettySexpr(FirstOf(x), 0);
          x:= RestOf(x)
        END;
      PrettySexpr(FirstOf(x), MarginReserve + 1)
    END;
  SuppressBlank;
  Emit(')');
  EndBlock
END;
```

In determining whether the list will fit on the remainder of the current line, the margin reserve is subtracted from the amount of space available. During printing of the list elements, however, the margin reserve parameter to `PrettySExpr` is specified as 0 for all but the last element. If a line break is needed before the last element, there is no need to reserve any right-margin space for the line just completed. For the last element, however, the margin reserve is specified as that passed in for the entire list plus an additional space for the) at the end of the list.

This approach to pretty-printer construction is relatively straightforward but has some drawbacks. First of all, it may be criticized on efficiency grounds because the calculations that determine whether a construct fits on the remainder of a line often duplicate work performed in the corresponding calculations for the enclosing constructs. Nevertheless, the resultant pretty-printers do seem to perform well enough for practical purposes. Second, the `SpaceAfter...` procedures duplicate information about token sizes and spacing also found in the corresponding `Pretty...` procedures. This creates a maintenance problem if some of the pretty-printing actions are to be changed. However, if the procedures are generated by a pretty-printer generator as in Exercise 12.6, this problem is also unimportant. Oppen [Opp80] describes a more elaborate approach to pretty-printer design which also remedies these difficulties.

12.5 EXERCISES

12.1. Develop an infix notation and its EBNF grammar for formulas of the propositional calculus using appropriate operator symbols and the following precedence and associativity rules. Logical negations should have the highest precedence level, followed by conjunctions at the second level and then disjunctions at the third level. Conjunctions and disjunctions should be left-to-right associative. Implications and equivalences should have the lowest precedence level and should be right-to-left associative.

12.2. The special end-of-stream marker `EOFchar` used in the Pascal version of the lexical analyzer for algebraic expressions is called a *sentinel*. It allows the next character in the input stream to be examined without an explicit end-of-stream test (if the current character is not `EOFchar`). Modify the GRAIL grammar of Figure 12.7 to include an appropriate sentinel and show how the Small Lisp version of the lexical analyzer can be simplified by assuming that this sentinel is always found as the last element of the input list.

12.3. Construct a recursive descent parser for the propositional calculus notation developed in Exercise 12.1.

12.4. Design and implement a generator of recursive-descent parsers for BNF grammars meeting the following restrictions. Grammar rules are of three types, namely lexical rules, construction rules, and alternation rules, each of which defines a nonterminal symbol in a different way. A lexical rule will simply indicate a nonterminal that corresponds to a class of tokens produced by the lexical analyzer. A construction rule will specify how its nonterminal is produced as composition of other nonterminal and terminal symbols. This is similar to a GRAIL construction rule, except that no repetition nonterminal symbols are allowed and no parentheses are required. Also similar to GRAIL, an alternation rule will specify that its nonterminal may be produced by one of several alternatives. Each of the alternatives must be a nonterminal defined by a construction or lexical rule, and each must begin with a distinct marker symbol. The output of your parser-generator should be a a symbolic representation of a Pascal recursive descent parser.

12.5. Devise a suitable pretty-printing strategy and implement the corresponding pretty-printer for algebraic expressions in the notation of Figure 12.4. Make sure that your pretty-printer inserts parentheses as appropriate so that the textual notation can be correctly interpreted according to the normal associativity and precedence rules for arithmetic operators.

12.6. Devise an extended form of EBNF grammars suitable for automatic generation of pretty-printers. Incorporate appropriate notation for specifying blank suppression, line breaks, margin reserves, and so on. Also develop a suitable symbolic representation for the Pascal space calculation and pretty-printing procedures. Implement the pretty-printer generator.

A

EBNF

EBNF or extended Backus-Naur form is an enhancement of the BNF metalanguage commonly used in many programming language texts for formally specifying the syntactic structure of a given language. While many other formal notations exist for such specification, BNF is one of the oldest and most widely used. Therefore, we have adopted an extension of it, which we shall refer to as EBNF, as one of the two notational systems used in the text for providing grammar definitions of formal languages and abstract data types.[1] In addition, the notation is used in Appendix B to provide the formal definition of the grammar of Small Lisp itself.

For completeness, and for the benefit of those who wish to review the rules and symbols used in the representation of a grammar using EBNF, we have summarized in this appendix some of the conventions commonly followed. In particular, we have identified those extensions we have adopted in the book. For more details on BNF and its extensions as well as other notation systems for defining programming language syntax the interested reader can consult Pagan [Pag81].

An EBNF grammar consists of a finite set of statements called *production rules*, which are defined in terms of *terminal* and *nonterminal* symbols. Terminal symbols, or simply *terminals*, comprise the set of symbols which actually appear in the language being defined. In the book, terminals are distinguished by the use of a typewriter font:

---

[1] The other notation system is GRAIL, whose syntax is described in detail in Chapter 4.

for example, CONS denotes that "CONS" is a terminal. Nonterminals, on the other hand, represent classes of syntactic constructs in the language and are represented by enclosing the name of the class within ⟨ and ⟩: for example, ⟨expression⟩ or ⟨digit⟩. For each nonterminal, a production rule specifies how objects of the corresponding class are constructed from other terminal and nonterminal symbols. Conventionally, one nonterminal, called the *start symbol*, is used to define the "top-level" syntactic class in the language. Working from the rule for the start symbol, the set of all possible sequences of terminal symbols that can be produced by repeated application of the production rules is referred to as the language *generated* by the grammar.

The production rules of a grammar can be recursive, and therefore it is possible to represent infinite languages with a finite number of rules. To terminate the generative process, at least one nonterminal in the language must be defined in such a way that it may be expanded to produce only terminal symbols. An EBNF grammar is therefore a recursive definition for a language, and so provides a means both for constructing valid instances and for analyzing whether given symbol sequences are within the language defined by the grammar.

Generally, the rules of the grammar provide a way of describing in what order to combine a sequence of terminals and nonterminals to obtain an instance of the language defined by the grammar. The syntax of an EBNF rule consists of a nonterminal, followed by the metasymbol ::=, followed by a sequence of terminals, nonterminals, and metasymbols: for example,

$$\langle\text{clause}\rangle \ ::= \ \langle\text{expression}\rangle \ \texttt{-->} \ \langle\text{expression}\rangle$$

In this instance the nonterminal ⟨clause⟩ is defined in terms of the nonterminal ⟨expression⟩ and the terminal -->. If the rule is to be used to construct an instance of a ⟨clause⟩, the metasymbol ::= can be read as "is constructed from," and the use of the grammar in this way is called *generation*. Alternatively, the grammar can be used to identify the components of a purported ⟨clause⟩ to validate that it possesses the structure defined by the rule. In this case the metasymbol ::= seems more appropriately interpreted as "consists of," and the use of the grammar is termed *analytical*. Thus, for the example given, the notation system provided by EBNF provides a concise way of representing the statement: "A ⟨clause⟩ consists of an ⟨expression⟩, followed by the symbol -->, followed by another ⟨expression⟩."

The rules may also identify alternative representations, in which case the syntax of a rule consists of a nonterminal followed by ::=, followed by each alternative, expressed as a sequence of terminals and nonterminals, separated by the metasymbol |. For example, the statement that an ⟨expression⟩ can be a ⟨value⟩, ⟨variable⟩, ⟨function-call⟩, ⟨conditional-expression⟩, or ⟨let-expression⟩ can be expressed by the rule

$$\langle\text{expression}\rangle \ ::= \ \langle\text{value}\rangle \mid \langle\text{variable}\rangle \mid \langle\text{function-call}\rangle \mid$$
$$\langle\text{conditional-expression}\rangle \mid \langle\text{let-expression}\rangle$$

From this example it is easy to see that The metasymbol ::= is conveniently read as "can be a" and the symbol | is interpreted as "or."

The notation system provided by the metasymbols ::= and |, together with the use of terminals and nonterminals as described above, constitutes the formalism

known as *Backus-Naur form* (BNF). A common occurrence in the formulation of production rules for a BNF grammar is illustrated by the following:

$$\langle\text{numeric-atom}\rangle \; ::= \; \langle\text{positive-integer}\rangle \mid \langle\text{negative-interger}\rangle$$
$$\langle\text{positive-integer}\rangle \; ::= \; \langle\text{digits}\rangle$$
$$\langle\text{negative-integer}\rangle \; ::= \; -\langle\text{digits}\rangle$$
$$\langle\text{digits}\rangle \; ::= \; \langle\text{digit}\rangle \mid \langle\text{digit}\rangle \; \langle\text{digits}\rangle$$
$$\langle\text{digit}\rangle \; ::= \; 0\mid1\mid2\mid3\mid4\mid5\mid6\mid7\mid8\mid9$$

In this instance what is captured by the grammar is the rather simple statement that
"a $\langle\text{numeric-atom}\rangle$ is a sequence of digits optionally preceded by a -." The frequency
with which the need to include "optional" terminals (or nonterminals) arises moti-
vates the extension of the BNF grammar notation system to include a means of more
conveniently identifying optional parameters. This extension consists of enclosing the
optional terminal (or nonterminal) with the metasymbols [and]. This permits the first
three rules used in the previous example to be replaced by the single rule

$$\langle\text{numeric-atom}\rangle \; ::= \; [-] \; \langle\text{digits}\rangle$$

This example also serves to motivate a second extension to BNF. The fourth rule
of the original definition of $\langle\text{numeric-atom}\rangle$ defines $\langle\text{digits}\rangle$ to be a $\langle\text{digit}\rangle$ followed by
zero or more $\langle\text{digit}\rangle$s. In EBNF, an extension is provided which simplifies the for-
mulation of such rules. A nonterminal which can be repeated indefinitely (zero or
more times) is enclosed within the metasymbols { and }. Thus the fourth rule can be
eliminated in the example and the definition of $\langle\text{numeric-atom}\rangle$ replaced by

$$\langle\text{numeric-atom}\rangle \; ::= \; [-] \; \langle\text{digit}\rangle \; \{ \; \langle\text{digit}\rangle \; \}$$
$$\langle\text{digit}\rangle \; ::= \; 0\mid1\mid2\mid3\mid4\mid5\mid6\mid7\mid8\mid9$$

While the two extensions described result in a more convenient notational representation for some rules, it is nevertheless the case that the expressive power of
BNF grammars is not increased; *context-free* grammars remain the class of grammars
capable of description using the BNF or EBNF notations.

B

Small Lisp Reference Manual

This appendix describes the Small Lisp programming language and the operation of its standard interpreter under the MS-DOS operating system.

B.1 LEXICAL STRUCTURE

A Small Lisp program consists of a stream of tokens and comment lines embedded in *white space*. White space is a sequence of one or more blanks, horizontal tabs, and newlines. Any amount of white space may separate tokens and/or comment lines, but none is generally required. The only exceptions are that some white space is required to separate consecutive atoms or identifiers (see below). White space may not appear within any token. Blanks and tab characters may appear within comment lines, however.

Small Lisp tokens can be divided into the following categories: symbolic atoms, numeric atoms, identifiers, and punctuation marks. Symbolic and numeric atoms are the elementary data objects of Small Lisp.

$$\begin{aligned}
\langle\text{symbolic-atom}\rangle &::= \langle\text{letter}\rangle \{ [-] \langle\text{letter}\rangle \mid [-] \langle\text{digit}\rangle \} \mid \\
&\quad \langle\text{special}\rangle \{ \langle\text{special}\rangle \} \\
\langle\text{letter}\rangle &::= \mathtt{A} \mid \mathtt{B} \mid \mathtt{C} \mid \ldots \mid \mathtt{Z} \mid \mathtt{a} \mid \mathtt{b} \mid \mathtt{c} \mid \ldots \mid \mathtt{z} \\
\langle\text{digit}\rangle &::= \mathtt{0} \mid \mathtt{1} \mid \mathtt{2} \mid \mathtt{3} \mid \mathtt{4} \mid \mathtt{5} \mid \mathtt{6} \mid \mathtt{7} \mid \mathtt{8} \mid \mathtt{9}
\end{aligned}$$

$$\langle special \rangle \; ::= \; + \mid - \mid * \mid / \mid < \mid > \mid = \mid \& \mid \mid \mid ! \mid @ \mid$$
$$\# \mid \$ \mid \% \mid ? \mid :$$
$$\langle numeric\text{-}atom \rangle \; ::= \; [-] \langle digit \rangle \{ \langle digit \rangle \}$$

Identifiers are used as function and variable names and have a similar syntax to that of symbolic atoms.

$$\langle identifier \rangle \; ::= \; \langle letter \rangle \{ [-] \langle letter \rangle \mid [-] \langle digit \rangle \}$$

The distinction between symbolic atoms and identifiers is context-dependent.

Small Lisp is case-sensitive. Thus foo, Foo, f00, and F00 are distinct entities, whether interpreted as identifiers or as symbolic atoms.

The following single characters are used as punctuation marks in Small Lisp:

$$[\;] \; \{ \; \} \; (\;) \; " \; = \; ; \; :$$

In addition, the three-character sequence --> is also a punctuation mark. Note that some of the punctuation marks are also acceptable as symbolic atoms; again, the distinction is context-dependent.

Comment lines are lines of source text beginning with three semicolons (;;;). One or more consecutive comment lines comprise a comment.

$$\langle comment \rangle \; ::= \; \{ \langle comment\text{-}line \rangle \}$$
$$\langle comment\text{-}line \rangle \; ::= \; a \; line \; of \; source \; text \; beginning \; ; ; ;$$

Comments are descriptive text which may appear only at the level of global declarations (see Section B.4.2).

B.2 SYMBOLIC DATA

The data objects of Small Lisp are called *S-expressions*.

$$\langle S\text{-}expression \rangle \; ::= \; \langle atom \rangle \mid \langle list \rangle$$
$$\langle atom \rangle \; ::= \; \langle numeric\text{-}atom \rangle \mid \langle symbolic\text{-}atom \rangle$$

Atoms are the elementary data objects of the S-expression domain. Lists are structured data objects which may be composed of atoms and other lists.

$$\langle list \rangle \; ::= \; (\{ \langle S\text{-}expression \rangle \})$$

A list may be empty, in which case it is denoted thus: ().[1] Note that identifiers, and punctuation marks other than (and), do not appear in S-expressions.

The atoms T and F are used to represent the Boolean values "true" and "false," respectively. Outside of the Boolean domain, however, T and F are simply ordinary atoms which may be used for other purposes.

B.3 EXPRESSIONS

Expressions specify the computation of values in the context of sets of function definitions and variable bindings. The value of an expression is always either an S-expression

---

[1]In contrast to other Lisp dialects, the empty list is not an atom in Small Lisp.

or the special value ⊥ ("bottom"), indicating an undefined or erroneous computation. However, if ⊥ is the result of an evaluation, an implementation may instead report that the computation is in error with a suitable error message.

There are several kinds of expression in Small Lisp.

$$\langle expression \rangle ::= \langle value \rangle \mid \langle variable \rangle \mid \langle function\text{-}call \rangle \mid$$
$$\langle conditional\text{-}expression \rangle \mid \langle let\text{-}expression \rangle$$

B.3.1 Value Expressions

A value expression allows an S-expression to be represented as a value without further computation.

$$\langle value \rangle ::= \langle numeric\text{-}atom \rangle \mid " \langle symbolic\text{-}atom \rangle " \mid \langle list \rangle$$

Numeric atoms and lists can be used directly to represent themselves. Symbolic atoms must be enclosed in quotation marks to distinguish them from variable identifiers.

B.3.2 Variables

Variable names use the identifier syntax.

$$\langle variable \rangle ::= \langle identifier \rangle$$

An identifier has a denotation as a variable if it is

1. One of the predefined variables T, F or otherwise
2. Globally defined in a constant definition (Section B.4.1)
3. Locally defined as a function parameter (Section B.4.2)
4. Locally defined in a let expression (Section B.3.4).

If an identifier denotes a variable, its value is the current binding of the variable established at the point of definition. The variables T, F, and otherwise are predefined to have the values T, F, and T, respectively. If an identifier does not denote a variable, its value is ⊥.

The use of an identifier as a variable name does not preclude its simultaneous use as a function name (i.e., the namespaces of variables and functions are distinct). In the context of an expression, however, an identifier is always interpreted as a variable.

B.3.3 Conditional Expressions

Conditional expressions specify alternative ways for computing a value depending on given logical conditions.

$$\langle conditional\text{-}expression \rangle ::= [\langle clause\text{-}list \rangle]$$
$$\langle clause\text{-}list \rangle ::= \langle clause \rangle \{ ; \langle clause \rangle \}$$
$$\langle clause \rangle ::= \langle expression \rangle \text{-->} \langle expression \rangle$$

A conditional expression of n clauses each of the form p_i --> r_i for $1 \leq i \leq n$ evaluates to

1. The value of r_i, if for each k such that $1 \leq k < i$, p_k evaluates to F and p_i evaluates to T.

2. $\perp$, if for each k such that $1 \leq k < i$, p_k evaluates to F and evaluation of p_i yields a value other than T or F.

3. $\perp$, if for each k such that $1 \leq k \leq n$, p_k evaluates to F.

B.3.4 Let Expressions

Let expressions allow expressions to be evaluated in the context of local variable assignments.

$$\langle\text{let-expression}\rangle ::= \{ \langle\text{let-list}\rangle : \langle\text{expression}\rangle \}$$
$$\langle\text{let-list}\rangle ::= \langle\text{local-definition}\rangle \{ ; \langle\text{local-definition}\rangle \}$$
$$\langle\text{local-definition}\rangle ::= \langle\text{variable}\rangle = \langle\text{expression}\rangle$$

Given an initial set of variable bindings E, a let expression having a final expression a and n local definitions each of the form $v_i = e_i$ for $1 \leq i \leq n$ evaluates to

1. The value of a in the context of E', where E' is E with the additional or updated bindings of the variables v_i to the respective values of e_i each evaluated in the context of E, provided that no such evaluation yields $\perp$.

2. $\perp$, if for any i, e_i evaluated in the context of E yields $\perp$.

B.3.5 Function Calls

Function calls allow user-defined or primitive functions to be called with specified argument values.

$$\langle\text{function-call}\rangle ::= \langle\text{function-name}\rangle [\langle\text{argument-list}\rangle]$$
$$\langle\text{function-name}\rangle ::= \langle\text{identifier}\rangle$$
$$\langle\text{argument-list}\rangle ::= \langle\text{expression}\rangle \{ ; \langle\text{expression}\rangle \}$$

A function call evaluates to $\perp$ if

1. The function name specified is neither the name of a user-defined function or a primitive function.

2. The function name is that of a primitive function and the number of arguments given is not equal to the number of parameters specified in Section B.5 for that primitive.

3. The function name is that of a user-defined function and the number of arguments given is not equal to the number of parameters specified in its function definition (see Section B.4.2).

4. Any of the arguments evaluates to $\perp$.

Otherwise, the value of a function call is computed by applying the named function to the list of evaluated arguments according to the rules of Section B.5 for primitive functions and Section B.4.2 for user-defined functions.

B.4 DEFINITIONS AND PROGRAMS

A Small Lisp program is a list of constant and function definitions.

⟨definition-list⟩ ::= { ⟨definition⟩ }
⟨definition⟩ ::= ⟨function-definition⟩ | ⟨constant-definition⟩

B.4.1 Constant Definitions

A constant definition establishes a variable as a globally bound constant.

⟨constant-definition⟩ ::= [⟨comment⟩] ⟨variable⟩ = ⟨expression⟩

The value bound to a global constant is determined by evaluating the R.H.S. of the constant definition in the context of previously defined functions and constants. It is illegal to redefine the variables T, F, and otherwise, which have predefined values as described in Section B.3.2.

B.4.2 Function Definitions

Functions may be defined by specifying a defining expression for the function which is to be evaluated in the context of argument values bound to parameter names.

⟨function-definition⟩ ::= [⟨comment⟩] ⟨function-name⟩
                    [⟨parameter-list⟩] = ⟨expression⟩
⟨parameter-list⟩ ::= ⟨variable⟩ { ; ⟨variable⟩ }

The values of the arguments are established by a function call as described in Section B.3.5 and are bound to the parameter names by position (i.e., the ith argument is bound to the ith parameter). The function is applied by evaluating the defining ⟨expression⟩ in the context of these bindings plus the bindings for any globally defined constants. The value computed is then returned as the result of the function application.

Function definitions may refer to any global definitions that exist at the time the function is called. This includes both self-recursive and mutually recursive function references. It is illegal to redefine any of Small Lisp's primitive functions described in Section B.5.

B.5 PRIMITIVE FUNCTIONS

Small Lisp provides 18 primitive functions as described below. Each function takes exactly the number of arguments shown.

symbolp[x] determines whether or not an object x is a symbolic atom, returning

> **1.** T if x is a symbolic atom.
> **2.** F if x is a numeric atom or a list.

numberp[x] determines whether or not an object x is a numeric atom, returning

> **1.** T if x is a numeric atom.
> **2.** F if x is a symbolic atom or a list.

listp[x] determines whether or not an object x is a list, returning

1. T if x is a list.
2. F if x is an atom.

endp[x] determines whether or not a list x is empty, returning

1. T if x is the empty list.
2. F if x is a nonempty list.
3. ⊥ if x is not a list.

first[x] returns

1. The first element of x if x is a nonempty list.
2. ⊥ if x is an empty list or an atom.

rest[x] returns

1. The tail sublist following the first element of x if x is a nonempty list.
2. ⊥ if x is an empty list or an atom.

cons[x; y] returns

1. The list whose first element is x and whose remaining elements are those of the list y in the same order, if y is a list.
2. ⊥ if y is not a list.

eq[x; y] determines whether x and y are equal symbolic atoms, returning

1. T if x and y are both symbolic atoms having the same name.
2. ⊥ if neither x nor y is a symbolic atom.
3. F, otherwise.

plus[x; y] returns

1. $x + y$ if x and y are both numeric atoms.
2. ⊥ if either x or y is not a numeric atom.

minus[x; y] returns

1. $x - y$ if x and y are both numeric atoms.
2. ⊥ if either x or y is not a numeric atom.

times[x; y] returns

1. $x \cdot y$ if x and y are both numeric atoms.
2. ⊥ if either x or y is not a numeric atom.

divide[x; y] computes the integer quotient of x and y, returning

1. $\operatorname{sgn} x \cdot \operatorname{sgn} y \cdot \lfloor |x/y| \rfloor$ if x and y are both numeric atoms and $y \neq 0$.
2. ⊥ if $y = 0$, or either x or y is not a numeric atom.

rem[x; y] computes the integer remainder of x and y, returning

1. $x - \text{divide}[x; y] \cdot y$ if x and y are both numeric atoms and $y \neq 0$.

2. $\perp$ if $y = 0$ or either x or y is not a numeric atom.

`eqp[x; y]` determines whether numeric atoms x and y are equal, returning

   1. T if x and y are both numeric atoms such that $x = y$.
   2. F if x and y are both numeric atoms such that $x \neq y$.
   3. $\perp$ if either x or y is not a numeric atom.

`lessp[x; y]` determines whether x is strictly less than y, returning

   1. T if x and y are both numeric atoms such that $x < y$.
   2. F if x and y are both numeric atoms such that $x \geq y$.
   3. $\perp$ if either x or y is not a numeric atom.

`greaterp[x; y]` determines whether x is strictly greater than y, returning

   1. T if x and y are both numeric atoms such that $x > y$.
   2. F if x and y are both numeric atoms such that $x \leq y$.
   3. $\perp$ if either x or y is not a numeric atom.

`sym-lessp[x; y]` determines whether x and y are lexicographically ordered symbolic atoms, returning

   1. T if x and y are both symbolic atoms such that x is lexicographically less than y.
   2. F if x and y are both symbolic atoms such that x is lexicographically greater than or equal to y.
   3. $\perp$ if either x or y is not a symbolic atom.

`explode[x]` returns

   1. The list of single-character symbolic atoms and single-digit numeric atoms which taken together comprise the name of x if x is a symbolic atom.
   2. $\perp$ if x is a numeric atom or list.

`implode[x]` returns

   1. The symbolic atom whose name is formed from the characters and digits of the atoms in the list x if x is a list of atoms.
   2. $\perp$ if x is not a list of atoms or the characters and digits of the atoms within x do not form a valid symbolic atom name.

`error[x]` reports a run-time error, printing out x as an error message. The `error` "function" always returns $\perp$.

B.6 THE COMPLETE GRAMMAR

The complete grammar of Small Lisp is collected together below.

$\langle$definition-list$\rangle$ ::= { $\langle$definition$\rangle$ }
$\langle$definition$\rangle$ ::= $\langle$function-definition$\rangle$ | $\langle$constant-definition$\rangle$

⟨function-definition⟩ ::= [⟨comment⟩] ⟨function-name⟩
                          [⟨parameter-list⟩] = ⟨expression⟩
⟨parameter-list⟩ ::= ⟨variable⟩ { ; ⟨variable⟩ }
⟨constant-definition⟩ ::= [⟨comment⟩] ⟨variable⟩ = ⟨expression⟩
⟨expression⟩ ::= ⟨value⟩ | ⟨variable⟩ | ⟨function-call⟩ |
                 ⟨conditional-expression⟩ | ⟨let-expression⟩
⟨variable⟩ ::= ⟨identifier⟩
⟨value⟩ ::= ⟨numeric-atom⟩ | " ⟨symbolic-atom⟩ " | ⟨list⟩
⟨function-call⟩ ::= ⟨function-name⟩ [⟨argument-list⟩]
⟨function-name⟩ ::= ⟨identifier⟩
⟨argument-list⟩ ::= ⟨expression⟩ { ; ⟨expression⟩ }
⟨conditional-expression⟩ ::= [⟨clause-list⟩]
⟨clause-list⟩ ::= ⟨clause⟩ { ; ⟨clause⟩ }
⟨clause⟩ ::= ⟨expression⟩ --> ⟨expression⟩
⟨let-expression⟩ ::= { ⟨let-list⟩ : ⟨expression⟩ }
⟨let-list⟩ ::= ⟨local-definition⟩ { ; ⟨local-definition⟩ }
⟨local-definition⟩ ::= ⟨variable⟩ = ⟨expression⟩
⟨list⟩ ::= ({ ⟨S-expression⟩ })
⟨S-expression⟩ ::= ⟨atom⟩ | ⟨list⟩
⟨identifier⟩ ::= ⟨letter⟩ { [-] ⟨letter⟩ | [-] ⟨digit⟩ }
⟨atom⟩ ::= ⟨numeric-atom⟩ | ⟨symbolic-atom⟩
⟨numeric-atom⟩ ::= [-] ⟨digit⟩ { ⟨digit⟩ }
⟨symbolic-atom⟩ ::= ⟨letter⟩ { [-] ⟨letter⟩ | [-] ⟨digit⟩ } |
                    ⟨special⟩ { ⟨special⟩ }
⟨letter⟩ ::= A | B | C | ... | Z | a | b | c | ... | z
⟨digit⟩ ::= 0 | 1 | 2 | 3 | 4 | 5 | 6 | 7 | 8 | 9
⟨special⟩ ::= + | - | * | / | < | > | = | & | | | ! | @ |
              # | $ | % | ? | :

B.7 IMPLEMENTATION LiMITS

A Small Lisp implementation may impose limits on the lengths of source lines, identifiers, and symbolic atom names and may also limit the range of representable numeric values. The MSDOS implementation of Small Lisp limits the length of source lines to 254 characters. Consequently, identifiers and symbolic atom names are also limited to this length, but no further limits are imposed. The values of numeric atoms are restricted to the interval $[-2147483648, 2147483647]$.

B.8 THE STANDARD INTERPRETER

The standard interpreter under MSDOS provides facilities for interactively evaluating Small Lisp expressions in the context of specified sets of Small Lisp definitions. The interpreter may be invoked with the command

```
smlisp [configfile]
```

The optional argument specifies an initial *configuration file* to be read in; see Section B.8.4. If no configuration file is specified, the only constants and functions that are initially available are those that are predefined by the Small Lisp language. Once the interpreter has been invoked, the user may enter Small Lisp expressions to be evaluated, Small Lisp definitions to be used in subsequent evaluations, and interpreter commands.

B.8.1 Expression Entry

Small Lisp expressions may be entered directly, using as many lines as necessary. Expression input continues until the numbers of left and right parentheses, brackets, and braces are each balanced, or until input is aborted by a syntax error. The user may force an abort by typing any illegal character (e.g., a control character) followed by a return. If a function call is to be entered, note that its initial left bracket must be on the same line as the function name; otherwise, it will instead be interpreted as a variable whose value is to be looked up.

B.8.2 Definition Entry

Small Lisp definitions can be entered interactively by prefixing the definition with the "@" character. As with expression entry, definitions may be entered over multiple lines, continuing until parentheses, brackets, and braces are balanced, or input is aborted by a syntax error. Alternatively, definitions may be prepared in files or configurations (see Section B.8.4) and read in with the commands /read and /reset described in Section B.8.3.

B.8.3 Interpreter Commands

Interpreter commands are entered on a single line beginning with a "/". The following commands are available.

/help prints out some reminders about using the interpreter.

/quit stops the interpreter, returning control to the operating system.

/read *smlispfile* reads in the list of Small Lisp definitions contained in *smlispfile*, adding them to the current set.

/reset [*configfile*] clears all current definitions and optionally reads in a new configuration from *configfile*.

/save *file-name* saves all the interactively entered definitions in *file-name*.

/show *function-name* prints out the current function definition associated with *function-name*.

/log [*logfile*] closes any current log file and starts a new log on *logfile*, if specified.

B.8.4 Configuration Files

Configuration files allow sets of files containing Small Lisp definitions to be grouped together as a *configuration*. The name of each file in the configuration is placed on a separate line in the configuration file. The entire configuration can then be read in with either the `smlisp` command, which starts the interpreter, or the `/reset` command, described in Section B.8.3.

B.9 UTILITY PROGRAMS

Three utility programs are provided with the MSDOS implementation of Small Lisp.

B.9.1 `prettysl`

The `prettysl` program pretty-prints a file of Small Lisp function and definitions. It may be invoked from MSDOS using the following syntax:

> `prettysl` *file1* [*file2*]

The list of definitions is read from *file1* and pretty-printed to *file2*, if specified, or the standard output, otherwise.

B.9.2 `slispify`

The `slispify` program converts a Small Lisp program in m-Lisp form into its S-Lisp equivalent. It may be invoked from MSDOS using the following syntax:

> `slispify` *file1* [*file2*]

The list of definitions is read from *file1* and pretty-printed in S-Lisp form to *file2*, if specified, or the standard output, otherwise.

B.9.3 `mlispify`

The `mlispify` program converts a Small Lisp program in S-Lisp form back into its m-Lisp equivalent. It may be invoked from MSDOS using the following syntax:

> `mlispify` *file1* [*file2*]

The list of definitions is read from *file1* and pretty-printed in m-Lisp form to *file2*, if specified, or the standard output, otherwise.

C

Pascal Implementation of Small Lisp: A Case Study

Throughout this book we have described algorithms and data structures for symbolic computing primarily in the context of implementations in Lisp. As mentioned in Section 1.4, however, the concepts involved can be applied more widely to develop symbolic computing solutions in procedural languages as well. In this appendix, we present a case study of such an application, namely an interpreter for Small Lisp implemented in the Pascal programming language (specifically, Turbo Pascal version 5.5). The full implementation of this interpreter is provided in source code form on the disk accompanying this book.

The strategy for the development of the interpreter follows the rapid prototyping methodology described in Section 4.1. Working from the Lisp-in-Lisp interpreter presented in Section 6.3 as the prototype, implementation of the Pascal version involves the following steps:

1. Development of suitable Pascal representations for the symbolic data domains involved, that is, Small Lisp expressions and programs as input and Small Lisp values (S-expressions) as output.

2. Reimplementation of the interpreter data structures (i.e., the function and value environments of Section 6.3.2) using appropriate Pascal data types.

319

3. Straightforward translation of interpreter main algorithms, (e.g., sl-eval and sl-apply).

4. Construction of input/output routines to convert between the m-Lisp (textual) representation of Small Lisp programs and the corresponding internal representation as Pascal data objects.

5. Design of an appropriate main program to tie all the pieces together and provide an interactive user interface to the interpreter.

The following sections describe how these requirements are carried out in the construction of the Small Lisp interpreter accompanying this book.

C.1 SYMBOLIC DATA DOMAINS

C.1.1 S-Expressions

The sExpressions module provides an implementation of the S-expression data type (i.e., atoms and lists) in Pascal. This data type is used to represent the values being computed by the interpreter.

Note that the use of the S-expression data type in the Pascal-based interpreter is considerably restricted in comparison to the usage in the Small Lisp version of Section 6.3. In Small Lisp, all data objects must ultimately be represented as S-expressions. The Pascal version of the S-expression data type is rather awkward to use as an implementation type, however, because of the extra tag information that must be maintained to distinguish between numeric and symbolic atoms and lists. In general, then, the data structures used by the Pascal interpreter will not be implemented using S-expressions but in terms of some more natural Pascal data type.

The S-expression data type has been extended to include a special value TheUndefinedValue to represent the value ⊥ specified in Section B.3 as the value of undefined or erroneous evaluations.

C.1.2 The m-Lisp ADTs

The mLisp module provides the abstract data types for Small Lisp expressions and definitions as data objects. These data domains were defined together with their S-Lisp representation in Section 4.5. Although the representation of these domains is changed to use Pascal data structures, the abstract structure of the domains remains virtually unchanged. This is the essence of data abstraction. Thus the mLisp unit provides all the recognizer, selector, constructor, and converter functions defined in Section 4.5, but implemented on the Pascal representations instead.

A slight change to the abstract structure of Small Lisp programs as data objects has been incorporated into the mLisp module, namely the inclusion of comments as syntactic components of constant and function definitions. This requires a new selector function Comments (overloaded) to select comments from either type of definition, and a corresponding additional parameter to each of the MakeFnDef and MakeConstDef constructors. Comments are represented as lists of comment lines, which are each represented as character strings.

C.1.3 Generic List Routines

Several of the symbolic subdomains provided by the mLisp module are list domains of a given type. For example, the ExpressionListType domain consists of ⟨expression⟩ lists, while the ClauseListType domain consists of the ⟨clause⟩ lists that comprise conditional expressions. The GenericLists module provides appropriate Lisp-like list processing facilities for these domains, including such functions as EndP, SingleP, First, Rest, and Cons.

The routines provided by the GenericLists module are designed to be "generic" in nature, that is, defined to allow the creation and manipulation of lists of various different element types, but restricting the elements of any one particular list to be all of the same type. It is not possible to provide true generic capabilities in Turbo Pascal. However, using Turbo Pascal's Pointer type to represent the base type of list elements, the GenericLists module allows lists of any pointer type to be processed. Since all the symbolic data domains are represented as pointers, this works out quite well. The main drawback to this approach is that no type checking on list operations is provided; arbitrary pointer objects may thus be inserted into lists of a given base type.

C.2 ENVIRONMENTS

The principal internal data structures used by the interpreter are the environment structures for storing variable values and function definitions. The value environment data structure is provided by the ValueEnv module and retains substantially the same ADT specification as that described in Section 6.3.2 for the Lisp-in-Lisp interpreter. The data structure design also parallels the Lisp-in-Lisp prototype, making use of a Pascal version of association lists.

The FnEnv module provides the ADT defining function environments for the Pascal implementation of the interpreter. As a concession to efficiency, the ADT has been changed from the specification of Section 6.3.2 to allow the destructive updating of the environment, but otherwise remains the same. The implementation uses ordered binary trees, again paralleling the Lisp-in-Lisp prototype.

C.3 MAIN ALGORITHMS: THE EVALUATOR

The Evaluate module contains the heart of the interpreter, consisting of slEval and slApply and their associated routines. Working from the sl-eval and sl-apply prototypes of Section 6.3.1, the Pascal versions of these routines are initially developed by straightforward translation using the techniques of Section 9.3.1. They are then extended to incorporate additional error checks as described at the end of Section 6.3.3. When an error condition does occur, the evaluation routines report the condition and gracefully terminate with the value TheUndefinedValue representing ⊥ (see also Exercise 6.7).

The Primitives module contains the routines necessary to implement the Small Lisp primitive functions on the sExpression data type. These functions are called by slApply. Note that the Lisp-in-Lisp interpreter does not provide corresponding implementations of these functions—rather, `sl-apply` directly uses the primitives built-in to Small Lisp, as shown in Figure 6.2.

C.4 INPUT/OUTPUT

The input/output facilities provide for reading and writing the m-Lisp representation of Small Lisp programs. The input process follows the lexical analysis and parsing strategies described in Sections 12.2 and 12.3. Output is provided by a pretty-printer constructed according to the scheme of Section 12.4.2.

C.4.1 Lexical Analysis

Based on either interactive user input or input from a file, the role of the lexical analyzer is to divide the input stream into a sequence of tokens for use by the parser. The lexical analyzer follows the basic strategy of Section 12.2. An `InputStreams` module provides a character-stream abstraction of the input; this abstraction is used by the lexical analyzer proper in the `LexicalAnalyzer` module.

The `InputStreams` module uses object-oriented techniques to provide two slightly different abstractions, one for input from a file and another for interactive input. Interactive input is initiated when an interactive command line is read and is found to contain no / command (see Section B.8.3). In this case, the command line that was just read must be made available as the first line of the interactive input stream. Thus the constructor for an interactive input stream allows the first line of text to be passed in as a parameter.

The `LexicalAnalyzer` also provides slightly different abstractions for interactive input versus input from a file, again using object-oriented techniques. File input is straightforward. In the case of interactive input, the token stream keeps track of the number of outstanding left brackets, braces, and parentheses. When there are no more such opening delimiters and no "=" symbol is pending, it is assumed that the end of the user's input has been reached, and an end-of-stream token is inserted automatically.

It is not possible to separate Small Lisp tokens completely into distinct classes because identifier tokens and certain punctuation marks (=, :, and -->) are also acceptable as symbolic atoms. The lexical analyzer therefore introduces a token class `IdentifierSymbol`, used to denote a token that may be either an identifier or a symbolic atom. Punctuation marks such as `'='` are denoted as tokens of a class `OperatorSymbol` with an appropriate `SymbolString` field.

C.4.2 Parsing

The `Parser` module provides a recursive-descent parser for Small Lisp in the style of Section 12.3. The interface to the parsing procedures is somewhat unusual. For example, to parse a list of Small Lisp definitions, the function `ParsesAsDefnList` is first used to determine if the stream of input tokens can in fact be parsed as such a list. If this is the case, the `ParsesAsDefnList` also constructs and saves the symbolic representation of the longest such list in the variable `ParsedDefinitionList`. Otherwise, the point at which the parsing would fail is reported in the interface variables `FailureLineNo` and `FailureCharNo`, together with an appropriate error message in `FailureMessage`.

The parser implements error processing in the following way. When a parse is attempted, a global variable `ParseHasFailed` is initially set to `FALSE`. When a parsing error is first encountered, this variable is set to `TRUE` and the error is reported. At this point, the parsing process conceptually terminates, returning the indication of parse failure to the original calling routine. However, since Turbo Pascal has no mechanism for nonlocal control transfers, the parser is allowed to continue until it terminates normally (it always will). Typically, a number of further errors may be detected, but these are not reported because they may be artifacts of a parsing process misdirected by the first error. When control finally returns to the top-level parsing routines, the heap space used for any objects allocated by the parser is reclaimed and the appropriate indication of parsing failure is returned.

C.4.3 Pretty-Printing

Section 12.4.2 presents the detailed design of the Small Lisp pretty-printer. Its implementation is organized into two modules, `OutputStreams` and `PrettyPrinter`. The `OutputStreams` module implements the basic formatting abstractions, such as `Emit`, `Indent`, `NewBlock`, and `LineBreak`. The `PrettyPrinter` provides the pretty-printing logic for each type of Small Lisp construct, expressed in terms of calls to the output stream abstraction.

C.5 THE INTERPRET MAIN PROGRAM

The module `SmLisp` implements the interpreter main program as specified in Section B.8. The main loop reads and processes interactive commands from the user as specified in Section B.8.3. This includes the facilities for reading configuration files, displaying the current definitions of functions and constants and saving interactively entered definitions to an output file. Input lines beginning with a "@" character are treated as the first line of an interactively entered definition. Lines beginning with neither a "/" command character or "@" definition character are interpreted as the first line of an expression to be evaluated in the context of the current set of definitions.

Bibliography

[All78] John Allen. *Anatomy of LISP*. McGraw-Hill, New York, 1978.

[AS85] Harold Abelson and Gerald J. Sussman. *Structure and Interpretation of Computer Programs*. MIT Press, Cambridge, Mass., 1985.

[ASU86] Alfred V. Aho, Ravi Sethi, and Jeffrey D. Ullman. *Compilers: Principles, Techniques and Tools*. Addison-Wesley, Reading, Mass., 1986.

[AU72] Alfred V. Aho and Jeffrey D. Ullman. *The Theory of Parsing, Translation and Compiling*, Vol. 1, *Parsing*. Prentice Hall, Englewood Cliffs, N.J., 1972.

[Chu41] A. Church. The calculi of lambda-conversion. *Annals of Mathematical Studies*. Princeton University Press, Princeton, N.J., 1941.

[CM81] W. F. Clocksin and C. S. Mellish. *Programming in PROLOG*. Springer-Verlag, New York, 1981.

[CM84] Eugene Charniak and Drew McDermott. *Introduction to Artificial Intelligence*. Addison-Wesley, Reading, Mass., 1984.

[Cus87] Steven Cushing. Some quantifiers require two-predicate scopes. *Artificial Intelligence, 32*, 1987.

[Dav73] D. Julian M. Davies. *POPLER 1.5 Reference Manual, T.P.U. Report 1*. School of Artificial Intelligence, University of Edinburgh, Edinburgh, Scotland, 1973.

[Del87] James P. Delgrande. A first-order conditional logic for prototypical properties. *Artificial Intelligence, 33*, 1987.

[Gib85] Alan Gibbons. *Algorithmic Graph Theory.* Cambridge University Press, Cambridge, 1985.

[GMW81] M. Gordon, A. Milner, and C. Wadsworth. LCF Edinburgh: A mechanized logic of computation. *Lecture Notes in Computer Science*, Vol. 78. Springer-Verlag, New York, 1981.

[GPP71] R. E. Griswold, J. F. Poage, and I. P. Polonsky. *The SNOBOL4 Programming Language*, 2nd ed. Prentice Hall, Englewood Cliffs, N.J., 1971.

[Har69] Frank Harary. *Graph Theory.* Addison-Wesley, Reading, Mass., 1969.

[Hen80] Peter Henderson. *Functional Programming, Application and Implementation.* Prentice Hall International, 1980.

[Hew72] Carl Hewitt. *Description and Theoretical Analysis (Using Schemata) of PLAN-NER: A Language for Proving Theorems and Manipulating Models of a Robot*, Ph.D. Thesis AI-TR-258. Massachusetts Institute of Technology, Cambridge, Mass., 1972.

[HWe90] P. Hudak and P. Wadler (editors). Report on the programming language Haskell, a non-strict purely functional language (Version 1.0), *Technical Report YALEU/DCS/RR777.* Yale University, Department of Computer Science, New Haven, Conn., April 1990.

[Knu73] Donald E. Knuth. *The Art of Computer Programming*, Vol. 3, *Sorting and Searching.* Addison-Wesley, Reading, Mass., 1973.

[Kow79] Robert A. Kowalski. *Logic for Problem Solving.* Elsevier (North-Holland), New York, 1979.

[McC60] John McCarthy. Recursive functions of symbolic expressions and their computation by machine, part I. *Communications of the ACM, 3*(4), June 1960.

[Mey90] Bertrand Meyer. *Introduction to the Theory of Programming Languages.* Prentice Hall, Englewood Cliffs, N.J., 1990.

[MTH90] Robin Milner, Mads Tofte, and Robert Harper. *The Definition of Standard ML.* MIT Press, Cambridge, Mass., 1990.

[Neu86] Peter G. Neumann. Risks to the public in computer systems. *ACM Software Engineering Notes, 11*(5):3–28, October 1986.

[Opp80] Derek C. Oppen. Prettyprinting. *ACM Transactions on Programming Languages and Systems, 2*(4):465–483, October 1980.

[Pag81] Frank G. Pagan. *Formal Specification of Programming Languages: A Panoramic Primer.* Prentice Hall, Englewood Cliffs, N.J., 1981.

[Rea72] Ronald C. Read (editor). *Graph Theory and Computing.* Academic Press, New York, 1972.

[SM72] Gerald Sussman and Drew McDermott. *Why Conniving Is Better Than Planning, AI-M-255A.* Massachusetts Institute of Technology, Cambridge, Mass., 1972.

[Ste90] Guy Steele. *Common LISP: The Language*: 2nd ed. Digital Press, Burlington, Mass., 1990.

[Sto77] Joseph E. Stoy. *Denotational Semantics: The Scott-Strachey Approach to Programming Language Theory*. MIT Press, Cambridge, Mass., 1977.

[SWC71] Gerald Sussman, Terry Winograd, and Eugene Charniak. *MICROPLANNER Reference Manual, AI-M-203A*. Massachusetts Institute of Technology, Cambridge, Mass., 1971.

[Tof89] Mads Tofte. *Four Lectures on Standard ML*. LFCS Report Series. Department of Computer Science, University of Edinburgh, Edinburgh, Scotland, 1989.

[Tur85] D.A. Turner. Miranda: a non-strict functional language with polymorphic types. *Functional Programming Languages and Computer Architecture*, Vol. 201, *Lecture Notes in Computer Science*. Springer-Verlag, New York, 1985.

[Wad87] Philip Wadler. Views: a way for pattern matching to cohabit with data abstraction. In *Conference Record of the Fourteenth Annual ACM Symposium on Principles of Programming Languages*, pages 307–313, 1987.

[Wan60] Hao Wang. Towards mechanical mathematics. *IBM Journal of Research and Development, 4*(1):2–22, 1960.

[Wat83] Richard C. Waters. User format control in a LISP prettyprinter. *ACM Transactions on Programming Languages and Systems, 5*(4):513–531, October 1983.

[Wei65] Joseph Weizenbaum. ELIZA: a computer program for the study of natural language communication between man and machine. *Communications of the Association for Computing Machinery, 9*(1):36–45, 1965.

[WH89] Patrick Henry Winston and Berthold Klaus Paul Horn. *LISP: Third Edition*. Addison-Wesley, Reading, Mass., 1989.

Index

Θ notation, 46
* (Common LISP function), 138
UNDEF, 154
+ (Common LISP function), 138
- (Common LISP function), 138
/ (Common LISP function), 138
< (Common LISP function), 140
> (Common LISP function), 140
&optional, 141
&rest, 142
⊥(bottom), 133, 311

Abstract syntax tree, 294
AcceptToken, 295
Access expressions, (setf), 159
Accumulating parameters, 45
  accumulator introduction, 214
  with reduce, 178–79
add-associations, 126
add-local-var-types, 206
AdvanceTokenStream, 291

Algebraic expressions
  data access functions, 21–25
  evaluation of, 119–21
  GRAIL grammar for, 73–74
  pretty-printing, 305
  representation, 19–21
  simplification of, 88–95, 107–11
  symbolic differentiation, *see* deriv
  textual notation for, 281–85
algebraic-lexer, 289
Alternation rules, 68
Ambiguous grammars, 281
Analysis
  application category, 2, 121
  metaprograms, 200
and, 132, 140
AND node, 57
AND/OR tree, 57, 61, 197
Antecedent, 74
append, 39, 55, 140
  destructive version, nconc, 156
append1, 46